The Ultimate Food Allergy Cookbook and Survival Guide

How to Cook with Ease for a Food Allergy Diet and Recover Good Health

Nicolette M. Dumke

The Ultimate Food Allergy Cookbook and Survival Guide:

How to Cook with Ease for a Food Allergy Diet and Recover Good Health

Published by

Adapt Books
Allergy Adapt, Inc.
1877 Polk Avenue
Louisville, Colorado 80027
(303) 666-8253

©2006 by Nicolette M. Dumke
First Printing, January, 2007
Printed in the United States of America

Cover design and typesetting by Ed Nies, Mel Typesetting,
1523 S. Pearl St., Suite B, Denver, CO 80210

Editing by Joan Hinkemeyer, Editorial Services,
2465 S. Humboldt, Denver, CO 80210

Publisher's Cataloging in Publication
(Provided by Quality Books, Inc.)

Dumke, Nicolette M.
    The ultimate food allergy cookbook and survival guide
: how to cook with ease for a food allergy diet and
recover good health / Nicolette M. Dumke.
        320 p. 24.6 cm.
        Includes bibliographical references and index.
        LCCN 2006900080
        ISBN-13: 978-1-887624-08-4
        ISBN-10: 1-887624-08-2

    1. Food allergy--Popular works. 2. Food allergy--
Diet therapy--Recipes.   I. Title.

RC596.D87 2007   616.97'50654
            QBI06-600026

Dedication

This book is dedicated to
all of the men in my life:

To my husband Mark,
whose love, hard work and
commitment to me and to our family
has made living through
the trying times possible,

To my son Joel,
whose encouragement and
whose positive and mature attitude
toward his allergies
are an inspiration to adults,

To my son John,
whose sensitive, thoughtful,
and generous nature
makes him a joy and delight,

and to the memory of my father,
Eugene Jiannetti,
whose love and example
showed all of us how to live
with challenges.

Disclaimer

The information contained in this book is merely intended to communicate food preparation material and information about possible treatment options which are helpful and educational to the reader. It is not intended to replace medical diagnosis or treatment, but rather to provide information and recipes which may be helpful in implementing a diet prescribed by your doctor. Please consult your physician for medical advice before embarking on any treatment or changing your diet.

The author and publisher declare that to the best of their knowledge all material in this book is accurate; however, although unknown to the author and publisher, some recipes may contain ingredients which may be harmful to some people.

There are no warranties which extend beyond the educational nature of this book. Therefore, we shall have neither liability nor responsibility to any person with respect to any loss or damage alleged to be caused, directly or indirectly, by the information contained in this book.

If you do not wish to be bound by the above, you may return this book to the publisher for a full refund.

Table of Contents

Foreword

Nickie Dumke's books are very high on our "office bestseller list." She has written several books and booklets which we advise our patients with food intolerance and allergy to utilize as routine "guides." Some of her books include *Allergy Cooking With Ease* and *Easy Breadmaking For Special Diets*. She has been writing about foods since 1988.

Nickie has had her share of food problems. Fortunately, they've improved, but certainly not by accident. Hopefully, low dose immunotherapy has now played a major role, but her ability to "do what needs to be done" with the food-related aspects of low dose immunotherapy has made a great deal of difference. If we have a patient on low dose immunotherapy who happens to go through a period of increased problems with foods, Nickie's recent booklet, *The Low Dose Immunotherapy Handbook,* is the one I recommend. This booklet contains the only "American" version of the British "Very Mixed Diet," an essential part of the program for our patients on low dose immunotherapy who "unmask" to foods.

The Ultimate Food Allergy Cookbook and Survival Guide is the next episode of what I hope will be a continuing series of easily readable guides for patients with food allergy and intolerance. The concepts of intestinal dysbiosis are paramount in this whole scheme, and food rotation is certainly the best tool many patients have to keep themselves stable enough to function on a daily basis. Since the content of this book comes from "someone who's been there," it is insightful. The "tips" here are designed for readers to use immediately, complete with more helpful recipes.

I highly recommend Nickie's latest book to readers who wish to add to their armamentarium of tools to deal with food problems of all kinds. Don't leave home without it!

W. A. Shrader, Jr., M.D.

Author's note: I wish to give special thanks to Dr. Shrader for reviewing this book and for his input into the chapters which contain medical information.

Survival

In My Fair Lady, Henry Higgins says, "Speech separates class from class and soul from soul." If you have food allergies, you know that allergies are also a divisive and isolating force in our society. On holidays and special occasions you watch the people around you partake of sumptuous feasts while your plate contains very little, and those few items may be foods that no one recognizes. Even the most polite individuals look at you askance, while others think (and say) that you are downright neurotic. Indeed, the pressure of constant malnourishment and continual allergic reactions can make you wonder if you are losing your mind.

People with food allergies are also separated from those around them by weight problems. Those who are underweight are "obviously" malnourished, but overweight people with food allergies are also malnourished. Their bodies are crying out for missing nutrients or craving a fix with allergic foods, and this, not lack of self-control, is why they are obese.

In 1991, I was diagnosed with Crohn's disease, an inflammatory bowel disease that often necessitates repeated surgical removal of parts of the patient's small intestine. I was told that the condition was incurable. I had food allergies for many years before this. While I could not eat much "normal" food, prior to the Crohn's disease my diet was adequate. I ate most vegetables and fruits, non-grains such as amaranth and quinoa, goat and sheep dairy products, legumes, nuts, and game meats. The Crohn's disease began a downward spiral in my health and diet until I was literally allergic to all food. I ate only exotic fish and exotic starches such as malanga, cassava, lotus, and true yam. I reacted somewhat to even those foods. I could eat no vegetables or fruits and was emaciated and malnourished.

By the grace of God I was led to the information and treatments in this book and I survived. I am now back to being well nourished. I can eat most vegetables and fruits, game meat (and even some "normal" meat like turkey), grain alternatives, nuts, and occasionally some goat milk products. I have enough energy to do what I want to do. My weight is normal and my cheeks are rosy. I feel as if I have been given my life back. I am optimistic about making further progress.

This book is the outgrowth of my journey back from near starvation. In it you will find out how you too can make that journey back to better health.

Hope

A speaker once said that we can live a few weeks without food, a few days without water, a few minutes without air, but only a few seconds without hope. Hope is indeed essential to life, to living rather than just surviving or existing.

Some people with food allergies discover what they are allergic to, avoid those foods, and by practicing avoidance faithfully, enjoy stable health for the rest of their lives. Some avoid their problem foods for a time, and then their allergies improve to the point that they can eat freely again. Yet others develop allergies to more and more foods as time goes on regardless of how faithful they are about their diets.

I was once involved in a discussion on how to prevent the development of new food allergies. One person said that using a rotation diet and not eating any one food too often was the way to keep from developing more allergies. Another said that rotation diets could lead to eating single foods in large quantities, and that eating too much of any food could cause one to become allergic to it. Finally someone asked, "So what will prevent the development of more food allergies?" The answer given was, "Death!" This does indeed seem to be the situation for some people – a situation without hope.

The purpose of this book is to give you hope. Just as a rainbow comes after the rain, so too can you enjoy good health again. By treating the underlying root causes of your food allergies, you may become healthier than you have ever been before. It might not be a quick process, and most of the time you will eat differently from those around you (at least at first), but you can again be healthy enough to enjoy your activities, friends, and family. You can truly live again rather than just survive.

Cicero said, "While there is life, there is hope." Our bodies were designed to heal themselves. As long as we have life, if we tip the balance in favor of the healing process, our bodies will heal. We are amazingly resilient creatures. Our Creator has not left us in the midst of our problems alone. The Psalmist said of God, "My hope is in Thee."[1] The Source of all life is the One who gives us hope and leads us through the process of restoring health to our bodies.

Footnotes

1. Psalm 39:7.

All About Food Allergies

What Are Food Allergies?

When the term "allergy" was first coined, it meant an adverse reaction to any substance that does not bother most people. Then, in the 1920's, it was discovered that a type of antibody called "Reagin" or IgE was involved in many allergic reactions, especially those to inhalants. So conventional medicine defined allergy as an IgE-mediated response.

IgE-mediated allergies are easily detected by standard blood or skin tests. The reactions happen rapidly, usually within a few minutes of exposure to inhaled substances or eating a food. Small amounts of the offending substance trigger the reactions, which commonly occur in the respiratory tract, digestive system, or skin. IgE-mediated food reactions are often "fixed." This means that after months or years of avoiding a problem food, eating any amount of it will still cause symptoms.

Many adverse reactions to foods do not involve IgE antibodies. They are often called food "sensitivities" or "intolerances." The absence of IgE does not make them any less real; other immune mechanisms, such as IgG antibodies, immune complexes, or cell-mediated reactions are involved instead. These reactions can happen quickly or can be delayed for two to seventy-two hours or longer. This makes home challenge testing for them much more difficult. (See page 6 for an explanation of this kind of testing). However, there are tests which are performed on "live patients" (in vivo testing) in a doctor's office which can diagnose food allergies, and blood tests can detect the antibodies that may be involved in causing allergic reactions. Standard IgE-based blood tests and skin tests are often negative. Virtually any part of the body can be affected by these types of allergies. About 95% of IgG-mediated reactions are not fixed.[1] Therefore, after several months of avoidance, problem foods can be reintroduced into the diet in moderate amounts without causing symptoms as long as they are not eaten too frequently.

In this book, the word "allergy" will be used in its original sense. Any immune-system related adverse reaction to a food will be called a food allergy without debate about the immune mechanism involved. Indeed, many adverse reactions can involve more than one mechanism.

Over seventy medical conditions are thought to be associated with food allergies. These conditions can be respiratory (hayfever, asthma, bronchitis, recurring ear infections, sinus conditions, rhinitis, laryngitis, allergic sore throat, hoarseness); digestive (gastroenteritis, irritable bowel syndrome, celiac disease, inflammatory bowel disease, diarrhea, constipation, colic, malabsorption); cerebral (headaches, dizziness, sleep disorders, learning disorders, tension-fatigue syndrome, foggy thinking, irritability, depression); skin-related (dermatitis, eczema, angioedema, hives, rashes); or related to other body systems (arthritis, myalgia, urinary irritation, conjunctivitis, edema, hypoglycemia, diabetes, overweight, underweight, premenstrual syndrome, fatigue).[2] This list is not exhaustive. Virtually any symptom can be associated with food allergy or intolerance. By identifying and eliminating or treating food allergies, many of our seemingly insolvable chronic health problems can be improved or eradicated.

Why Do We Have Food Allergies?

"Why?" is a difficult question. When my food allergies were first diagnosed, I asked the doctor, "Why did I suddenly develop all of these food allergies?" His reply was, "You may have had them for a long time without realizing it." His answer may have been partially correct, because I was always an allergic person from a family of allergic people, but he did not consider what had suddenly caused a change in the level of my allergies. It is only by addressing the "whys" of our food allergies that we can hope to actually solve the problem.

Heredity is often cited as a cause of food allergies, and certainly plays a role since a recessive gene has been identified as being linked to IgE-mediated food allergies.[3] Repeated exposure to the same foods, especially in large quantities, is also implicated.[4] Yet other factors also contribute to the severity and number of allergies most allergy-prone people endure.

The most common cause of multiple food allergies, in my opinion, is having a "leaky gut," or increased intestinal permeability. (This can be debated as a "chicken or egg" story though; which came first, the increased intestinal permeability or the food allergies?) Small openings can occur in the lining of the intestine, which allow large molecules of undigested or incompletely digested food to enter the bloodstream. If the quantity is too great for the liver to "clear" almost immediately, the immune system has a chance to recognize these molecules as being foreign to the body and produces antibodies against them. When the food is eaten again and again passes into the bloodstream undigested or only partially digested, the antibodies bind with the food. These antibody-food complexes can travel through the bloodstream to any part of the body where they then cause problems.

There are many causes of "leaky gut." Immaturity is one of them. Babies are born with higher intestinal permeability than older children or adults. Therefore, ideally infants should consume only breast milk for the first several months of life and other foods should be introduced cautiously.[5] If breast feeding is impossible, a completely hydrolyzed formula such as Nutramigen™ should be used because it is already "broken down" into simple sugars, free amino acids, and other very small units.[6] Cow's milk is highly allergenic and should not be given to babies.

Toxins of many kinds can also increase intestinal permeability. These include alcohol, nonsteroidal anti-inflammatory drugs (aspirin, ibuprofen, arthritis medications, and many others), cytotoxic drugs used to treat cancer, corticosteroid drugs, and, by their action on bowel flora, antibiotics. Radiation therapy to the abdomen also increases intestinal permeability.[7]

Then too, internal factors in a patient's body can cause or contribute to a leaky gut. These include nutritional deficiencies, inflammatory bowel disease, poor digestion, and food allergies. There is a vicious cycle involved with these internal factors since the leaky gut also causes them or contributes to their severity.[8]

Last, but by no means least, "unfriendly" organisms present in the digestive tract can cause increased intestinal permeability. These infections can involve protozoan parasites, yeasts such as *Candida albicans,* bacteria that are conventionally considered "pathogens," such as *Salmonella,* or an overgrowth of bacteria usually considered nonpathogenic, such as *Klebsiella, Proteus,* or *Pseudomonas.* Many other organisms not mentioned here can also increase intestinal permeability. (See pages 17 to 20 for more information on intestinal infections).

Most of the factors that increase intestinal permeability can be treated or eliminated from the lives of patients with food allergies. (See pages 13 to 21 for details). By doing this, the "why" of our leaky guts can be treated, and therefore our food allergies can be lessened and our health can be greatly improved.

FOOTNOTES

1. Braly, James, M.D. *Dr. Braly's Food Allergy and Nutrition Revolution,* Keats Publishing, Inc., New Canaan, CT, 1992, p. 39.

2. Reno, Liz, M.A. and Joanna Devrais, M.A. *Allergy Free Eating,* Celestial Arts, Berkeley, CA, 1995, pp. 22-23 and Braly, James, M.D. *Dr. Braly's Food Allergy and Nutrition Revolution,* pp. 44-45.

3. Reno, Liz, M.A. et al, *Allergy Free Eating,* p. 26.

4. Ibid, p. 18.

5. Ibid, p. 19.

6. Ibid, p. 27.

7. Galland, Leo, M.D. "Leaky Gut Syndromes: Breaking the Vicious Cycles," *Townsend Letter for Doctors,* August/September 1995, p. 62, and Reno, Liz, et al, pp. 19-20.

8. Galland, Leo, M.D. "Leaky Gut Syndromes," pp 62-63 and Reno, Liz, et al, pp. 19-20.

The Diagnosis And Treatment of Food Allergies

The diagnosis of food allergies can seem complicated because reactions to foods are often delayed and may be affected by many factors, including insufficient rest, stress, and other allergens we are exposed to at the same time. Indeed, it is usually impossible to determine what you are allergic to on your own if you have more than a very few food allergies. Therefore, medical testing and help from the right health professionals is important. There are associations you can consult to find someone who can help you in your area. (See "Sources," page 299).

The treatment of food allergy can, like its diagnosis, seem complex. Food allergy is definitely not a problem that fits the preconceived notions of our "for every ill there is a pill" society. Food allergies are often treated from several directions at the same time, such as eliminating allergens, strengthening the patient nutritionally, and modifying the patient's immune response. It is not something your doctor can do for you by himself or herself. (Indeed, many physicians do not understand allergies other than those mediated by IgE). As a patient with food allergies, YOU must be actively involved in your treatment. The most important parts of your treatment YOU will do, not your doctor. Food allergy is a very individual problem, and you know your body better than anyone else does. It may be difficult to take action because of your health, but if you want to get well, YOU must take responsibility for yourself. YOU must make the necessary changes in your lifestyle. YOU must become a well-informed, active participant in your own health care. Then YOU will be the one to enjoy the benefits of improved health.

Diagnostic Tools

Elimination and challenge was the first type of testing used for food allergies. It is still often used in the clinical ecology units of hospitals or clinics and is considered the "gold standard" method of allergy testing for foods. The patient either fasts for several days (in a clinic under medical supervision) or at home eliminates the foods to be tested from the diet for five to ten days. The suspected foods are then eaten one at a time and symptoms are recorded. This method is difficult to use for delayed (non-IgE) food allergies. In severely allergic patients, it can be dangerous and should be used only under medical supervision, such as in a clinic setting.[1]

Intradermal or scratch skin tests are used by many conventional allergists and are good for inhalant allergies. However, they are usually not reliable for food allergies because they detect only IgE-mediated food allergies, which make up only about five percent of all food reactions.[2]

Provocation-neutralization testing is the most common in-office, or in-vivo test for food allergies. A small amount of a dilute extract of the food to be tested is injected into the skin of the patient's arm or given under the tongue. Any symptoms that result are recorded and the skin reaction is monitored. Then injections or sublingual drops of weaker or stronger dilutions of the same food extract are given. The dilution which does not provoke a skin reaction and clears up the patient's symptoms is the "neutralizing dose" and is used for neutralization treatment. (See page 10 for more information about neutralization). This test works best with food reactions that happen quickly whether mediated by IgE or IgG[3] It is about 80% accurate.[4]

Only in vivo tests (such as elimination-and-challenge or provocation-neutralization) are considered definitive for food allergies because they have been tested in double-blind studies. However, although our allergist uses the provocation-neutralization method for all food allergy testing for adults, when my son needed allergy testing at age 4, the doctor used a blood test to spare such a young child the trauma of multiple needle sticks. We were instructed to re-test all the foods that showed up as possible problems for my son by doing elimination and challenge tests at home. In this time of economic struggle and medical insurance which covers less and less every year (if you are fortunate enough to have it), some patients chose to pay out-of-pocket for blood tests for food allergies rather than bear the cost in both time and money of allergy testing in a doctor's office. There are several types of blood tests including RAST (Radio-Allergo-Sorbent Test), ELISA (Enzyme Linked Immuno-Sorbent Assay), and ELISA/ACT (Enzyme Linked Immuno-Sorbent Assay/Activated Cell Test). RAST and ELISA tests can detect either IgE or IgG antibodies to foods in the blood sample.[5] ELISA/ACT tests can detect IgG, IgA, and IgM antibodies, immune complexes, and cell activated reactions.[6] Thus, blood tests can detect the factors implicated in delayed as well as immediate food allergies, but to be definitive, food allergies that show up on a blood test should be confirmed by elimination and challenge.[7] If you elect to have a blood test, consult your doctor about the advisability and safety of confirming food allergies that show up as positive by an elimination and challenge test. Laboratories that perform blood tests are listed in "Sources," page 300. These laboratories may also be able to direct you to a nearby allergy clinic.

Treatments

Special diets are the most commonly used treatment for food allergies. If the patient is allergic to only one or two foods, eliminating the offending foods may be the only treatment necessary. This is the course usually taken in the case of children with peanut anaphylaxis. My father was able to treat the milk allergy he got from drinking large quantities of milk for an ulcer by simply eliminating dairy products.

When a patient has multiple food allergies, the offending foods must be eliminated and all other foods should be eaten at intervals of four to five days or longer. This is know as a "rotation" or "rotary diversified" diet. Rotation diets are necessary for patients with multiple allergies because if you have overt allergies to many foods, it is likely that you have slight, subclinical allergies to many other foods that you consider safe. Eating them on a rotated basis reduces your exposure to them and hopefully will help preserve your tolerance for them.

Doctors prescribe rotation diets of varying degrees of strictness depending on the severity of your allergies. On the most strict diets each food is eaten only once on its rotation day and the length of the rotation cycle may be much longer than four to five days. One very allergic person I talked to had been put on a one food per meal, three meals per day, twelve day cycle diet by a prominent allergy clinic.

Some doctors consider rotation diets with very long cycles to be counterproductive.[8] For most patients, a four to five day interval between eating foods gives the best masking of symptoms. A longer cycle may lead to "unmasking;" the patient reacts to and "loses" yet another food. However, there are patients who find that some foods agree with them better if they are rotated at longer intervals. I personally have many foods that I can tolerate if I eat them at one week or two week intervals, but which will bother me if I eat them every fourth to fifth day. The ideal rotation interval can vary from patient to patient and from food to food, but should never be less than four days because it takes at least that long for foods and immune factors to clear.

On most patients' rotation diets each food may be eaten more than once on the rotation day and the cycle is usually four to five days long. The rotation day can be any twenty-four hour period, not necessarily a calendar day. This means that leftovers from dinner can be eaten for tomorrow's lunch. No food should be eaten in extremely large quantities. (For example, rice should not make up half of the food you eat on its rotation day). As long as many foods are included in the diet, this is an easy rule to follow. However, if patients become allergic to almost all foods and find themselves left with only two or three foods per rotation day, they will of necessity be eating those foods in large quantities. In this situation they will probably eventually become sensitive to the few foods they are eating. Efforts must be made to seek out new and unusual foods so the number of foods they are eating can be increased. For sources of unusual starches and game meats, see "Sources," pages 298 and 299.

On a rotation diet, foods are rotated according to their biological classification in food families because foods in the same family have similar antigens. Usually the entire family is kept on the same rotation day. However, some doctors allow their less severely allergic patients to eat a different member of certain families on each day of the cycle. The families most often treated this way are the grain family and the cattle family. The rotation diet in this book, found on pages 39 to 45, treats the grain and cattle families this way. If your doctor advises against, for example, eating a different grain every day, simply eliminate grains from three days (or two days, if he allows you to "split" the grain family, as in the next paragraph) and instead eat the listed non-grain alternative on those days.

On a rotation diet, food families that are not a major problem for you can be "split." This means that you eat some of the foods in the family on, for example, day 1 of a four day cycle, and others of them on day 3. I like to split the vegetable families that contain dark green leafy vegetables so I can eat some of these extremely nutritious foods every day. Using the rotation diet in this book, you could eat goosefoot family vegetables on days 1 and 3 (chard on day 1 and spinach on day 3, for example) and cabbage family vegetables on days 2 and 4 (collards on day 2 and arugula on day 4, for example). For more information on how to use the rotation diet in this book, see pages 34 to 38.

When you first start on rotation, you may find it easiest to follow a set rotation diet such as the one in this book. However, after a while you may tire of eating the same combinations of foods every fourth day. For variety you may wish to rotate different categories of foods on different lengths of cycles. For example, rotate your grains or non-grain alternatives, oils (and other foods in the same family), and fruit sweeteners used in baking (and therefore also the fruits they come from) on a four day cycle, so leftover baked goods from Monday can be frozen and eaten on Friday. Rotate meats or other protein foods and vegetables on longer cycles. Decide each day what vegetables and proteins you want to eat and record them so you can be sure you have not eaten the same or related foods for at least four days. Rotating foods at longer intervals this way may also improve your tolerance for them, although this is not the case for all patients.

Since most food allergies are not "fixed," after you have avoided your problem foods for several months, your doctor may advise you to try to reintroduce them into your diet. When you are ready to liberalize your diet, you should eat your problem foods in moderate amounts and on a strictly rotated basis. You may find that you can eat some of them every fourth day with no problems, but that others must be rotated at longer intervals in order for you to tolerate them. For example, after six months of avoidance, my son, Joel, was able to add most of his problem foods back into his diet at five day intervals, but he could eat corn only once or twice a month. If he ate it weekly, his eczema would flare up. Several years ago when I was able to eat grains occasionally, I could eat one serving about once a month during the winter months without having problems. If I ate them more often or during pollen season, I could not tolerate them.

Medications and supplements may be used to help deal with food allergy symptoms. Gastrocrom™ is a prescription medication that can give people with food allergies some relief. It is sodium cromolyn, a drug which is taken by inhalation for hayfever and asthma and orally for food allergies. It must be used before exposure to an allergen, and works by preventing the release of histamine and other chemicals which initiate and mediate the allergic response. Because Gastrocrom™ suppresses symptoms without having any effect at all on the causes of food allergies, I have heard of patients getting progressively worse while taking it, although they may initially feel better. Other allergy medications such as antihistamines may also help suppress your symptoms.

Digestive enzymes help you break down your food into smaller less allergenic molecules, thus decreasing your reaction to the foods you eat. They can be quite useful for short term use as part of the recovery process. Because digestive enzymes are large complex protein molecules, you may not want to use them for long periods of time without rotating the sources they come from or you could become allergic to the enzyme preparations themselves. For more information on digestive enzymes and how to rotate them, see pages 15 to 16.

Vitamin C is a general anti-allergy supplement. We experience allergic symptoms when an allergen-antibody complex causes mast cells to release histamine and other allergy-mediating chemicals. Vitamin C helps stabilize mast cells so they are less likely to release these substances.

Large doses of quercitin, such as 4 to 6 grams per day, may also be helpful to some allergy patients.

Pantothenic acid is sometimes used for general allergy relief. It supports the function of the adrenal glands which make hormones that help us cope with allergic reactions.

Bicarbonate preparations such as Alka Seltzer Gold™, Vital Life Bi-Carb Formula™, or Tri-Salts are useful as a "quick fix" for food reactions. The pH of the body becomes more acid during an allergic reaction, and these supplements help alkalinize the blood, thus making you feel better. However, they should not be over-used because they neutralize stomach acid, which is essential to good digestion and to the support of healthy intestinal flora. (See pages 16 to 17 for more about hydrochloric acid). Bicarbonate preparations are best used twenty minutes to an hour following the meal to which you react so they do not interfere with the digestion of your next meal. The bicarbonate preparations, as all supplements you use, should be hypoallergenic themselves. Alka Seltzer Gold™ contains corn and thus is not appropriate for corn-sensitive patients. See "Sources," page 300, to locate brands that you can tolerate.

Immunotherapy may also be used to treat food allergies by modifying the immune response to allergenic foods. While standard conventional allergy shots are not effective for food allergies, two types of immunotherapy were developed in the 1960's that are useful. In this country, neutralization is the most widely used type of immunotherapy for food allergies. The patient is tested using the provocation-neutralization method described on page 7, and the dilutions of food extracts which "neutralize" the patient's reactions are determined. These dilutions are called "neutralizing doses." The doctor's office then prepares a solution containing neutralizing doses of extracts for all the foods to which the patient is allergic. The patient takes this neutralizing solution either under the tongue or by self-injection. When an allergenic food is eaten, the neutralizing solution should turn off the patient's reaction to the food. Because neutralizing doses change, patients must be retested frequently to keep their neutralizing drops current and working effectively.

The second kind of immunotherapy for food allergies is low dose immunotherapy. The first treatment of this type was enzyme potentiated desensitization (EPD) which was developed in England over 40 years ago and has been used around the world. It was used in the United States for about 10 years as part of a study conducted under an Investigational Review Board. An EPD shot contains a very minute amount of many allergens plus an enzyme which naturally occurs in the human body, beta-glucuronidase.

An American-made form of low dose immunotherapy called LDA (for Low Dose Allergens) was developed in 2003. Both EPD and LDA are used to treat inhalant allergies, adverse reactions to chemicals, and food allergies all at the same time. They stimulate the body to make T-suppressor lymphocytes specific for allergen suppression. These lymphocytes retrain the body not to react to allergenic substances.[9] Because the shot's effectiveness is dependent on having the correct, very low dose exposure to allergens at the time the shot is given, patients must avoid exposure to high amounts of allergens around the time of their shots. For severely allergic persons, it may take two years of treatment to achieve good results with food allergens, but after that, most patients' diets are unrestricted except for around the time of their shots. About 70-80% of LDA patient have a good response to treatment for food allergies. The success rate for inhalant allergies is 80-85% (90% if the patient has no food allergies) and the response is usually rapid, within one to a few shots.[10] Retesting is never required for low dose immunotherapy.[11]

LDA contains uniquely American allergens such as cottonwood, mountain juniper, New World evergreens, sage, avocadoes and other foods not commonly eaten in the UK and which are not in EPD, perfumes, etc. This broader antigenic coverage makes LDA a more complete treatment for Americans.[12] Part of the reason low dose immunotherapy is more effective than conventional allergy shots or neutralization may be because it treats all of the patient's allergies at the same time, including those not tested for and those which may be latent or causing subclinical reactions.[13] Thus, having a unique form of low dose immunotherapy for Americans makes sense on many levels.

Most American patients who have taken both EPD and LDA find them to be equally effective. In my own personal experience, I have done better on LDA than I did previously on EPD, but whether this is due to being better covered by the Americanized antigen mixture or just my improving health is impossible to determine. However, conversations with other patients also lead me to believe that more complete coverage for one's allergies is important. I have talked to many patients who say things like, "My doctor didn't think I had major problems with inhalants. When my food allergies didn't respond to treatment as expected, he reconsidered and added the inhalant concentrate to my shots. Then suddenly I could eat everything."

Before low dose immunotherapy treatment is begun, factors which could interfere, such as dysbiosis, hormonal imbalances, heavy metal toxicity, and poor nutritional status, should be corrected as well as possible. Dr. Leo Galland estimated that in his practice of patients with digestive problems, after he treated their dysbiosis, nutritional and other problems, and promoted intestinal healing, only 25% of those who came to him for low dose immunotherapy treatment for their food allergies still needed it.[14] If low dose immunotherapy has seemed to fail, interfering factors should be tested for and treated.

To learn more about low dose immunotherapy and for recipes and organizational tips which will help you with this treatment, see *The Low Dose Immunotherapy Handbook* as described on the last page of this book. To find a doctor who can treat you with LDA, visit this website: www.drshrader.com.

By using these options for the diagnosis and treatment of food allergies, and especially by getting to the root of the problem as discussed in the next chapter, those of us with food allergies can progress towards optimal health.

FOOTNOTES

1. Reno, Liz, M.A. and Joanna Devrais, M.A. *Allergy Free Eating*, Celestial Arts, Berkeley, CA, 1995, p.28.

2. Ibid, pp. 29-30.

3. Ibid, pp. 29-30.

4. Personal communication from W. A. Shrader, Jr., M.D., April, 1997.

5. Reno, Liz, M.A. et al, pp. 30-31.

6. Interview with Russell Jaffe, M.D., Ph.D., "Allergy Testing," *Mastering Food Allergies Newsletter*, #44, April 1990, p. 3.

7. Personal communication from W. A. Shrader, Jr., M.D., April, 1997.

8. Personal communication from W. A. Shrader, Jr., M.D., April, 1997.

9. Interview with W. A. Shrader, Jr. M.D. "Enzyme Potentiated Desensitization (EPD): Exciting New Hope for Food Allergies," *Mastering Food Allergies Newsletter*, #74, July/August 1993, pp. 1-2.

10. Personal communication from W. A. Shrader, Jr., M.D., January, 2006.

11. Interview with W. A. Shrader, Jr. M.D. "Enzyme Potentiated Desensitization (EPD): Exciting New Hope for Food Allergies," *Mastering Food Allergies Newsletter*, #74, July/August 1993, pp. 1-2.

12. Personal communication from W. A. Shrader, Jr., M.D., June, 2003.

13. Interview with Len McEwen, M.D. and W. A. Shrader, Jr. M.D. "EPD Update," *Mastering Food Allergies Newsletter*, #88, November/December 1995, p. 3.

14. Ibid, p. 1.

Getting to the Root of the Problem

The most effective treatments for any health problem are those that address the root cause of the condition rather than just treat the symptoms. By correcting the factors that contribute to food allergies and leaky gut, you can enhance the effectiveness of the treatments described in the last chapter and overcome your allergies.

Nutrition and Diet

Our bodies depend on the nutrients from our food for energy, repair, and all the functions of life. (That is why many nutrients are called "essential.") Even with a good diet, those of us with food allergies are often malnourished because our nutritional status does not depend only on what we eat, but also on what we digest and absorb. Therefore, attention to diet and nutrition is crucial to repairing our leaky guts and recovering our health.

Because we may not absorb nutrients from foods to which we are allergic, and because these foods contribute to the irritation of our intestine and further decrease absorption, the first thing to consider in planning your diet is that you do not eat foods to which you are allergic. If you have reached the point of having some degree of allergy to most common foods, seek out new foods which you have never tried before. Read the food family tables on pages 269 to 280 to get ideas. Sources for unusual starches, flours, and game meats are listed on pages 298 and 299. Large health food stores often carry unusual vegetables and fruits in their produce departments. You might also shop for produce at an international market or in the "exotics" section of the produce department in a large supermarket. As your health improves, or if your diet still contains only a few foods after you have added all the new ones possible, add back some of your least problematic foods on a carefully rotated basis, possibly using a longer cycle than four to five days. The extremely restricted diets often required by the severely allergic may add to the problem of malnourishment. A highly varied diet is the most healthy kind of diet for everyone to eat.

Dr. Leo Galland, who is one of the foremost authorities on food allergies and gastrointestinal health, recommends an oligoallergenic (low in allergens) nutrient dense diet for "gut repair."[1] This means that your diet should not contain foods to which you are allergic nor the chemically adulterated, nutrient stripped, highly processed foods that are a major part of the "standard American diet."

Vegetables and fruits should make up a large part of your diet because of the vitamins, minerals, phytochemicals, and fiber they contain. Dark green leafy vegetables are nutritional powerhouses in every way, and even contain good quantities of essential fatty acids.[2] (To "legally" eat them on every day of rotation, see page 9).

High quality, non-allergenic protein is essential for the tissue repair involved in healing your intestine. Vegetarian diets are popular among those with health problems and, properly used, can supply this protein. (Dr. Paul Eck suggests that the prevalence of impaired secretion of stomach acid and the associated difficulty in digesting flesh proteins is the reason for the popularity of these diets.[3] See pages 16 to 17 for more about this problem). However, if you are allergic to the beans and grains that are the best protein sources on vegetarian diets and must omit them or not eat them frequently, you will often be better off eating unusual fish or game meat and taking a hydrochloric acid supplement to help your digestion.

You also should pay attention to the types of fats you eat. While the fat in commercially raised beef is unhealthy, game meat is a good source of essential fatty acids.[4] Essential fatty acids are important to intestinal integrity and are especially high in fatty fish, such as salmon and mackerel, and cold pressed oils, such as flaxseed oil. As with all foods, if you take flax oil every day, you may become allergic to it. Rotating a variety of oils is safer. For more information on the fatty acid profiles of oils and fatty acid nutrition, call Omega Nutrition at (800) 661-3529 and ask for their pamphlet, "Fats: Facts and Fiction."

Supplementation is an excellent way to improve your nutritional status. The supplements you take should be hypoallergenic because, as with foods, you may not absorb nutrients well from preparations which come from or contain fillers made from foods to which you are allergic.[5] (For sources of hypoallergenic supplements, see page 300). The need for certain nutrients can vary as much as 30-fold from person to person.[6] Food allergy patients can be profoundly deficient in some nutrients, so restoring the balance is essential to recovery. However, taking large quantities of single nutrients can cause deficiencies of other nutrients. Nutrient imbalances, like food allergies, can be complicated to determine without, or sometimes even with, professional help. If your doctor is not experienced in this area, you may benefit from consulting a nutritionist who, from your history, symptoms, and laboratory tests, can help determine your individual needs. (See "Sources," page 299, for help in finding a qualified nutritionist near you).

What we eat also affects our health through the presence of undesirable organisms in our food. All animal foods should be thoroughly cooked before you eat them. Thorough cooking is also the only way to be completely certain that plant foods contain no infectious agents. Plant foods that will be eaten raw should be treated with a disinfectant before you eat them. In *Guess What Came to Dinner*, Ann Louise Gittleman gives detailed instructions on how to disinfect food using Clorox™ and how to prevent getting a parasitic infestation from your food, water, travel, or pets. (See "References," page 296). If you are not able to use Clorox™ due to chemical sensitivities, Nutribiotic™, a grapefruit seed extract, can be used instead. In laboratory testing, it has been shown to be active against a wide range of bacteria, yeasts, fungi, and parasites.[7] At our house, any produce that we will be eating raw is soaked in a sink of cool water with about 30 drops of Nutribiotic™ added for at least 30 minutes as soon as we bring it home from the store.

Finally, consider the effect that your attitude toward food has on your nutritional status. So often when we think of food, those of us with food allergies think of what we cannot eat, and our whole focus is on the elimination of foods. A friend told me that, after consulting a naturopath, her whole attitude toward food changed. She changed her perspective from the avoidance of foods to an emphasis on putting good and healthy foods into her body. Seek out the most nutritious foods you can tolerate and eat them with enjoyment.

Digestion

Many people with food allergies have impaired digestion. Incomplete digestion of foods which then pass through a leaky gut into the bloodstream is a major contributing factor to the problem of food allergies.[8]

There are several things you can do to improve your digestion. The most basic is to pay attention to how you eat. Try to be in a relaxed frame of mind when you eat. Chew your food very thoroughly. Chewing breaks the food down into smaller particles that can be acted on more easily by your digestive system, starting in the mouth. When you chew well, you begin the process of starch digestion by mixing the food with the enzyme salivary amylase.

Drinking water with meals is a controversial subject. Some have suggested that it "dilutes the digestive juices." Using large quantities of water to wash down food rather than taking the time to chew thoroughly is a practice to be avoided. However, studies have shown that a moderate intake of one to two glasses of water with a meal improves digestion by facilitating both the production of gastric secretions at the time you eat and also the secretion of bicarbonate into the small intestine that normally occurs one to two hours after a meal.[9]

The presence of undigested food in the stool indicates a deficiency in the secretion of hydrocholoric acid by the stomach, of digestive enzymes by the pancreas, or both. These deficiencies can be helped by supplementation. Digestive enzymes are available as supplements in several forms. Pancreatin is an extract of the pancreas of cows or pigs and is a very potent, broad-spectrum aid for the digestion of proteins, fats, and carbohydrates. However, if you are allergic to beef or pork, you will probably not tolerate pancreatin.

Broad-spectrum plant enzymes are derived from the fungus *Aspergillus orazeae*. They are also active in the digestion of fats, proteins, and carbohydrates. I took plant-based enzymes for several months, and during that time gained weight easily for the first time since I developed Crohn's disease. (Note: Although being underweight is a problem for some with food allergies, improving digestion, and especially removing addictive allergic foods from the diet, allows overweight patients to lose weight easily. The treatment of maldigestion and food allergies should lead to normal weight). However, after using digestive enzymes daily for several months, I became sensitized to them. Digestive enzymes are large, complex protein molecules, and thus we may sensitize to them more easily than to other supplements.[10]

Dr. William Philpott recommends the rotation of digestive enzymes on a four-day cycle.[11] This can be accomplished by using pancreatin (from pork and beef), plant enzymes (from *Aspergillus orazeae*), bromelain (from pineapple), and papain (from papaya). Bromelain and papain are active in the digestion of protein only. I personally found that I did not gain weight using papain and bromelain. Studies have shown them to be much less potent than pancreatin.[12]

In his book, *Digestive Enzymes,* Dr. Jeffrey Bland says that while enzyme supplements can be an important part of breaking the vicious cycle of maldigestion and starting us on the road back to health, we should not have to take them forever. He recommends a regimen of vitamin C, vitamin A, zinc, and pantothenic acid to improve digestive health in general.[13] You might want to discuss this protocol with your doctor or nutritionist and consider trying it. After about a month on these supplements, I again found it easier to gain weight, and because of that, I assume than I am now producing my own digestive enzymes.

It is estimated that 80% of patients with food allergies suffer from some degree of impairment of hydrochloric acid secretion by their stomachs.[14] This can range from the complete absence of hydrochloric acid (achlorhydria) to a deficiency in the amount of hydrochloric acid secreted (hypochlorhydria). The passage of acidic stomach contents into the small intestine is the stimulus for the pancreas to release digestive enzymes and bicarbonate. Therefore, if you have hypochlorhydria or achlorhydria, you may not secrete digestive enzymes properly even if your pancreas is fully able to do so. This is one of several reasons that hydrocholoric acid supplements may be essential to your return to health.

However, hydrocholoric acid supplements, if not needed or if taken in too large amounts, can cause ulceration of the stomach. Supplementation with betaine-HCl (from beets) or glutamic-HCl (from grains) should be done only under medical supervision. Your doctor may perform a Heidelberg gastrogram, which is a test that determines your ability to secrete hydrocholoric acid. To do this test, the patient swallows an instrument the size of a large capsule which has a string attached to it for retrieval. The instrument then transmits information about the pH of the digestive tract and how it changes when the patient drinks a bicarbonate solution. Or your doctor might suspect hypochlorhydria because of the presence of undigested food in a stool analysis. Rather than doing a Heidelberg gastrogram, he or she may have you take gradually increasing amounts of a hydrocholoric acid supplement and report your symptoms to determine your degree of need for hydrochloric acid.

Surprisingly, a common symptom of hypochlorhydria is heartburn. Television commercials tell us when we have heartburn we should neutralize our stomach acid with various antacids, or, even more drastically, take medications which have recently become available "over the counter," such as ranitidine, cimetidine, nizatidine, or famotidine, which reduce our production of stomach acid. For those who have heartburn because of hypochlorhydria, these medications may bring relief of heartburn but could lead to poor digestion and thus to dysbiosis, leaky gut, and food allergies. Before you risk compromising your health with these medications, ask your doctor to help you find out if your real problem might be inefficient production of hydrochloric acid.

In addition to stimulating the release of digestive enzymes, hydrocholoric acid plays other roles in your health. It is essential for the ionization of minerals so they can be absorbed. It is interesting to note that some cases of iron deficiency anemia and other mineral deficiencies can be traced to low hydrocholoric acid production. Protein cannot be digested without sufficient hydrocholoric acid. This acid is responsible for nearly sterilizing food in the stomach, so insufficient secretion can result in bacterial overgrowth of the small intestine, as discussed in the section on dysbiosis, pages 17 to 20. Finally, hydrocholoric acid promotes a friendly pH for the growth of *Lactobacillus* and *Bifidobacterium* in the small and large intestine.[15]

A final possible way to improve your digestion, in addition to chewing thoroughly, relaxing at mealtimes, and taking any necessary hydrocholoric acid or digestive enzyme supplements, is the system of "food combining." I practiced food combining faithfully for several months and did not notice a change, but there are many testimonials about its effectiveness, so it must help some people. *The Body Ecology Diet* by Donna Gates is based in part on the principals of food combining. In my opinion, if other ways of improving your digestion seem ineffective, the body ecology diet and food combining are worth a try as long as they do not severely restrict your nutrition.

Dysbiosis

A healthy person lives in harmony with his or her intestinal flora. The person provides a home and food to over 400 species of bacteria.[17] The bacteria, which in a healthy person will be predominantly "friendly" types, do a myriad of health-promoting things for the person, as will be discussed in the next chapter. This state is called "symbiosis."

Sometimes this state of happy balance does not exist because of the presence of frankly pathogenic organisms, the overgrowth of unfriendly organisms that are often not considered pathogenic, or the absence of friendly bacteria. Then, dys-symbiosis, or dysbio-sis exists. Dysbiosis can be caused by protozoan parasites *(Entamoeba histolytica, Entamoe-ba coli,* other *Entamoeba, Dientamoeba fragilis, Endolimax nana, Giardia lamblia, Blastocys-tis hominis, Chilomastix mesnili,* and others); yeast *(Candida albicans,* other *Candida* species, *Torulopsis glabrata,* and others); or bacteria *(Salmonella, Shigella, Campylobacter jejuni, Yersinia enterocolitica, Klebsiella pneumoniae, Citrobacter freundii, Citrobacter diver-sus, Proteus mirabilis, Pseudomonas aeruginosa,* some strains of *Escherichia coli, Staphylococ-cus aureus,* some strains of *Bacteriodes, Clostridium difficile,* and others). Some of these organisms are not considered "pathogenic" by conventional medicine. However, weak pathogens, or a predominance of "unfriendly" organisms can cause severe illness in a chron-ically ill, weakened, or malnourished patient.[18] The eradication of these organisms can make a dramatic difference in the patient's health.

A very common cause of bacterial or fungal dysbiosis is often the repeated or long term use of antibiotics. Antibiotics kill both the bacteria you want them to kill and the "friendly" bacteria in the intestine and the vagina. This leaves these areas open to be colo-nized by yeast, unfriendly bacteria, and parasites.

Parasitic infestations are on the increase because of changes in our lifestyles that have occurred over the last few decades. International travel is now commonplace. If you are not a traveler, the world and its parasites will come to you, brought by imported pro-duce and immigrants from countries where sanitation is sub-standard. Eating out in restau-rants frequently and the close contact of day care centers contribute to the spread of para-sites.

Maldigestion can also promote dysbiosis. Dr. Martin Lee says, "Colonic flora is a reflection of what it is fed."[19] If food is completely and rapidly digested and absorbed in the small intestine, it is not available to nourish unfriendly bacteria or yeast in either the small or large intestine. Almost all that is left to reach the large intestine is fiber, which is a favorite food for friendly bacteria such as *Lactobacillus* and *Bifidobacterium* and promotes their growth.

Diet can also contribute to dysbiosis. A diet high in flesh protein and low in plant foods promotes the growth of *Bacteroides* species, but a lacto-vegetarian diet, based on milk products and plant foods, promotes the growth of *Lactobacillus* and *Bifidobacterium.*[20] Elaine Gottshalls's book *Breaking the Vicious Cycle* prescribes the "specific carbohydrate diet" for patients with inflammatory bowel disease.[21] This diet eliminates all grains, sugar, lactose, other disaccharides, and some starches that such patients may be unable to digest and absorb. This leads to a shift in bowel flora towards normal and improvement in symp-toms.

The ideal diet for patients with candidiasis is the subject of considerable debate. Several years ago, high-protein, low-carbohydrate diets, on which the grams of carbohydrate may have even been counted, were used. Then Dr. William Crook began using diets higher in complex carbohydrates for his patients. Simple carbohydrates, such as fruits, were still restricted initially.[22] When Dr. Crook was in Colorado in 1995, I heard him speak to a group of health professionals, and the question of the best diet for candidiasis was raised. Dr. Crook said that, in his many years of experience, the only absolute he had determined to be essential for the diet was that sugar had to be avoided. He said that all the Nystatin™ or Diflucan™ in the world will not eradicate *Candida* if a patient continues to eat sugar. Recent German studies suggest that very low carbohydrate diets may be counterproductive because they cause the *Candida* to become invasive and penetrate deeper into the tissues in search of food.[23]

Dysbiosis caused by bacteria or yeast can be diagnosed using a stool test called a comprehensive digestive stool analysis (CDSA). The microbiology part of this test differs from a standard "stool culture," which usually only reports the presence or absence of aerobic (oxygen-loving) bacteria considered "pathothenic" by conventional medicine, such as *Salmonella* and *Shigella*. A CDSA tests for the presence and amount or absence of all aerobic organisms and, although they are not strictly aerobic, friendly organisms such as *Lactobacillus* and *Bifidobacterium*. The organisms a CDSA reports include yeast of all kinds, all normal and abnormal aerobic bacteria, *Bacteroides Lactobacillus,* and *Bifidobacterium.* A CDSA also gives your doctor chemical information that reflects the health of your digestive system. This information includes the presence and amount or absence of undigested protein and plant fibers, fats, fatty acids, occult blood, and other metabolic markers. This information may be suggestive of conditions that are affecting your health in general. Tests for dysbiosis, such as a CDSA or a parasitology test, as discussed below, may be the most important tests you do and should not be omitted for any patient with severe food allergies or digestive problems. Great Smokies Diagnostic Laboratory can refer you to doctors in your area who use the CDSA to evaluate their patients. (See "Sources," page 300). To learn more about the CDSA, visit this page of the Great Smokies Laboratories website: http://gsdl.com/home/assessments/cdsa/appguide/.

In-depth parasitology testing should also be done to determine if parasites are causing dysbiosis. Such in-depth testing can be done best by a specialized parasitology lab such as the Parasitology Center. (See "Sources," page 300). The parasitology testing you should have done differs from the standard "ova and parasites" test done at most hospital laboratories in several ways. This testing will report organisms that would not be reported on a standard test because they are not considered "pathogenic" by many in conventional medicine, such as *Blastocystis homonis*. Also, since specialized laboratories have more experience in looking for parasites, they are more likely to find any that are there. However, even when the test is done by an experienced laboratory, Dr. Leo Galland says that parasitology testing should be "taken with a grain of salt."[24] Stool samples, by their very nature, contain a

lot of debris mixed with a very few parasites, eggs, or cysts. It is not always easy to distin-
guish a degrading white blood cell or other material from something significant. For this
reason the test may be reported as negative when the patient DOES have parasites, even if
it is done by a competent technician at an excellent laboratory. The more samples submit-
ted, the more likely a parasite will be picked up. The use of purged stool specimens or rec-
tal swabs also increases the chance of recovering parasites because they are dislodged from
the intestinal wall. A patient may have several negative tests and still have parasites.

Intestinal dysbiosis can be treated with a variety of prescription and botanical medicines to rid your body of unfriendly organisms. Your CDSA results include sensitivity testing which indicates which medicines are effective against your particular unfriendly bacteria and yeast. Treatment of dysbiosis caused by bacteria and/or yeast will also usually
include supplementation with friendly probiotic organisms such as *Lactobacillus* and *Bifidobacterium*. Dr. Leo Galland does not recommend taking probiotics while under treatment for parasitic infestations because bacteria are "food" for protozoal parasites: save your
probiotics to take after the course of anti-parasitic treatment is completed.[25] Your doctor
may also direct you to take nutrients that help your intestine heal, such as L-glutamine (the
major source of nourishment for the cells lining the small intestine), N-acetyl-glucosamine
(which stimulates the production of intestinal secretory IgA, a protective factor), and
butyric acid (which promotes healing in the large intestine), or other nutrients.

A few supplements you may be taking can be counterproductive to the treatment
of dysbiosis and are mentioned here so you can avoid them. Iron supplements feed
unfriendly bacteria and protozoan parasites.[26] Fructooligosaccharides (FOS) also feed some
unfriendly bacteria, especially *Klebsiella pneumoniae,* hemolytic *E. coli, Bacteroides species,*
and *Staphylococcus aureus.*[27] As mentioned above, protozoal parasites "eat" bacteria, so your
doctor may advise you to avoid probiotics during the course of anti-parasitic treatment.
Cysteine, glycine, and glutathione, while important antioxidants, can stimulate the growth
of yeast in some patients with candidiasis.[28] If you are taking botanical remedies for dysbiosis, your doctor may tell you to temporarily avoid all antioxidants because botanical
medicines kill parasites and bacteria by oxidizing them, and thus, antioxidants reduce the
effectiveness of these remedies.[29]

Other Factors That May Be
Harming Your Intestine

Some substances cause increased intestinal permeability and can compound the
problem of "leaky gut" and contribute to food allergies. They include alcoholic beverages,
nonsteroidal anti-inflammatory drugs (aspirin, ibuprofen, ketoprofen, naproxen, prescrip-

tion arthritis medications, etc.), chemotherapeutic drugs for cancer, radiation therapy to the abdomen, and corticosteroid drugs. There may be times, such as if you have cancer, when you have to take some of these treatments. But "just say no" to using the ones that you have a choice about, such as alcohol and nonsteroidal anti-inflammatory drugs for pain relief.[30]

Nonsteroidal anti-inflammatory drugs are now being sold without a prescription and without much warning about their side effects. I consider this very unfortunate, as is the sometimes seemingly indiscriminate prescribing of these drugs. For anyone with even the possibility of compromised intestinal health, a single dose of a nonsteroidal anti-inflammatory drug can increase intestinal permeability tremendously.[31] Food allergy patients and first degree relatives of people with Crohn's disease, such as my children, fall into the "possibly compromised" category.[32] (I half-jokingly tell my children that if they ever have an injury or other circumstance that requires a painkiller, they should ask for morphine!) If you need pain relief medication, try using heat, herbal pain relief remedies, supplements such as DL-phenylalanine, or acupuncture rather than resorting to nonsteroidal anti-inflammatory drugs.

In a study of factors that might cause inflammatory bowel disease in mice, indomethacin, a prescription nonsteroidal anti-inflammatory drug, induced symptoms of Crohn's disease in normal mice, but not in germ-free mice. The study concluded that some interaction between the indomethacin and intestinal flora produced inflammation.[33] Perhaps the indomethacin caused "leaky gut," which then allowed the mice to become sensitive to their intestinal flora. The *Physician's Desk Reference* warns about the possibility of gastrointestinal bleeding, ulceration, and perforation when using nonsteroidal inflammatory drugs, and reports that one arthritis drug can lead to the development of inflammatory bowel disease.[34] Dr. W. A. Shrader, Jr. says that all nonsteroidal anti-inflammatory drugs cause some degree of mucosal atrophy in the intestine.[35] In my opinion, it is wise to avoid nonsteroidal anti-inflammatory drugs to prevent such problems.

If people with food allergies avoid harmful substances and address the factors at the root of their problems, such as nutrition, digestion, and dysbiosis, their allergies CAN be overcome. It may take time and some of the medical treatments discussed in the last chapter may also be needed, but good health can be possible.

FOOTNOTES

1. Galland, Leo, M.D. "Leaky Gut Syndromes: Breaking the Vicious Cycles," *Townsend Letter for Doctors,* August/September 1995, p. 63.

2. Braly, James, M.D. *Dr. Braly's Food Allergy and Nutrition Revolution,* Keats Publishing, Inc., New Canaan, CT, 1992, p. 143.

3. Eck, Paul, N.D. "Adrenal Burnout Syndrome," Eck Institute Articles, Eck Institute of Applied Nutrition and Bioenergetics, Ltd., 8650 N. 22nd Avenue, Phoenix, AZ 85021, pp. 2-3.

4. Braly, James, M.D. *Dr. Braly's Food Allergy and Nutrition Revolution,* p. 143.

5. Ibid, p. 89.

6. Lipski, Elizabeth, M.S., C.C.N. *Digestive Wellness,* Keats Publishing, Inc., New Canaan, CT, 1996, p.9.

7. Testing on many organisms done by an independent laboratory for BioChem Research, Inc.,
        865 Parallel Drive, Lakeport, CA 95453, (707) 263-1475, 1994 and previously.
        Independent testing on several organisms also done in 1996 at Western Illinois University by
        Kathy Jeffries, B.S.

8. Bland, Jeffrey, Ph.D. *Digestive Enzymes,* Keats Publishing, Inc., New Canaan, CT, 1993,
        pp. 13 and 15.

9. Ibid, p. 9.

10. Jaffe, Russell, M.D., "Dysbiosis," American Academy of Environmental Medicine Conference,
        October 1992.

11. Phillpott, William H., M.D. *Victory Over Diabetes,* Keats Publishing, Inc., New Canaan, CT, 1983, p.
        69.

12. Bland, Jeffrey, Ph.D. *Digestive Enzymes,* p. 11.

13. Ibid, p. 20.

14. Braly, James, M.D. *Dr. Braly's Food Allergy and Nutrition Revolution,* p. 73.

15. Chaitow, Leon, and Natasha Trenev, *Probiotics,* Hohm Press, P.O. Box 2501, Prescott, AZ 86302,
        p. 12.

16. Gates, Donna, *The Body Ecology Diet,* B.E.D. Publications, 1266 W. Paces Ferry Road, Suite
        505, Atlanta, GA 30327, p. 13.

17. Chaitow, Leon, et al, *Probiotics,* p. 11.

18. Lee, Martin J., Ph.D. "Parasites, Yeast, and Bacteria in Health and Disease," *Journal of Advancement in
        Medicine,* Volume 8, Number 2, Summer 1995, pp. 121 and 127-128.

19. Lee, Martin J., Ph.D. "Gastrointestinal Function," Solving the Digestive Puzzle Symposium,
        May 1995.

20. Galland, Leo, M.D. "Dysbiotic Relationships in the Bowel," American College of Advancement in
        Medicine Conference, Spring 1992.

21. Gottschall, Elaine, B.S., M.Sc., *Breaking the Vicious Cycle: Intestinal Health Through Diet,*
        The Kirkton Press, Kirkton, Ontario, Canada, 1994, pp. 53-59.

22. Crook, William G., M.D. and Marjorie H. Jones, R.N., *The Yeast Connection Cookbook,* Professional
        Books, Jackson, TN, 1989, pp. 39-45.

23. Naugle, Elizabeth, "Dietary Update," Candida and Dysbiosis Information Foundation,
        P.O. Drawer JF, College Station, TX 77841, p. 1.

24. Galland, Leo, M.D. "Gut Parasites," Enzyme Potentiated Desensitization Conference,
        October 1995.

25. Ibid.

26. Galland, Leo, M.D. "Gut Parasites and Bacteria," Enzyme Potentiated Desensitization Conference, October 1995.

27. Barrager, Eleanor, R.D. "Clinical Therapeutics and Case Studies," Solving the Digestive Puzzle Symposium, May 1995; Mitsuoka, Tomotari, "Intestinal Flora and Aging," *Nutrition Reviews,* Volume 50, Number 12, December 1992, p. 442-443; and Mitsuoka, Tomotari, Hidemasa Hidaka, and Toshaki Eida, "Effect of Fructo-oligosaccharides on Intestinal Microflora," *Die Nahrung* 31 (1987), 5-6, pp. 427-436.

28. Rogers, Sherry, M.D. *Tired or Toxic,* Prestige Publishing, Box 3161, Syracuse, NY 13220, 1990, p. 252, also personal communication from Dr. Sidney Baker to nutritionist Katherine Gibbons.

29. Galland, Leo, M.D. "Dysbiotic Relationships in the Bowel," American College of Advancement in Medicine Conference, Spring 1992.

30. Galland, Leo, M.D. "Leaky Gut Syndromes," p. 62, and Reno, Liz, M.A. and Joanna Devrais, M.A. *Allergy Free Eating,* Celestial Arts, Berkeley, CA, 1995, pp. 19-20.

31. Galland, Leo, M.D. "Leaky Gut Syndromes," p. 63.

32. Interview with Leo Galland, M.D., "Leaky Gut – What Is It? What Factors Cause It? What Can Be Done?" *Mastering Food Allergies Newsletter,* #86, July/August 1995, p. 4.

33. Martin, Peter, "Closing In On the Cause," *IBD Digest,* November 1991, p. 12.

34. 1996 *Physician's Desk Reference,* pp. 817, 862, 1619, 1681, 2579.
(On p. 1681, it says of indomethacin, "The development of ulcerative colitis and regional ileitis have been reported to occur rarely.")

35. Personal communication from W. A. Shrader, Jr., M.D., April, 1997.

Our Unseen Allies

Each of us carries within our bodies about three and one-half pounds of bacteria. There is a greater number of bacterial cells present in each of us than the number of our own cells. Normally over four hundred species of bacteria live in our intestines. If the predominant organisms are friendly, our intestinal flora does us an amazing amount of good.[1]

Before birth, babies have sterile digestive tracts. As they are born and pass through the vagina, babies pick up bacteria, including *Lactobacillus* and *Bifidobacterium*. By the age of six days, 60% of vaginally born babies have *Bifidobacterium infantis* in their intestines. (Only 9% of babies born by Caesarian section are so colonized).[2] Breast milk contributes *Bifidobacterium* to an infant's body, and is the perfect food for both the child and friendly intestinal bacteria.

By the age of three months, a healthy breast-fed baby will have a thriving, self-sustaining colony of friendly intestinal bacteria.[3] As the child's diet changes, the bowel flora will also change. Other organisms will join the original pure culture of *Bifidobacterium* that a breast-fed child has. *Lactobacillus, E.coli,* and other normal intestinal flora will appear and produce a balanced, healthy bacterial ecosystem that should last throughout life.

However, nowadays our bacterial ecosystems are subjected to antibiotics, corticosteroid drugs, and other stresses of modern life; thus unfriendly organisms can become the predominant flora. Then we must start over to eradicate the unfriendly organisms, put friendly bacteria back, feed them well, and create a good environment for them so they can once again become a thriving colony that contributes to our health.

In discussing lactose intolerance, the point is often made that many adults (indeed most adults who are not of Northern European descent) lack the ability to produce the enzyme lactase. The conclusion drawn from this is that adults were not "naturally" meant to drink milk or consume dairy products of any kind. However, we were also not "naturally" meant to be exposed to antibiotics and other stresses on our friendly intestinal flora. Milk is the "favorite food" of *Lactobacillus* and *Bifidobacterium*. Fermented milks, such as yogurt, acidophilus milk, and kefir, contain almost no lactose if properly made. The protein in them is partially pre-digested and therefore less allergenic. If made from alternative milks, such as goat, sheep, or soy milk, they are more likely to be tolerated by allergic people. Because milk is the best food for *Lactobacillus* and *Bifidobacterium* and, as in my case, may be the only thing that will get them to implant, and because there are alternative milks to use in place of cow's milk, I must differ with the "all milk products are bad for everyone" stand that many books on food allergy take. Therefore, this chapter will discuss both our unseen allies, *Lactobacillus* and *Bifidobacterium,* and their favorite foods, fermented milks.

What Does Our Friendly Flora Do for Us?

Lactobacillus and *Bifidobacterium* are called "probiotic" organisms because they are for ("pro" means for) life ("bios" means life). These unseen allies belong to several species in the *Lactobacillus* and *Bifidobacterium* genera. *Lactobacillus acidophilus* is the only *Lactobacillus* that can colonize our bodies with a self-sustaining population. Other members of the *Lactobacillus* group, such as *Lactobacillus bulgaricus* from yogurt and *Lactobacillus plantarum* from cultured vegetables are transient organisms. They will live in our intestines for several days after ingestion and improve our intestinal environment so *Lactobacillus acidophilus* can implant more easily. *Bifidobacterium bifidum* is the *Bifidobacterium* species most commonly found in adults. *Bifidobacterium infantis* is found in infants and small children. *Lactobacillus* lives mostly in the small intestine and the vagina. *Bifidobacterium* lives mostly in the large intestine. As all of these organisms live in us, they support and enrich our lives in a multitude of ways.

First, they improve our nutrition. They manufacture vitamins, including vitamin K and the B vitamins biotin, niacin, pantothenic acid, pyridoxine, and folic acid.[4] They produce the enzyme lactase which digests lactose in dairy products. Therefore, a thriving colony of friendly flora can make a lactase-deficient person better able to tolerate dairy products and derive nutrients such as calcium and protein from them.[5]

Second, they enhance digestion and bowel function. *Bifidobacteria* are supplemented in bottle-fed babies who fail to thrive because these organisms help the babies absorb nutrients from their food. In adults and older children, establishing normal flora can help lessen constipation, diarrhea, and flatulence.[6]

Our friendly flora also helps protect us from cancer. They produce anti-tumor substances, and also reduce the risk of colon cancer by blocking the conversion of nitrates in the bowel into potentially harmful nitrites and nitrosamines. In addition, they may have an anti-cancer effect by stimulating immunity in general.[7]

They even relieve the liver of some of its workload of detoxification. By creating an acid pH in the bowel, friendly organisms cause ammonia to remain in its ionized form. It cannot be absorbed into the bloodstream in this form; so instead of being absorbed and having to be detoxified by the liver, it passes out of the body in the feces.[8]

Last, but certainly not least in importance, our friendly flora protects us from other, less friendly organisms, including parasites, yeast, and harmful bacteria. They keep unfriendly organisms from establishing a home inside us by making lactic acid, hydrogen peroxide, and an assortment of natural antibiotic substances. The biotin they produce prevents *Candida albicans* from turning into its more harmful and aggressive mycelial form.[9]

By suppressing the growth of unfriendly organisms in the digestive tract, *Lacto-bacillus* and *Bifidobacterium* protect us from a host of diseases. As mentioned in the last chapter, dysbiosis with parasites, yeast, or bacteria causes "leaky gut" and thus contributes to food allergies. Some autoimmune diseases have been linked to the presence of unfriendly bacteria in the gut. In ankylosing spondylitis, the body attacks tissue antigens that are the same as those found on *Klebsiella pneumoniae.* In rheumatoid arthritis, the same type of cross-reaction exists with *Proteus mirabilis.*[10] One wonders how many other diseases have similar, but as yet undiscovered, causes.

How Can We Cultivate Healthy Intestinal Flora?

Establishing thriving colonies of *Lactobacillus* and *Bifidobacterium* is harder for us to do as adults than it is for infants to do with their initially sterile intestines. The presence of unfriendly organisms may be directly antagonistic to *Lactobacillus* and *Bifidobacterium.*[11] Therefore, any unfriendly organisms or potential pathogens that show up on a patient's CDSA or parasitology test should be treated and eradicated. (See pages 19 to 20).

Taking probiotic supplements is the next step in establishing normal intestinal flora. What kind, how much, how, and when to take probiotics is the subject of considerable debate. Most probiotic supplement manufacturers recommend taking one capsule or ¼ to ½ teaspoon of powder one to three times per day. Following the manufacturer's instructions is always a sensible place to start, and is also the most economical dose. However, I have talked to many people who assumed that they had friendly intestinal flora because they faithfully took probiotics every day in the recommended amounts. Then they have a CDSA and find out that they have no *Lactobacillus* or *Bifidobacterium.*

Dr. Sidney Baker advises his patients to take their whole week's worth of probiotics at one time. This amounts to taking one to two tablespoons of powder once a week. His reasoning is that if ninety percent of the dose is going to be killed before it reaches the site at which it should implant, if the original dose is larger, enough may still get through to implant.[12] When asked how much *acidophilus* one should take, Dr. William Crook's reply was, "Take as much as you can afford."

In *The Body Ecology Diet,* Donna Gates suggests that the dose of probiotics that it may take to achieve implantation is probably much higher than the suggested dose on most supplement bottles. She recommends taking one to two tablespoons of probiotic powder per day. She says to take it all in one dose first thing in the morning on an empty stomach and to wait at least a half-hour before eating breakfast. By taking it with a full glass of non-chlorinated water, you should be able to wash it through your stomach and into your small intestine before you eat and your stomach produces acid. She suggests continuing this daily for at least three months.[13]

There are many different brands of probiotic supplements containing many different strains of organisms. Which brand or strain will be able to implant and transform your personal intestinal ecosystem is a very individual issue. I have heard, "This probiotic made an incredible difference in my health" from countless people and about many different probiotics. The probiotic organism that has the most clinical data supporting its effectiveness is *Lactobacillus GG*.[14] This strain is of human origin, readily attaches to human intestinal cells, and is resistant to stomach acid and bile, so therefore it is more likely to survive the journey to the intestine and implant there. I took many different probiotics in large quantities for years but never had *Lactobacillus* show up in a CDSA until after I began taking Culturelle™, a probiotic supplement which contains only this organism, in the late 1990's. Also, Culturelle™ is the most "potent" culture for making acidophilus milk. You can start a full quart of milk and have it congeal using half the amount of culture it takes to start a cup of milk using other strains. However, if Culturelle™ does not work for you, another highly recommended strain of *Lactobacillus* is the NCFM strain which can be purchased as Ultradophilus™. Before *Lactobacillus GG* was available, Drs. Michael Rosenbaum and Murray Susser reported in *Solving the Puzzle of Chronic Fatigue Syndrome* that the NCFM strain was particularly good at implanting in their patients, often causing their gastrointestinal symptoms to improve dramatically.[15] To purchase either of these supplements, see "Sources," page 300.

You should consider your individual needs when you choose a probiotic supplement. Naturally, your probiotic supplement should not contain substances to which you are allergic. Keep your probiotic powders or capsules refrigerated, and purchase them from a health care professional or health food store that refrigerates them. Tablets are not recommended because the tableting process may kill many of the organisms.

It is crucial that you create an environment in your intestine that is hospitable to *Lactobacillus* and *Bifidobacterium* and inhospitable to unfriendly organisms when you are trying to reestablish normal intestinal flora. My husband likens growing *Lactobacillus* and *Bifidobacterium* in the intestine to growing grass. The first year we had a lawn it had terrible dry spots and brown patches. We watered it more and more and the problem got worse and worse. Finally, we took a sample to a nursery. They told us that our lawn had fungus and sold us a $26 bag of an antifungal powder called Daconil.™ We put on several bags of Daconil™ but our lawn still looked terrible. Then my father told us that we were watering too often. He recommended watering heavily but no more often than every third day and doing it in the early morning when grass is the most active and fungus is the least active. His recommended antifungal remedy was laundry detergent at a fraction of the cost of Daconil.™ When we followed his advice, our lawn recovered and we saved money.

Similarly, we must create an intestinal environment that encourages the growth of *Lactobacillus* and *Bifidobacterium* and discourages the growth of their competitors if we want to have normal intestinal flora. "Acidophilus" means acid-loving. The pH (degree of acidity) of your intestine is crucial when you are trying to get healthy flora to grow. Hypochlorhydria must be corrected by taking a supplement of betaine-HCl or glutamic-HCl with your meals.[16] Your digestion should be improved as much as possible by improving your eating habits and taking digestive enzymes if necessary. Good digestion insures that you digest and absorb most of the foods that unfriendly organisms prefer, leaving mostly fiber for the *Lactobacillus* and *Bifidobacterium* to consume. (See pages 15 to 17 for more on improving your digestion).

Stagnation of the intestinal contents favors the growth of unfriendly organisms. The temporary slowing of peristaltic action during stress may affect intestinal flora by this mechanism, so try to relax. Chronic constipation should be corrected.[17] Eat a lot vegetables and fruits as tolerated, and, if necessary, take an insoluble fiber supplement. Dr. Leo Galland recommends methylcellulose rather than soluble fiber supplements, such as psyllium seed, which can foster the overgrowth of bacteria in the small intestine.[18] With your doctor's or nutritionist's approval, magnesium supplements may also be used to speed transit time through the intestine.

Diet also affects the flora present in the intestine. A high meat diet favors the growth of *Bacteroides* over *Bifidobacteria* in the large intestine. A lactovegetarian diet favors the growth of *Lactobacillus* and *Bifidobacterium*. If you cannot get your protein from vegetable (bean or grain) or milk (including alternative milk) sources because you are allergic to these foods, game meat does not have a detrimental effect on bowel flora.[19] A study was done that showed that when fat from beef was added to the diet without the meat, the composition of the bowel flora deteriorated.[20] Perhaps the fat from commercially raised beef is the real culprit rather than the meat. The fat from feed-lot-fed beef is low in essential fatty acids (EFAs); however the fat in game meat and grass-grazed beef is high in EFAs. A diet high in sugar is also detrimental to the intestinal flora.[21] Varying the types of foods you eat tends to produce a more balanced intestinal flora.[22] But, according to Dr. Leon Chaitow in the book *Probiotics*, the best thing you can do diet-wise to encourage the growth of *Lactobacillus* and *Bifidobacterium* is to feed your intestinal flora fermented milks, such as yogurt, acidophilus milk, and kefir.[23]

Fermented Milks

Yogurt has been credited with almost miraculous health enhancing properties. The Greek physician Galen prescribed it for stomach problems in about A.D. 150. King Francis I of France paid a fortune for the formula for "the milk of eternal life." In 1902, the Russian microbiologist Elie Metchnikoff published *The Prolongation of Life,* which claimed that yogurt was a veritable fountain of youth.[24] While yogurt and other fermented milks do not actually have miraculous powers, they can greatly contribute to our health and the health and vitality of our unseen allies, *Lactobacillus* and *Bifidobacterium.*

Fermented milks are milk in their most allergically tolerable, digestible, and absorbable form because they are predigested by the organisms that make them. The lactose-free specific carbohydrate diet for inflammatory bowel disease allows yogurt that has been fermented for twenty four hours because after twenty four hours of fermentation virtually all of the lactose has been predigested by the yogurt bacteria.[25] The proteins are also predigested to short peptides and free amino acids. This makes the milk less allergenic.[26] Also, the calcium in fermented milks helps *Lactobacillus acidophilus* adhere and implant in the intestine.[27]

Yogurt is very nutritious. It is higher in B vitamins and vitamin K than the milk from which it is made. Its protein is highly bioavailable because it has been predigested by the yogurt bacteria. On a 100-point scale comparing the biological value of the protein in foods to that of human breast milk (at 100 points), cow's milk scores 84.5, cow's yogurt scores 89.3, and goat's yogurt scores 90.5.[28] Because of the acid pH of yogurt, the calcium in it is more easily absorbed than from milk.[29]

The organisms used to make fermented milks differ for the various kinds of fermented milks. Acidophilus milk contains *Lactobacillus acidophilus* only. The health benefits conferred by this organism are described at the beginning of this chapter. *Lactobacillus acidophilus* is the only organism in fermented milks that can implant in the human digestive tract. Sweet acidophilus milk is milk that has been inoculated with *Lactobacillus acidophilus* and then held at refrigerated temperatures. It retains the original nutrient profile of the milk from which it is made. Fermented acidophilus milk is inoculated with *Lactobacillus acidophilus* and then incubated so that the organism grows and multiplies. It contains a higher number of organisms and more vitamins than milk or sweet acidophilus milk, is low in lactose (or essentially lactose free if it has been fermented for twenty four hours), and its protein is predigested. A recipe for fermented acidophilus milk appears on page 61 of this book.

Yogurt contains *Lactobacillus bulgaricus* and *Streptococcus thermophilus.* It is incubated after it is inoculated with these organisms, so it is higher in vitamins than milk, low in lactose, and its protein is predigested. Many commercial yogurts claim to also contain

Lactobacillus acidophilus and have indeed been inoculated with it. However, as the *Lactobacillus bulgaricus* grows, it creates a pH that is too acid for *Lactobacillus acidophilus,* so by the time we eat it there is little or no *Lactobacillus acidophilus* present.[30] However, the *Lactobacillus bulgaricus* and *Streptococcus thermophilus* are transient friendly flora which live in our intestines for up to twelve days. They create an acid environment and assist any probiotic supplements we are taking to implant, or cause small colonies of *Lactobacillus acidophilus* already present in our intestines to grow.[31]

Not all commercial yogurts are equal in health value. Yogurts that have been pasteurized after they are incubated do not contain any live organisms. Likewise, the organisms in frozen yogurt are dead.[32] Fruit-flavored yogurts may contain chemicals to keep the organisms from digesting the sugar and fruit.[33] The best yogurt to buy is plain yogurt with live cultures. You can mix it with fresh fruit when you eat it if you prefer fruit-flavored yogurt.

Kefir is a fermented milk which contains a blend of cultures including *Saccharomyces kefir, Torula kefir* (these two organisms are yeasts), *Lactobacillus caucasus, Streptococcus lactis,* and other organisms. According to Dr. Leon Chaitow in the book *Probiotics,* kefir is the most nutritious fermented milk and the most helpful in aiding *Lactobacillus acidophilus* to implant.[34] A recipe for kefir is found on page 65 of this book. (Note: Personally, I was unable to tolerate kefir, possibly because of the antigenic similarity between *Saccharomyces kefir* and *Saccharomyces cerevisiae,* which is baker's/brewer's yeast, a common food allergen).

Fermented milks are indeed marvelous foods for our health. But the "catch" is that cow's milk is a major food allergen for most of the readers of this book. Even predigested, as it is in fermented milks, it is likely to cause allergic symptoms. How can we feed fermented milks to our unseen allies within, *Lactobacillus* and *Bifidobacterium,* without having reactions ourselves?

The solution is to eat fermented milks made from alternative milks. Soy, goat and sheep yogurts are commercially available. (See "Using Commercially Prepared Foods," page 294). Or you can make acidophilus milk, yogurt, or kefir at home with goat's, sheep's, or any other available animal milk. Soy milk also makes good yogurt. Rice and nut milks, however, cannot be used to make fermented milks at home.

When you make your own fermented milks, you know that they are fresh, that the organisms in them are alive, and that no additives have been used. It is a craft which is easy to master and may be one of the best things you ever do for yourself and your family.

Dr. Gruia Ionescu, director of a large allergy clinic in Germany, has his patients eat at least a pint of yogurt a day in addition to taking probiotic supplements. He says, "The yogurt is milk in its most digestible form, and the *Lactobacillus* in it is just so beneficial that if they can handle the yogurt at all, we want them to eat it."[35]

When I first began eating goat yogurt, I could tolerate it if it was homemade and fermented for twenty four hours, but could not tolerate commercial goat yogurt, which I assumed had not been fermented as long, and was therefore less predigested. Do not give up on trying fermented milks until you have made them using alternative milks yourself. See pages 57 to 66 of this book for instructions and recipes for making fermented milks. If you have trouble tolerating fermented milks, try eating them in small amounts and gradually increasing the quantity or eat them on an off-and-on basis as I do. Make every effort to rotate fermented milks from different animal sources if you eat them on a daily basis.

If there is no way that you can tolerate any type of alternative fermented milk, another way to add friendly organisms to your diet is to eat cultured vegetables. Rejuvenative Foods makes unpasteurized sauerkraut and other unpasteurized cultured vegetables that contain live *Lactobacillus plantarum*. This organism is a transient in our digestive systems, like the *Lactobacillus bulgaricus* in yogurt. It creates a more acid environment in the intestine which helps the organisms in the probiotic supplements you may be taking to implant, or helps any *Lactobacillus acidophilus* already present in your intestine to thrive. It also inhibits unfriendly organisms in the intestine.[36] Many health food stores carry Rejuvenative Foods cultured vegetables, or see "Using Commercially Prepared Foods," page 292 for information on ordering them. Do not heat these vegetables before eating them, or you will kill the beneficial organisms. If you have trouble tolerating these vegetables, eating them in small amounts and gradually increasing the quantity may help. *Lactobacillus plantarum* is also available in supplement form. (See "Sources," page 300).

Consider eating these foods as a way to "send in the reinforcements" and help the organisms in the probiotic supplements you are taking or the friendly flora already present in your body to thrive. By helping your unseen allies, you will be helping yourself in many ways.

Footnotes

1. Chaitow, Leon, and Natasha Trenev, *Probiotics,* Hohm Press, P.O. Box 2501, Prescott, AZ 86302, p. 11.

2. Ibid, p. 13.

3. Gates, Donna, *The Body Ecology Diet,* B.E.D. Publications, 1266 W. Paces Ferry Road, Suite 505, Atlanta, GA 30327, p. 6.

4. Chaitow, Leon, et al, *Probiotics,* p. 14.

5. Ibid, p. 25.

6. Ibid, pp. 15, 29, and 133.

7. Ibid, pp. 29 and 109-122.

8. Ibid, p. 129.

9. Ibid, pp. 54-66 and p. 87.

10. Lipski, Elizabeth, M.S., C.C.N. *Digestive Wellness,* Keats Publishing, Inc., New Canaan, CT, 1996, p. 81.

11. Chaitow, Leon, et al, *Probiotics,* p. 45.

12. Personal communication from Dr. Sidney Baker to nutritionist Katherine Gibbons.

13. Gates, Donna, *The Body Ecology Diet,* pp. 131-132.

14. Multiple sources including these by Goldin and Gorbach who isolated *Lactobacillus GG* (GG is for their names) and others listed below, plus more at this website: http://www.live-well.com/reference/biblio.html

   Goldin, B. R., Gorbach, S. L., Saxelin, M., et al. "Survival of *Lactobacillus* species (strain GG) in Human Gastrointestinal Tract." *Digestive Diseases Science,* 1992. 37(1):121-128.

   Gorbach, S. L., Chang, T. W. and Goldin, B. R. "Successful Treatment of Relapsing *Clostridium difficile* Colitis with *Lactobacillus GG.*" *Lancet,* December, 1987. 26:1519.

   Alander, M., Korpela, R., Saxelin, M., et al. "Recovery of *Lactobacillus rhamnosus GG* from Human Colonic Biopsies." *Letters of Applied Microbiology,* 1997. 24:361-364.

   Colodner, R., Edelstein, H., Chazan, B., et al. "Vaginal Colonization by Orally Administered *Lactobacillus rhamnosus GG.*" *Israeli Medical Association Journal,* November, 2003, 5(11):812-813.

15. Rosenbaum, Michael, M.D., and Murray Susser, M.D., *Solving the Puzzle of Chronic Fatigue Syndrome,* Life Sciences Press, Tacoma, WA, 1992.

16. Chaitow, Leon, et al, *Probiotics,* pp. 30-31.

17. Ibid, p. 30.

18. Interview with Leo Galland, M.D., "Leaky Gut – What Is It? What Factors Cause It? What Can Be Done?" *Mastering Food Allergies Newsletter,* #86, July/August 1995, p. 7.

19. Chaitow, Leon, et al, *Probiotics,* pp. 114-115.

20. Ibid, p. 58.

21. Ibid, p. 125.

22. Ibid, pp. 155-156.

23. Ibid, pp. 174-175.

24. Alth, Max, *Making Your Own Cheese and Yogurt,* Funk & Wagnalls, New York, NY, 1973, pp. 12-16.

25. Gottschall, Elaine, B.S., M.Sc., *Breaking the Vicious Cycle: Intestinal Health Through Diet,* The Kirkton Press, Kirkton, Ontario, Canada, 1994, p. 133.

26. Chaitow, Leon, et al, *Probiotics,* p. 36.

27. Mitsuoka, Tomotari. "Intestinal Flora and Aging." *Nutrition Reviews,* December, 1992. 50(12):442.

28. Chaitow, Leon, et al, *Probiotics,* p. 36.

29. Ibid, p. 39.

30. Ibid, p. 171.

31. Ibid, p. 176.

32. Ibid, p. 171.

33. Ibid, p. 168.

34. Ibid, p. 173.

35. Interview with Gruia Ionescu, Ph.D., "Candida – A Different Approach," *Mastering Food Allergies Newsletter,* #37, July/August 1989, p. 6.

36. Chaitow, Leon, et al, *Probiotics,* p. 200.

About the
Rotation Diet

If you have multiple food allergies, one of the best ways to help yourself is to "rotate" your foods, or eat a rotation diet. A rotation diet is a system of controlling food allergies by eating biologically related foods on the same day and then waiting at least four days before eating them again. Such a diet can help those with food allergies in several ways.

Rotation diets may help prevent the development of allergies to new foods. Any food, if eaten repetitively, can cause food allergies in allergy-prone individuals or people with "leaky guts." When my food allergies were first diagnosed, I was not told to rotate my foods. I simply eliminated the foods to which I was allergic. Four years later I had developed allergies to the foods I had used to replace the original problem foods in my diet.

A rotation diet helps you pick out allergies to foods for which you were not tested and may not have suspected were problems. If you eat a food on Monday, for example, by Friday, when you eat it again, the "masking" antibodies your body makes specifically for that food will be diminished. Therefore, you will realize you are reacting to it, even though you did not have obvious symptoms when you ate it on a daily basis.

A rotation diet allows you to eat foods to which you have a mild or borderline allergy and which you might not tolerate if you ate them often. Sometimes your reaction to borderline foods may depend on your stress level, other illness or infection, lack of adequate rest, or the season of the year. (For example, grain allergies tend to be more pronounced when the grass is pollinating).

On a rotation diet each food is eaten only every fourth to fifth day or at even longer intervals. Depending on the severity of your allergies, your doctor may suggest that you eat a food only once during the rotation day. Or, if your allergies are not too severe, you may tolerate eating each food more than once during a 24-hour rotation day. Usually all of the members of a food family are eaten on the same day. However, some doctors allow their patients to "split" food families for a more nutritious or more palatable diet. In this case, you eat different members of the same family on more than one day of the rotation cycle with a day off from that family between. (For example, you might eat apples on day 1 and pears on day 3). Some doctors permit their patients to eat a different member of the grain or cattle family on each day of their rotation cycle, depending on the patient's degree of sensitivity to grains or cattle family meats.

On a rotation diet, you eat members of the same biological food family on the same day because foods in the same family have similar antigens. The classification of the plants and animals we use for food is not an exact science; thus, various classification schemes differ on the level of relatedness they assign to some foods. What one botanist or zoologist calls a family, another may call a suborder, meaning that the foods are less closely related than on the family level.

In my opinion some allergy patients cross-react to foods related on a higher classification level than the family level, such as the suborder or order level. I have talked to several people whose sensitivity to amaranth carries over to quinoa, or vice versa. This may happen because amaranth and quinoa are in different families in the same order. Personally, I have reacted to several kinds of fish I had never eaten before. When I looked up what they were related to, I found that they were in the same suborder as kinds of fish to which I was already sensitive, although they were not in the same family.

Because some allergy patients seem to cross-react to foods which are related on the order or suborder level, the complete classification of the plants and animals we use as foods is listed in the back of this book, rather than just a listing of the food families. Using this complete classification, you can rotate foods at whatever level you personally need.

The food family tables in this book list members of the same species on the same line. When you "split" food families as part of your rotation, you may wish to keep all of the members of the same species on the same day because they are very closely related – so closely related that they can interbreed. For example, you will find beets, sugar beets, and chard all listed together because they are the same species. I always keep chard and beets on the same day of rotation, even when I "split" spinach off to eat it two days later. In the cases of the bean and cabbage families where there are several foods in a single species, a small list of foods is given for that species.

For more information about rotation diets, see pages 8 to 9.

HOW TO USE THE ROTATION DIET IN THIS BOOK

A rotation diet can seem confusing, overwhelming, or confining at first. However, like hearing aids, bifocals, or any other health aid, once you get used to your rotation diet, it will become easier to use and your health will be improved by using it.

The rotation diet in this book is designed to help you get started on rotation. It is not set in stone and can and should be individualized. Rotation group numbers (written as [64], for example) are listed with each food so you can easily move whole families of foods from one rotation day to another. For example, if you find that you do not have any vegetables that you like or can tolerate on one day of the diet, but have two families of vegetables on a different day, move one of those families to the day on which you do not have vegetables. (Be sure to move ALL of the members of the family or all of the foods with the same rotation group number). You might instead choose a vegetable family from the "extra foods" list and assign it to the day on which you have no vegetables. If your doctor allows, another option is to "split" a food family, eating some members of it on the day of your cycle for which you have no vegetables, and other members two days later.

There are many options for variety on a rotation diet. In addition to moving foods permanently as described in the last paragraph, you can also move a food to another day temporarily if you want to try a recipe that does not exactly fit your rotation cycle or if you want to eat the food for a special occasion. For example, suppose that on your rotation diet you have assigned cranberries to day 1. If Thanksgiving falls on day 2 of your cycle, you can "borrow" cranberries from day 1 to make cranberry sauce with grape juice (a day 2 food) to go with your turkey (also a day 2 food). If Thanksgiving falls on day 3 of your cycle, "split" cranberries from blueberries to make cranberry sauce with apple juice and eat buffalo for your meat on day 2 so you can have turkey on day 3. If you are "borrowing" a food that is not a major problem for you and moving it only one day (such as turkey in this situation), you will probably do all right eating it at a five day interval one cycle and a three day interval the next. If the food is one that you do not tolerate well, you might be better off to omit it from the short cycle so you do not eat again it too soon.

Some people can eat no gluten (due to celiac disease or allergy) or no grains (due to allergies to all members of the grain family). The inclusion of gluten-containing grains in the diet in this book does not imply that celiacs or people with any type of gluten sensitivity should eat gluten-containing grains. They are included in the standard rotation diet to contribute to the nutrition of those who can tolerate them. Do not eat any food on the diet if you are allergic to it or intolerant of it.

Ask your doctor for advice on how you should rotate the grains you tolerate. Some doctors permit their patients who are not extremely grain-sensitive to have a grain on each day of their rotation cycle. (If this is what your doctor tells you to do, you can use the grains section of the diet each day). Other patients may be allowed to "split" the grain family. They are advised to have two grain days out of their four rotation days, with different grains assigned to them, and with non-grain days between them. In this case, you could eat, for example, amaranth and arrowroot on day 1, rye and teff on day 2, quinoa and tapioca on day 3, and oats and rice on day 4. Because some doctors allow their less sensitive patients to eat a grain or cattle family meat on each day of their diet, each of these foods has a different rotation group number in this book even though they are all in the same grain or meat family.

You will notice that the rotation diet in this book contains a long list of "extra foods" that are not assigned to a specific day. One purpose of the extra foods list is to give you flexibility. For example, the families containing beef, white potatoes, and lettuce are in the extra foods list because it is usually possible to get these foods plain in a restaurant. Thus, you may want to save these foods for when you eat out so you have the flexibility of eating out occasionally when you find it necessary or convenient rather than being restricted to eating out only on potato-and-lettuce day.

Other foods, such as tomatoes (which should be rotated with potatoes, since they are in the same family), seasonings in the mint and onion families, carrots and celery, are on the extra foods list to allow you more versatility in your cooking. You can use carrots in chicken soup one cycle and in game stew the next, rather than always being stuck with carrots on "chicken day." Be sure to write down when you use an extra food on your calendar so you will wait at least four days before using it again.

Foods such as wheat, corn, cow's milk, legumes, and citrus fruits are on the extra foods list because they are common allergens. If you have a "borderline" allergy to them, you may need to rotate them at a longer interval than less allergenic foods. However, if you tolerate them well, you can assign them to any rotation day you choose.

Finally, many foods are on the extra foods list because we have so many foods to choose from that it would complicate the diet to assign all of them – especially the ones that are less readily available – to specific days.

As you plan your rotation diet, the process of moving and shuffling food families between days, remembering to move the whole family or correctly "splitting" families, etc. can seem daunting. If you need help making the rotation diet in this book "fit" your doctor's advice and your allergies or if you need to "start from scratch" on a diet, customized rotation diets will be available starting in 2007. Visit www.food-allergy.org details about when they become available, price, and ordering information

When you first start a rotation diet, you may have to modify the diet based on your reactions. If you find that you are reacting to foods that you previously did not suspect to be problems, eliminate these foods from your diet, at least temporarily, and replace their food families with others from the "extra foods" section. This situation is sometimes called "unmasking" because on a rotation diet the days off from a certain food allow your level of antibodies to that food to decrease. Then when you eat the food again several days later, there no longer are "masking" antibodies to diminish your reaction to the food.

After you have been on rotation for several months, if you find you are reacting to foods that you previously tolerated, you may be overloaded with seasonal pollens or other allergic exposures. These foods, which are tolerated at some times but not others, are your "borderline" foods. If you find that you are reacting to previously tolerated foods even after the time of allergic overload is over, you may need to change to a longer rotation cycle of five or more days.

Make use of a calendar with room to write on to help you with your rotation diet. Mark your rotation day numbers on the calendar. After many years of rotating, I do not have trouble remembering which foods we eat on which days of the diet, but sometimes I cannot remember what day it is! In addition, if you use a food from the "extra foods" section of your diet or rotate some foods on a more flexible longer cycle, record on your calendar when you use them. Then you will know how soon you can use them or another member of their food family.

Your health is important to all of the members of your family, so take the time to make some special treats for yourself as well as for other family members. For example, make yourself a large batch of "special" pizza and freeze some. Then the next time your family or friends decide to order pizza, you will be prepared with a pizza you can eat.

Freeze portions of allowable desserts for each day of your rotation cycle. When there is a birthday party or when others are having a treat, pull your dessert out of the freezer and join the celebration.

If you eat out or travel, you may find it difficult to stay on rotation. It is better to eat a food to which you are not allergic but which you just had yesterday than to choose a food to which you are allergic. This advice also applies in other situations. For example, in the pizza illustration above, it would be better to eat your special pizza from the freezer even if it is made with the same grain you ate yesterday than to eat the "normal" pizza.

Occasionally I am asked how much of each food should be eaten on a rotation diet. Assuming you are not eating sugar or foods to which you are allergic, your hunger should be a good indicator of how much food you need. You should not need to weigh portions or count calories because weight tends to normalize when food allergies are controlled and allergic cravings and food addictions are eliminated. If your weight is not beginning to normalize after several months on a rotation diet that eliminates ALL of your problem foods, you should be evaluated for thyroid or other metabolic problems. Individuals with Wilson's disease can exhibit symptoms of hypothyroidism in spite of normal blood tests for thyroid hormones because their thyroid hormones do not have normal activity in their bodies.[1]

Although you do not need to count calories or weigh portions, you should try to eat a balanced diet, getting complex carbohydrates, protein, a little fat which includes essential fatty acids, and lots of vitamins and minerals from vegetables and fruits, as tolerated. Those of us with food allergies may not find it reasonable to follow the USDA's food pyramid strictly and eat eleven servings of grains per day. I have talked to more than one person who developed food allergy symptoms when they decided to eat a "healthier" diet including large quantities of grains. This made their latent grain allergies more pronounced. If you are allergic to a few grains, you may have some degree of allergy to all of them, so do not overeat your safe grains. Let common sense, your body, and your doctor be your guide to how much of any food you should consume on a rotation diet.

Keep yourself from getting too hungry or feeling deprived. This will increase your ability to resist eating your problem foods and thus will improve your health. After you have successfully eliminated your allergic foods for the length of time your doctor suggests, you may be able to add them back to your diet in moderation and on a rotated schedule.

A rotation diet alone is not "the answer" to food allergies. You must also get to the root of your problem, pursue appropriate treatment for the underlying causes of your food allergies, and heal your leaky gut. However, a properly used, highly diversified rotation diet will give you the most nutrition for the least amount of allergic reaction. Improved nutrition can only lead to improved health.

FOOTNOTES

1. Interview with E. Denis Wilson, M.D., "Wilson's Syndrome: New Light on Thyroid Dysfunction," *Mastering Food Allergies Newsletter,* #71, January/February 1993, pp. 4-7.

The Standard Rotation Diet — Day 1 Foods

GLUTEN* GRAINS	Barley* [84] Kamut* [85]
NON-GLUTEN GRAINS	Milo (Sorghum) [95]
NON-GRAIN ALTERNATIVES	Amaranth [33] Arrowroot [109][a] White sweet potato flour [71]
MEAT	Pork [272] Wild Boar [272] Goat [282][c]
FISH	Cod (Scrod) [226] Haddock [226] Pollack [226] Whiting [226] Albacore [242] Tuna [242]
PROTEIN ALTERNATIVES	Pecan or walnut butter [29] Goat milk [282] Goat cheese [282] (also cheese mold, [2])
NUTS	Walnut, all types [29] Butternut [29] Pecan [29] Hickory nut [29]
VEGETABLES	Okra [54] Jicama [71][s] Sweet Potato [71] White Sweet Potato [71] Commercial "yam" [71] Artichoke, globe [78] Plantain [109]
SEA VEGETABLES	Wakame [17]
FRUITS	Pineapple [102] Banana [109]
SWEETENERS	Malt (barley) [84] Sorghum molasses [95] Pineapple juice concentrate [102]
OILS	Walnut oil [29] Safflower oil [78]
SEASONINGS	Cardamon [110] Ginger [110] Turmeric [110]
BEVERAGES	Hibiscus tea [54]

The Standard Rotation Diet — Day 2 Foods

GLUTEN* GRAINS	Rye* [86]	
NON-GLUTEN GRAINS	Teff [91]	
NON-GRAIN ALTERNATIVES	Buckwheat [28] True yam flour [104]	
MEAT	Turkey [260] American buffalo (bison) [278]c	
FISH	Perch [233] Mutton snapper [234]	Walleye [233] Red snapper [234] Other types of snapper [234]
PROTEIN ALTERNATIVES	Cashew butter [50] Turkey eggs [258]	
NUTS	Cashew [50] Pistachio [50]	
VEGETABLES	Sorrel [28]s Broccoli [40] Cabbage, all varieties [40]s Collards [40] Kale [40] Mustard greens [40] Daikon radish [40]	Arugula [40]s Brussels sprouts [40] Cauliflower [40] Cress, all types [40] Kohlrabi [40] Radish [40] Rutabaga [40] Turnip [40]
SEA VEGETABLES	Dulse [14]	
FRUITS	Mulberry [26] Rhubarb [28] Grape [53] Commercial "currant" [53]	Fig [26] Mango [50] Raisin [53] Guava [60]
SWEETENERS	Maple syrup or sugar [52] Grape juice concentrate [53]	
OILS	Grapeseed oil [53]	Canola oil [40]
SEASONINGS	Canola seeds [40] Mustard seeds [40]	Horseradish [40] Allspice [60] Cloves [60]
BEVERAGES	Yerba mate tea [51]	
MISCELLANEOUS FOODS	Cream of tartar [53] Vinegar, wine [53] (also fungus, [2])	

The Standard Rotation Diet — Day 3 Foods

GLUTEN* GRAINS	Spelt* [87]	
NON-GLUTEN GRAINS	Millet [94]	
NON-GRAIN ALTERNATIVES	Quinoa [32] Tapioca [48] Cassava [48]	
MEAT	Chicken [259] Pheasant [259]	Cornish hen [259] Quail [259] Sheep (lamb) [283]C
FISH	Turbot [248] Dab [248] Plaice [248] Freshwater catfish [223]	Halibut [248] Flounder [248] Sole [248] Sea catfish [224]
PROTEIN ALTERNATIVES	Filbert (hazelnut) butter [31] Sheep milk [283]	Eggs, chicken [259] Sheep cheese [283] (also cheese mold, [2])
NUTS	Filbert (hazelnut) [31]	
VEGETABLES	Beet [32] Spinach [32]S	Chard [32] Avocado [38] Olive, black or green [69]
SEA VEGETABLES	Nori [15]	
FRUITS	Blackberry [42] Dewberry [42] Longberry [42] Strawberry [42] Apple [43] Pear [43]	Boysenberry [42] Loganberry [42] Raspberry [42] Youngberry [42] Loquat [43] Quince [43]
SWEETENERS	Beet sugar [32] Apple juice concentrate [43]	
OILS	Olive oil [69] Sesame oil [80]	
SEASONINGS	Wintergreen [31] Bayleaf [38] Cinnamon [38] Sesame seeds [80]	
BEVERAGES	Sassafras tea [38] Rosehip tea [43]	
MISCELLANEOUS FOODS	Vinegar, cider [43] (also fungus, [2])	

The Standard Rotation Diet — Day 4 Foods

GLUTEN* GRAINS	Oats* [90]	
NON-GLUTEN GRAINS	Rice [92] Wild rice [93]	
NON-GRAIN ALTERNATIVES	Chestnut flour [30] Water chestnut flour [82]	Jerusalem artichoke flour [76] Malanga flour [101] Poi flour [101]
MEAT	Duck [257] Goose [257] Rabbit [265]	
FISH	Salmon [217] Orange roughy [227]	Trout [217] Other types of roughy [227]
PROTEIN ALTERNATIVES	Almond butter [44] Goose eggs [257] Duck eggs [257]	
NUTS	Chestnut [30] Pumpkin seeds [75]	Almond [44] Sunflower seeds [76] Coconut [100]
VEGETABLES	Cucumber [75] Summer squash [75]S Zucchini [75]S Water chestnut [82]	Pumpkin [75] Winter squash [75] Artichoke, Jerusalem [76] Taro [101]
SEA VEGETABLES	Arame [13] Irish moss [13]	
FRUITS	Apricot [44] Chokecherry [44] Peach [44] Cantaloupe [75] Watermelon [75]	Cherry [44] Nectarine [44] Plum [44] Honeydew [75] Other melons [75] Date [100]
SWEETENERS	Rice syrup [92] Date sugar [100]	
OILS	Almond oil [44] Sunflower oil [76] Coconut oil [100]	
SEASONINGS	Nutmeg [36] Mace [36]	
BEVERAGES	Dacopa [76] Poi [101]	

The Standard Rotation Diet – Extra Foods

GLUTEN* GRAINS	Triticale* [88] Wheat* [89] Job's tears* [99]	FISH (continued)	Herring [215] Sardine [215] Anchovy [216] Smelt [218]

GLUTEN*
GRAINS
   Triticale* [88]
   Wheat* [89]
   Job's tears* [99]

NON-GLUTEN
GRAINS
   Corn [98]

NON-GRAIN
   Lotus flour [34]
   Bean starch [45]
   Garbanzo (chickpea) flour [45]
   Kudzu [45]
   Lupine flour [45]
   Soy flour [45]

MEAT
   Frog [250]
   Turtle [251]
   Alligator [252]
   Crocodile [253]
   Rattlesnake [254]
   Ostrich [255]
   Emu [256]
   Grouse (partridge) [258]
   Guinea hen [261]
   Pigeon (squab) [262]
   Kangaroo [264]
   Bear [269]
   Lion [270]
   Caribou [274]
   Deer (venison) [274]
   Elk [274]
   Pronghorn [275]
   Antelope [276]
   Other game meat
   Beef [277]
   Yak [281]

FISH
   Abalone [201]
   Snail (escargot) [202]
   Mussel [203]
   Scallop [204]
   Oyster [205]
   Thick shell clam [206]
   Soft shell clam [207]
   Cockle [208]
   Squid [209]
   Cuttlefish [209]
   Octopus [210]
   Prawn [211]
   Shrimp [211]
   Crayfish [212]
   Lobster [212]
   Crab, all types [213]
   Other shellfish
   Sturgeon (caviar) [214]

FISH (continued)
   Herring [215]
   Sardine [215]
   Anchovy [216]
   Smelt [218]
   Whitefish, true [219]
   Blackfish [220]
   Pickerel [220]
   Pike [220]
   Carp [222]
   Chub [222]
   Minnow [222]
   John dory [228]
   Oreo dory [229]
   Other types of dory,
     except oreo [228]
   Butterfish [230]
   Grouper [231]
   Sea bass [231]
   Dolphinfish (mahi mahi) [232]
   Black bass [235]
   Crappie [235]
   Freshwater bass [235]
   Sea trout [236]
   Bluefish [238]
   Mackerel [240]
   Bonito [241]
   Swordfish [243]
   Marlin [244]
   Sailfish [244]
   Other types of fish

PROTEIN
ALTERNATIVES
   Soy milk [45] (Check oils & sweeteners).
   Soy cheese [45]
     (also cheese mold, [2])
   Cow's milk [277]
   Cow's milk cheese [277]
     (also cheese mold, [2])
   Peanut butter [45]
     (Check for other ingredients
     besides peanuts).
   Macadamia nut butter [25]

NUTS
   Pine nut [22]
   Macadamia nut [25]
   Peanut [45]
   Brazil nut [63]
   Paradise nut [63]
   Lychee nut [112]

VEGETABLES
   Morel [3]
   Truffle [4]
   Common (cultivated) mushroom [5]
   Field or meadow mushroom [5]
   Horse mushroom [5]

Extra Foods – continued

VEGETABLES
(continued)

Oyster mushroom [5]
Parasol (umbrella) mushroom [5]
Shitake mushroom [5]
Porcino (cep) mushroom [6]
Green russula [7]
Chanterelle [8]
Puffball [9]
Wood ear [10]
Alfalfa [45]
Beans, all types [45]
Black-eyed pea [45]
Chickpea (garbanzo bean) [45]
Green pea [45]
Lentil [45]
Lupine bean [45]
Carrots [65]
Celeriac [65]
Celery [65]
Fennel [65]
Parsnip [65]
Parsley root [65]
Eggplant [73]
Pepino [73]
Pepper, anaheim,
   banana, bell, cherry,
   green, jalapeno, etc. [73]
Tamarillo [73]
Tomatillo [73]
Tomato [73]
White potato [73]
Belgian endive [79]S
Chicory [79]S
Dandelion [79]S
Endive, all types [79]S
Escarole [79]S
Lettuce, all types[79]S
Radicchio [79]S
Romaine [79]S
Salsify [79]S
Bamboo shoots [83]
Asparagus [103]
Chives [103]
Garlic [103]
Leeks [103]
Onion [103]
Shallot [103]
Yucca [105]

SEA
VEGETABLES

Gracillaria seaweeds [12]
Laminaria seaweeds [16]
Kombu [16]
Kelp [18]

FRUITS

Atemoya [35]
Custard apple [35]
Cherimoya [35]
Papaw [35] (different from papaya)
Gooseberry [41]
Currant, true [41]
Carambola [47]
Citron [49]
Clementine [49]
Grapefruit [49]
Kumquat [49]
Lemon [49]
Lime [49]
Mandarin [49]
Orange [49]
Pumello [49]
Tangelo [49]
Tangerine [49]
Ugli fruit [49]
Kiwi fruit [56]
Passion fruit [58]
Papaya [59]
Pomegranate [62]
Blueberry [66]
Cranberry [66]
Huckleberry [66]
Persimmon [67]
Prickly pear [81.5]

SWEETENERS

Orange juice concentrate [49]
Stevia [77]
Molasses [96]
Sugar, cane [97]
Corn syrup [98]
Aguamiel [105]
Honey [113]
FOS (fructooligosaccharides)
   [32 or 97] for the sugar it is made
   from, also *Aspergillus* mold, [2]

OILS

Peanut oil [45]
Soy oil [45]
Flaxseed oil [46]
Evening primrose oil [61]
Butter [277]
Ghee (clarified butter) [277]

SEASONINGS

Pepper, black [24]
Pepper, white [24]
Poppyseed [39]
Caper [29]
Tamarind [45]

Extra Foods — continued

SEASONINGS
(continued)

Licorice [45]
Anise [65]
Caraway [65]
Celery seed or leaf [65]
Chervil [65]
Cilantro [65]
Coriander [65]
Cumin [65]
Dill [65]
Parsley [65]
Basil [72]
Marjoram [72]
Mint [72]
Oregano [72]
Peppermint [72]
Rosemary [72]
Sage [72]
Savory [72]
Spearmint [72]
Thyme [72]
Paprika [73]
Pepper, cayenne [73]
Pepper, chili [73]
Tarragon [77]
Saffron [106]
Vanilla [112]

BEVERAGES

Cocoa [55]
   (Check for other ingredients
   in cocoa mixes).
Cola nut [55] (Check for other
   ingredients in cola drinks).
Black tea [57]
Green tea [57]
Peppermint tea [72]
Spearmint tea [72]
Coffee [74]
Chamomile tea [77]
Chicory [79]
Sarsaparilla [103]

MISC.
FOODS

Baker's yeast [1]
Brewer's yeast [1]
Citric acid molds, citric acid [2]
Cheese molds [2]
Agar [11 or 12]
Carob [45]
Flaxseed [46]
Chocolate [55]
   (Check for other ingredients).
Cocoa, baking [55]
Gelatin [272 and 277]

NOTES

The number, such as [64], that follows the name of each food, is a rotation group number. Except for the cattle and grain families, all of the foods with the same number are usually in the same family, although sometimes they may be in the same tribe, or suborder. If you wish to move a food to another day of your diet, be sure to move all of the members of the group (all of the foods which have the same number).

a Arrowroot: There are several types of arrowroot from several different food families. Only two of them are from families that contain frequently eaten foods (bananas, ginger, and turmeric). Therefore, since it is usually impossible to determine the source of the arrowroot you purchase, arrowroot is rotated on the same day as bananas, ginger, and turmeric.

c Cattle family meats: Many allergy doctors allow their patients to eat a different member of the cattle family each day on rotation, as they appear on this diet.

s Vegetables that are good eaten raw in salads. If they are not leafy, such as carrots, jicama, cabbage, zucchini, etc., they may be shredded.

NOTE ABOUT
GLUTEN-CONTAINING GRAINS

* The inclusion of gluten-containing grains in the diet in this book does not imply that celiacs or people with any type of gluten sensitivity should eat gluten-containing grains. They are included in the standard rotation diet to contribute to the nutrition of those who can tolerate them.

About the Recipes and Ingredients Used In This Book

Hippocrates said, "Let your food be your medicine and your medicine be your food." The purpose of the recipes in this book is to give you food that will enhance and improve your health, as well as being delicious and enjoyable.

This book differs from many allergy cookbooks in that the recipes are compatible with a rotation diet. Some allergy cookbooks combine several flours in each recipe. If you do this on a rotation diet, you may not have enough grains for all of your rotation days. In this book there is usually only one grain or grain alternative used in each recipe. Exceptions are made to this rule for some of the non-grain or gluten-free grain flours. For them a starch is usually necessary to provide a "glue" to hold your muffin or cracker together. The grain or grain-alternative and starch combinations used are consistent throughout the book and are geared to the standard rotation diet on pages 39 to 45.

Another difference between this book and some allergy cookbooks is that no sugar is used in the recipes. Yet, you will find recipes for delicious desserts, cookies, and snacks on pages 201 to 260 which are sweetened with fruit, stevia, or FOS. Sometimes using sugar seems unavoidable. For example, if you are planning a birthday party for an allergic child and feel that you must use sugar to make foods that your child's friends will also enjoy, refer to *Allergy Cooking With Ease* for such cakes, cookies, and candies.

People with food allergies often miss ethnic foods more than any other foods they have had to eliminate. Those who practice food combining take exception to some ethnic foods, especially Italian foods as they are eaten in this country, because they contain both meats and grains in large amounts. Therefore you will find suggestions for vegetable "pastas" to use with meat sauces and vegetarian versions of your favorite Italian recipes in this book.

Allergy cooking is more exacting than cooking with more forgiving "normal" ingredients. In allergy cooking, the measurements often cannot be rounded off to the nearest half teaspoon or fourth cup without changing the quality of the completed food. Therefore, some of the recipes in this book use less common amounts of ingredients, such as $\frac{1}{16}$ teaspoon or $\frac{3}{8}$ cup. A chart is included on page 295 to help you measure such amounts. It is worthwhile to invest in a liquid measuring cup that has eighth cup markings, an $\frac{1}{8}$ cup coffee measure for dry ingredients, and a set of measuring spoons that has an $\frac{1}{8}$ teaspoon. If you are measuring very small amounts of dry ingredients such as stevia in measuring spoons, you can fill the $\frac{1}{8}$ or $\frac{1}{4}$ teaspoon, level it off, and then used a butter knife to divide it down the middle and scrape half or three-quarters of it out.

Most of the recipes in this book contain several choices of sets of ingredients, or options within a set of ingredients. If the directions refer to an ingredient not in the list of ingredients you are using, just ignore that reference. For example, if you are making oat granola, which is sweetened with date sugar, ignore references to fruit juice (the sweetener in the other granolas) in the directions.

Finally, the recipes in this book are designed to be as simple as possible. Since you will be making most of your food "from scratch," simplicity in cooking is essential. The recipe directions aim to be simple and very detailed. Some of the most desperate people I have talked to are non-cooks who have just been diagnosed as having multiple food allergies. The instructions in this book are written with them in mind. Also, those who have not done a lot of cooking (or even experienced cooks who want to know more about nutrition) may wish to read *Easy Cooking for Special Diets* to learn more about nutrition and diets, cooking techniques and terminology, shopping for food, food safety, and time-saving techniques and organization which can help you stay on a special diet.

The Ingredients Used in this Book
Milks

To make the various fermented milks in the next chapter, you must begin with a milk. All of the fermented milk recipes in this book can be made with cow's milk of any kind: whole, skim, or reduced fat. The higher fat milks will produce a thicker fermented milk.

GOAT'S MILK is the most commonly available alternative animal milk. Most health food stores and some grocery stores sell fresh pasteurized goat's milk, powdered goat's milk, or canned goat's milk. If you cannot purchase it from a store, see "Using Commercially Prepared Foods," page 293. Goat's milk is lower in protein than cow's milk, so yogurt or acidophilus milk made from it has a very soft curd that reliquifies if the milk is stirred. If you make your yogurt or acidophilus milk from powdered milk or if you enrich fresh or canned milk with additional powdered milk, the curd will be thicker. If you wish to reduce your fat intake, skim goat milk is commercially available. However, it makes very thin, watery yogurt and acidophilus milk.

SHEEP'S MILK is higher in protein and fat than goat's milk. Therefore, sheep's milk yogurt is very thick and creamy. I have not been able to locate a source for canned or dried sheep's milk in this country. To get fresh sheep milk, you will have to find a nearby sheep dairy or a local farmer who milks sheep.

COMMERCIAL SOY MILK, such as EdenSoy,™ makes tolerable yogurt and acidophilus milk. Nut milks, rice milk, and home-ground soy milks that do not contain additional carbohydrate are not suitable for making fermented milks at home.

OTHER ANIMAL MILKS, such as llama milk, should work in the recipes in the next chapter. Unfortunately, I have not had the opportunity to try any other milks because I do not live in an area where these animals are kept and milked.

Cultures

YOGURT CULTURES or starters contain the friendly bacteria *Lactobacillus bulgaricus* and *Streptococcus thermophilus.* Some also contain *Lactobacillus acidophilus.* However, this organism will not be present in the final yogurt in very high numbers. (See page 30 for more about this). All of the yogurt cultures I have seen contain some cow's milk. If you wish to use a commercial culture and are allergic to cow's milk, start a quart batch of yogurt with the contents of one packet of starter. Start the next batch using yogurt from the first batch, and use the second batch to make a third batch. Give away the first few batches of yogurt you make. By the time you get to your fourth or fifth batch, there will be very little of the original starter powder in your yogurt.

You do not need to use a commercial yogurt starter to make yogurt. You can use any live-culture plain yogurt. If you want to make goat or sheep yogurt you can use commercial goat or sheep yogurt for the starter. (See "Using Commercially Prepared Foods," page 294 to get goat or sheep yogurt). Then there will be no cow's milk in your yogurt beginning with the first batch.

ACIDOPHILUS MILK CULTURES contain only *Lactobacillus acidophilus.* The starters sold for the purpose of making acidophilus milk, like commercial yogurt starters, contain cow's milk. However, Culturelle™ and Ultradophilus™, which are sold as dairy-free probiotic supplements, make excellent acidophilus milk. If your health food store does not have these brands of supplements, see "Sources," page 297, to order them. Other brands of probiotic supplements I have tried have not made good acidophilus milk. Dairy-free Ultra-dophilus™ contains rice. If you use it and are very allergic to rice, give away your first few batches of acidophilus milk as explained above.

KEFIR CULTURES contain *Saccharomyces kefir, Torula kefir* (these two organisms are yeasts), *Lactobacillus caucasus, Streptococcus lactis* (these are bacteria), and other organisms. These organisms clump together with the milk protein to form cauliflower-like particles called "grains" in the kefir. The grains must be strained from the kefir to use them to start the next batch. The best kefir culture I tried came with a small plastic receptacle called a "kefir bug" that held the grains of the culture and could be transferred from one batch of kefir to the next. To order this culture, see "Sources," page 297.

SOURDOUGH CULTURES contain wild yeast and bacteria of the genus *Lacto-bacillus* in a symbiotic relationship. The *Lactobacillus* is what gives the bread its characteristic sour flavor. The degree of sourness varies from culture to culture. Because the yeast is a different strain than commercial baker's yeast, some people who are allergic to bread made with baker's yeast can eat sourdough. (Ask your doctor whether this might be true for you before trying it). Wild yeast leavens bread much more slowly than baker's yeast.

Purchased sourdough cultures also contain wheat flour. As you feed the culture with an alternative flour and transfer it many times in the process of activating it, the wheat flour is diluted out. Sparing you the arithmetic, I calculated that by the time I had fed my culture from Sourdoughs International nine times to activate it, my first loaf of bread contained about $1/32$ teaspoon of wheat flour in a 2-pound loaf of white spelt bread. To order sourdough cultures, see "Sources," page 297.

BAKER'S YEAST is available in many forms. Active dry yeast is yeast that has been freeze-dried to retain its activity. An expiration date is usually stamped on the package and the yeast should be good until that date if you store it in the refrigerator after opening it. Active dry yeast is available in ¼ ounce (2¼ teaspoon) packets or 4 ounce jars in most grocery stores. Also, you can purchase it in 1 pound bags and store the yeast in your freezer. Do not thaw and refreeze this yeast; instead occasionally take out a small amount to use within a few weeks and keep it in a jar in the refrigerator. Leave the remainder of the yeast frozen. Red Star™ yeast is free of grains and preservatives and works well in bread machines. Instant or quick-rise yeasts leaven bread more rapidly than active dry yeast. They are useful for making bread by hand more quickly. If you wish to use them in your bread machine, decrease the amount you use by about one fourth. These "fast" types of yeast are not recommended for most of the non-wheat bread machine breads because their gluten structure is more fragile. If quick-rise yeasts are used, the bread may over-rise and then collapse during baking. However, they do work well for white spelt bread.

Main and Side Dish Ingredients

Main and side dishes are usually made from vegetables, protein foods such as meats and beans, grains, and grain alternatives such as quinoa and amaranth.

When you choose your **VEGETABLES**, there is more to consider than just what kinds you enjoy most. Nutrition is the most important factor to consider. Testing done at Rutgers University showed that organic vegetables are much higher in minerals than their conventionally raised counterparts.[1] Since vegetables are relatively inexpensive and we eat them mainly for their vitamin and mineral content, it makes sense to spend an extra few pennies per serving to buy organic vegetables when possible even if chemical sensitivity does not force you to eat organic foods. Eating a variety of vegetables rather than just a few kinds will supply you with a wider range of nutrients. Another factor to consider is convenience. If you do not have the time to clean, wash, peel, and prepare fresh vegetables, by all means use frozen vegetables rather than not eating vegetables at all. Most of the nutritional value is preserved through the freezing process. Many health food stores carry a limited selection of frozen organic vegetables.

BEANS, GRAINS, and GRAIN ALTERNATIVES such as amaranth and quinoa are some of the most inexpensive, satisfying, and nutritious foods we have. There are many cookbooks devoted exclusively to bean and grain cooking; therefore, only basic preparation techniques for these foods are covered in this book. (See pages 90 to 94 and 104 to 106). However, you will find several legume soup recipes on pages 118 to 120. Keep in mind that grains and beans are fairly allergenic foods. If you overuse them or fail to rotate them you may become allergic to them.

GAME MEATS are used extensively in the main dish recipes in this book. As discussed in previous chapters, game is lower in fat than many "normal" meats and higher in essential fatty acids (see page 14). Game also does not have the detrimental effect that beef does on your intestinal flora (see page 28). In spite of its health benefits, some people are reluctant to try game because they expect it to taste "gamey" or to be expensive and hard to get. Indeed, if your neighbor goes hunting and gives you some game, it may taste "gamey" because of the way it was handled. Proper cooking can usually overcome this problem. Commercial game has a much better flavor than home-hunted game and does not have to be expensive. Call around for prices when you are shopping for game.

Game animals live very natural lives. They get a lot of exercise all throughout their lives and do not spend time in feed lots where they are force fed, cannot move around much, and are given hormones. Therefore, their meat tends to be tougher and less well marbled with fat than most of the meat in your grocery store. Long slow cooking with liquid, such as crockpot cooking, tenderizes game meat. You can also grind game in your food processor to overcome toughness and use it in casseroles and burgers. If your home-hunted game has a wild taste, rub the frozen meat with salt before you put it in your refrigerator to thaw. Trimming the fat before cooking also reduces the gamey taste.

Flours

There are many different kinds of flours that can be used in place of wheat flour in allergy cooking. The gluten-containing grain flours are the most allergenic for many people. Non-gluten grains may be easier to tolerate. Then there are non-grain alternative flours for those who are allergic to all grains. To find recipes that you can use for your allergies, see the listing of the grain-containing recipes on pages 301 to 303 in this book. This list also indicates which grains or grain alternatives are/are not members of the grain family and which are gluten-containing or gluten-free.

The gluten-containing grain flours include spelt, kamut, rye, barley, oats, and wheat. Among the non-gluten grains are teff, rice, wild rice, millet, milo (also called sorghum or jowar), and corn. Non-grain flours include amaranth, quinoa, buckwheat, tapioca, cassava meal, arrowroot, chestnut flour, water chestnut flour, and various legume flours and starches such as garbanzo flour, soy flour, carob powder, lupine flour, bean starch, and kudzu starch. In addition, tropical tubers can be made into flours, such as malanga flour, white sweet potato flour, true yam flour, cassava flour, lotus flour, and others. See "Sources," pages 297 to 298 for information on how to get these flours.

The **GLUTEN-CONTAINING GRAINS** make the most "normal" baked goods. Spelt, kamut, and rye make good yeast breads. Spelt and kamut are very closely related to wheat, being in the same genus but different species. (This, with recent help from the government, has led to confusion about spelt. See the note below*).

Baked goods made with barley flour are slightly more crumbly but still have great texture and flavor. The "crumbliness" of barley makes it especially well suited for making tender pie crusts. Oat flour also has a great flavor, although some oat-based baked goods are quite dense and can occasionally be gummy. Perhaps the most delicious way to bake with oats is in crackers where the denseness is not a problem.

Be sure to purchase high-quality flour. Arrowhead Mills and Bob's Red Mill flours are good for most grains and grain alternatives. For spelt, I recommend using Purity Foods flour. No, I have no connections to the company and am not being paid to say this; this recommendation is based on my experience in baking. I have found more variability in spelt flour from different sources than for any other kind of flour. All of the recipes in this book were developed using Purity Foods spelt flour. Their flour is milled from a European strain of spelt that is higher in protein than other strains, and produces consistently excellent baked goods. Purity Foods also sells a sifted spelt flour called "white spelt" that you may want to try if you are coking for company. If your health food store does not carry Purity Foods flour, see "Sources," page 298, for information on ordering it. If you cannot get Purity Foods flour and must use another brand, you will need to add more spelt flour to the recipes in this book to achieve the right consistency in your non-yeast baked goods. Other brands of spelt flour are not recommended for yeast breads.

> *NOTE ABOUT SPELT: A great deal of confusion has risen concerning spelt recently. The United States Government is now requiring that foods be labeled to indicate whether they contain any of eight food allergens. As part of the implementation of this law, the FDA has declared that spelt is wheat! Although spelt and wheat are indeed closely related, they are two different species in the same genus. Spelt is *Triticum spelta* and wheat is *Triticum aestivum*. When asked why they had decided that spelt is wheat,

an FDA official said that it was because spelt contains gluten. (They had no answer to the question of whether rye would also be considered wheat because it contains gluten). Spelt does indeed contain gluten and should not be eaten by anyone who is gluten-sensitive or has celiac disease, but the presence of gluten does not make spelt wheat.

The gluten in spelt behaves differently than the gluten in wheat in cooking. It is extremely difficult to make seitan from spelt. When making it from wheat, a process of soaking in hot water is used to remove the starch from the protein. If the same process is followed with spelt, the protein structure also dissolves in the hot water. Spelt seitan must be washed by hand very carefully under running cold water.

Because the gluten in spelt is more soluble than wheat gluten, making yeast bread with spelt is also different than making it with wheat. The individual gluten molecules join up more readily to form long chains and sheets that trap the gas produced by yeast. This means that it is possible to over-knead spelt bread. There are some bread machines that work quite well for wheat and even other allergy breads but are unacceptable for spelt bread because they knead so vigorously that they over-develop the gluten.

It is possible that the greater solubility of spelt protein makes it easier to digest than wheat. Undoubtedly, most people have had much less prior exposure to spelt than to wheat resulting in less opportunity to become allergic to spelt. Whatever the reason, there are many people who suffer allergic reactions after eating wheat but do not react to spelt. (I have talked to hundreds of them). Restricting one's diet unnecessarily, as the new law will undoubtedly lead people to do, is counterproductive to good nutrition. Consult your doctor about your own food allergy test results and follow the diet recommended for you, but do not unnecessarily restrict spelt consumption based on faulty government labeling requirements.

Baked goods made with the **NON-GLUTEN GRAINS** are more crumbly than those made with the gluten grains. Some people also find rice and teff gritty. Many of the recipes using these flours contain a starch for "glue," but still you have to expect some crumbs and heaviness. Some of the recipes in this book do not include non-gluten versions because of the fragility of baked goods made with these flours. However, the flavor of the non-gluten grains is excellent. Millet and milo (jowar) have an especially good flavor, and since you have probably rarely eaten them, you may tolerate them better than rice. To order milo, see "Sources," page 298.

The **NON-GRAIN** flours are surprisingly versatile. Their flavor may take a little getting used to, but you will eventually come to enjoy them. If quinoa is used with apple juice, sesame seeds, or carob, its distinctive flavor will be masked. The recipes in this book which use these flours also usually contain a starch to improve the texture of the final product. Most of the non-grains, especially amaranth, quinoa, and buckwheat, when used with a starch, produce an excellent texture in baked goods which is not crumbly at all. However, an occasional batch of amaranth flour might yield gummy baked goods. Amaranth pancakes and yeast breads are especially prone to gumminess. However, if you cannot eat grains, you cannot afford to be too fussy, so when my pancakes turn out gummy, I just toast them until they are crisp.

Sweeteners

The recipes in this book are sweetened without sugar. Most of them are sweetened with liquid **FRUIT SWEETENERS** of various kinds. The least concentrated of these are pureed fruits and fruit juice concentrates. More concentrated fruit sweeteners include Fruit Sweet™ which is a blend of peach, pear, and pineapple juices, Pear Sweet™ and Grape Sweet™. Using these sweeteners, you can make desserts so similar to sugar-containing desserts that no one will know they do not contain sugar. (See page 293 for information about ordering these sweeteners from Wax Orchards). Fruit sweeteners contain fructose, a simple sugar which can be directly absorbed without any digestion and does not cause wide swings in our blood sugar level like refined sugar (sucrose) does.

DATE SUGAR is ground dried dates. It is a fairly concentrated sweetener and is very useful in desserts where more sweetness is desired. It also helps keep your baked goods moist.

RICE SYRUP is rice that has been exposed to enzymes (often from fungi) which break down the starch into sugars. It is less sweet than fruit sweeteners. Baked products made with rice syrup do not brown as much as those made with fruit sweeteners.

STEVIA is an herb that is very sweet. It has no effect on blood sugar and contains no calories. You can bake and cook with stevia at any temperature and for any length of time without it breaking down. It has a slight licorice aftertaste. The aftertaste is less noticeable with the white crystalline extract of stevia, which is used in the recipes in this book, than with the whole herb. Expect your stevia sweetened desserts to be light colored; baked goods made with stevia do not brown much. A great baking combination is stevia and carob because the carob masks stevia's aftertaste and contributes a rich brown color.

FOS (fructooligosaccharides) are long-chain carbohydrates that have a clean, sweet taste like sugar, although the flavor is not as intense. FOS can be used in baking and candy making as long as it is not heated for longer than 45 minutes. (If it is heated too long and begins to caramelize, it breaks down into sucrose). We do not digest FOS, so it has no effect on our blood sugar. It is digested by our intestinal flora. If you do not have dysbiosis with one of the unfriendly organisms that FOS can nourish, it is a great sweetener to use for making "normal" treats for parties, such as the FOS candies found on pages 250 to 255. However, FOS can contribute to dysbiosis involving some types of bacteria, so use it with caution. (See page 20 for more information about this).

   HONEY and **BLACKSTRAP MOLASSES** are used in a very few of the special occasion recipes in this book. While usually considered refined sweeteners because they do affect our blood sugar, they have not been stripped of their mineral content as sugar has been. Blackstrap molasses is a byproduct of the sugar manufacturing process and is very high in minerals, especially iron. I like to make gingerbread with a combination of a little blackstrap molasses for flavor and minerals and fruit sweeteners for the rest of the sweetening needed. Sorghum molasses, which comes from milo, can be used in place of light molasses if you are allergic to the sugar cane from which "regular" molasses is made.

Leavening Ingredients

   Non-yeast baked goods are leavened by using baking soda with an acid ingredient. When these two components become wet, they react with each other to release gas into your batter or dough, thus making it rise. Commercial **BAKING POWDER** contains both components plus a starch (usually cornstarch) to keep them dry so they do not react before you want them to. Featherweight™ baking powder contains potato starch instead of cornstarch. Since potato should be rotated, be careful to rotate this baking powder and use it only on your "potato day."

   BAKING SODA is a simple, pure chemical which you do not need to rotate. The various acid ingredients that can be used with it to produce leavening include unbuffered vitamin C powder, cream of tartar, vinegar, citrus juices, pineapple juice, rhubarb concentrate, and, although not used in baking in this book, yogurt and buttermilk. (See page 248 for a recipe for rhubarb concentrate).

   Most of the recipes in this book call for **UNBUFFERED VITAMIN C POWDER** as the acid component of leavening. This powder is available in very hypoallergenic forms and from several plant sources, so you can rotate types of vitamin C if you need to. (Vitamin C powder can also be made from corn, so seek out a hypoallergenic brand as listed in "Sources," page 299). Be sure to purchase unbuffered vitamin C because buffered vitamin C will not provide the acid needed for the leavening process. Unbuffered vitamin C powder and unbuffered vitamin C crystals may be used interchangeably in the same amounts.

CREAM OF TARTAR comes from grapes as a byproduct of wine making. It should be rotated on your "grape day." If you wish to substitute cream of tartar for the vitamin C called for in a recipe, use about the same amount of cream of tartar as the recipe calls for of baking soda, or about four times as much vitamin C as is called for. For example, if a recipe calls for 1 teaspoon of baking soda and ¼ teaspoon of vitamin C, use 1 teaspoon of baking soda and 1 teaspoon of cream of tartar. You may have to experiment with the amounts a little to produce the best results.

VINEGAR, CITRUS JUICES, or RHUBARB CONCENTRATE can be substituted for vitamin C as the acid component in leavening. Use about three times as much of each of these liquids as the amount of baking powder the recipe calls for. For instance, if a recipe calls for 1 teaspoon of baking powder and ¼ teaspoon of vitamin C, use 1 teaspoon of baking powder and 3 teaspoons of vinegar, citrus juice, or rhubarb concentrate. In some recipes, you may need to decrease the amount of other liquids to compensate for the volume of vinegar, citrus juice, or rhubarb concentrate you are using.

All of these acid leavening ingredients can also be used to make salad dressings. If you cannot use vinegar, substitute citrus juices in an amount equal to the vinegar or rhubarb concentrate in a slightly greater amount. You can also substitute ½ teaspoon to 1 teaspoon of a tart-tasting brand of unbuffered vitamin C powder mixed with ¼ cup water for the vinegar in your favorite salad dressing recipe. Ecological Formulas produces a tapioca-source vitamin C that is great tasting in salads. (See "Sources," page 299, for information on ordering this brand of vitamin C). Adjust the amount of vitamin C to your taste preference. For salad dressing recipes using these ingredients, see pages 138 to 143.

Other Ingredients

OILS vary widely in health benefits. Some of these benefits are discussed on page 14 of this book. For purposes of cooking, it is best not to heat oils other than olive, coconut, avocado, or peanut oils to sauteing temperatures. (Peanut oil can be a problem for those with food allergies and chemical sensitivities). Coconut oil is a saturated fat, but recently has been exonerated from being harmful for you, if used in moderation, because it does not contain trans fats like margarine does.[2] Because it is solid at room temperature, coconut oil is very useful for making some types of cookies and waffles and for greasing waffle irons.

SALT is an unappreciated food and recipe ingredient. In addition to adding flavor to foods and moderating the growth of yeast in yeast breads, it can contribute to our health if properly used. People with food allergies often have "overworked" adrenal glands which cannot make enough of the hormone aldosterone. The judicious use of salt in the diet can help compensate for this problem.[3] A new treatment for chronic fatigue syndrome with the associated problem of low blood pressure is a diet moderately high in salt. However, some people have high blood pressure which is aggravated by a high salt diet, and on their doctor's advice, should restrict their intake of salt. Dr. Paul Eck suggests that the adverse effect of salt on those with high blood pressure may be due to the fact that salt is usually a highly refined food, devoid of other minerals to balance the sodium. He recommends that those with high blood pressure find out if they are deficient in calcium, magnesium, potassium or zinc, and that they supplement with these minerals if necessary to correct their blood pressure problems.[4] He suggests that all of us use high quality sea salt rather than refined salt.[5]

LECITHIN is an oil-like substance that can be used in place of part of the oil in yeast breads to keep them from drying out. It improves the texture and general quality of breads made in bread machines. Lecithin is usually derived from soybeans.

AGAR is a seaweed product that may be used like gelatin for thickening yogurt and making aspics or pies. It is usually available in the form of flakes. Therefore, the recipes in this book call for agar flakes. If you wish to use agar powder instead, reduce the amount of agar called for in the recipe by about one third.

GUAR GUM and **XANTHUM GUM** are two types of soluble fiber that can be used in making breads and other baked goods from non-gluten grains and non-grains. When used in yeast breads, they help to strengthen bread's structure so it can rise well. They can also be used to thicken oil-free salad dressings. Guar gum is derived from a legume and therefore should be rotated on your "bean day." Xanthum gum is derived from the bacteria, *Xanthomonas compestris*.

FOOTNOTES

1. McHerron, Elena, "Eating Organic Means More Minerals," *Organic Living,* Volume 57, Late Spring 1996, p. 6.

2. Interview with Mary Enig, Ph.D., "Fats – The Real Story," *Mastering Food Allergies Newsletter,* #89, January/February 1996, p. 4.

3. Eck, Paul, N.D. "Common Misconceptions Associated with Salt," Eck Institute Articles, Eck Institute of Applied Nutrition and Bioenergetics, Ltd., 8650 N. 22nd Avenue, Phoenix, AZ 85021, pp. 1-2.

4. Ibid, pp. 2-3.

5. Ibid, p. 1.

Lactobacillus-
Containing Foods

Healthy bowel flora is an essential defense factor for health. One way to encourage healthy flora is to consume *Lactobacillus*-containing foods. Also, the "friendly flora" in these foods partially digest the foods before we eat them, making them easier for us to digest and to tolerate if they are foods to which we are allergic.

Foods that contain live *Lactobacillus* include yogurt, acidophilus milk, kefir, and unpasteurized fermented vegetables such as sauerkraut. In frozen yogurt and sourdough breads the organisms are no longer alive, but we still get the nutritional benefits conferred by the organisms, such as increased vitamin content and the predigestion of the foods, making it easier for us to derive nutrition from them.

This chapter gives recipes and instructions for making your own *Lactobacillus*-containing foods. However, if you do not have the time to make your own *Lactobacillus*-containing foods, there are many good commercial products available. Goat, sheep, and soy milk yogurts which contain live cultures are available and delicious. (See page 294 for information on how to get them). Health-food store refrigerators are loaded with live-culture cow's milk yogurts. Occasionally one can even find acidophilus milk or kefir. But if you make your own *Lactobacillus*-containing foods, you will know that the organisms are alive and potent when you eat them.

Several factors influence the quality of homemade fermented milks such as yogurt, acidophilus milk, and kefir. The most important are the temperature at which they are made, the milk used, and the culture used.

Since yogurt, acidophilus milk, and sourdough breads rely on being kept at about body temperature so *Lactobacillus* can grow, you will have to make a small investment in equipment to incubate these foods if you are going to make them at home. There are several yogurt makers on the market. Choose a system that uses electricity to keep your yogurt warm for up to 24 hours. Systems that do not use electricity are basically thermos bottles and do not keep the yogurt at a high enough temperature for more than several hours. If you wish to make a 24-hour yogurt or acidophilus milk, thus insuring that all of the lactose in the milk will be predigested, you will need a longer incubation time than thermos-type yogurt makers can give. Also, fermented alternative milk products do not thicken as quickly as cow's milk products, and therefore require longer incubation.

Most commercial yogurt makers make between one and two quarts of yogurt at one time. They may make it all in one container or in individual cups. Their prices range from about $20 to $70. I have tried several brands, and they all work well. Some of them incubate the yogurt at about 110°F, which is a perfect temperature to make cow's milk yogurt quickly, but can result in a "buttermilk" type of texture in a 24-hour goat yogurt or acidophilus milk. Fermented milks made at this temperature are still nutritious and perfectly safe to eat, but most people prefer a more creamy texture. The yogurt makers which use an incubation temperature of about 95°F, such as the Yogourmet™, make excellent acidophilus milk and yogurt of all kinds.

My favorite incubator for yogurt and acidophilus milk is my inexpensive homemade "proofing box" incubator which I originally made to incubate sourdough bread. To make a homemade incubator, you will need a styrofoam cooler (mine cost about $3), a "shop light," preferably with plastic rather than metal casing (costing about $10), a 25-watt light bulb, and a thermometer. Install the light bulb into the shop light. Discard the lid of the cooler. Make a small hole in the bottom of the cooler near one end and thread the cord of the shop light through it until the base of the shop light touches the inside of the cooler. Tape the cord on the outside of the cooler to keep it from slipping. Use wire or tape to attach the "hook" end of the shop light to the bottom of the cooler near the other end of the cooler. Turn the cooler upside down on a table or countertop and plug in the light. Put the thermometer in the "proofing box." After about an hour, read the temperature on the thermometer. If it is between 90°F and 98°F, your proofing box is ready to use. If it is higher, experiment with propping one end of the box up ½ inch or so until you find how much you need to prop it up to maintain the temperature in the proper range. I use the ring from the lid of a canning jar to prop up the end of my box, thus maintaining the temperature at about 95°F. If the temperature is lower than 90°F, check it in another hour or two; the temperature will almost certainly have risen into the right range by then. If it has not, change the light bulb to one with higher wattage. The first few times you use your proofing box, it is a good idea to check the temperature every hour or two to be sure that the temperature is staying at about 95°F.

A homemade proofing box is very versatile. It can be used to make sourdough breads as well as fermented milks. (Mine has even been used as an incubator for science projects!) If you are making more than one kind of fermented milk at a time, you can incubate several jars of different kinds of milks at the same time. You can also make larger batches of fermented milks using a proofing box than you can using a yogurt machine. You do not need special containers when making yogurt in a proofing box, so you can store your yogurt in the same jars in which you made it, rather than having to empty a special container that fits a yogurt maker before you can make another batch of yogurt.

The type of milk used also influences the character of your yogurt or acidophilus milk. Cow's and sheep's milk, being relatively high in fat and protein, make thick, creamy yogurt and acidophilus milk. Whole goat's milk makes thinner fermented milks than cow's milk; but when the culture is at its "peak," these milks are quite creamy. Non-fat goat's milk makes very watery fermented milks; however, they still are very nutritious and contain lots of health-promoting "friendly flora." Reconstituted powdered milk can be used to make fermented milks. In some cases, such as with goat's milk, I find that reconstituted powdered milk makes thicker yogurt and acidophilus milk than fresh whole milk does.

Non-animal milk can also be used to make fermented milks, although the texture will not be as thick or creamy. The milk used must contain enough fermentable carbohydrate to support the growth of your culture. I have had good results using soy milks such as Edensoy™. The nut and rice milks I tried did not work.

The type of organisms in the culture and age of the culture you use also affect your fermented milks. Yogurt is thicker and creamier than acidophilus milk due to the action of

Lactobacillus bulgaricus on the milk protein. You can use either "live" yogurt or a powdered yogurt culture as a starter with good results. All of the powdered yogurt cultures I have seen contained some cow's milk. If you wish to make cow's milk-free yogurt, you may use goat or sheep yogurt as a starter.

To make acidophilus milk, I prefer to use Culturelle™ as a starter. The consistency of your acidophilus milk will vary with the age of the culture. The batch made directly from the powdered acidophilus culture will be creamy, but not extremely thick. Then as the culture reaches its peak, your acidophilus milk will become much thicker. When the acidophilus milk becomes thinner again with subsequent batches, it is time to start a new culture from acidophilus powder.

The cultures used for kefir are considerably more complex than yogurt or acidophilus milk cultures. They contain several strains of bacteria and yeast growing in a synergistic relationship, which form hard, cauliflower-like kefir grains in a mature culture. Traditionally, these grains are strained out of the milk and used to start the next batch of kefir. The GoodLife Company of Australia produces an ingenious contraption called a kefir bug that holds the culture and floats on the top of the milk as it ferments. GoodLife's kefir cultures also work well; I did not succeed in making kefir with several other commercial kefir cultures. To get a GoodLife Kefir Bug™ and kefir culture, see "Sources," page 297.

Cultured vegetables, such as unpasteurized sauerkraut, are also dietary sources of "healthy flora" such as *Lactobacillus plantarum*. To make these vegetables at home, refer to *The Body Ecology Diet* by Donna Gates for a recipe. (See "References," page 296). I have not included a recipe for fermented vegetables in this book because these vegetables are made using what I consider to be an uncontrolled fermentation process, and therefore I feel the process is best left to the professionals. The vegetables are not sterilized before the fermentation process, as the milk is essentially sterilized by boiling it in the following fermented milk recipes. One hopes that the proper organisms are present on the vegetables to start the fermentation rather than adding a starter containing organisms of known identity. When I took a course in food microbiology in college, our class made several crocks of sauerkraut as part of the laboratory section of the course. Only one of the crocks underwent the desired fermentation. Therefore, I am more comfortable eating natural unpasteurized sauerkraut I buy from a health food store than making it myself. To obtain fermented vegetables, ask for them at your health food store, or see "Using Commercially Prepared Foods," page 292.

Good hygiene is always important in all cooking, but when you are making fermented foods, it is paramount to the outcome of your recipe. Wash your hands thoroughly before you start, and wash them again whenever they may have become contaminated with anything as you proceed. Use scrupulously clean pans, spoons, and other utensils. I like to use a long-handled spoon to stir the milk as it is coming to a boil and just leave the spoon in the pot; it is then sterilized along with the milk. However, if you must remove the spoon from the pan, set it on a clean dish, and get a new spoon if it may have become contaminated. If you introduce organisms into the milk besides the "friendly flora" yogurt, acidophilus milk, or kefir organisms you want to grow, the results of your fermentation may not be what you desire.

Yogurt

Yogurt has been called "the milk of life," and is indeed a great health-promoting food. It is made by fermenting milk with the organisms *Lactobacillus bulgaricus* and *Streptococcus thermophilus.* Although these organisms do not permanently colonize the human intestine, they assist colonization by *Lactobacillus acidophilus* and *Bifidobacterium bifidum.*

DAY 1 if goat's milk is used
DAY 3 if sheep's milk is used
EXTRA FOODS if soy or cow's milk is used

> 1 quart of goat's, sheep's, cow's, or soy milk
> (Whole, low-fat, non-fat, or reconstituted powdered milk may be used).
> ¼ to ⅓ cup of yogurt containing live cultures OR 1 envelope of powdered yogurt
> culture (See note about cultures on the next page).

1. Bring the milk to a boil in a saucepan and boil it for one minute if the milk is pasteurized or for five minutes if it is raw.

2. Cool the milk to about 95°F, using a bread or yogurt thermometer to monitor the temperature as it cools. If you are in a hurry, you can speed this process by putting the pan in a sink of cold water.

3. Stir a little of the warm milk into your yogurt starter or powdered culture; then stir the starter into the rest of the milk in the saucepan.

4. Pour the milk into yogurt maker container(s) or glass jar(s) to go into your proofing box. (See page 58 for more about proofing boxes).

5. Place the container(s) into your yogurt maker or proofing box.

6. Incubate the yogurt until it thickens (5 to 10 hours) or for up to 24 hours. Yogurt that is incubated for 24 hours will contain almost no lactose and the protein will be partially digested, which makes it easier to tolerate.

   > NOTE: If the yogurt does not thicken or has an off odor, do not eat it – begin again with fresh starter. If it has been 3 to 4 weeks since you started with a fresh culture, start over with fresh culture next time. If you have made several batches since you used fresh starter and the quality of the yogurt has begun to deteriorate, begin with fresh starter next time.

7. Save some of the yogurt in a clean container in the refrigerator to use to make your next batch of yogurt. Reserve ¼ to ⅓ cup of yogurt for each quart of yogurt you plan to make.

8. Serve the rest of the yogurt immediately or you can refrigerate it for up to one week. Serve it plain or with fresh fruit and/or stevia, if desired.

NOTE: If you must use cow's milk yogurt or a powdered starter containing cow's milk to make an alternative milk yogurt, you can minimize the amount of cow's milk in your yogurt as follows: Heat about 1 cup of alternative milk and cool it as above. Make a batch of yogurt with it using about 2 teaspoons of cow's yogurt or culture. Then, the next day, use this yogurt to start a 1-quart batch of yogurt. As you make successive batches of yogurt, each batch will contain less and less cow's milk.

Makes about 1 quart of yogurt.

Acidophilus Milk

Acidophilus milk is a fermented milk that tastes much like yogurt. It is made with a pure culture of *Lactobacillus acidophilus*. It does not get as thick as yogurt, especially if made with goat's milk. It has traditionally been used as a treatment for gastrointestinal disorders.

DAY 1 if goat's milk is used
DAY 3 if sheep's milk is used
EXTRA FOODS if soy or cow's milk is used

   1 to 1¼ quarts goat's, sheep's, or cow's milk (Whole milk, reconstituted powdered milk, low-fat, or non-fat milk may be used).
   2 teaspoons Ultradophilus™, 1 teaspoon Culturelle™ (empty out four capsules), 1 envelope Hansen's™ acidophilus milk culture, or other culture which contains only *Lactobacillus acidophilus* (See note in step 11 on the next page and "Sources," page 297).

First Day
1. Bring 1 cup of milk to a boil in a saucepan over medium heat and boil it for one minute if the milk is pasteurized or for five minutes if it is raw milk. If you are using Culturelle™ and would like to consume your acidophilus milk the next day, you may bring a quart of milk to a boil and use a one-stage rather than two-stage process to make your acidophilus milk.

2. Cool the milk to about 95°F, using a bread or yogurt thermometer to monitor the temperature as it cools.

3. Stir the culture into the warm milk and put the milk in a yogurt maker container(s) or glass jar(s). (For the one-day method of making acidophilus milk with Culturelle™, open the four capsules and empty them into about ½ cup of the milk. Stir very thoroughly to mix all of the powder into the milk well. Then combine this mixture with the rest of the milk, stir thoroughly, and put it into the yogurt maker containers. Continue with step 9 below).

4. Incubate the milk overnight in a yogurt maker or proofing box. (See page 58 more about proofing boxes).

Second Day

5. The next day, when the acidophilus milk has thickened (after about 12 to 24 hours of incubation, the length of time depending on the culture used), bring the remaining milk to a boil over medium heat and boil it for one minute if the milk is pasteurized or for five minutes if it is raw.

6. Cool the milk to 95°F, using a bread or yogurt thermometer to monitor the temperature as it cools. If you are in a hurry, you can speed this process by putting the pan in a sink of cold water.

7. Stir a little of the warm milk into of the previous day's batch of acidophilus milk; then stir this mixture into the rest of the milk in the saucepan.

8. Pour the milk into yogurt maker container(s) or glass jar(s) to go into your proofing box.

9. Incubate it for 24 hours. A 24-hour acidophilus milk will contain almost no lactose and the protein will be partially digested, which makes it easier to tolerate.

    NOTE: Acidophilus milk does not get very thick. However, if does not thicken at all or has an off odor, do not eat it – begin again with fresh starter. If it has been 3 to 4 weeks since you started with a fresh culture, start over with fresh culture next time. If you have made several batches since you used fresh starter and the quality of the acidophilus milk has begun to deteriorate, begin with fresh starter next time.

10. Save some of the acidophilus milk in a clean container in the refrigerator to use to make your next batch. Reserve ¼ to ⅓ cup of acidophilus milk for each quart of it you plan to make next time. Use what you reserve to start at step 5 of this recipe when making your next batch of acidophilus milk.

11. Serve the rest of the acidophilus milk immediately or refrigerate it for up to one week. Serve it plain, with fresh fruit and/or stevia, or as a smoothie, below.

    NOTE: Culturelle™ (*Lactobacillus GG)*, Metagenics/Essential Nutrients' NCFM strain-containing Ultradophilus,™ and Hansen's™ acidophilus milk culture are the only three cultures I have used that make good acidophilus milk. The DDS-1 strain-containing probiotics I tried either did not work, produced a bubbly "off" fermentation, or, in the case of Megadophillus™, seemed to work but produced an inferior acidophilus milk which did not taste quite right and which developed an "off" odor after refrigeration. Never eat acidophilus milk or yogurt that has an "off" odor – The old wives' advice, "When in doubt, throw it out" is sound.

ACIDOPHILUS SMOOTHIE VARIATION: Stir one cup of acidophilus milk until it is smooth. Add a pinch of white stevia powder and ½ teaspoon of corn-free natural flavoring OR ¼ cup pureed fresh fruit. Stir thoroughly and drink.

Makes about 1 quart of acidophilus milk

Extra-Thick Yogurt or Acidophilus Milk

DAY 1 if made with goat yogurt; borrow tapioca from **DAY 3**
DAY 3 if made with sheep yogurt
EXTRA FOODS if made with cow or soy yogurt

Ingredients for one batch of yogurt or acidophilus milk, above
One or more of the following additions:
  1 envelope of plain gelatin OR 3 to 4 teaspoons of agar flakes
  ⅓ cup powdered milk
  2 tablespoons tapioca flour

1. To make your yogurt or acidophilus milk extra-thick and creamy using gelatin or agar, sprinkle the gelatin or agar onto the surface of the one quart of milk before bringing it to a boil. Stir it in as the milk heats. Proceed as in the preceding recipes.

2. If you are going to thicken your yogurt using powdered milk, use powdered goat's milk in goat yogurt, powdered cow's milk in cow yogurt, etc. If you are lactose-intolerant, do not use powdered milk to thicken your yogurt because all of the lactose may not be fermented in 24 hours. Stir the powdered milk into the one quart of milk before bringing it to a boil. Then proceed as in the preceding recipes.

3. If you wish to thicken your yogurt or acidophilus milk with tapioca flour, reserve about ¼ cup milk from the one quart of milk to be used in the recipe. Bring the rest of the milk to a boil. Stir the tapioca flour into the reserved ¼ cup of milk and stir it into the rest of the milk just as it begins to boil. Proceed with the recipe as directed, except cool the milk rapidly by putting the pan in a sink of cold water and stirring it continually rather than allowing it to cool slowly. If it cools too slowly, the tapioca may burn onto the bottom of the pan.

Yogurt "Sour Cream" or Yo-Cheese

DAY 1 if made with goat yogurt
DAY 3 if made with sheep yogurt
EXTRA FOODS if made with cow or soy yogurt

One batch of yogurt, page 60, made without gelatin or tapioca to thicken it OR one quart of commercial yogurt which does not contain thickeners

1. Line a colander with two double layers of cheesecloth, or use a "yogurt strainer" purchased from a cooking store or catalogue. (See "Sources," page 300).

2. Place a pan or bowl beneath the colander or strainer, allowing plenty of room for the liquid to drain without touching the bottom of the colander or strainer.

3. Place the yogurt in the colander or strainer, and refrigerate it for 4 to 6 hours, overnight,

or for a full 24 hours. The length of time you must drain your yogurt to obtain the consistency you desire will depend on how thick the yogurt was to begin with; a very thick sheep yogurt will achieve a "sour cream" or soft cheese consistency sooner than goat yogurt will.

4. Serve immediately or refrigerate for up to a week. Yogurt sour cream is delicious on baked potatoes. Yo-cheese is great as a spread or in recipes such as lasagne.

Makes about 1½ to 2½ cups of yogurt sour cream or yo-cheese.

Frozen Yogurt

DAY 1 if made with goat yogurt and pineapple juice
DAY 3 if made with sheep yogurt and apple juice or Pear Sweet™
EXTRA FOODS if made with cow or soy yogurt

> 2 cups plain yogurt
> ¼ teaspoon white stevia extract powder, or slightly more to taste OR
> > ⅜ cup Fruit Sweet™, Grape Sweet™, Pear Sweet™, or honey OR ¾ cup apple or pineapple juice concentrate, thawed
> 1 cup fruit (strawberries, blueberries, peaches, etc.)
> > OR ¾ teaspoon corn-free natural vanilla OR 2 tablespoons carob powder

1. To make frozen yogurt in an ice cream maker, puree the fruit (if you are using it), combine it with the rest of the ingredients, and chill and freeze as the machine's instructions direct.

2. To make frozen yogurt using a food processor, freeze the yogurt in an ice cube tray for several hours or overnight.

3. The next day remove the yogurt cubes from the freezer and allow them to stand for five to fifteen minutes at room temperature, or until they are no longer rock hard.

4. If you are making carob or vanilla frozen yogurt, put the Fruit Sweet™, Grape Sweet™, Pear Sweet™, honey, fruit juice concentrate, or stevia and vanilla or carob in the processor bowl.

5. If you are making a fruit yogurt, put the fruit and sweetner in the processor bowl and puree it briefly.

6. With the processor running, add the yogurt cubes one or two at a time, processing until smooth after each addition.

NOTE: If you are making this recipe with homemade yogurt, you may wish to use a short (5 to 10 hour) incubation rather than a 24 hour incubation to reduce the tanginess of the yogurt. However, the lactose level will be almost negligible in a 24-hour yogurt, making it easier for some people to tolerate.

ICE CREAM VARIATION: For ice cream, substitute any animal milk or cream, soy milk, rice milk, nut milk, or coconut milk for the yogurt.

Makes 1½ to 2 pints of frozen yogurt

Kefir

Kefir is milk that has been fermented by a number of organisms, both bacteria and yeast, including *Saccharomyces kefir, Torula kefir, Lactobacillus caucasus, Streptococcus lactis,* and others. In a mature culture, these organisms form clumps called "grains" in the milk, which are strained out and used to start your next batch of kefir. The most convenient way to make kefir is with a "kefir bug" which contains the grains and floats in the milk as it ferments. To order a "bug" with a kefir culture see "Sources," page 297.

DAY 1 if made with goat's milk
DAY 3 if made with sheep's milk
EXTRA FOODS if made with cow's milk

> 1 quart of any animal milk – cow's, goat's, sheep's, etc.
> 1 "kefir bug"
> 2 tablets of kefir culture

1. If you are using raw milk, put it into a saucepan and bring it to a boil. Reduce the heat and simmer it for five minutes, then allow it to cool to room temperature before proceeding with the recipe.

2. Fresh pasteurized milk may be used straight from the refrigerator. However, if it has been open for more than a day or two, begin with a new carton.

3. Wash all the parts of the kefir bug with soap and very hot water, rinse them, and allow them to air dry.

4. Put the two culture tablets into the cone of the kefir bug and snap on the perforated lid. Snap the floater top onto the top of the assembly.

5. Put just enough milk into a clean jar to float the kefir bug. Add the bug and set the jar in a warm spot (around 70°F to 80°F) for 24 hours. Do not set it in direct sunlight.

6. The next day, put enough milk into another clean jar to float the kefir bug. Using clean utensils, remove the bug from the first jar and transfer it to the second jar. Discard the milk from the first jar. Set the jar in a warm spot (around 70°F to 80°F) for 24 hours. Do not set it in direct sunlight.

7. Repeat step 6 once more.

8. On the fourth day, using a clean fork or knife, pry the floater top off the kefir bug. Do not remove the perforated top from the cone. Swish the cone in a small bowl of bottled water to dislodge excess milk from the kefir grains that should be starting to form inside the cone. Wash and rinse the floater top and put it back on the "bug."

9. Put one cup of fresh milk into a clean jar. Float the kefir bug in it and allow it to stand for 24 to 48 hours in a warm spot. When it thickens slightly and begins to smell alcoholic, you have kefir!

10. Remove the kefir bug from the jar and clean it as in step 8. Put it into another cup of milk in a clean jar as in step 9 to make more kefir.

1. Choose one set of ingredients from the previous page.

2. If you bake with your sourdough starter infrequently, bring it back to a full activity level as described on the previous page.

3. The night before you plan to make bread, thoroughly mix the starter with 1½ cups of the flour in a glass, plastic, or ceramic mixing bowl. (Do not use a metal bowl.)

4. If you are going to use your bread machine to make the dough, and its pan does not have a hole in the bottom, you may mix the starter and 1½ cups flour in your bread machine pan in the machine. Put the starter and flour in the pan, start the dough cycle, and allow the machine to mix the starter and flour for a few minutes. Then turn the machine off and remove the pan from the machine.

5. Cover the bowl or bread machine pan with plastic wrap or a towel and put it in a warm place overnight. (If you made a "proofing box" to activate your culture, this is an ideal place).

6. The next morning, add the salt, caraway seeds, and enough of the remaining flour to make a firm dough. To make the dough by hand, stir in as much flour as possible and then knead in enough of the rest of the flour to make a stiff dough. Knead the dough by hand for 10 to 15 minutes. To use a heavy-duty mixer to make the dough, knead the dough for as long as your mixer book suggests for yeast breads.

7. If you are using a bread machine, put the pan back into the machine or transfer the mixture in the bowl to your machine pan. Add the salt and enough flour so the total amount you have used is the smallest amount flour listed above and start the dough cycle. If the dough is sticky, add more flour during the initial kneading cycle. After mixing, remove the dough from the pan and knead in enough of the remaining flour by hand to make a firm dough.

8. Shape the dough into either a round loaf or long loaf and put it on a baking sheet that has been oiled or liberally sprinkled with flour.

9. Slash the top of the loaf with a very sharp knife.

10. Put the loaf in a warm place, such as a proofing box, to rise until doubled. For the San Francisco sourdough culture, this takes about 3 to 5 hours. Other cultures can take a shorter time or as long as 10 to 14 hours. Also, if you do not use your starter regularly, it will take longer to leaven bread than if you use it often.

11. Preheat your oven to 375°F. Moisture in the oven contributes to a crisp crust, so I like to put a few potatoes into the oven when I turn it on for added moisture.

12. Bake the bread for 65 to 80 minutes or until brown.

13. Immediately remove the loaf from the baking sheet and cool it on a wire rack.

Makes one very dense loaf of bread.

Main Dishes

When you have food allergies, it is often best to keep meals simple. If you react to something that you have eaten, the detective work needed to identify the offending food will be easier if your meal consists of just a few foods. Therefore, most of the recipes in this chapter are simple. For more complex casseroles, pot pies, pasties, and ethnic dishes, refer to *Allergy Cooking With Ease*.

Many of the recipes in this chapter are made with game meat. If you are allergic to "normal" meats, do not hesitate to try game. It is a great source of the high-quality protein necessary for healing, as well as essential fatty acids, zinc, and B vitamins. Game from a good commercial source, properly prepared for tenderness, is as delicious as any "normal" meat, and does not taste gamey.

Game requires some special attention in cooking. If you are using frozen game, rub the meat with the salt called for in the recipe when you take it from the freezer. Then allow it to thaw in the refrigerator. Trim as much fat and gristle from the meat as possible. Long, slow cooking, such as crock pot cooking or braising, tenderizes game. Grinding the meat also overcomes the problem of toughness. If you cannot buy your game already ground, you can grind it yourself using a food processor or blender. Cut the meat into one to two inch cubes. If it is still slightly frozen when you grind it, that makes the process easier. Use the metal blade for pureeing in your processor. Put the chunks of meat into the processor or blender. (If you use a blender, you will have to grind the meat in small batches; in a food processor, you can grind about a pound at a time). Pulse the processor or blender until the meat is ground. Then use it in any of the recipes below which call for ground meat.

Poached Fish

ANY DAY, depending on the fish used

  1 pound of fish fillets or steaks
  Water
  ⅛ to ½ teaspoon salt, or to taste
  2 tablespoons oil (optional)
  1 tablespoon lemon juice OR
     ⅛ teaspoon tart tasting unbuffered vitamin C powder (optional)
  Dash of paprika (optional)
  ½ teaspoon dry sweet basil OR 1 teaspoon chopped fresh sweet basil (optional)

1. Put the fish in a baking dish in a single layer.

2. If you are cooking a tender, mild flavored type of fish, add about ¼ cup of water to the baking dish. If you are cooking a tough, strong flavored fish, add water to a depth of about ½ inch.

3. Sprinkle the fish with salt and any of the optional ingredients you wish to use.

4. Turn on your oven to 350°F.

5. Bake the fish for 15 to 25 minutes (bake longer for thicker fish) until the fish flakes easily when pierced with a fork.

Makes 2 to 4 servings.

Breaded Fish

DAY 1 – cod or haddock, borrow cassava from **DAY 3**
DAY 3 – turbot or halibut

    1 pound cod, haddock, turbot, halibut, or other white fish fillets or steaks
    2 to 3 teaspoons oil
    Salt
    1 to 2 tablespoons cassava meal (See "Sources," page 297).

1. Brush oil on both sides of the fish.

2. Sprinkle the fish lightly with salt on both sides.

3. Pat the cassava meal onto both sides of the fish.

4. Put the fish on a broiler pan.

5. Turn your broiler on to 450°F.

6. Broil the fish for five minutes if your fish is one inch thick or less.

7. Turn the fish over with a spatula and broil the other side for five minutes.

8. Pierce the fish with a fork. If it is white all the way through and flakes easily, it is done.

9. If the fish is more than one inch thick, increase the broiling time on each side so that the total time is at least ten minutes per inch of thickness. Test it with a fork for doneness as in step 8.

10. When the fish is done, remove it from the broiler and serve it immediately.

Makes 2 to 4 servings

Braised Alligator or Rattlesnake

Any day – both alligator and rattlesnake are assigned to "**EXTRA FOODS**" on the rotation diet

    1 pound alligator meat (sirloin is the most tender) or boneless rattlesnake meat or one snake with the bones
    Salt
    Water

1. If you are using rattlesnake with the bones, put it in a baking dish and proceed with step 5 below.

2. If you are using boneless meat, slice the alligator or boneless rattlesnake meat into ½ inch slices or cut it into ½ to ¾ inch cubes.

3. Pound the slices or cubes with a meat tenderizer mallet.

4. Put the slices or cubes in a baking dish or casserole with a lid.

5. Salt the meat generously and add water to a depth of ¼ to ½ inch so that the water is about ⅔ the depth of the meat. For rattlesnake with the bones, add ½ inch of water.

6. Cover the dish with its lid or with foil.

7. Turn your oven on to 350°F.

8. Bake for 40 to 60 minutes. If you wish to uncover the baking dish the last ten to fifteen minutes of the cooking time and let the meat dry out and brown a little, it will improve the appearance of the meat.

9. If you cooked rattlesnake with the bones, pick the meat from the bones.

10. Serve immediately. Both kinds of meat are good shredded and wrapped in a tortilla.

Makes 4 servings

Turtle

ANY DAY – turtle is assigned to "EXTRA FOODS" on the rotation diet

2½ pounds turtle meat
4 cups water, plus additional water
1 teaspoon salt

1. Put the turtle, 4 cups of water (or enough to cover the meat), and salt in a saucepan.

2. Bring it to a boil and skim the foam off of the top of the liquid.

3. Reduce the heat and simmer it for 2½ to 3 hours, or until the meat is tender. Check it occasionally while it is cooking and add more water if necessary to keep the meat covered with water.

4. Strain the broth from the meat.

5. Cool the meat until you can handle it; then pick the meat from the bones.

6. Serve the meat "as is," or return it to the broth and add cooked vegetables of your choice for turtle soup.

Makes 4 to 6 servings

Braised Frog Legs

ANY DAY – frog is assigned to "EXTRA FOODS" on the rotation diet

    1 pound frog legs
    Water
    Salt

1. Put the frog legs in a baking dish in a single layer.

2. Salt them generously and add water to the dish to a depth of about ½ inch.

3. Cover the baking dish with a lid or with foil.

4. Turn the oven on to 350°F.

5. Bake the frog legs for 30 to 40 minutes, or until the meat is white and opaque all the way to the bone.

6. Serve "as is," or remove the meat from the bones and serve it wrapped in tortillas.

Makes 2 to 4 servings

Roasted Poultry

DAY 2 – turkey
DAY 3 – chicken, pheasant, or cornish hen
DAY 4 – duck or goose
EXTRA FOODS – guinea hen, partridge, or squab

    1 bird of any type
    Salt

1. Clean the bird and cut off the excess skin and fat.

2. Rub the inside of the cavity with salt.

3. Place the bird on a rack in an uncovered roasting pan.

4. Turn your oven on to 350°F.

5. Bake the bird until it is nicely browned and when pierced with a fork, the juice runs clear. You may baste the bird with the drippings during the roasting time if you wish. Approximate cooking times are listed below. For large birds, like turkeys, use a meat thermometer and cook the bird until the temperature in the deepest part of the meat is at least 185°F.

Approximate cooking times:

    Turkey: 20 minutes per pound
    Chicken or pheasant: 1½ to 2½ hours
    Duck or goose: 2½ to 3½ hours
    Guinea hen: 1½ to 2 hours
    Cornish hen, partridge, or squab: 1 to 1¼ hours

6. Remove the bird from the oven when it is done.

7. Allow large birds to stand for about 15 minutes before slicing the meat. Medium-sized birds may be cut into breasts, legs and wings and served immediately. Serve the small birds whole immediately.

Serves one (cornish hen, partridge, or squab) to many (turkey)

Arrowroot Gravy

ANY DAY – Borrow arrowroot from Day 1

If you roast a large bird (recipe above) and have drippings, you can use them to make gravy. Skim most of the fat from the drippings with a spoon. Combine ¼ cup arrowroot with ¾ cup cold water in a jar and shake thoroughly. Remove the bird from the roasting pan and place the pan on the stovetop, over two burners if the pan is large. Turn the burners on to medium heat. Pour about half of the arrowroot mixture into the drippings and cook, stirring, until thickened and bubbly. If the gravy is not thick enough, and the rest of the arrowroot mixture and cook. If it is still not thick, make more arrowroot mixture and continue adding it and cooking until the gravy is thick. Taste the gravy and add salt if needed.

Poultry Stuffing

This is an easy and tasty stuffing for "Roasted Poultry," above. The celery and onion are assigned to "**EXTRA FOODS**" on this book's rotation diet, so the grain used determines the rotation day on which you will use this stuffing.

DAY 1 – kamut
DAY 3 – millet
DAY 4 – rice

> 1 cup finely chopped celery
> ½ cup finely chopped onion OR an additional ½ cup chopped celery
> 2 tablespoons oil
> ¼ teaspoon salt
> ⅛ teaspoon pepper (optional)
> 1½ cups puffed cereal – puffed kamut on **DAY 1**,
>   puffed millet on **DAY 3**, or puffed rice on **DAY 4**

1. Chop the celery and onion. Put them in a saucepan with the oil and cook them over medium heat until they begin to brown.

2. Stir in the seasonings and cereal.

3. Stuff the cavity of a chicken, duck, or other medium sized bird with the mixture and roast it as in the recipe above, adding ½ hour to the roasting time.

4. For small birds, stuff four birds and roast for 1 to 1½ hours as in the recipe above.

5. This recipe may be doubled or tripled to stuff a turkey. Roast the turkey as in the recipe above but increase the cooking time to 25 minutes per pound. Test the turkey for done-

Braised Chops or Steak

DAY 1 – goat or pork
DAY 2 – buffalo
EXTRA FOODS – game meat or beef

> 1 to 1½ pounds of chops, round steak, shoulder steak,
>   or other cut of any red game meat, goat, pork, buffalo, or beef
> 2 bell peppers (optional)
> Salt
> Pepper (optional)
> Water

1. If you are using frozen game, rub it with salt while it is still frozen and then allow it to thaw in the refrigerator.

2. Trim the fat and gristle from the meat.

3. Put the meat in a baking dish.

4. If you wish to use the bell peppers, remove the stems and seeds from them, slice them into strips, and put them on top of the meat in the baking dish.

5. Add water to the dish to a depth of about ¾ the thickness of the meat.

6. Sprinkle the meat with the seasonings.

7. Cover the baking dish with foil or a lid.

8. Turn the oven on to 350°F.

9. Bake the meat for two hours. Watch it as it is cooking and add more water if necessary to keep it from drying out completely. The water should have almost completely evaporated by serving time. If it seems to be evaporating too slowly, remove the lid or foil during the last half hour of baking to allow most of the water to evaporate and the meat to brown.

Makes 4 to 6 servings

Any Meat Crockpot Roast

For Saint Patrick's Day, or just for an exciting change of pace, make this dish with potatoes, carrots, cabbage wedges, and corned buffalo.

DAY 2 – buffalo
EXTRA FOODS – game or beef

> One 2 to 3 pound roast of any kind of red meat – buffalo, antelope, kangaroo,
>   venison, elk, beef, etc.
> ½ to 1 teaspoon salt (omit with corned meats)
> 2 to 3 pounds of vegetables of your choice such as carrots, potatoes,
>   parsnips, etc. (optional)
> Water

1. If you are using frozen game, rub the frozen roast with the salt and allow it to thaw overnight in the refrigerator.

2. The next morning, put the roast in a 3-quart crockpot. If you are using the vegetables put them in the pot around and underneath the roast.

3. Add enough water to almost come to the top of the meat. If you did not salt the meat before thawing it, add the salt to the pot.

4. Cook the roast on low for 8 to 10 hours.

5. Remove the roast from the crockpot, slice it, and serve it with the vegetables.

Makes 6 to 8 servings

Any Meat Burgers or Sausage Patties

DAY 1 – pork or goat
DAY 2 – turkey or buffalo
DAY 3 – lamb or chicken
DAY 4 – duck
EXTRA FOODS – game meat or ostrich

> 1 pound ground meat or poultry of any kind
> ½ teaspoon salt
> Water, if you are braising the burgers rather than broiling them
> Extra ingredients for sausage:
> > 1 to 2 tablespoons finely minced onion (optional)
> > 1½ teaspoons fennel seeds
> > ⅛ teaspoon seeded and finely crumbled dried red chili pepper
> > > OR ¼ teaspoon black pepper to make mild sausage
> > > (double the amounts of pepper for hot sausage)

1. If you are making burgers, put the meat and salt in a bowl. If you are making sausage, also add the extra seasonings for sausage.

2. Mix the ingredients together thoroughly with your hands and shape them into four patties.

3. If you are using a high-fat meat or a tender game meat, turn the broiler on to 450°F to 500°F. Put the patties on a broiler pan and broil them for ten minutes on each side, turning them halfway through the cooking time. (The total cooking time is 20 minutes).

4. If you are using a low-fat or less tender meat, put the patties in a baking dish and add water to a depth of ¼ to ½ inch.

5. Cover the baking dish with a lid or with foil.

6. Turn on your oven to 350°F.

7. Bake the patties for 30 minutes.

8. Uncover them and bake them for an additional 15 minutes or until the tops of the patties are brown.

9. Turn the patties over and bake them for another 15 minutes or until the other side of the patties is also brown on the top.

10. Serve immediately.

Makes 4 servings

Any Day Meat Loaf With Vegetables

Day 1 – pork or goat with carrots
Day 2 – turkey or buffalo with cabbage
Day 3 – lamb with spinach
Extra Foods – game meat, ostrich, or beef with carrots or other vegetables for the rotation day

　　1 pound ground meat of any kind
　　1 cup grated or shredded vegetables such as cabbage (**Day 2**), spinach (**Day 3**), zucchini or yellow squash (**Day 4**), or carrots (**Extra Foods**)
　　¼ small onion, finely chopped (optional – **Extra Foods**)
　　⅓ cup finely chopped green pepper (optional – **Extra Foods**)
　　¾ teaspoon salt
　　¼ teaspoon pepper
　　¼ teaspoon dry mustard (optional – **Day 2**)
　　¼ cup water
　　¼ cup catsup (optional – **Extra Foods**; see the recipe on page 136)

1. Put the meat, vegetables, and seasonings in a bowl and mix them together thoroughly with your hands.

2. Shape the mixture into a loaf.

3. Put it into a 2 to 3 quart casserole dish.

4. Add the water to the bottom of the dish.

5. Cover the dish with a lid or with foil.

6. Turn the oven on to 350°F.

7. Bake the meat loaf for 45 minutes. Then uncover it and bake it for another 30 minutes to allow it to brown.

8. If you wish to use the catsup, pour it on top of the meat loaf during the last 15 minutes of the baking time.

9. Slice and serve.

Makes 6 servings

Meat 'n Veggie Burgers

DAY 1 – pork or goat with carrots
DAY 2 – turkey or buffalo with cabbage
DAY 3 – lamb with spinach
EXTRA FOODS – game meat, ostrich, or beef with carrots or other vegetables for the rotation day

1 pound of ground meat of any kind
¾ cup total of any combination of vegetables, choosing from:
    Grated carrots (**EXTRA FOODS**, use any day)
    Very finely shredded cabbage (**DAY 2**)
    Very finely shredded spinach (**DAY 3**)
    Grated zucchini or yellow squash (**DAY 4**)
    ¼ small onion, finely chopped (**EXTRA FOODS**)
    ⅓ to ½ small green pepper, finely chopped (**EXTRA FOODS**)
½ to ¾ teaspoon salt
⅛ to ¼ teaspoon pepper (optional)
Water, if you are braising rather than broiling the burgers

1. Put the meat, vegetables, and seasonings in a bowl and mix them together thoroughly with your hands.

2. Shape the mixture into four to six patties.

3. If you are using a high-fat or tender meat, turn the broiler on to 450°F to 500°F. Put the patties on a broiler pan and broil them for ten minutes on each side, turning them halfway through the cooking time. (The total cooking time is 20 minutes).

4. If you are using a low-fat or less tender meat, put the patties in a baking dish and add water to a depth of ¼ to ½ inch.

5. Cover the baking dish with a lid or with foil.

6. Turn on your oven to 350°F.

7. Bake the patties for 30 minutes.

8. Uncover them and bake them for an additional 15 minutes or until the tops of the patties are brown.

9. Turn the patties over and bake them for another 15 minutes, or until the other side of the patties is also brown on the top.

10. Serve immediately.

Makes 4 to 6 servings

Crockpot Stew

This is a great way to prepare any kind of meat, including lion, kangaroo, antelope, buffalo, elk, venison, lamb, or even beef.

ANY DAY depending on the meat used; the vegetables are all from "**EXTRA FOODS,**" borrow tapioca from **DAY 3**

 2 pounds of any red meat
 1 pound of carrots (about 5)
 5 stalks of celery
 1½ pounds of potatoes (about 3 to 4, optional)
 ½ cup quick-cooking tapioca
 2 teaspoons salt
 ¼ teaspoon pepper (optional)
 2¼ cups water

1. If you are using frozen game, rub it with part of the salt and let it thaw in the refrigerator.

2. Trim the fat and gristle from the meat. Cut the meat into one inch cubes.

3. Peel the carrots and cut them into one inch pieces.

4. Slice the celery into one inch pieces.

5. If you are using the potatoes, thoroughly scrub or peel them and cut them into one inch cubes.

6. Put the meat, vegetables, tapioca, seasonings, and water into a 3-quart crockpot. Stir thoroughly to evenly distribute the tapioca.

7. Cook the stew on low for 8 to 10 hours or on high for 6 hours.

8. If you prefer a "juicier" stew, add some boiling water to it about one hour before the stew will be finished cooking.

Makes 6 to 8 servings

Four Way Chili

TRADITIONAL CHILI CON CARNE

DAY 1 – pork or goat
DAY 2 – buffalo or turkey
DAY 3 – chicken or lamb
DAY 4 – rabbit
EXTRA FOODS – game meat or ostrich

> 1½ pounds of ground meat of any kind
> 1 tablespoon oil (optional)
> 3 cups tomato sauce or 1¾ pounds fresh tomatoes
> ½ to ¾ teaspoon chili powder, or to taste
> ¼ teaspoon salt
> ½ cup water
> 5 cups cooked kidney beans or other cooked beans, drained

1. If you are using a very low-fat meat, put the oil in a large saucepan. No oil is necessary if the meat contains the slightest bit of fat.

2. Put the meat in the saucepan and brown it over medium heat, stirring often.

3. If you are using fresh tomatoes, while the meat is cooking, wash and stem them. Put them in a blender in small batches or in a food processor with the metal pureeing blade and puree them.

4. When the meat is well browned, pour off the fat from the meat.

5. Add the tomato sauce or puree, seasonings, water, and beans to the saucepan.

6. Bring the chili to a boil, reduce the heat, and simmer it for 30 minutes to an hour.

Makes 6 to 8 servings

TRADITIONAL VEGETARIAN CHILI

EXTRA FOODS

> ¾ cup dry textured vegetable protein (optional)
> ¾ cup water if you are using the textured vegetable protein
> 5 cups cooked kidney beans or other cooked beans, drained
> 3 cups tomato sauce or 1¾ pounds fresh tomatoes
> ½ cup water
> ½ teaspoon salt
> ½ to ¾ teaspoons chili powder, to taste

1. If you are using the textured vegetable protein, bring the ¾ cup water to a boil in a large saucepan. Add the textured vegetable protein and allow it to stand for five to ten minutes or until the water is absorbed.

2. If you are using fresh tomatoes, wash and stem them. Chop them into small pieces or put them in a blender in small batches or in a food processor with the metal pureeing blade and puree them.

3. Combine all the ingredients in the saucepan with the textured vegetable protein.

4. Bring the chili to a boil, reduce the heat, and simmer it for 30 minutes to one hour.

Makes 6 to 8 servings

TOMATO-FREE CHILI

DAY 1 – pork or goat with arrowroot
DAY 2 – buffalo or turkey with bean starch or borrow arrowroot from **DAY 1**
      or tapioca starch from **DAY 3**
DAY 3 – chicken or lamb with tapioca starch
DAY 4 – rabbit with water chestnut starch
EXTRA FOODS – game meat or ostrich with bean starch or a starch appropriate for the
      rotation day

> ½ to 1 pound of ground meat of any kind (optional)
> 1 cup water
> 1 tablespoon arrowroot, tapioca starch, water chestnut starch, or bean starch
> ¼ to ½ teaspoon chili powder, or to taste
> 1 tablespoon paprika (for color)
> ½ teaspoon salt
> 3 to 5 cups cooked kidney beans or other cooked beans, drained
> 1 to 1¼ teaspoons tart tasting unbuffered vitamin C powder

1. If you are using the meat, put it in a frying pan and cook it over medium heat, stirring often, until it is well browned. Pour off the fat.

2. Mix together the water, starch, and seasonings in a saucepan. Bring the mixture to a boil, stirring it often.

3. Add the cooked meat and beans to the saucepan. If you prefer a thicker "juice," crush a few of the beans against the side of the pan.

4. Bring the chili to a boil, reduce the heat, and simmer it for 30 minutes.

5. Stir in the vitamin C powder and serve immediately.

Makes 4 to 6 servings

LENTIL VEGETARIAN CHILI

Extra foods

    1 pound dry lentils
    Water
    4 cups chopped peeled tomatoes (about 2 pounds fresh or canned)
       or 4 cups tomato sauce
    1 teaspoon salt
    1 tablespoon chili powder, or to taste
    ½ cup chopped celery (optional)
    1 medium onion chopped (optional)

1. The day before you plan to serve this chili, wash and sort over the lentils, discarding any shriveled ones.

2. Put the lentils in a 3-quart crockpot and fill the pot almost to the top with water. Allow the lentils to soak overnight.

3. In the morning drain the lentils. Rinse them by adding fresh water to the pot and draining it three times.

4. Add 5 cups of water to the drained lentils and cook them for 4 to 5 hours on high.

5. Drain about half of the liquid from the crockpot, reserving it if you like "thin" chili and think you might use it in step 6 below.

6. Add the rest of the ingredients to the crockpot and cook the chili for another 4 hours on high, adding more water or the reserved liquid from step 5 if necessary to reach the chili consistency you prefer.

Makes 8 to 10 servings

Meat 'n Veggie Bundles

Day 2

    1 pound ground buffalo, turkey, or game meat
    3 tablespoons finely chopped onion (optional)
    3 tablespoons finely chopped collards, arugula, or parsley
    ¾ teaspoon salt
    8 to 12 large collard, cabbage, or mustard green leaves
    Water

1. In a bowl combine the meat, chopped vegetables, and salt.

2. Bring a large pot of water to a boil.

3. Add the large vegetable leaves to the water, return the water to a boil, and boil for 2 minutes for collards or mustard greens or for 4 minutes for cabbage.

4. Pour off most of the water from the vegetables and refill the pot with cold water to stop the vegetable leaves from cooking more.

5. Divide the meat mixture into 8 to 12 portions, or as many portions as you have large vegetable leaves.

6. Place each meat portion near the stem end of a vegetable leaf.

7. Fold the end of the leaf over the meat.

8. Then fold both sides of the leaf to the center of the leaf over the meat.

9. Roll the leaf up from the stem end to make a bundle with the meat in the center.

10. Use a toothpick to skewer the loose end of the leaf to the bundle.

11. Put the bundles in a baking dish.

12. Add ½ cup water to the dish and cover it with a lid or with foil.

13. Turn your oven on to 350°F.

14. Bake the bundles for one hour.

15. Remove them from the oven and serve them immediately.

Makes 4 to 6 servings

Stuffed Peppers

DAY 1 – kamut, barley, milo, or amaranth with shredded carrots
DAY 2 – rye, teff, or buckwheat with chopped collards, kale, or mustard greens
DAY 3 – spelt, millet, or quinoa with chopped spinach
DAY 4 – rice or wild rice with shredded zucchini

3 cups cooked grain or grain alternative from the list above
1 pound of vegetable from the list above
2 tablespoons oil
Water
2 teaspoons salt
¾ teaspoon pepper
3 tablespoons chopped fresh or 3 teaspoons dry sweet basil
2 tablespoons paprika (optional – for color)
6 bell peppers

1. Cook the grain or grain alternative according to the directions on pages 90 to 94. Depending on the grain, you should cook 1 to 1½ cups of raw grain to get 3 cups of cooked grain.

2. Wash and chop or shred the vegetable.

3. Combine the vegetable, oil, and 2 tablespoons water in a saucepan and bring it to a boil. Reduce the heat and simmer it for 15 minutes or until the vegetable is tender. There should be little or no water remaining in the pan.

4. Mix the grain and seasonings into the vegetable.

5. Wash, core, and seed the peppers.

6. Bring a large pot of water to a boil; add the peppers, return the water to a boil, and boil them for five minutes.

7. Drain most of the water from the peppers and refill the pot with cold water to stop the cooking process.

8. After the peppers have had a minute or two to cool in the cold water, remove them from the water and drain them.

9. Stuff the grain mixture into the peppers.

10. Oil a deep casserole dish.

11. Stand the stuffed peppers upright in the casserole dish.

12. Cover the dish with a lid or with foil.

13. Turn your oven on to 350°F.

14. Bake the peppers for 40 to 50 minutes.

EASY NO PEPPER VARIATION: For a quick main or side dish, serve the grain-vegetable stuffing hot without the bell peppers.

Makes 4 to 6 servings

Grandma Capraro's Zucchini Casserole

This is a great way to use up a summer over-abundance of zucchini because the zucchini does not get mushy when frozen in this dish.

DAY 4

4 cups of "Tomato and Meat Sauce," page 133
2 to 2½ pounds of zucchini

1. Make the sauce as directed in the "Tomato and Meat Sauce" recipe using game or a **DAY 4** meat. Put 4 cups of the sauce into a large pan.

2. Wash and stem the zucchini. Slice it about ¾ inch thick.

3. Add the zucchini to the sauce in the pan.

4. Bring the sauce to a boil, reduce the heat, and simmer it for 10 to 15 minutes, or until the zucchini is tender.

Makes 4 to 6 servings

Pizza

ANY DAY depending on the grain or grain alternative used for the crust and the toppings used

Dough:
2 batches of any "Handmade Non-Yeast Bread," pages 151 to 153
OR a double batch of any "Mixer/Hand Made Yeast Bread," pages 184 to 188 OR
    a double 1-pound batch of any "Bread Machine Yeast Bread,"
    pages 189 to 194

Sauce:
1 batch of "Mrs. Calabra's Pizza Sauce," page 134
OR ½ batch of "Grandma Jiannetti's Tomato Sauce," page 131
OR 1½ cups of "Any day Pesto," page 130

Toppings:
2 cups of assorted toppings such as sliced black olives, chopped green peppers,
    chopped onions, pineapple tidbits, etc.
4 to 6 ounces of goat jack or Mozarella cheese (optional)
2 tablespoons grated pecorino Romano (sheep) or parmesan cheese (optional)
¼ to ½ pound of ground meat (optional)

1. If you are using a yeast dough, make the dough according to the instructions in the recipe you are using. If you are using a bread machine to make it, use the "dough" cycle. A 1½ or 2 pound machine should be capable of mixing a double 1-pound batch of dough; for a 1½ pound machine, just watch the dough as it rises so it does not go over the sides of the pan.

2. If you are using a non-yeast dough, wait to make the dough until all of the toppings and the pans are ready and the oven is preheated (step 9, below).

3. Make the sauce as directed in the recipe for the sauce you have chosen.

4. If you wish to use cheese and meat on your pizza, grate the cheese and cook the meat in a frying pan on medium heat, stirring often, until it is brown.

5. Chop the vegetable and fruit toppings you are going to use.

6. If you are making yeast pizzas, very lightly oil two 12-inch pizza pans by rubbing them with an oiled paper towel.

7. If you are making non-yeast pizzas, generously oil two 12-inch pizza pans and shake flour in them so the bottom and sides of the pans are coated.

8. Preheat your oven to 400°F.

9. If you are making non-yeast pizzas, make the non-yeast bread dough as directed in the recipe at this point.

10. For thick non-yeast pizzas, divide the non-yeast dough equally between the two prepared pans. Flour your hands and pat the dough out to fill the pans. If you prefer thinner pizzas, put less of the dough in the pizza pans. Put the remaining dough in a muffin tin and bake it as directed in the "Muffins" recipe on page 159.

11. If you are making yeast pizzas, when the yeast dough has finished rising once or when the dough cycle on the bread machine is finished, divide the dough in half and stretch it out to fit the two prepared pizza pans.

12. Spread the sauce of your choice on top of your pizzas.

13. Sprinkle the toppings of your choice on top of the sauce.

14. Bake the pizzas for 20 to 30 minutes or until the edge of the pizzas begins to brown.

15. Cut any uneaten pizza into wedges, wrap them, and freeze them for a "rainy day." Pizza in the freezer is like money in the bank.

Makes two 12-inch pizzas

Lasagne

For grain-free lasagne, you can make this dish using layers of vegetable leaves in place of the pasta.

DAY 1 – any vegetable listed with goat cheese; borrow cabbage or collards from **DAY 2** or "split" the spinach family and use spinach or chard from **DAY 3**

DAY 2 – cabbage or collards; borrow goat cheese from **DAY 1** or sheep cheese from **DAY 3**

DAY 3 – spinach, chard, or spelt pasta with sheep cheese

DAY 4 – rice pasta; borrow goat cheese from **DAY 1** or sheep cheese from **DAY 3**

1 head of cabbage OR 2 to 3 bunches of collards or chard with large leaves OR 2 bunches of spinach with large leaves (If you wish to use pasta instead, substitute one 8-ounce box of spelt or rice lasagne for the vegetable leaves).
2 cups of yo-cheese (recipe on page 63) or 1 pound of goat or sheep ricotta cheese, feta cheese, or other soft cheese
¼ teaspoon salt (omit if you use feta cheese)
⅛ teaspoon pepper (optional)
2 teaspoons finely chopped fresh or dried parsley (optional)
¾ pound goat jack cheese or mozzarella (optional)
Oil
½ batch of "Tomato and Meat Sauce," page 133

1. Make the "Tomato and Meat Sauce" as directed in the recipe, using a kind of meat appropriate for the rotation day.

2. While the sauce is cooking, separate the leaves from the head of cabbage if you are using it.

3. Wash the vegetables if you are using them.

4. Slice the jack cheese or mozzarella thinly if you are using it.

5. Mash together the soft cheese with the salt, pepper, and parsley.

6. Generously rub the inside of an 8 inch or 9 inch square baking dish with oil.

7. If you are going to use pasta rather than vegetables, bring a large pot of salted water to a boil.

8. Add the lasagne, bring the water back to a boil, reduce the heat slightly, and cook the pasta for two to three minutes less than the box recommends as a cooking time.

9. Pour most of the boiling water from the pot; then replace it with cold water to stop the cooking process.

10. Put several layers of vegetable leaves (about ⅓ of the leaves) or one layer of pasta in the bottom of the baking dish.

11. Spread this with about 1½ cups of the sauce.

12. Top the sauce with about half of the soft cheese, and top the soft cheese with half of the slices of jack cheese mozzarella if you are using it.

13. Add another layer of vegetable leaves or pasta to the dish and then additional layers of sauce and cheese as above.

14. Top this with a third layer of vegetables or pasta.

15. Spread the top layer of vegetables or pasta with ¾ to 1 cup more of the tomato and meat sauce.

16. Cover the baking dish with its lid or with foil.

17. Bake the lasagne at 350°F for one hour or until it is bubbly and hot all the way through.

18. Serve the lasagne with the remaining tomato sauce.

Makes 4 to 6 servings

Mineral Sandwiches

This is a very palatable way to eat seaweed, which is an excellent source of minerals. These sandwiches are especially good made with dulse and spicy arugula.

ANY DAY, depending on the bread and vegetables used

4 pieces of bread, waffles, pancakes, or tortillas
Dry sea vegetables, such as dulse, wakame, arame, or other seaweed of your choice
Arugula, cabbage, spinach, lettuce, zucchini, or yellow summer squash

1. Wash and dry the vegetables. Shred the cabbage or squash.

2. Top the bread, waffles, pancakes, or tortillas with a generous sprinkling of sea vegetables.

3. Put the fresh vegetables on top of the sea vegetables.

4. Add another layer of bread, waffles, pancakes, or tortillas if desired.

Makes 2 to 4 servings

Side Dishes, Vegetables, and Soups

This chapter will give you recipes for cooking grains, beans, pasta, vegetables and soups. These foods can be used to go along with a main dish. However, most of them are substantial enough to be the main part of a meal all by themselves.

GRAINS AND CEREALS

Stovetop Grains

In the past we were taught not to rinse rice before cooking because rinsing removes the vitamins that must by law be added to enrich white rice. However, natural whole grains benefit from rinsing. Quinoa especially must be thoroughly rinsed to remove its natural soapy coating.

KAMUT (DAY 1)

1 cup kamut
3 cups water
¼ teaspoon salt

Cooking time: 2 hours

AMARANTH (DAY 1)

1 cup amaranth
2½ cups water
¼ teaspoon salt

Cooking time: 30 to 35 minutes

BARLEY (DAY 1)

1 cup barley
3 cups water
¼ teaspoon salt

Cooking time: 1½ to 1¾ hours for whole barley or 45 to 55 minutes for pearled barley

MILO (DAY 1)

1 cup milo
3½ cups water
¼ teaspoon salt

Cooking time: 1 to 1¼ hours

RYE (DAY 2)

1 cup rye
4 cups water
¼ teaspoon salt

Cooking time: 1½ to 2 hours

TEFF (DAY 2)

1 cup teff
3 cups water
¼ teaspoon salt

Cooking time: 15 to 20 minutes

BUCKWHEAT, white or raw (DAY 2)

1 cup buckwheat
3 cups water
½ teaspoon salt

Cooking time: 20 to 25 minutes

BUCKWHEAT, roasted (DAY 2)

1 cup buckwheat
2½ cups water
½ teaspoon salt

Cooking time: 20 to 30 minutes

SPELT (DAY 3)

1 cup spelt
3 cups water
¼ teaspoon salt

Cooking time: 1½ to 2½ hours
    (Soaking spelt for several hours
    before cooking is highly
    recommended).

QUINOA (DAY 3)

1 cup quinoa
2 cups water
¼ teaspoon salt

Cooking time: 20 minutes; quinoa
    should be thoroughly rinsed under
    running water in a strainer before
    cooking.

MILLET (DAY 3)

1 cup millet
3 cups water
¼ teaspoon salt

Cooking time: 25 to 35 minutes

OAT GROATS (DAY 4)

1 cup oat groats
3 cups water
¼ teaspoon salt

Cooking time: 2 to 2½ hours

WHITE RICE (DAY 4)

1 cup white rice
2 cups water
¼ teaspoon salt

Cooking time: 20 minutes

BROWN RICE (DAY 4)

1 cup brown rice
2½ cups water
¼ teaspoon salt

Cooking time: 45 to 50 minutes

WILD RICE (DAY 4)

1 cup wild rice
4 cups water
¼ teaspoon salt

Cooking time: 60 minutes

QUINOA (DAY 3)

1 cup quinoa
2½ cups water
1 tablespoon oil
½ teaspoon salt

Cooking time: 1 hour; quinoa should be thoroughy rinsed under running water in a strainer before cooking it

BROWN RICE (DAY 4)

1 cup brown rice
2½ cups water
1 tablespoon oil
½ teaspoon salt

Cooking time: 1 to 1½ hours

WHITE RICE (DAY 4)

1 cup white rice
2½ cups water
1 tablespoon oil
½ teaspoon salt

Cooking time: 1 to 1¼ hours

WILD RICE (DAY 4)

1 cup wild rice
4 cups water
1 tablespoon oil
½ teaspoon salt

Cooking time: 1½ to 2 hours

OAT GROATS (DAY 4)

1 cup oat groats
2¾ cups water
1 tablespoon oil
½ teaspoon salt

Cooking time: 2 hours

1. Choose one set of ingredients from above or the previous page.

2. Turn your oven on to 350°F or the temperature needed for other dishes you will be baking with the grain.

3. Combine the grain, water, oil, and salt in a 2 to 3 quart casserole dish with a lid. Put the lid on the casserole.

4. Bake until the grain is tender and all the water is absorbed.

5. The first time you make this recipe with each grain, or if you are using a different oven temperature, check the grain during baking and add more water if it is beginning to dry out.

6. If you wish to bake a grain for the same amount of time as the entree of an oven meal, the baking time can be extended. The first time you extend the baking time, be sure to check the grain and add water as it bakes. Record how much extra water you add, and the next time you use the longer baking time, you can add the extra water initially.

7. Fluff the grain and serve.

Makes 4 to 6 servings

Grains Pilaf

The vegetables and seasonings used in this recipe are from "EXTRA FOODS" on the rotation diet in this book, so the recipe may be used on ANY DAY of the diet depending on the grain used.

ANY DAY

SAVORY CELERY VERSION:

2 cups sliced celery
¼ small onion, chopped (optional)
4 tablespoons oil
1 cup of any grain in the "Stovetop Grains" recipe, page 90
Water in the amount specified in the "Stovetop Grains" recipe
½ to 1 teaspoon salt, to taste
¼ teaspoon black pepper
3 tablespoons finely chopped fresh parsley OR 1 tablespoon dried parsley
1 tablespoon finely chopped fresh sweet basil OR 1 teaspoon dried sweet basil

SPICY CARROT VERSION:

1 cup of any grain in the "Stovetop Grains" recipe, page 90
Water in the amount specified in the "Stovetop Grains" recipe PLUS 1 cup
2 to 2½ cups shredded carrots
4 tablespoons oil
½ teaspoon salt (optional)
1 teaspoon cinnamon (optional – use or borrow from DAY 3)
¼ teaspoon cloves (optional – use or borrow from DAY 2)

1. Choose one set of ingredients from above.

2. If you are making the savory celery version, combine the celery, onion, and oil in a saucepan and cook over medium heat until the vegetables begin to brown. Add the grain and water to the pan.

3. If you are using the spicy carrot version and a grain that cooks in 45 minutes or less, combine grain, water, and carrots in a saucepan. If you are using a grain that cooks for more than 45 minutes, put only the grain and water in the pan initially. Add the carrots to the pan 30 minutes before the simmering time for the grain is finished (step 4, below).

4. Bring the mixture to a boil, reduce the heat, and simmer it for the length of time specified in the "Stovetop Grains" recipe on page 90. If you are using the carrots with a long-cooking grain, add them to the pan 30 minutes before this time will be up.

5. Stir the seasonings into the grain thoroughly and allow it to stand for a few minutes so that the flavors can blend before serving.

Makes 4 to 6 servings

Three-Way Mush

MILLET (DAY 3)

1 cup whole millet
4½ cups water
½ teaspoon salt, or to taste

CASSAVA (DAY 3)

1⅓ cups cassava meal (To mail order cassava meal, see "Sources," page 297).
4 cups water
1 teaspoon salt, or to taste

CORN (EXTRA FOODS)

2 cups finely ground cornmeal flour (not regular cornmeal)
4 cups water
1½ teaspoons salt, or to taste

1. If you are making millet mush, put the millet in a strainer and rinse it with cold water.

2. Combine the millet with the water and salt in a saucepan.

3. Bring to a boil, reduce the heat, and simmer for 35 minutes.

4. Remove the pan from the heat and beat the millet with a spoon until it is smooth.

5. If you are making cassava or corn mush, stir together the cassava meal or cornmeal flour with 2 cups of cold water in a small bowl.

6. Put the remaining 2 cups of water and the salt in a large saucepan and bring it to a boil.

7. Add the wet cassava meal or cornmeal to the boiling water a little at a time, stirring the mush constantly.

8. Return the mush to a boil; then reduce the heat to a low simmer and cook it over very low heat for 1 hour for the cornmeal flour or for 30 minutes for the cassava meal.

9. Stir the mush thoroughly every five minutes while it is cooking. It will be very stiff when it is done.

THREE WAYS TO SERVE MUSH:

AS IS: Serve the mush plain as a side dish. Millet mush is an especially good substitute for mashed potatoes. You may also serve it for breakfast with fresh fruit or any fruit sauce in the next chapter.

AS POLENTA: Serve the mush with the following toppings: (Tomato sauces are assigned to "**EXTRA FOODS**," pesto is **ANY DAY** as given in the recipe, goat cheese is **DAY 1**, and sheep cheese is **DAY 3**).

Any tomato sauce, pages 131 to 134, or "Any day Pesto," page 130
Yo-cheese (page 63), grated goat or sheep cheese, or crumbled goat or
   sheep feta cheese (optional)

1. Spread the millet, cassava, or cornmeal mush on a platter and top it with sauce and cheese.
2. Serve it with extra sauce and cheese.

AS SCRAPPLE:

1. After the mush is cooked, pack it into an oiled loaf pan and refrigerate it until it is very firm. (The cassava mush will not get stiff).
2. Turn the mush out of the pan and slice it about ½ inch thick. (The cassava meal may not slice well; if you need to, just remove spoonfuls of the mush and flatten them to ½ inch thickness. Freeze any leftover cassava mush in ½ inch thick patties so it will be easy to fry).
3. Put a tablespoon or two of oil into a small skillet and heat it for about a minute over medium to medium high heat.
4. Put the mush slices in the skillet a few slices at a time and cook them until they are brown on one side. Then turn them and cook until the other side is brown.

Makes 4 to 6 servings

Hot Grain Cereals

KAMUT (DAY 1)

   1 cup kamut flakes
   2 cups water
   ¼ teaspoon salt

Cooking time: 20 minutes

BARLEY (DAY 1)

   1 cup barley flakes
   3 cups water
   ¼ teaspoon salt

Cooking time: 20 minutes

RYE (DAY 2)

   1 cup rye flakes
   3 cups water
   ¼ teaspoon salt

Cooking time: 30 minutes

SPELT (DAY 3)

   1 cup spelt flakes or quick spelt flakes
   3 cups water for regular spelt flakes, 2½ cups for quick spelt flakes
   ¼ teaspoon salt

Cooking time: 20 minutes for regular spelt flakes, 3 to 5 minutes for quick spelt flakes

OAT (DAY 4)

   1 cup rolled oats or quick rolled oats
   3 cups water for regular oats, 2½ cups for quick oats
   ¼ teaspoon salt

Cooking time: 20 minutes for regular rolled oats, 6 to 10 minutes for quick rolled oats

1. Choose one set of ingredients above.
2. Bring the water and salt to a boil in a saucepan.
3. Add the grain flakes, stir, cover the pan, and allow the water to return to a boil.
4. Reduce the heat to a simmer and cook the cereal for the time listed above or until it is soft.
5. Serve with fresh fruit if desired.

Makes 2 to 3 servings.

Hot Tuber Cereals

These are very soothing to the gastrointestinal system and easy for severely allergic persons to digest. You can make them with tuber flours instead of cereals for an especially smooth, baby-food texture. See "Sources," page 298, for ordering information.

WHITE SWEET POTATO (DAY 1)

1¼ cups water, divided
A dash of salt
⅓ cup cream of white sweet potato cereal or ¼ cup white sweet potato flour

TRUE YAM (DAY 2)

1¼ cups water, divided
A dash of salt
¼ cup cream of true yam cereal or a scant ¼ cup true yam flour

CASSAVA (DAY 3)

1¼ cups water, divided
A dash of salt
⅓ cup cream of cassava cereal or ¼ cup cassava flour

MALANGA (DAY 4)

1¼ cups water, divided
A dash of salt
⅓ cup cream of malanga cereal or ¼ cup malanga flour

1. Choose one set of ingredients, above.

2. Put ¾ cup of the water and the salt in a saucepan. Bring it to a boil.

3. Combine the remaining ½ cup of water with the cereal or flour.

4. Stir the wet cereal or flour into the boiling water, cover the pan, and allow it to return to a boil.

5. Reduce the heat and simmer the cereal for five minutes.

6. Remove the pan from the heat and, if you can wait, let the cereal stand for another five minutes before serving.

Makes 1 serving

PASTA

Pasta is one of the most versatile main or side dishes. It can be served with many of the sauces in the next chapter. There are excellent commercial non-wheat pastas available at health food stores, or see "Using Commercially Prepared Foods," pages 291 to 292, to order the less common non-wheat pastas. You can also make your own pasta using the recipes below. Pay attention to how you cook your pasta; cooking can either bring out the best in pasta or turn it into mush. However, some non-wheat pastas do not hold together well even when carefully cooked. You should just lower your standards a little and enjoy these pastas as they are.

Cooked Pasta

ANY DAY depending on the pasta used

    10 ounces to 1 pound of pasta
    3 to 6 quarts of water
    1 to 2 teaspoons of salt

1. Put the water and salt in a large saucepot.

2. Bring the water to a rolling boil.

3. Add the pasta and stir it to keep it from sticking together.

4. Return the water to a boil and reduce the heat slightly to keep the water from boiling over while maintaining a good boil. Begin timing the cooking of the pasta when the water returns to a boil after you add it.

5. Boil the pasta until it is *al dente* or offers some resistance "to the tooth." The time this will take varies with the size and shape of the pasta, quality of the flour used, etc., but approximate cooking times are given on the boxes of commercial pastas and in the recipes below.

6. Put a large colander in your sink.

7. When the pasta is cooked, pour it into the colander to drain.

8. Immediately put the pasta back into the pan or into a serving bowl and toss it with sauce or oil.

9. Serve it immediately.

Makes 4 to 6 servings.

Rolled Pasta

KAMUT (DAY 1)

    3 cups kamut flour
    1⅛ cups water
        (1 cup plus 2 tablespoons)

BARLEY (DAY 1)

    3 cups barley flour
    1⅛ cups water
        (1 cup plus 2 tablespoons)

RYE (Day 2)

3 cups rye flour
¾ cup water

SPELT (Day 3)

3 cups spelt flour
1 cup minus 1 tablespoon water

WHITE SPELT (Day 3)

3 cups white spelt flour
⅝ cup water
(½ cup plus 2 tablespoons)

QUINOA (Day 3)

1½ cups quinoa flour
1½ cups tapioca flour
⅞ cup water (¾ cup plus 2 tablespoons)

(No **Day 4** pasta recipes are given because oat flour does not make good pasta and rice pastas are widely available in health food stores).

1. Choose one set of ingreedients from the previous page or above.

2. Put the flour(s) into a large bowl.

3. Make a well in the center of the flour and pour the water into it.

4. Using a fork, begin stirring the water and flour together in the center of the crater, gradually stirring in more flour.

5. When the dough becomes very thick, mix it with your hand instead of the fork until all of the flour is mixed in.

6. Knead the dough, which will be very stiff, on a lightly floured board for 5 to 10 minutes.

7. Lightly rub the ball of dough with oil. Cover it with plastic wrap or with an inverted bowl and let it stand for 30 minutes.

8. Roll it out as thinly as possible with a rolling pin, and cut it into noodles with a knife, or use it to layer with the other ingredients in lasagne.

9. The more sturdy pastas, such as kamut, rye, and spelt, can be rolled using a crank-type pasta machine, following the directions that come with the machine.

10. Cook the pasta immediately as described above in "Cooked Pasta" or spread it out on paper towels or dishcloths and allow it to dry overnight.

11. Approximate cooking times for rolled pastas are:

    Kamut: 3 to 5 minutes
    Barley: 2 to 3 minutes
    Rye: 6½ to 8 minutes
    Whole spelt: 10 to 13 minutes
    White spelt: 4 to 8 minutes
    Quinoa: 3½ to 4 minutes.

Makes 4 to 6 servings

Extruded Pasta

The water measurements in this recipe are given in milliliters because it is easier to get a very precise measurement using the "other side" of the measuring cup. However, the amount of water your flour will take may vary depending on the quality of the flour, humidity, etc. Record how much extra flour or water you add when you make this pasta so you can use your own measurements the next time you make it.

KAMUT (DAY 1)

> 3 cups kamut flour
> 170 milliliters water

BARLEY (DAY 1)

> 3 cups barley flour
> 180 milliliters water

RYE (DAY 2)

> 3 cups rye flour
> 160 milliliters water

WHOLE SPELT (DAY 3)

> 3 cups whole spelt flour
> 145 milliliters water

WHITE SPELT (DAY 3)

> 3 cups white spelt flour
> 115 milliliters water

QUINOA (DAY 3)

> 3 cups quinoa flour
> 180 milliliters water

(No **DAY 4** pasta recipes are given because oat flour does not make good pasta and rice pastas are widely available in health food stores).

1. Choose one set of ingreedients from the previous page.

2. Stir the flour to loosen it, lightly spoon it into the measuring cup, and level it off with a straight-edged knife. (Accurate measurement is very important in making extruded pasta). Put the flour into the mixing bowl of your pasta machine.

3. Measure the water.

4. Start the machine and add the water as directed in the machine's instructions.

5. After the pasta has mixed for a minute or two, pick up a few crumbs of the dough with your thumb and index finger and pinch them together. (This is called the "pinch test"). They should stick together, but the dough should be dry rather than sticky.

6. If the dough is sticky, add 1 tablespoon of flour to the machine. Allow the pasta to mix another minute and retest it using the "pinch test" again.

7. Keep adding flour 1 tablespoon at a time until the dough sticks together but is dry when you pinch the crumbs of dough together.

8. If the crumbs of dough do not stick together when you do the pinch test, add 1 teaspoon of water to the machine. Allow it to mix for another minute and retest it with the pinch test.

9. Keep adding water one teaspoon at a time until the crumbs stick together but are dry.

10. Extrude the pasta according to the machine's instructions.

11. Spread out the pasta on paper towels or dishcloths to dry overnight, separating the strands as you lay them down, or cook the pasta immediately as described in the "Cooked Pasta" recipe on page 100.

12. Approximate cooking times for extruded pastas are:

Kamut: 4 to 6 minutes
Barley: 2½ to 3 minutes
Rye: 6½ to 8 minutes
Whole spelt: 11 to 14 minutes
White spelt: 7 to 10 minutes
Quinoa: 3 to 3½ minutes

Makes 4 to 6 servings

VEGETABLES

Stovetop Cooked Legumes

All of the legumes listed below are assigned to "**Extra foods**" on the rotation diet in this book. If you tolerate beans well, you may want to "split" the food family and eat beans of different species (see page 272) on two different rotation days with a day off from legumes between.

Extra foods

LENTILS OR SPLIT PEAS

    1 cup of dry lentils or split peas
    2 cups water
    ¼ teaspoon salt

ADZUKI, BLACK, SOY, OR GREAT NORTHERN BEANS

    1 cup of dry beans
    3 cups water
    ¼ teaspoon salt

ANASAZI, CRANBERRY, CANELLINI, GARBANZO, KIDNEY, LIMA, NAVY, PINTO, OR RED BEANS OR BLACK-EYED PEAS

    1 cup of dry beans
    4 cups water
    ¼ teaspoon salt

1. Wash the dry legumes and discard any shriveled ones.

2. Lentils and split peas do not absolutely have to be soaked, but for the best digestibility, all legumes benefit from overnight soaking and rinsing.

3. Put the legumes in a saucepan and cover them with three times their volume of water. Soak them overnight.

4. The next morning pour the water off the beans and replace it with fresh water three times. This removes indigestible carbohydrates.

5. Drain and discard all of the rinse water. Add the amount of water specified above to the drained legumes.

6. Put the pan on the stove and bring it to a boil.

7. Reduce the heat and simmer the legumes until they are tender to soft. (Beans are more digestible if they are cooked until they are soft rather than just tender). Check them during cooking and add more water if necessary.

8. Add the salt during the last ten minutes of cooking.

9. Approximate cooking times are:

   Adzuki beans: 2 to 2½ hours
   Anasazi beans: 2 to 2½ hours
   Black-eyed peas: 1½ to 2 hours
   Black beans: 2 to 2½ hours
   Canellini beans: 1½ to 2 hours
   Cranberry beans: 1½ to 2 hours
   Garbanzo beans: 3 to 3½ hours
   Great northern beans: 2 to 2½ hours
   Kidney beans: 2½ to 3 hours
   Lentils: 1 to 2 hours
   Lima beans: 1 to 1 ½ hours
   Navy (small white) beans: 3 to 3½ hours
   Pinto beans: 2 to 2½ hours
   Red beans: 2 to 2½ hours
   Soybeans: 3½ to 4½ hours
   Split peas: 1 to 2 hours

Makes 2 to 2½ cups of cooked legumes, or 4 to 5 servings

Crockpot Cooked Legumes

If you have the time, the easiest way to cook dried legumes is using a crockpot.

EXTRA FOODS

   1 pound any dry legume
   Water
   1 teaspoon salt

1. The night before you plan to serve the dry legumes for dinner, wash the legumes, removing any shriveled ones.

2. Put the legumes in a 3-quart crockpot and fill the pot almost to the top with water. (The volume of the water should be two to three times the volume of the legumes).

3. The next morning, pour the water off the beans and replace it with fresh water three times. This removes indigestible carbohydrates. Drain off all of the water after the last rinse.

4. Add 4 cups of water to the pot and put the cover on.

5. Cook the legumes on low for 8 to 10 hours or on high for 4 to 6 hours. Check them during cooking and add more water if necessary.

6. Stir the salt into the legumes during the last fifteen minutes of the cooking time.

Makes 8 to 10 servings

Crockpot Baked Beans

Extra foods

    1 pound small white or small navy beans
Water
¾ cup pineapple (**Day 1**), white grape (**Day 2**), or apple (**Day 3**)
    juice concentrate OR ¾ cup water plus ⅓ cup date sugar (**Day 4**) or
    1⁄16 teaspoon white stevia powder (**Extra foods**)
1½ teaspoons salt
¼ teaspoon pepper (optional)
1 tablespoon finely chopped onion, or 1 teaspoon dried onion flakes (optional)
1 tablespoon finely chopped fresh sweet basil OR 1 teaspoon dried sweet basil
1½ teaspoons paprika

1. The night before you plan to serve the beans for dinner, wash the beans, removing any shriveled ones.

2. Put the beans in a 3-quart crockpot and fill the pot almost to the top with water. (The volume of the water should be two to three times the volume of the beans).

3. The next morning, pour the water off the beans and replace it with fresh water three times. This removes indigestible carbohydrates. Drain off all of the water after the last rinse.

4. Add 4 cups of water to the pot and cover the pot.

5. Cook the beans on high for 4 to 5 hours or until they are very tender. Check them during cooking and add more water if necessary.

6. Add the fruit juice concentrate or ¾ cup water plus the date sugar or stevia and seasonings to the crock pot. Stir them into the beans thoroughly.

7. Cover the pot and cook the beans on high another 2 to 3 hours.

8. If you like a thick sauce, smash a few beans against the side of the pot an hour or so before they finish cooking.

9. Check the beans during cooking and add more water if necessary.

Makes 6 to 8 servings

Greens

These vegetables are powerhouses of nutrition; they are very rich in vitamins, minerals, and even contain essential fatty acids. If you can tolerate them well, you may want to "split" the cabbage and spinach families so you have some greens every day of rotation.

Collards, kale, or mustard greens (**DAY 2**, or **DAYS 2 & 4** if the family is "split")
Spinach, beet tops, or chard (**DAY 3**, or **DAYS 1 & 3** if the family is "split")
Dandelion greens (**EXTRA FOODS**)

    1 bunch of any of the greens listed above
    Water

1. Wash the greens in several changes of water to remove all of the dirt.

2. Remove the greens from the water you washed them in, and with water still clinging to the leaves, put them in a large saucepot.

3. Cover the pot with a lid and cook them over low heat. Some people find these vegetables hard to digest and should cook them for 20 to 25 minutes, adding a tablespoon or two of water during the cooking time if necessary. People with strong digestive abilities may cook them for 5 to 8 minutes.

4. These vegetables are so flavorful that they really do not require salt or seasoning, but if you wish to, you can dress them with a little oil.

Makes 3 to 4 servings

Oven Vegetables

Vegetables roasted in the oven with oil and just a little or no water are very flavorful. You can put them into the oven with a main dish and oven grain for a complete, no-fuss meal.

SWEET POTATOES (Day 1)

2 pounds regular (orange) or white
    sweet potatoes
¼ teaspoon salt
2 tablespoons oil

TURNIPS (Day 2)

2 pounds turnips
¼ teaspoon salt
2 tablespoons oil

CABBAGE (Day 2)

1 head of cabbage
    (about 1½ to 1¾ pounds)
½ teaspoon salt
¼ teaspoon ground black pepper
    (optional)
½ cup water
3 tablespoons oil

CAULIFLOWER (Day 2)

1 head of cauliflower
    (about 1½ to 1¾ pounds)
½ teaspoon salt
¼ teaspoon ground black pepper
    (optional)
½ cup water
3 tablespoons oil

BUTTERNUT SQUASH (Day 4)

2½ pounds butternut squash
¼ teaspoon salt
2 tablespoons oil

CARROTS (Extra foods)

2 to 2½ pounds carrots
½ cup water
½ teaspoon salt
2 tablespoons oil

PEAS OR BEANS (Extra foods)

2 10-ounce packages frozen lima
    beans, cut green beans, or peas
    OR 1¼ pounds of fresh cut green
    beans or shelled peas
⅔ cup water
¼ teaspoon salt
2 tablespoons oil

WHITE POTATOES (Extra foods)

1 to 1½ pounds white potatoes
½ teaspooon salt
Dash of black pepper (optional)
2 tablespoons oil

Choose one set of ingredients from above.

DIRECTIONS FOR SWEET POTATOES, TURNIPS, SQUASH, OR WHITE POTATOES:

1. If you are using sweet potatoes, turnips, squash, or white potatoes, peel the vegetables and cut them in half lenghtwise. Seed the squash.

2. Slice the vegetables into ¼ inch slices. For variety, you may wish to cut the white potatoes into ¾ inch cubes or leave them unpeeled.

3. Put the slices or cubes into an 11 inch by 7 inch baking dish, sprinkle them with the seasoning(s), and drizzle the oil over them.

4. Stir them to coat all of the slices or cubes with the oil.

5. Turn your oven on to 400°F for cubed white potatoes or to 350°F for sliced white potatoes or any of the other vegetables.

6. Bake cubed white potatoes for 45 minutes to one hour without turning them. Bake sliced white potatoes or the other vegetables for 1½ to 2 hours, turning the slices after the first hour.

DIRECTIONS FOR CABBAGE, CAULIFLOWER, OR CARROTS:

1. If you are using the cabbage, coarsely shred it and put it into a 3 quart glass casserole dish with a lid.

2. If you are using the cauliflower, cut it into very small florets and dice the core. Put it into a 3 quart glass casserole dish with a lid.

3. If you are using the carrots, peel them and cut them in half lengthwise, or into quarters if they are large. Lay the carrot sticks parallel to each other in a 2 to 3 quart glass casserole dish with a lid.

4. Add the seasoning(s) and water to the dish, and drizzle the oil over the top of the vegetables.

5. Cover the dish with its lid and bake at 350°F for 1 to 1½ hours.

   *NOTE on pre-peeled mini-carrots: Pre-peeled carrots absorb a lot of water in the peeling process so they don't caramelize well in this recipe. If you want to use them, bake them without anything else for one hour. Drain off the water. Add the salt and oil and bake for another hour or more until they dry out and begin to caramelize.

DIRECTIONS FOR BEANS OR PEAS:

1. Stir together all of the ingredients in a 2 to 3 quart glass casserole dish with a lid.

2. Cover the dish with the lid.

3. Bake at 350°F for 1 to 1½ hours for the beans or 1 hour for the peas.

Makes 4 to 6 servings

Cooked Plantains

If you have never eaten these starchy cousins of bananas because you do not know what to do with them, now is the time to give them a try.

DAY 1

2 plantains
Water OR up to 3 tablespoons of oil

1. If the plantains are green when you buy them, keep them on a countertop until they turn yellow or yellow with brown spots.
2. Cut across the end of each plantain with a knife. If they are very ripe and have many brown spots, you may be able to peel them like bananas. If not, slit the skin down the length of the plantain and peel it off with your fingers, or slice it off with a knife.
3. Slice the peeled plantains into ½ inch slices.
4. If you wish to boil the plantains, put the slices in a saucepan and cover with water.
5. Bring the water to a boil and simmer the plantains for 20 minutes. Serve immediately.
6. If you wish to fry the plantains, heat 1 to 2 tablespoons of oil in a skillet over medium heat for a minute or so.
7. Add one layer of the plantain slices and cook them until they are brown on the bottom.
8. Turn them and cook them until the other side is brown.
9. Remove them from the pan and cook the remaining slices the same way, adding more oil if necessary.
10. Drain the slices on paper towels for a minute or two before serving.

Makes 4 servings

Artichokes

Here is another kind of vegetable you may not have eaten because you are not sure how to handle it. Artichokes are delicious and, with a nut sauce, can be a whole meal.

Day 1

Artichoke(s)
Water

1. Wash the artichokes thoroughly, being careful to rinse out any dirt that may be trapped between the leaves.

2. Trim off most of the stem, any bad leaves, and the tiny leaves at the bottom of the artichoke. Most cookbooks suggest using a scissors to trim the spiny end off of each leaf; but if you eat your artichoke carefully, it is not really necessary to go to this much trouble.

3. Place the artichoke(s) in a saucepan with water to cover.

4. Bring the water to a boil, reduce the heat, and simmer for 30 to 40 minutes, or until the stem end is tender when pierced with a fork.

5. To eat an artichoke, peel off each leaf and dip the edible end into a dip if you wish. Hold on to the spiny end of the leaf, put the meaty end of the leaf into your mouth, and pull off the edible part between your teeth.

6. Serve artichokes with "Super Smooth Sauce," page 135, or a mixture of 2 tablespoons oil with a dash of salt and/or pepper for dipping.

Each artichoke serves one person.

Exotic Tubers

International grocery stores often sell exotic tubers such as yucca root or taro root, or sometimes you can even find them in the produce section of large supermarkets. They are a great substitute for potatoes.

Taro (**DAY 4**)
Yucca (**EXTRA FOODS**)

BOILED AND MASHED TUBERS:

12 ounces of yucca root or taro root (about one medium-sized root)
1½ cups water
¼ teaspoon salt

SAUTEED TUBERS:

Yucca or taro roots
Oil
Salt

1. Choose one set of ingredients from above.

2. Peel the roots. For boiled and mashed tubers, cut them into ½ inch cubes. For sauteed tubers, cut them into ¼ inch slices.

3. For boiled and mashed tubers, combine the tuber cubes and water in a saucepan. Bring it to a boil, reduce the heat, and simmer for 45 minutes or until the roots are tender when pierced with a fork.

4. Drain all but about ¼ cup of water from the pan. The yucca root will probably have absorbed most of the water and will not need to be drained.

5. Add the salt to the boiled tuber.

6. Mash with a potato masher and serve.

7. For sauteed tubers, put oil into a frying pan to a depth of about ¼ inch.

8. Heat the oil over medium heat briefly.

9. Add the tuber slices to the oil in a single layer. Cook them for a few minutes until they are brown on the bottom. Turn them and cook until the other side is also brown.

10. Drain the slices on paper towels briefly and serve.

Makes 2 to 3 servings

Braised Fennel

Fennel is delicious eaten raw; but if you need to cook your vegetables to be able to digest them, this is a great way to eat fennel.

EXTRA FOODS

1 large bulb of fennel, weighing about 1 pound
½ cup water
1 tablespoon oil
⅛ teaspoon salt

1. Wash the fennel, trim off any brown spots, and remove the fine leaves.

2. Slice it into ½ inch slices crosswise.

3. Put the slices in a saucepan with the rest of the ingredients.

4. Cover the pan, bring it to a boil, reduce the heat, and simmer for 20 to 30 minutes.

5. For the best flavor, while watching the fennel closely, cook it until the liquid is completely gone, and the fennel begins to turn brown on the bottom of the pan.

Makes 3 to 4 servings

Oven Fries

TARO (DAY 4)

YUCCA OR WHITE POTATO (EXTRA FOODS)

1 pound of yucca root, taro root, or white potatoes
1 tablespoon oil (optional)
¼ teaspoon salt

1. Turn your oven on to 400°F.

2. Peel the roots or potatoes.

3. Cut them into ⅜ to ½ inch sticks or "fries."

4. Toss the sticks with the oil and salt.

5. Spread them out in a single layer on a non-stick baking sheet. (You can use a regular baking sheet if you use the oil. You may wish to use slightly more oil to make them easier to turn).

6. Bake them for 15 to 20 minutes.

7. Remove the baking sheet from the oven and turn the fries over with a spatula.

8. Bake them for another 15 to 20 minutes, or until they are nicely browned.

Makes 2 to 4 servings

Braised Thin-Leaf Cabbage

DAY 2

> 1 medium head of savoy or napa cabbage (about 1½ pounds)
> ¾ cup water
> ¼ teaspoon salt
> 2 tablespoons oil

1. Wash the cabbage. Quarter the head, core it, and cut the leaves into small squares.

2. Put the cabbage in a saucepan with the water, salt, and oil.

3. Bring it to a boil, reduce the heat, and simmer for 15 to 20 minutes, stirring every 5 minutes. The water will be almost gone with the savoy cabbage; napa cabbage is juicier and may be cooked longer with the lid off to evaporate the water if desired.

4. Serve over baked or mashed potatoes for a delicious meal.

Makes 4 to 6 servings

Roasted Peppers

EXTRA FOODS

> Green, red, or yellow bell peppers
> About 1 teaspoon of oil per pepper (optional)
> Salt

1. Preheat your oven to 400°F.

2. Wash and dry the peppers. Do not remove the stems.

3. Put the peppers on a baking sheet. Place them in the oven and bake for 45 minutes to 1 hour.

4. Check the peppers every 10 to 15 minutes and turn them over as they cook so that all of the sides of the peppers become blistered and turn brown.

5. When the peppers are blistered all over, remove them from the oven and allow them to cool slightly.

6. Peel the outer skin off them using your fingers.

7. Slice, core, and seed the peppers and season them with oil and salt if desired.

8. Serve as a side dish or put them on bread, tortillas, or waffles to make a great sandwich.

Makes 1 to 2 servings per pepper used

SOUPS

Rich Poultry Broth or Soup

Here is a good way to get some roast duck meat for sandwiches and use the bones too.

DAY 4

1 duck (about 5 to 6 pounds), 1 goose (about 8 to 10 pounds),
    or any other high-fat poultry
3 stalks of celery with leaves
2 carrots, peeled and cut into large chunks
½ small onion, sliced (optional)
2 tablespoons chopped fresh parsley OR 1 tablespoon dried parsley (optional)
3 teaspoons salt
¼ teaspoon pepper (optional)
4 quarts (16 cups) water

Additional ingredients for soup, optional:
    3 stalks celery
    4 carrots
    1 cup of chopped cabbage, peas, or other vegetables of your choice

1. Clean the bird and rub the cavity with ½ teaspoon of the salt.

2. Put the bird on a rack in a large roaster. Do not cover it with the lid.

3. Bake at 325°F for 3 hours. Tip the bird on end a few times during baking so that the cavity juices drain into the fat and brown.

4. When the bird is finished roasting, remove it and the rack from the roaster. Drain as much of the fat as possible from the roaster without pouring off any of the brown bits in the bottom of the roaster.

5. Remove the breast and leg meat from the bones and reserve the meat for future use.

6. Put the bones, skin, and small bits of meat remaining on the carcass back into the roaster.

7. Put the roaster on the stove top, across two burners if possible.

8. Add the 3 stalks of celery, 2 carrots, onion, remaining salt, pepper, parsley, and water to the roaster.

9. Turn both burners on if the roaster is large enough to fit across two burners, cover the roaster, and bring the soup to a boil.

10. Reduce the heat and simmer the soup for 2 hours.

11. Cool the soup slightly. Pour it through a strainer to remove the vegetables, skin and bones. (The broth will be cloudy due to the calcium leaching out of the bones). Reserve any meat. Discard the skin, bones, and vegetables.

12. Refrigerate the broth overnight and remove the congealed fat from the top of it.

13. If you wish to have plain broth, reheat the broth before serving it.

14. If you wish to have soup, peel and slice the additional 4 carrots, slice the additional 3 stalks of celery, and chop about 2 cups of the meat you strained from the broth or the meat removed from the bones initially.

15. Add the carrots, celery, meat, and any optional vegetables you wish to use to the broth, bring it to a boil, and reduce the heat and simmer the soup for 30 minutes. Serve the soup immediately.

Makes about 2½ quarts of broth or 8 to 10 servings of soup

Lean Poultry Broth or Soup

DAY 2 – turkey
DAY 3 – chicken or cornish hen
EXTRA FOODS – guinea hen, partridge, or other game birds

> 1 large chicken (3½ to 4 pounds), 2 guinea hens, 1 3- to 4-pound turkey leg, or about 4 pounds of any lean poultry, such as cornish hens, partridge, etc.
> 3 quarts (12 cups) water
> 5 to 7 carrots (1 to 1½ pounds)
> 3 stalks of celery
> ½ medium-sized onion (optional)
> 4 teaspoons salt
> ¼ teaspoon pepper (optional)
>
> Additional ingredients for soup (2 to 3 cups total ingredients), optional:
> 1 to 2 cup of peas, beans, chopped cabbage,
> or other vegetables of your choice
> 1 cup cooked pasta, rice, or barley

1. Clean the poultry.

2. Combine the poultry and water in a large kettle.

3. Bring them to a boil, reduce the heat, and simmer the broth for 30 minutes. Skim the foam from the top of the soup while it is simmering.

4. Peel the carrots.

5. If you wish to make soup, slice the carrots and celery and chop the onion. If you are making broth, cut the vegetables in half.

6. Add the carrots, celery, onion, salt, and pepper to the soup.

7. Return the soup to a boil, reduce the heat, and simmer it for 2 more hours.

8. Cool the soup slightly. Pour it through a strainer to remove the vegetables, meat, skin, and bones. (The broth will be cloudy due to the calcium leaching out of the bones).

9. If you wish to have broth, reheat the broth and serve it.

10. If you wish to have soup, return the vegetables to the broth. Remove the bones and skin from the meat strained from the broth in step 8. Chop the meat and return it to the pot. If you wish to use the optional extra vegetables, add them to the pot.

11. Return the soup to a boil, reduce the heat, and simmer it until the extra vegetables are tender.

12. Add the optional pasta or grains and simmer a few more minutes until they are heated through.

13. Serve the soup immediately. Alternative pastas may fall apart if they are allowed to stand in the soup for a long time.

Makes 8 to 10 servings

Seven-Way Legume Soup

These soups are so different that you can eat one variety every few days and never get bored. They are all made the same easy way in a crockpot.

NAVY BEAN SOUP (Extra foods)

1 pound dry navy beans
Water
2 carrots, peeled and sliced
3 stalks of celery, sliced
2 teaspoons salt
½ teaspoon pepper (optional)
3 tablespoons fresh chopped parsley
    or 1 tablespoon dry parsley
1 tablespoon fresh chopped sweet
    basil or 1 teaspoon dry sweet basil
1 potato, peeled and grated (optional)

LIMA BEAN SOUP (Extra foods)

1 pound dry baby lima beans
Water
1 large or 2 small carrots,
    peeled and sliced
3 to 4 stalks of celery, sliced
2 teaspoons salt
½ teaspoon pepper (optional)
1 bay leaf
3 tablespoons fresh chopped parsley or
    1 tablespoon dry parsley
1 tablespoon fresh chopped sweet basil
    or 1 teaspoon dry sweet basil

BLACK BEAN SOUP (Extra foods)

1 pound dry black beans
Water
2 bell peppers, preferably one green
    and one red, seeded and diced
1 small onion, diced (optional)
1 pound tomatoes, chopped (optional)
1 teaspoon ground cumin (optional)
2 teaspoons salt
2 tablespoons fresh chopped oregano
    OR 2 teaspoons dry oregano
½ teaspoon black pepper
    OR a 2 inch chili pepper,
    seeded and crumbled

WHITE BEAN AND ESCAROLE SOUP (Day 2)

1 pound dry white beans
Water
½ small head of cabbage, chopped
    (about ¾ pound)
2 teaspoons salt
¼ teaspoon pepper (optional)
1 tablespoon fresh chopped sweet basil
    or 1 teaspoon dry sweet basil
1 head of escarole, washed and
    chopped (about ¾ pound)
2 medium potatoes, peeled and diced

LENTIL SOUP (Extra foods)

1 pound lentils
Water
3 to 5 carrots, peeled and sliced
3 stalks of celery, sliced
2 teaspoons salt
¼ teaspoon pepper (optional)

SPLIT PEA SOUP (Extra foods)

1 pound split peas
Water
3 to 4 carrots, peeled and sliced
3 stalks of celery, sliced
2 teaspoons salt
¼ teaspoon pepper (optional)
1 bay leaf (optional)

MULTI-BEAN SOUP (EXTRA FOODS)

A total of 1 pound dried beans, composed of as many of the varieties below as
  you tolerate, OR 2 ounces each of 8 of the following kinds of beans:
   Lentils
   Yellow split peas
   Green split peas
   Black beans
   Small navy beans
   Medium lima beans
   Blackeyed peas
   Small red beans
   Kidney beans
   Pinto beans
Water
3 carrots, about ½ pound, peeled and sliced
3 stalks of celery, sliced
2 teaspoons salt
¼ teaspoon pepper (optional)

1. Choose one set of ingredients from the previous page or above.

2. The night before you plan to serve the soup for dinner, wash the legumes, discarding
   any shriveled ones.

3. Put the legumes in a 3-quart crockpot and cover them with two to three times their
   volume of water.

4. Soak them overnight.

5. The next morning, pour the water off the beans and replace it with fresh water three
   times. This removes indigestible carbohydrates. Drain off all of the water after the last
   rinse.

6. Add water to the beans in the pot in the following amounts:

   Navy bean soup: 6 cups
   Lima bean soup: 6 cups
   Black bean soup: 3 cups if you are using the tomatoes, or 4 cups if you are
        not using the tomatoes
   White bean and escarole soup: 5½ cups
   Lentil soup: 5 cups
   Split pea soup: 5 cups
   Multi-bean soup: 6 cups

7. Add the rest of the ingredients to the pot EXCEPT for the potatoes and escarole in the navy bean and white bean and escarole soups.

8. Cover the crockpot with the lid and cook the soup on high for 5 to 6 hours or on low for 8 to 10 hours.

9. Add the potatoes and escarole, if you are using them, about two hours before the end of the cooking time.

10. Check the soup near the end of the cooking time and add a little boiling water if you like your soup thinner.

Makes 6 to 8 servings or about 2½ quarts of soup

Broccoli Soup

DAY 2, borrow goat milk products from DAY 1
      or sheep milk products from DAY 3,
      borrow optional spelt from DAY 3

    1 cup sliced carrots (1 large or 2 small)
    1 cup sliced celery (1½ to 2 stalks)
    1 pound of frozen chopped broccoli OR a 1-pound head of fresh broccoli
    3 cups of poultry broth (recipes on pages 115 to 117)
        OR 3 cups of water
    ½ teaspoon salt only if water is used rather than broth
    Dash of black pepper (optional)
    2 cups goat or sheep milk or yogurt
    6 tablespoons of white spelt flour (optional – use if a thicker soup is desired)

1. Peel and slice the carrots. Slice the celery. Wash and chop the broccoli if you are using fresh broccoli rather than frozen broccoli.

2. Combine the vegetables with the broth or water and seasonings in a large saucepan.

3. Bring to a boil, lower the heat, and simmer for 15 to 20 minutes or until the vegetables are tender.

4. Thoroughly combine the optional spelt flour with the milk or yogurt; stir them into the soup.

5. Reheat the soup. Serve immediately.

Makes 4 to 6 servings

All-Potato Soup or Potato and Arugula Soup

DAY 2 if arugula is used, otherwise **EXTRA FOODS**

> 2 medium potatoes, about 1 pound
> Water – 1¾ cups without arugula or 2 cups with arugula
> ¾ teaspoons salt
> 1½ to 2 cups of chopped arugula, about 2 to 3 ounces (optional)

1. Peel the potatoes. Cut one into ½ inch cubes. Quarter the other potato.

2. Combine the potatoes with the other ingredients in a saucepan.

3. Bring to a boil, reduce the heat, and simmer the soup for 20 to 30 minutes, or until the potatoes are tender.

4. Remove the quartered potato from the soup. Also remove about ½ cup of the liquid. Put the quartered potato and liquid in a food processor or blender and puree.

5. Return the potato puree to the pan and reheat the soup. Serve immediately.

Makes 2 servings

Hearty Meat and Vegetable Soup

DAY 2 if buffalo and cabbage are used, otherwise **EXTRA FOODS**

> 1 pound of round steak or stew meat of buffalo, beef, antelope, kangaroo,
>   or any mild tasting red game meat
> 1 tablespoon oil
> 6 to 8 cups water
> 1½ teaspoons salt
> ⅛ teaspoon black pepper (optional)
> 5 carrots (about 1 pound)
> 4 to 5 stalks of celery
> 1 cup chopped cabbage or other vegetable (optional)

1. Cut the meat into small cubes.

2. Put the meat and oil into a large saucepan and cook them over medium heat until the meat is browned.

3. Add 6 cups of the water to the pan, bring the soup to a boil, reduce the heat, and simmer for one hour.

4. Peel and slice the carrots. Wash and slice the celery.

5. Add the salt, pepper, carrots, and celery to the pan. Add more of the water if the soup is getting too thick.

6. Return the soup to a boil, reduce the heat, and simmer it for another half hour.

7. Add the cabbage and simmer the soup for another 15 minutes. Serve immediately.

Makes 4 to 6 servings.

Meatball Soup

DAY 2 if buffalo is used; otherwise **EXTRA FOODS**

1 pound ground buffalo, beef, antelope, or other mild tasting red game meat
1½ teaspoons salt, divided
¼ teaspoon pepper (optional)
2 teaspoons oil (optional)
2 to 3 stalks of celery, sliced
4 to 5 carrots, peeled and sliced
8 cups water

1. Mix together the ground meat, ½ teaspoon salt, and pepper with your hands.

2. Form the meat mixture into 1inch meatballs.

3. If you are using a very lean meat, put the oil into a large saucepan. Add the meatballs.

4. Brown the meatballs on all sides over medium heat. When they are browned, drain and discard the fat.

5. Add the vegetables, remaining salt, pepper, and water to the stockpot.

6. Bring the soup to a boil, reduce the heat, and simmer the soup for 1½ hours.

Makes 6 to 8 servings

Sauces and Condiments

When you are on a very limited diet, you may sometimes seem to be eating tasteless food day after day. Hopefully this chapter will give you recipes for sauces and condiments to brighten up your diet.

SWEET SAUCES

Pancake Syrup

FOS*-SWEETENED (Extra foods)

¼ teaspoon arrowroot (DAY 1), tapioca starch (DAY 3),
    water chestnut starch (DAY 4), or bean starch (EXTRA FOODS)
½ cup water
¾ cup FOS*
½ teaspoon corn-free natural maple flavoring
½ teaspoon corn-free natural vanilla (optional)

STEVIA-SWEETENED (Extra foods)

1 teaspoon arrowroot (DAY 1) or water chestnut starch (DAY 4)
    OR 1½ teaspoons tapioca starch (DAY 3)
1 cup water
⅛ teaspoon white stevia extract powder
½ teaspoon corn-free natural maple flavoring
½ teaspoon corn-free natural vanilla (optional)

1. Choose one set of ingredients from above. *If you are using the FOS, please read pages 20 and 250 of this book and be aware that FOS can support the growth of a few types of "unfriendly" bacteria that may contribute to dysbiosis. If you do not have these bacteria, FOS may be better for you than sugar, but it should be used with caution.

2. Combine the starch and water in a saucepan.

3. Bring the mixture to a boil. The mixture will thicken slightly and become clear.

4. Stir in the FOS or stevia. If you are using the FOS, stir it in one tablespoon at a time, allowing each addition to dissolve before adding more. The stevia may be added all at once. Stir until it completely dissolves.

5. Stir in the flavorings.

6. Serve the syrup immediately. Store any leftover syrup in the refrigerator. If it becomes quite cloudy, reheat it slightly before serving.

Makes about 1 cup of syrup

Any Day Fruit Sauce

These sauces are great over frozen yogurt, pancakes, waffles, cereal, mush, or even roasted poultry or meat.

PINEAPPLE (DAY 1)

     1 8-ounce can crushed pineapple packed in its own juice OR ¾ cup finely chopped fresh pineapple
     1 cup pineapple juice
     2 teaspoons arrowroot

BLUEBERRY-GRAPE (DAY 2)

     1 pound unsweetened frozen blueberries OR 1 pound fresh blueberries
     ½ cup white or purple grape juice concentrate
     2 teaspoons bean starch (**EXTRA FOODS**), arrowroot (borrowed from **DAY 1**), OR tapioca starch (borrowed from **DAY 3**)

APPLE (DAY 3)

     2 large apples, or about 3 cups diced apples
     ¾ teaspoon cinnamon
     ⅞ cup (¾ cup plus 2 tablespoons) thawed apple juice concentrate, divided
     2 teaspoons tapioca starch

STRAWBERRY (DAY 3)

     1 pound thawed unsweetened frozen strawberries OR 1 pound fresh strawberries
     ½ cup apple juice concentrate, thawed
     2 teaspoons tapioca starch

CHERRY (DAY 4)

     1 16-ounce can tart pie cherries, packed in water
     ½ cup cherry juice, drained from above can
     1 cup pineapple juice concentrate (borrowed from **DAY 1**) or apple juice concentrate (borrowed from **DAY 3**), thawed
     4 teaspoons water chestnut starch, arrowroot (borrowed from **DAY 1**), OR tapioca starch (borrowed from **DAY 3**)

1. Choose one set of ingredients from above.

2. If you are making pineapple sauce using canned pineapple, drain the pineapple juice from the pineapple and reserve it. It can be used for part of the juice in the sauce.

3. If you are making apple sauce, peel, core, and dice the apples. Combine them with ¾ cup of the apple juice and the cinnamon in a saucepan and bring them to a boil. Reduce the heat and simmer for 15 to 20 minutes or until the apples are tender. Combine the remaining 2 tablespoons apple juice with the starch and stir it into the pan. Proceed with step 8, below.

4. If you are making strawberry sauce, slice the fresh strawberries or cut the frozen strawberries into pieces.

5. If you are making cherry sauce, drain the cherries, reserving ½ cup of the juice.

6. For all of the kinds of fruit sauce except apple, stir together the juice(s) and starch in a saucepan.

7. Add the fruit to the pan.

8. Cook the mixture over medium heat stirring it often, until the sauce thickens and boils.

9. Remove the pan from the heat. Serve the sauce warm or refrigerate it. The cherry sauce is best after overnight refrigeration.

Makes about 2 cups of sauce

Butterscotch Sauce

DAY 1 – borrow the peach in the Fruit Sweet™ from **DAY 4**
       and the pear in the Fruit Sweet™ or Pear Sweet™ from **DAY 3**

¼ cup water
3 to 4 tablespoons arrowroot
¾ cup Fruit Sweet™ or Pear Sweet™
4 teaspoons corn-free natural vanilla extract
2 tablespoons goat butter or ghee

1. Stir together the water and arrowroot in a saucepan. Use 3 tablespoons arrowroot if you prefer a thin sauce, or 4 tablespoons if you prefer a thicker sauce.

2. When they are mixed, stir in the Fruit Sweet™ or Pear Sweet™.

3. Cook the sauce over medium heat, stirring often.

4. As the sauce begins to steam and nears boiling, stir it continuously.

5. When the sauce comes to a full boil, cook it for one more minute, stirring continuously. It will thicken and become darker during this time.

6. Cool the sauce to room temperature. Using a hand blender or electric mixer, beat in the vanilla and goat butter or ghee. The sauce will lighten in both texture and color.

7. Serve immediately or refrigerate and stir before serving.

Makes about 1 cup of sauce

Any Day Cranberry Sauce

PINEAPPLE-SWEETENED (DAY 1)

2½ cups pineapple juice concentrate, thawed

4 cups cranberries (about 12 ounces)

GRAPE-SWEETENED (DAY 2)

2 cups thawed white grape juice concentrate OR

1 cup Grape Sweet™

4 cups cranberries (about 12 ounces)

APPLE-SWEETENED (DAY 3)

2 cups apple juice concentrate, thawed

4 cups cranberries (about 12 ounces)

DATE-SWEETENED (DAY 4)

1 cup water

4 cups cranberries (about 12 ounces)

1 cup date sugar

STEVIA-SWEETENED (EXTRA FOODS)

1 cup water

4 cups cranberries (about 12 ounces)

¼ teaspoon white stevia extract powder

1. Choose one set of ingredients from above.

2. If you are using the pineapple, white grape, or apple juice concentrate, put it in a saucepan and bring it to a boil.

3. Boil it in an uncovered pan until the amount is reduced to about one cup in volume. Pour it out of the pan into a measuring cup occasionally to see how close you are getting to one cup. When it reaches about one cup, proceed with step 5 below.

4. If you are using water or Grape Sweet™ for the liquid, just put it into a saucepan.

5. Add the cranberries to the juice, sweetener, or water in the pan.

6. Bring the mixture to a boil, reduce the heat, and simmer, stirring often, for 15 to 20 minutes, or until the cranberries have popped.

7. If you are using the date sugar or stevia, stir it into the sauce. Stir the stevia in thoroughly, making sure it has completely dissolved.

8. Refrigerate the sauce until serving time.

Makes about 2 cups of cranberry sauce

Carob Sauce

DAY 1 (pineapple), **DAY 3** (pear) or **DAY 4** (peach) if you use
Fruit Sweet™ – borrow the other fruits from their respective days
DAY 2 if you use Grape Sweet™
DAY 3 if you use Pear Sweet™
EXTRA FOODS if you use honey

1 cup Fruit Sweet™, Grape Sweet™, Pear Sweet™, or honey
⅜ cup (¼ cup plus 2 tablespoons) carob powder

1. Put the carob powder in a wire mesh strainer.

2. Press it through the strainer with the back of a spoon to remove any lumps from the powder.

3. In a small bowl thoroughly stir together the sweetener and carob powder.

4. Serve the sauce immediately or refrigerate it.

Makes about 1 cup of sauce

SAVORY SAUCES

Easy Cheese Sauce

This recipe gives you a choice of two yeast-free cheese sauces to serve over cooked pasta or vegetables.

YOGURT CHEESE SAUCE

DAY 1 if goat products are used,
DAY 3 if sheep products are used

¾ cup goat or sheep yo-cheese (recipe on page 63)
Up to ¼ cup goat or sheep yogurt

1. Stir the yo-cheese until smooth.

2. Add yogurt one tablespoon at a time, stirring after each addition, until you reach the thickness you prefer in your sauce.

3. Stir into 2 to 3 cups of hot cooked pasta or serve over vegetables.

FETA CHEESE SAUCE

> **DAY 1** if goat cheese and arrowroot are used,
> **DAY 3** if sheep cheese and tapioca are used

> ¾ cup crumbled goat or sheep feta cheese (about ¼ pound)
> ½ cup water
> 1 tablespoon arrowroot or tapioca starch

1. Combine all the ingredients in a blender or food processor and puree until smooth, or blend with a hand blender.

2. Transfer the mixture to a saucepan.

3. Cook the mixture over medium heat until it thickens and just begins to boil.

4. Stir into 2 to 3 cups of hot cooked pasta or serve over vegetables.

Makes about 1 cup of either sauce

C-Guacamole

DAY 3

> 1 large ripe avocado, weighing about ½ pound
> ⅛ teaspoon tart-tasting unbuffered vitamin C powder
> 1 tablespoon finely chopped onion (optional)
> ¼ teaspoon salt
> ⅛ teaspoon pepper (optional)

1. Peel and seed the avocado.

2. Put the avocado in a bowl with the rest of the ingredients.

3. Mash all of the ingredients together thoroughly with a fork or potato masher.

4. Serve immediately. This sauce may darken if it stands for a long time.

Makes about ⅔ cup of sauce

PASTA SAUCES

My husband once commented about my family, "For Italians, food is love." Just as we all have our own individual ways of showing love, every Italian mamma has her own style of pasta sauce. Most of these recipes originated with my family members and were given with love. They are wonderful on pasta, but they can also be used on cooked vegetables such as spaghetti squash, french cut beans, shredded cabbage, or zucchini. Enjoy!

Spicy Oil Sauce for Pasta

ANY DAY, depending on the oil used

½ cup oil, traditionally olive oil
1 to 3 cloves of garlic (optional)
1 to 1½ teaspoons black pepper OR 2 to 4 red pepper pods, to taste
¼ cup finely chopped fresh Italian flat-leaf parsley
    OR 2 tablespoons dry parsley
¼ teaspoon salt

1. Peel the garlic, if you are using it. Cut each clove into quarters.

2. Combine the garlic and red pepper pods, if you are using them, with 2 to 3 tablespoons of the oil in a small skillet.

3. Cook the vegetables in the oil over medium heat until garlic is golden and the pepper pods are dark brown. Remove the vegetables from the oil.

4. Stir the parsley, salt, black pepper and remaining oil into the oil in the pan; or, if you are going to use the sauce on pasta immediately, sprinkle the pasta with the parsley, salt, and pepper and toss it with the oil.

5. If you wish to make this sauce ahead of serving time, store it in a jar in the refrigerator and use it in small amounts on individual servings of pasta.

Makes about ½ cup of sauce or enough for 2 to 3 pounds of pasta

Any Day Pesto

Although "pesto alla Genovese" is traditionally made with sweet basil, pine nuts, and olive oil, the combinations below are all delicious and will give you pesto sauce to use on **Any day** of your rotation. Because this sauce freezes well, I make it in large batches so I always have it on hand when I want it.

PARSLEY PESTO (Day 1)

½ pound (about 7 cups)
Italian flat-leaf parsley
1 to 3 cloves of garlic (optional)
1 cup walnuts
1 cup walnut oil
1 to 1½ teaspoons salt, or to taste
¼ teaspoon pepper (optional)

ARUGULA PESTO (Day 2)

½ pound (about 7 cups) arugula
1 to 3 cloves of garlic (optional)
1 cup pine nuts
1 cup canola oil
1 to 1½ teaspoons salt, or to taste
¼ teaspoon pepper (optional)

SPINACH PESTO (Day 3)

½ pound (about 7 cups) spinach
1 to 3 cloves of garlic (optional)
1 cup filberts
1 cup olive oil
1 to 1½ teaspoons salt, or to taste
¼ teaspoon pepper (optional)

BASIL PESTO (Day 4)

½ pound (about 7 cups) sweet basil
1 to 3 cloves of garlic (optional)
1 cup almonds
1 cup almond oil
1 to 1½ teaspoons salt, or to taste
¼ teaspoon pepper (optional)

1. Remove the stems from the vegetables and wash the leaves in several changes of water. Spread them out on a dishcloth or paper towel. Blot them to remove most of the water.

2. If you are using the garlic, chop it in a blender or a food processor with the metal blade using a pulsing action.

3. Add the vegetable leaves to the processor or blender and use a pulsing action to chop the leaves.

4. Add the nuts to the processor or blender and process continually until they are ground.

5. With the machine running, add the oil in a thin stream.

6. Add the seasonings and process briefly.

7. Serve the sauce over pasta or polenta or use it for a spread on bread, crackers, tortillas, or other baked goods.

8. This makes a large batch of pesto. Freeze any leftover sauce.

Makes about 2¼ cups of sauce, or enough for 2 to 4 pounds of pasta

Grandma Jiannetti's Tomato Sauce

EXTRA FOODS

6 pounds of ripe Italian plum tomatoes
Water
¼ cup olive oil or other oil
1 to 2 cloves of garlic, minced (optional)
¼ teaspoon pepper OR a 1-inch dried red pepper pod,
    seeded and crumbled (optional)
1 to 1½ teaspoons salt, or to taste
1 tablespoon chopped fresh or 1 teaspoon dry sweet basil, or to taste (optional)

1. Bring a large pan of water to a boil.

2. Add the tomatoes to the pan several at a time; return the water to a boil and boil for two minutes.

3. Remove the tomatoes from the pan with a slotted spoon. Return the water to a boil and continue to process tomatoes until they have all been scalded.

5. While the tomatoes are being processed, peel the garlic, if you are using it. Put it in a skillet with the oil and cook it over medium heat until it is brown. Remove the garlic from the oil.

6. After the tomatoes have cooled slightly, slip the skins off with your fingers.

7. Put the tomatoes in a food processor or blender and puree them until they are smooth.

8. In a large stockpot, combine the tomatoes, oil and seasonings.

9. Bring the sauce to a boil, reduce the heat, and simmer the sauce uncovered for 1 hour and then covered for another ½ to 1 hour or until it is very thick and the volume is reduced by almost one-half. Stir the sauce frequently while it is simmering.

Makes about 4 cups of sauce

VARIATIONS:

SAUCE WITH MEATBALLS: Make meatballs from 1 pound of ground meat, ¾ teaspoon salt, and a dash of pepper and brown them as directed in the "Tomato Sauce with Meatballs" recipe on page 132. Add them to this sauce during its simmering time in step 8 above. Remove them from the sauce after 1 hour of simmering.

PIZZA SAUCE: Make the sauce as directed above, except use the optional sweet basil and also add 1 tablespoon chopped fresh or 1 teaspoon dry oregano and 1 teaspoon chopped fresh or ½ teaspoon dry thyme.

Grandma Capraro's
Tomato Sauce with Meatballs

DAY 1 with pork or goat
DAY 2 with turkey or buffalo
DAY 3 with chicken
EXTRA FOODS with beef or red game meat

MEATBALL INGREDIENTS:

2½ pounds lean ground beef, pork, buffalo,
    goat, chicken, turkey, or red game meat
1 tablespoon chopped fresh or 1 teaspoon dry parsley (optional)
½ teaspoon salt
¼ teaspoon pepper
2 tablespoons oil (needed only if the meat is very low in fat)
1 clove of garlic, peeled (optional)

SAUCE INGREDIENTS:

1 28-ounce can tomato puree
3 6-ounce cans tomato paste
1 cup water
1 teaspoon chopped fresh or ¼ teaspoon dry oregano
    (optional – Grandma did not use)
1 teaspoon chopped fresh or ¼ teaspoon dry sweet basil
    (optional – Grandma did not use)
1 teaspoon salt
¼ teaspoon pepper

1. Combine the meat, ½ teaspoon salt, ¼ teaspoon pepper, and the parsley in a bowl.

2. Use your hands to press the mixture firmly into 10 to 12 meatballs.

3. If the meat you used is very low in fat, put the oil into a skillet. Put the meatballs into the skillet and cook them over medium heat, uncovered, turning them as they cook, until they are brown on all sides.

4. If you wish to use the garlic, add it to the skillet as soon as some fat has been rendered from the meat. Remove it from the pan when it is brown.

5. Remove the meatballs from the skillet and drain off all of the fat.

6. Add one can of the tomato paste to the skillet and heat it over medium heat, stirring to loosen all of the brown meat bits stuck in the pan.

7. In a large saucepot, combine the tomato puree, tomato paste (from both the cans and the skillet), water, 1 teaspoon salt, ¼ teaspoon pepper, oregano, and sweet basil.

8. Add the meatballs to the sauce.

9. Bring the sauce to a boil, reduce the heat, and simmer the sauce, stirring it frequently, for 1 hour.

10. Remove the meatballs from the sauce with a slotted spoon after the first hour of simmering.

11. Simmer the sauce for another hour. If you are planning to serve the sauce immediately, add the meatballs back to the sauce and simmer until they are heated through.

12. Serve the sauce immediately, or freeze it with the meatballs for future meals.

Makes about 6 cups sauce and 10 to 12 meatballs or enough for 2 to 3 pounds of pasta

Tomato and Meat Sauce

This recipe was adapted from a sauce I first ate many years ago at the home of my cousin Mary Lou DiManna.

DAY 1 with pork or goat
DAY 2 with turkey or buffalo
DAY 3 with chicken
EXTRA FOODS with beef or red game meat

    2 pounds lean ground beef, pork, buffalo, goat, chicken, turkey,
        or red game meat
    2 12-ounce cans tomato paste
    1 28-ounce can tomato puree
    3 cups water
    1 teaspoon salt
    ⅛ teaspoon pepper (optional)

1. Put the meat in a large saucepan and cook it over medium heat, stirring often, until it is well browned.

2. Drain off all of the fat from the meat.

3. Add the tomato paste, tomato puree, water, and seasonings.

4. Bring the sauce to a boil, reduce the heat, and simmer it, stirring frequently, for 1½ to 2 hours.

5. Serve over cooked vegetables or pasta, or use it to make the zucchini casserole or lasagne recipes on pages 85 and 88 of this book.

6. Freeze leftover sauce for future meals.

Makes 10 to 11 cups of sauce

Rich Vegetarian Tomato Sauce

The long cooking makes this sauce much tastier than tomato sauce out of a jar; yet it contains no meat.

Extra foods

2 tablespoons olive or other oil
1 clove of garlic (optional)
3 6-ounce cans tomato paste
1 28-ounce can tomato puree
2 cups water
1 tablespoon fresh chopped or 1 teaspoon dry oregano
1 teaspoon fresh chopped or ½ teaspoon dry sweet basil
1 teaspoon salt
⅛ teaspoon pepper (optional)

1. Put the oil into a large saucepan.

2. If you are using the garlic, peel it and cut it into quarters. Add it to the oil in the pan and cook it over medium heat until it turns golden brown. Remove the garlic from the pan and discard it.

3. Add the tomato paste to the oil, and cook it over medium heat, stirring frequently, for 10 minutes or until its color becomes darker red.

4. Stir the tomato puree, water and seasonings into the tomato paste.

5. Bring the sauce to a boil over medium heat, reduce the heat, and simmer the sauce for two hours, stirring it every 10 to 15 minutes.

6. Serve immediately or freeze the sauce for future meals.

Makes 6 to 7 cups of sauce

Mrs. Calabra's Pizza Sauce

My father had a friend with whom he went to school from kindergarten through college and remained in touch with for the rest of his life. This recipe is a modification of a sauce which his friend's mother made.

Extra foods

1 6-ounce can tomato paste
1 8-ounce can tomato sauce
½ cup water
1 tablespoon chopped fresh or 1 teaspoon dry oregano
1½ teaspoons chopped fresh or ½ teaspoon dry thyme
1½ teaspoons chopped fresh or ½ teaspoon dry sweet basil

1. Stir together all of the ingredients in a saucepan.

2. Bring the sauce to a boil, reduce the heat, and simmer it for 40 to 45 minutes, stirring it every 10 to 15 minutes.

3. Use this sauce in the pizza recipe on page 86.

Makes about 2 cups of sauce or enough sauce for two pizzas

CONDIMENTS

Super Smooth Sauce

This is a great dip for artichokes or substitute for mayonnaise.

CASHEW (DAY 2)

¼ cup cashew butter
1½ teaspoons tart-tasting unbuffered
     vitamin C powder
¼ cup water, rhubarb concentrate
     (recipe on page 248) OR lemon or
     lime juice (omit vitamin C if you
     use the concentrate or juice)
⅛ teaspoon salt
¼ cup oil

ALMOND (DAY 4)

¼ cup almond butter
1 teaspoon tart-tasting unbuffered
     vitamin C powder
¼ cup water
     OR lemon or lime juice (omit vita-
     min C if you use the juice)
⅛ teaspoon salt
¼ cup oil

MACADAMIA (EXTRA FOODS)

¼ cup macadamia nut butter
1 teaspoon tart-tasting unbuffered
     vitamin C powder
¼ cup water OR lemon
     or lime juice (omit vitamin C if
     you use the juice)
⅛ teaspoon salt
¼ cup oil

PINE NUT (EXTRA FOODS)

½ cup pine nuts
1 teaspoon tart-tasting unbuffered
     vitamin C powder
¼ cup water OR lemon
     or lime juice (omit vitamin C if
     you use the juice)
⅛ teaspoon salt
¼ cup oil

1. Choose one set of ingredients from above.

2. If you are making the pine nut dressing, process the nuts in a food processor until they are very finely ground. Add the water or juice and process until smooth. Add the rest of the ingredients except the oil and process. Proceed with step 5 below.

3. If you are making any of the other dressings, combine the nut butter, vitamin C, water, juice or concentrate, and salt in a blender or in the container for a hand blender.

4. Blend until smooth.

5. With the machine running, pour in the oil in a slow stream.

6. Serve immediately or refrigerate any leftover sauce.

Makes about ¾ cup sauce

Any day Catsup

DAY 1 – borrow cloves and mustard from **DAY 2**

3 pounds Italian plum tomatoes
OR 1 6-ounce can tomato paste
plus ½ cup water
¼ cup pineapple juice concentrate
1 tablespoon finely chopped onion
OR 1 teaspoon dry onion flakes
(optional)
2 whole cloves
½ teaspoon dry mustard (optional)
1 teaspoon salt
2 teaspoons tart tasting unbuffered
vitamin C powder

DAY 2

3 pounds Italian plum tomatoes
OR 1 6-ounce can tomato paste
plus ½ cup water
¼ cup white grape juice concentrate
1 tablespoon finely chopped onion
OR 1 teaspoon dry onion flakes
(optional)
2 whole cloves
½ teaspoon dry mustard (optional)
1 teaspoon salt
2 teaspoons tart tasting unbuffered
vitamin C powder

DAY 3 – borrow cloves and mustard from **DAY 2**

3 pounds Italian plum tomatoes
OR 1 6-ounce can tomato paste
plus ½ cup water
¼ cup apple juice concentrate
1 tablespoon finely chopped onion
OR 1 teaspoon dry onion flakes
(optional)
2 whole cloves
½ teaspoon dry mustard (optional)
1 teaspoon salt
2 teaspoons tart tasting unbuffered
vitamin C powder

EXTRA FOODS – use cloves and mustard from **DAY 2**

3 pounds Italian plum tomatoes OR
1 6-ounce can tomato paste plus
¾ cup water
⅛ teaspoon white stevia extract
powder, or to taste
1 tablespoon finely chopped onion
OR 1 teaspoon dry onion flakes
(optional)
2 whole cloves
½ teaspoon dry mustard (optional)
1 teaspoon salt
2 teaspoons tart tasting unbuffered
vitamin C powder

1. Choose one set of ingredients from above.
2. If you are using the fresh tomatoes, wash them, cut off the stem and any bad spots, put them in a food processor or blender, and puree them until they are smooth.
3. In a large saucepan stir together the pureed tomatoes or tomato paste plus water with the juice or stevia, onion, cloves, mustard, and salt.
4. Bring the catsup to a boil, reduce the heat, and simmer it. If you used the fresh tomatoes, simmer it for 1 to 1½ hours, or until it is very thick. If you used the tomato paste, simmer it for 30 minutes. Stir the catsup every 10 minutes during the simmering time.
5. Remove the catsup from the heat and stir in the vitamin C powder.
6. Refrigerate the catsup or freeze it in small portions.

Makes about 1 cup of catsup if you use the tomato paste or 2 cups of catsup if you use fresh tomatoes

ANY DAY Mustard

DAY 1 traditional mustard – borrow mustard from **DAY 2**

2 teaspoons dry mustard
1 cup water with the vitamin C
    or ¾ cup water with the
    lemon juice
1 tablespoon arrowroot
¼ teaspoon turmeric
½ teaspoon salt
1 teaspoon tart tasting
    unbuffered vitamin C powder OR
    ¼ cup lemon juice

DAY 3 traditional mustard – borrow mustard from **DAY 2** and turmeric from **DAY 1**

2 teaspoons dry mustard
1 cup water with the vitamin C
    or ¾ cup water with the lemon
    juice
1 tablespoon tapioca starch
¼ teaspoon turmeric
½ teaspoon salt
1 teaspoon tart tasting unbuffered
    vitamin C powder OR ¼ cup
    lemon juice

DAY 2 Chinese-style mustard

¼ cup dry mild dijon style mustard
    powder
3 tablespoons water

DAY 2 traditional mustard – borrow tapioca from **DAY 3** or arrowroot from **DAY 1** and turmeric from **DAY 1**

2 teaspoons dry mustard
1 cup water with the vitamin C
    or ¾ cup water with the lemon
    juice or ½ cup water with the
    rhubarb concentrate
1 tablespoon tapioca starch
    or arrowroot
¼ teaspoon turmeric
½ teaspoon salt
1 teaspoon tart tasting unbuffered
    vitamin C powder OR ¼ cup
    lemon juice OR ½ cup rhubarb
    concentrate (recipe on page 247)

DAY 4 traditional mustard – borrow mustard from **DAY 2** and turmeric from **DAY 1**

2 teaspoons dry mustard
1 cup water with the vitamin C
    or ¾ cup water with the lemon
    juice
1 tablespoon water chestnut starch
¼ teaspoon turmeric
½ teaspoon salt
1 teaspoon tart tasting unbuffered
    vitamin C powder OR ¼ cup
    lemon juice

1. Choose one set of ingredients from above.

2. If you are making Chinese-style mustard, stir together the mustard and water thoroughly. Serve the mustard immediately or refrigerate it.

3. If you are making traditional mustard, stir together the mustard and water in a saucepan and allow them to stand for 10 minutes.

4. Stir the starch, turmeric, and salt into the mustard mixture in the pan. Also stir in the lemon juice or rhubarb concentrate if you are using them.

5. Cook over medium heat, stirring it frequently, until it thickens and boils.

6. Stir in the vitamin C powder if you are using it.

7. Cool the mustard before serving it. Store the mustard in the refrigerator.

Makes about 1 cup of traditional mustard of ⅓ cup of Chinese-style mustard

Salads and Dressings

Vegetables are rich in vitamins, minerals, and enzymes when used raw. If you can digest them raw, this chapter of salad recipes is for you.

Salads do not have to be made with lettuce. Use a wide variety of vegetables and you will get a wide variety of nutrients. Dark colored vegetables, such as spinach and leaf lettuces, contain more minerals than light-colored iceberg lettuce. (Magnesium is in every molecule of the pigment chlorophyll). Vegetables that are not leafy can be shredded to make great salads. Strive for variety in your dressing ingredients too. If you must avoid vinegar, you can make dressings with tart-tasting vitamin C powder, citrus juices, or rhubarb concentrate instead.

Oil and "Vinegar" Dressing

ANY DAY, depending on the oil used

¼ cup oil
½ clove of garlic, crushed (optional)
1 teaspoon finely chopped fresh oregano, sweet basil, or parsley
    OR ¼ teaspoon dried oregano, sweet basil, or parley (optional)
¼ teaspoon salt
Dash of pepper (optional)
½ to ¾ teaspoon tart-tasting unbuffered vitamin C powder (to taste)
    plus 1 teaspoon water OR 3 tablespoons lemon juice or 4 tablespoons rhubarb
    concentrate (**DAY 2**, recipe on page 248)

1. If you are using the garlic, combine the oil and crushed garlic in a glass jar and refrigerate them at least overnight.

2. Take the garlic out of the oil and discard the garlic.

3. If you wish to prepare enough oil for several days' use, you can double or quadruple the amounts of oil and garlic and store the extra oil in the refrigerator until needed.

4. If you are using the vitamin C, mix the vitamin C powder with the water in a separate cup. Stir it until the vitamin C dissolves.

4. Add the vitamin C solution, the lemon juice, or the rhubarb concentrate to the oil in the jar.

5. Add the seasonings to the oil in the jar.

5. Shake the jar well before pouring the dressing on the salad.

Makes about ¼ cup of dressing

VARIATION: For a slightly sweet salad dressing, omit the garlic and herbs. Add 2 tablespoons of any thawed fruit juice concentrate to the dressing.

Creamy French Dressing

DAY 1 if arrowroot is used; borrow the pear and peach in the Fruit Sweet™ or Pear Sweet™ from days 3 and 4

DAY 3 if tapioca and Pear Sweet™ are used; borrow the pineapple and peach in the Fruit Sweet™ from days 1 and 4

¼ cup water
2 teaspoons tapioca starch or arrowroot
⅓ cup vinegar or lemon juice OR ⅓ cup water plus 1½ teaspoons tart-tasting
    unbuffered vitamin C powder
1 tablespoon paprika (optional – for color)
2 teaspoons Fruit Sweet™, Pear Sweet™, or honey
1 teaspoon salt
Dash of pepper
1 cup oil

1. Combine the ¼ cup water and starch in a saucepan.

2. Cook the mixture over medium heat until it reaches the boiling point, becomes thick and clears somewhat.

3. Allow it to cool slightly, then transfer it to a blender or food processor.

4. Add the vinegar, lemon juice, or ⅓ cup water plus vitamin C, paprika, Fruit Sweet™, Pear Sweet™, or honey, salt, and pepper to the blender or food processor and process briefly.

5. With the blender or processor running, add the oil in a very slow stream.

LOWER-FAT VARIATION: For a dressing that is lower in fat, use ¾ cup water in place of the ¼ cup water, 3 tablespoons starch, and ½ cup oil.

Makes about 1⅔ cups of dressing

Avocado Dressing

This dressing is delicious on spinach or sliced cucumbers.

DAY 3, borrow optional rhubarb from **DAY 2**

    1 large ripe avocado (½ to ¾ pound)
    1 teaspoon tart-tasting unbuffered vitamin C powder (or to taste)
        OR ⅓ cup rhubarb concentrate (recipe on page 248) OR 2 tablespoons
        lemon juice or vinegar
    Water
    ⅛ teaspoon salt
    Dash of pepper (optional)

1. Peel and seed the avocado.

2. Put the avocado flesh in a glass measuring cup and mash it with a fork. There should be about ⅔ cup of mashed avocado.

3. If you are using rhubarb concentrate, lemon juice, or vinegar, add them to the cup with the avocado.

4. Add water to the 1 cup mark on the measuring cup.

5. Transfer the avocado and liquid to a blender or food processor.

6. Add the vitamin C powder (if you are using it), salt, and pepper and puree the mixture until it is smooth.

7. Serve the dressing immediately. It may darken if it stands for very long.

Makes about 1 cup of dressing

No Oil Dressing

DAY 2

½ cup water
¾ cup rhubarb concentrate (recipe on page 247)
1 clove of garlic, crushed (optional)
3 teaspoons finely chopped fresh oregano, sweet basil, or parsley
    OR 1 teaspoon dried oregano, sweet basil, or parsley (optional)
1 teaspoon salt
⅛ to ¼ teaspoon pepper, or to taste
½ teaspoon xanthum gum

ANY DAY depending on the oil used

¾ cup water
½ cup lemon juice OR 2 teaspoons tart-tasting unbuffered vitamin
    C powder plus 1 tablespoon water
1 clove of garlic, crushed (optional)
3 teaspoons finely chopped fresh oregano, sweet basil, or parsley
    OR 1 teaspoon dried oregano, sweet basil, or parsley (optional)
1 teaspoon salt
⅛ to ¼ teaspoon pepper, or to taste
½ teaspoon xanthum gum

1. In a jar combine all of the ingredients except the xanthum gum and, if you are using the vitamin C, the vitamin C plus 1 tablespoon water.

2. Shake the jar thoroughly.

3. Add the xanthum gum and shake the jar for about two minutes.

4. Refrigerate the dressing overnight. It will thicken as it stands.

5. Remove the garlic.

6. In a separate cup, stir together the vitamin C and 1 tablespoon water until the vitamin C is dissolved. Add it to the jar and shake.

7. Serve the dressing immediately. It may lose some of its "tang" with storage if made with the vitamin C.

Makes 1¼ cups dressing if the lemon juice or rhubarb concentrate is used and ¾ cup dressing if the vitamin C is used

Sweet Yogurt Dressing

GOAT (DAY 1, borrow rhubarb from **DAY 2)**

> 1 cup thick goat yogurt or goat yogurt "sour cream" (See recipe, page 63).
> 2 tablespoons lemon juice OR 3 tablespoons rhubarb concentrate (recipe on
>   page 248) OR ¼ teaspoon tart-tasting unbuffered vitamin C powder
> ¼ cup pineapple juice concentrate, thawed
> ¼ teaspoon salt
> 1 teaspoon celery or poppy seeds (optional)

SHEEP (DAY 3, borrow rhubarb from **DAY 2)**

> 1 cup sheep yogurt
> 2 tablespoons lemon juice OR 3 tablespoons rhubarb concentrate (recipe on
>   page 248) OR ¼ teaspoon tart-tasting unbuffered vitamin C powder
> ¼ cup apple juice concentrate, thawed
> ¼ teaspoon salt
> 1 teaspoon celery or poppy seeds (optional)

1. If you are using the vitamin C powder, stir it into the fruit juice concentrate until it is completely dissolved.

2. Stir together all of the recipe ingredients.

3. Serve the dressing immediately or refrigerate leftover dressing.

Makes about 1⅓ cups of dressing

Herbed Yogurt Dressing

DAY 1 if goat products are used, **DAY 3** if sheep products are used; borrow rhubarb from **DAY 2**

1 cup goat or sheep yogurt or acidophilus milk
2 tablespoons lemon juice OR 4 tablespoons rhubarb concentrate (recipe on
   page 248) OR ¼ teaspoon tart-tasting unbuffered vitamin C powder
⅛ to ¼ teaspoon black pepper, to taste
¼ teaspoon salt
1 tablespoon fresh chopped oregano or sweet basil or 1 teaspoon dry oregano
   or sweet basil

1. If you are using the vitamin C powder, stir it into a few tablespoons of the yogurt or acidophilus milk until it is completely dissolved.

2. Stir together all of the recipe ingredients.

3. Serve the dressing immediately or refrigerate leftover dressing.

Makes about 1 cup of dressing

Health Dressing

Make this dressing with flax oil to get your essential fatty acids. The yogurt and herbs will mask the taste of the oil.

DAY 1 if goat yogurt is used, **DAY 3** if sheep yogurt is used

½ cup yogurt
¼ cup oil
⅛ to ¼ teaspoon salt, or to taste
Dash of pepper (optional)
1 to 3 teaspoons fresh oregano or sweet basil or ½ to 1 teaspoon dry oregano
   or sweet basil

1. Stir together all of the recipe ingredients.

2. Serve the dressing immediately or refrigerate any that is left over.

Makes ¾ cup of dressing

Any day Shredded Vegetable Salad

CREAMY JICAMA SLAW (Day 1)

1½ pounds jicama
¾ cup macadamia or pine nut
    "Super Smooth Sauce", page 135
    OR ¾ cup goat "Sweet Yogurt
    Dressing," page 142
⅛ to ¼ teaspoon tart-tasting
    unbuffered vitamin C powder
    with the "Super Smooth Sauce,"
    or to taste (optional)

JICAMA-RASPBERRY SALAD
(Day 1, borrow raspberries from Day 3)

1½ pounds jicama
Raspberry dressing:
    ¼ cup fresh or frozen
        unsweetened raspberries
    ⅓ cup oil
    ¼ to ½ teaspoon tart-tasting
        unbuffered vitamin C powder
        (Use the smaller amount if
        the raspberries are tart).
    ⅓ cup pineapple juice
        concentrate, thawed
Dash of salt

COLESLAW (Day 2, borrow goat yogurt from Day 1 or sheep yogurt from Day 3)

1 pound cabbage (½ of a large head)
¾ cup cashew "Super Smooth Sauce,"
    page 135 or ¾ cup goat or sheep
    "Sweet Yogurt Dressing," page 142
⅛ to ¼ teaspoon tart-tasting
    unbuffered vitamin C powder
    with the "Super Smooth Sauce,"
    or to taste (optional)
¼ teaspoon salt with the yogurt
    dressing only (optional)
Dash of pepper (optional)

CABBAGE-CANOLA SALAD (Day 2)

1 pound cabbage (½ of a large head)
Canola dressing:
    1 teaspoon water
    ½ to ¾ teaspoon tart-tasting
        unbuffered vitamin C
        powder, to taste
    ¼ teaspoon salt
    ⅛ teaspoon pepper (optional)
    2 tablespoons canola or other oil
    2 tablespoons canola seeds
        (optional)

BROCCOLI SALAD (Day 2)

1 pound broccoli cut into small pieces
Dressing:
    ½ teaspoon water
    ¼ to ⅜ teaspoon tart-tasting unbuffered vitamin C powder, to taste
    ⅛ teaspoon salt
    2 tablespoons oil

SWEET CARROT SLAW (Day 3)

1 pound carrots (about 5 carrots)
¾ cup macadamia or pine nut
    "Super Smooth Sauce", page 135
    or ¾ cup sheep "Sweet Yogurt
    Dressing," page 142
1 tablespoon apple juice concentrate,
    thawed, with the "Super Smooth
    Sauce" (optional)

SQUASH SLAW
(Day 4, borrow goat yogurt from Day 1
or sheep yogurt from Day 3)

1 pound zucchini or crookneck
    squash (about 2 medium
    or 3 small)
¾ cup almond "Super Smooth
    Sauce," page 135 or ¾ cup goat or
    sheep "Sweet Yogurt Dressing,"
    page 142
⅛ to ¼ teaspoon tart-tasting
    unbuffered vitamin C powder with
    the "Super Smooth Sauce," or to
    taste (optional)
¼ teaspoon salt, with the yogurt
    dressing only (optional)
Dash of pepper (optional)

CARROT-OLIVE SALAD (Day 3)

1 pound carrots (about 5 carrots)
1 cup sliced black olives
Dressing:
    3 tablespoons olive oil
    ¼ cup juice from the olives

DOUBLE SQUASH SALAD (Day 4)

1 pound zucchini or crookneck
    squash (about 2 medium or 3
    small)
Dressing:
    1 additional small zucchini or
    crookneck squash (about 5 ounces),
    cut into pieces
½ teaspoon tart-tasting unbuffered
    vitamin C powder
¼ teaspoon salt
⅓ cup oil

1. Choose one set of ingredients from above.

2. If you are using jicama or carrots, peel them.

3. Shred or grate the vegetables, except for the additional one small squash in the "Double Squash Salad" dressing. (A food processor is very handy for shredding vegetables). Put the vegetables into a large serving bowl.

4. If you are making any variety of slaw, mix the "Super Smooth Sauce" with the optional vitamin C powder, apple juice, or pepper, or mix the yogurt dressing with the optional salt and pepper. Toss the dressing with the shredded vegetables.

5. If you are making jicama-raspberry or double squash salad, put all of the dressing ingredients in a food processor or blender and puree until smooth. Toss the dressing with the shredded vegetables.

4. If you are making cabbage-canola or broccoli salad, stir together the vitamin C and water in a cup until the vitamin C is dissolved. Add the rest of the dressing ingredients and stir. Toss the dressing with the vegetables.

5. If you are making carrot-olive salad, stir together the carrots and olives in a serving bowl. Combine the oil and olive juice in a cup. Toss the dressing with the vegetables.

Makes about 4 cups of salad or 3 to 4 servings

Any day Leafy Vegetable Salad

You can make a meal out of many of these salads by serving them on a large tortilla.

LETTUCE OR ENDIVE (Extra foods)

4 cups lettuce or belgian endive torn into bite-sized pieces
Optional additions:
    ¼ cup crumbled crackers of the day, page 166
    ¼ cup chopped nuts
    ¼ cup crumbled goat or sheep cheese
    ½ cup cooked dried legumes, drained
Dressing (or use any dressing on pages 138 to 143):
    ¼ to ½ teaspoon tart-tasting unbuffered vitamin C powder, to taste
    1 teaspoon water
    ⅛ teaspoon salt
    Dash of pepper (optional)
    2 tablespoons oil

ARUGULA (Day 2)

4 cups arugula torn into bite-sized pieces OR, if this is too spicy, 1 to 2 cups of
    arugula with 2 to 3 cups of lettuce
Optional additions:
    ¼ cup crumbled rye, teff, or buckwheat crackers, page 166
    ¼ cup chopped cashews
Dressing (or use oil and "vinegar" dressing, on page 138):
    ¼ to ½ teaspoon tart-tasting unbuffered vitamin C powder, to taste
    1 teaspoon water
    ⅛ teaspoon salt
    Dash of pepper (optional)
    2 tablespoons canola oil

SPINACH (Day 3)

4 cups spinach leaves torn into bite-sized pieces
Optional additions:
    ¼ cup spelt, quinoa, or cassava crackers, page 166
    ¼ cup crumbled sheep cheese
    1 cup diced or sliced cooked beets
    ¼ cup chopped filberts
    1 avocado, peeled, seeded and diced

Dressing (or use any dressing on pages 138 to 143):
   ¼ to ½ teaspoon tart-tasting unbuffered vitamin C powder, to taste
   1 teaspoon water
   ⅛ teaspoon salt
   Dash of pepper (optional)
   2 tablespoons olive or avocado oil

1. Choose one set of ingredients from the previous page or above.

2. For the dressing, combine the vitamin C powder, salt, and pepper with the water in a small bowl or glass jar and stir or shake until the vitamin C is dissolved. Add the oil and mix or shake it again.

3. Put the salad greens in a large serving bowl.

4. Pour the dressing over the greens and toss.

5. Add whatever optional additional ingredients you wish and toss the salad again lightly.

6. Serve the salad immediately

Makes one "whole meal" or 2 side dish servings

Grandpa Capraro's Salad

DAY 4, borrow avocado from DAY 3

   2 medium-sized cucumbers
   1 large ripe avocado OR 2 regular or 4 to 6 Italian plum tomatoes
   2 tablespoons vinegar or lemon juice OR ¼ to ½ teaspoon tart-tasting
       unbuffered vitamin C powder plus ½ teaspoon water
   ⅛ teaspoon pepper
   ⅛ teaspoon salt
   2 tablespoons oil

1. Peel and slice the cucumbers and put them in a large serving bowl.

2. Peel and seed the avocado and cut it into cubes if you are using it. Add it to the serving bowl.

3. Slice the tomatoes, if you are using them. Add them to the serving bowl.

4. If you are using the vitamin C, stir it together with the water in a small cup or bowl until it is dissolved.

5. Combine the vitamin C solution, lemon juice, or vinegar with the seasonings and oil. Stir thoroughly.

6. Pour the dressing over the vegetables and toss the salad.

Makes 2 to 4 servings

Bean Salad

This salad can be made a myriad of ways depending on which beans you use. For traditional three bean salad, use one cup each of kidney, garbanzo, and cut green beans – or make this salad with a single kind of bean.

Extra foods

    3 cups of cooked beans, any kind or combination
    ½ to 1½ teaspoons tart-tasting unbuffered vitamin C powder, to taste
    1 teaspoon water
    ⅛ teaspoon salt, to taste
    Dash of pepper (optional)
    2 tablespoons oil
    1½ tablespoons pineapple, white grape, or apple juice concentrate, thawed (optional - use with three bean salad)

1. Stir the beans together in a serving bowl.

2. Mix the vitamin C with the water until it is dissolved. Use the larger amount if you are using the fruit juice.

3. Stir the salt, pepper, oil, and fruit juice into the vitamin C mixture.

4. Pour the dressing over the beans and toss the salad.

5. Serve the salad immediately; the vitamin C may lose its "tang" if it stands too long.

Makes 4 to 6 servings

Any day Meat or Poultry Salad

This salad is great served on a bed of lettuce or spinach or as a sandwich filling.

DAY 1 – pork or goat with jicama or celery and macadamia or pine nut sauce
DAY 2 – turkey with cauliflower or celery and cashew sauce
DAY 3 – chicken or cornish hen with celery and macadamia or pine nut sauce
DAY 4 – rabbit or duck with cucumber, zucchini, or crookneck squash
           and almond sauce

12 to 16 ounces cooked pork, goat, turkey, chicken, rabbit, or duck
    (about 3 cups cubed)
¾ cup diced celery or other chopped raw vegetables, such as jicama, cauliflower,
    cucumber, zucchini, or crookneck squash (optional)
½ cup "Super Smooth Sauce," page 135
⅛ to ¼ teaspoon salt, or to taste
Dash of pepper (optional)

1. Remove the meat or poultry from the bones; remove and discard any skin or fat.

2. Cut the meat or poultry into ½ inch cubes.

3. Dice or chop the vegetable.

4. Stir the meat or poultry and vegetable together in a serving bowl.

5. Stir together the sauce with the salt and pepper in a cup.

6. Add the sauce to the serving bowl, and stir thoroughly to coat the meat and vegetables
   with the sauce.

7. Serve immediately on a bed of salad greens or in sandwiches.

Makes 4 servings

Non-Yeast Breads and Baked Goods

The art of making non-yeast breads and baked goods is one of the most essential skills you must learn when you begin to cook for an allergy diet. Baking with alternative flours is different from baking with wheat. These flours are usually coarser and heavier than wheat and may not always offer the same consistency in each bag of flour. The leavening ingredients we use on allergy diets also demand more attention to mixing technique than do standard corn-containing baking powders. However, allergy baking is NOT DIFFICULT. Once you have mastered the information in the following paragraphs, you can make any type of non-yeast bread, cracker, muffin, cake, cookie, or dessert you desire.

In all baking, measuring your ingredients accurately is of the utmost importance. Therefore, you should invest in a good set of tools for measuring. (See "Sources," page 300, to mail order measuring utensils such as those described in this chapter). Measuring cups for dry ingredients are usually made out of metal or opaque plastic and come in nesting sets of various sizes. If possible, choose a set that has an eighth-cup measure or, to complete your set, get a coffee measure which equals ⅛ cup.

Glass or clear plastic measuring cups with markings on them are for liquid ingredients. Get a cup that has one ounce or ⅛ cup markings. This will make it easy to use the ⅛ cup measurements in this book without having to use measuring spoons in addition to the cup. To read the amount of liquid in a measuring cup, have your eyes down on the level of the cup. Fill the cup until the bottom of the meniscus (the curve that the surface of the liquid makes in the cup) lines up with the measurement you want to use. If you want fewer dirty dishes to wash, you can measure several liquid ingredients in the measuring cup at one time and then mix them together in the cup. For example, if your recipe calls for ½ cup water and ¼ cup oil, fill the cup with water to the ½ cup line. Then add oil until the level of the liquids reaches ¾ cup.

Measuring spoons are used for both liquid and dry ingredients. It is helpful to have a set which includes an ⅛ teaspoon. To measure liquids, fill the spoon with the liquid, making sure that it does not round up over the top of the spoon. To measure dry ingredients, stir up the ingredient with the spoon, dip the spoon in, and level it off with a straight-edged knife. For some of the recipes in this book you may need to measure an amount smaller than your smallest measuring spoon. For example, assume you need to measure ⅛ teaspoon of white stevia extract powder with a ¼ teaspoon. Fill the ¼ teaspoon and level it off with a straight-edged knife. Then use a dinner knife to divide the powder in the spoon in half and push half of it back into the bottle. If you need to measure ¹⁄₁₆ teaspoon, again divide the remaining ⅛ teaspoon and push half of it back into the bottle.

You do not need to sift flour before you measure it for the recipes in this book. Instead, get a large spoon, stir the flour, lightly spoon it into a measuring cup for dry ingredients, and then level it off with a straight-edged knife. Do not tap the cup or pack the flour into it.

Before you begin making non-yeast baked goods, preheat your oven to the temperature specified in the recipe. Oil your baking sheets or oil and flour your pan or muffin cups, using the same flour you are using in the recipe. It is important to do these things first so you do not have to spend time doing them after your dough or batter is mixed.

The procedure for making non-yeast breads follows. It can also be used for muffins, cookies, pancakes, cakes, and other non-yeast baked goods. They are all mixed the same way although some of them are cooked differently.

First, stir the dry ingredients together in a large bowl. Mix the liquid ingredients in another bowl or in the cup you used to measure them. Before the oil and water or other liquids can separate, quickly stir them into the dry ingredients until they are just mixed. It is better to undermix than overmix. If you undermix, the floury spots will probably moisten up in baking. If you overmix, you will "use up" the leavening power of the baking soda and acid ingredient during mixing, rather than having this power act in the oven where the leavening should cause your bread to rise.

As soon as the ingredients are mixed, quickly put the batter into the prepared pan and slide it into the preheated oven. Bake your bread for the shortest time specified in the recipe. Then look at it. Is it beginning to brown? (Some recipes, such as those containing stevia, will not brown much). Is the bread beginning to pull away from the sides of the pans slightly? If you think your bread might be done, stick a toothpick into the center of the loaf. If the toothpick remains dry, the bread is done. If there is moist batter (not dry crumbs) on the toothpick, bake the bread for another five to ten minutes and then test it with a toothpick again.

When the bread is done, remove it from the pan immediately. (Some recipes, such as cake recipes, will tell you to cool your cake in the pan for a short time before removing it). Put the bread on a cooling rack and cool it completely before slicing it.

Handmade Non-Yeast Bread

Non-yeast breads are more fragile than yeast breads. However, if you slice them and toast them until they are crisp, you can use them for a sandwich.

KAMUT (DAY 1)

3 cups kamut flour
1 teaspoon salt
1½ teaspoons baking soda
½ teaspoon unbuffered
   vitamin C powder
⅓ cup oil
1⅔ cups water

BARLEY (DAY 1)

3 cups barley flour
1 teaspoon salt
1½ teaspoons baking soda
½ teaspoon unbuffered
   vitamin C powder
⅜ cup (¼ cup plus 2 tablespoons) oil
2 cups water

MILO (Day 1)

3 cups milo flour
1⅛ cups (1 cup plus 2 tablespoons)
    arrowroot
1 teaspoon salt
1½ teaspoons baking soda
⅜ teaspoon (¼ teaspoon
    plus ⅛ teaspoon) unbuffered
    vitamin C powder
⅜ cup (¼ cup plus 2 tablespoons) oil
1⅜ cups (1¼ cups plus 2
    tablespoons) water
2 extra large eggs

AMARANTH (Day 1)

3⅜ cups (3¼ cups plus 2
    tablespoons) amaranth flour
1⅛ cups (1 cup plus 2 tablespoons)
    arrowroot
1½ teaspoons salt
3 teaspoons baking soda
¾ teaspoon unbuffered vitamin C
    powder
⅜ cup (¼ cup plus 2 tablespoons) oil
1½ cups water

RYE (Day 2)

3 cups rye flour
1 teaspoon salt
1½ teaspoons baking soda
½ teaspoon unbuffered vitamin C
    powder
⅓ cup oil
1½ cups water

TEFF (Day 2)

3 cups teff flour
¾ teaspoon salt
3 teaspoons baking soda
¾ teaspoon unbuffered vitamin C
    powder
⅜ cup (¼ cup plus 2 tablespoons) oil
2¼ cups water

BUCKWHEAT (Day 2)

3 cups roasted buckwheat flour
¾ teaspoon salt
3 teaspoons baking soda
¾ teaspoon unbuffered
    vitamin C powder
⅜ cup (¼ cup plus 2 tablespoons) oil
2 cups water

SPELT (Day 3)

3½ cups whole spelt flour
    OR 4 cups white spelt flour
1 teaspoon salt
2 teaspoons baking soda
½ teaspoon unbuffered
    vitamin C powder
½ cup oil
1¼ cups water

MILLET (Day 3)

2¼ cups millet flour
1⅛ cups tapioca flour
¾ teaspoon salt
1 teaspoon baking soda
¼ teaspoon unbuffered
    vitamin C powder
⅜ cup (¼ cup plus 2 tablespoons) oil
⅝ cup (½ cup
    plus 2 tablespoons) water
2 extra large eggs

MILLET-SQUASH
(Day 3, borrow squash from Day 4)

1½ cups millet flour
1 cup tapioca flour
¾ teaspoon salt
2 teaspoons baking soda
½ teaspoon unbuffered
    vitamin C powder
1¾ cups pureed baked winter squash
¼ cup oil

QUINOA (DAY 3)

2¼ cups quinoa flour
¾ cup tapioca flour
1 teaspoon salt
2 teaspoons baking soda
½ teaspoon unbuffered
    vitamin C powder
¼ cup oil
1½ cups water

RICE (DAY 4, borrow tapioca flour from DAY 3 or arrowroot from DAY 1)

3 cups brown rice flour or white rice
    flour
¾ cup tapioca flour, arrowroot, or
    water chestnut starch
1 teaspoon salt
1 tablespoon guar gum
2 teaspoons baking soda
½ teaspoon unbuffered
    vitamin C powder
¼ cup oil
2½ cups water

1. Choose one set of the above ingredients from the previous page or above.

2. Turn your oven on to 350°F.

3. Rub oil all around the inside of an 8 by 4 inch or 9 by 5 inch loaf pan. Put 1 to 2 tablespoons of flour of the same kind you are using in the recipe in the pan and shake it around until the bottom and all of the sides are coated with flour.

4. Stir together the flour(s), salt, baking soda, vitamin C powder, and guar gum (if used) in a large bowl.

5. Thoroughly mix the oil, water, squash (if used), and eggs (if used) in another bowl or measuring cup.

6. Before the liquid ingredients have time to separate, pour them into the bowl with the dry ingredients.

7. Stir together the liquid and dry ingredients until they are just mixed. DO NOT OVERMIX.

8. Quickly scrape the batter into the prepared pan.

9. Put the bread into the oven and bake it for 45 to 55 minutes, or until it is beginning to brown. Insert a toothpick into the center of the loaf. If it comes out dry, remove the loaf from the oven.

10. Turn the bread out onto a cooling rack and cool it completely before slicing it.

11. If you wish, you can freeze leftover sliced bread. When you want to eat it, toast the slices while still frozen.

12. If you want to make sandwiches with the more fragile varieties of this bread, toast the bread thoroughly using a toaster-oven in which you can lay the slices of bread flat.

Makes one loaf of bread.

Bread Machine
Non-Yeast Bread

You can make non-yeast breads in any bread machine that has a quick bread or cake cycle. However, since on most machines you cannot start the "bake" part of the cycle as soon as the dough is mixed, you have to use baking powder rather than baking soda and vitamin C powder for leavening. Featherweight™ baking powder does not contain corn; however, it contains potato starch, which you should rotate rather than using every day.

KAMUT (DAY 1)

3 cups kamut flour
3 teaspoons baking powder
¾ teaspoon salt
⅓ cup oil
1⅓ cups water

BARLEY (DAY 1)

3 cups barley flour
3 teaspoons baking powder
¾ teaspoon salt
¼ cup oil
1¼ cups water

RYE (DAY 2)

3 cups rye flour
3 teaspoons baking powder
¾ teaspoon salt
2 teaspoons caraway seed (optional)
⅓ cup oil
1¼ cups water

WHOLE SPELT (DAY 3)

3 cups whole grain spelt flour
3 teaspoons baking powder
½ teaspoon salt
¼ cup oil
1¼ cups water

WHITE SPELT (DAY 3)

3 cups white spelt flour
3 teaspoons baking powder
½ teaspoon salt
¼ cup oil
1 cup water

RICE (DAY 4, borrow arrowroot or tapioca from DAY 1 or 3)

1⅓ cups brown rice flour or white
    rice flour
⅓ cup tapioca flour, arrowroot, or
    water chestnut starch
⅓ cup potato flour
2¾ teaspoons guar gum
2¾ teaspoons baking powder
¾ teaspoon salt
1 tablespoon plus 1 teaspoon oil
2 extra large eggs
    (½ cup in total volume)
1⅓ cups water

1. Choose one set of ingredients from the previous page.

2. Put the flour(s), baking powder, salt, and guar gum, if used, in the bread machine.

3. Choose the "Cake" or "Quick bread" cycle from your bread machine's menu. This is a cycle that mixes and then bakes immediately.

4. Press "start" and allow the machine to mix for ½ to 1 minute. Begin timing AFTER the fast mixing starts if your machine mixes slowly at first.

5. Add the oil and allow the machine to mix for 1 minute.

6. Add the water and eggs, if used. (A few bread machines have mix cycles that are longer than the ideal 3 to 4 minutes for non-yeast breads. If the mixing phase of this cycle lasts more than four minutes on your machine, delay adding the water until about two minutes before the end of the mixing time. For instance, if your machine mixes for 6 minutes, instead of adding the water 1½ to 2 minutes after you start the machine, wait until it has been mixing for 4 minutes to add the water).

7. Use a rubber spatula to move flour from the corners of the pans to the center if it does not mix in by itself.

8. If the dough is not evenly distributed in the pan at the end of the mixing time, reach in with a rubber spatula and gently spread the dough so it covers the bottom of the pan fairly evenly. Scrape down the sides of the pan if necessary.

9. Allow the machine to bake. When the cycle is complete, remove the bread pan from the machine. Turn it upside down and shake it to get the loaf of bread out.

10. Cool the bread completely on a cooling rack before slicing it. You can freeze the sliced bread and toast frozen slices when you want to eat them if desired.

Makes one loaf of bread.

Fruited Non-Yeast Bread

KAMUT-BANANA (Day 1, borrow cloves from Day 2 or cinnamon from Day 3)

1¾ cups kamut flour
½ teaspoon salt
2 teaspoons baking soda
½ teaspoon unbuffered
    vitamin C powder
½ teaspoon cloves
    OR 1 teaspoon cinnamon
½ cup nuts (optional)
1¾ cups thoroughly mashed
    ripe bananas
¼ cup oil

BARLEY-BANANA (Day 1, borrow cloves from Day 2 or cinnamon from Day 3)

2½ cups barley flour
½ teaspoon salt
2 teaspoons baking soda
½ teaspoon unbuffered
    vitamin C powder
½ teaspoon cloves
    OR 1 teaspoon cinnamon
½ cup nuts (optional)
1¾ cups thoroughly mashed
    ripe bananas
¼ cup oil

AMARANTH-BANANA (Day 1, borrow cloves from Day 2)

2 cups amaranth flour
½ cup arrowroot
2 teaspoons baking soda
½ teaspoon unbuffered vitamin C
    powder
½ teaspoon ground cloves (optional)
½ cup chopped nuts (optional)
1¾ cups thoroughly mashed ripe
    bananas
¼ cup oil

MILO-BANANA (Day 1, borrow cloves from Day 2 or cinnamon from Day 3)

1½ cups milo flour
1 cup arrowroot
¾ teaspoon salt
2 teaspoons baking soda
½ teaspoon unbuffered vitamin C
    powder
¾ teaspoon cloves OR 2 teaspoons
    cinnamon
¼ teaspoon ginger
½ cup nuts (optional)
1¾ cups thoroughly mashed ripe
    bananas
¼ cup oil

MILLET-BANANA (Day 3, borrow bananas from Day 1)

1½ cups millet flour
1 cup tapioca flour
½ teaspoon salt
2 teaspoons baking soda
½ teaspoon unbuffered vitamin C powder
1 teaspoon cinnamon
½ cup chopped nuts (optional)
1¾ cups thoroughly mashed ripe bananas
¼ cup oil

QUINOA-APPLE (DAY 3)

    2 cups quinoa flour
    ½ cup tapioca flour
    ¼ teaspoon salt
    2 teaspoons baking soda
    ½ teaspoon unbuffered vitamin C powder
    2 teaspoons cinnamon
    1 cup unsweetened applesauce
    ¾ cup apple juice concentrate, thawed
    ¼ cup oil

SPELT-BANANA (DAY 3, borrow bananas from DAY 1)

    3 cups spelt flour
    2 teaspoons baking soda
    ½ teaspoon unbuffered vitamin C powder
    1 teaspoon cinnamon (optional)
    ½ cup chopped nuts (optional)
    1¾ cups thoroughly mashed ripe bananas
    ¼ cup oil

1. Choose one set of ingredients on the previous page or above.

2. Turn your oven on to 350°F.

3. Rub oil all around the inside of an 8 by 4 inch or 9 by 5 inch loaf pan. Put 1 to 2 tablespoons of flour of the same kind you are using in the recipe in the pan and shake it around until the bottom and all of the sides are coated with flour.

4. Stir together the flour(s), salt, baking soda, vitamin C powder, and spices in a large bowl.

5. Mash or puree and measure the bananas, if you are using them.

6. Thoroughly mix the oil, fruit juice (if used), and bananas or applesauce in another bowl or measuring cup.

7. Before the liquid ingredients have time to separate, pour them into the bowl with the dry ingredients.

8. Stir together the liquid and dry ingredients until they are just mixed. DO NOT OVERMIX.

9. Quickly scrape the batter into the prepared pan.

10. Put the bread into the oven and bake it for 50 to 60 minutes or until it is brown. Insert a toothpick into the center of the loaf. If it comes out dry, remove the loaf from the oven.

11. Cool the bread in the pan for ten minutes. Then turn the bread out onto a cooling rack and cool it completely before slicing it.

11. If you wish, you can freeze leftover sliced bread. When you want to eat it, toast the slices while still frozen.

Makes one loaf of bread.

Fruited Bread Machine Non-Yeast Bread

BARLEY-BANANA (Day 1, borrow allspice and cloves from **Day 2,** cinnamon from **Day 3,** and dates from day 4)

> 2 cups barley flour
> ½ cup date sugar
> 3 teaspoons baking powder
> 1½ teaspoons cinnamon
> ¼ teaspoon cloves
> ¼ teaspoon allspice
> ¼ cup oil
> 2¼ cups pureed or thoroughly mashed bananas

QUINOA-APPLE (Day 3, borrow optional raisins from day 2)

> 2½ cups quinoa flour
> ¾ cup tapioca flour
> 3 teaspoons baking powder
> ½ teaspoon baking soda
> 2 teaspoons cinnamon
> ¼ cup oil
> ¾ cup unsweetened apple juice concentrate, thawed
> ¾ cup unsweetened applesauce
> ½ cup raisins (optional)

SPELT-APPLE (Day 3, borrow optional raisins from day 2)

> 2⅜ cups white spelt flour
> 1 teaspoon baking powder
> ½ teaspoon baking soda
> ½ teaspoon salt
> 1 teaspoon cinnamon
> ¼ cup oil
> ½ cup unsweetened apple juice concentrate, thawed
> ¾ cup unsweetened applesauce
> ½ cup raisins (optional)

RICE-BANANA (Day 4, borrow bananas and arrowroot from **Day 1,** allspice and cloves from **Day 2,** and tapioca and cinnamon from **Day 3)**

> 2¼ cups brown rice flour
> ½ cup tapioca flour or arrowroot
> ½ cup date sugar
> 3 teaspoons baking powder
> 1½ teaspoons cinnamon
> ¼ teaspoon cloves
> ¼ teaspoon allspice
> ¼ cup oil
> 2¼ cups pureed or thoroughly mashed bananas

1. Choose one set of ingredients from above.

2. Mash or puree and measure the bananas, if you are using them.

3. Put the flour(s), baking powder, baking soda, salt, and spices, if used, in the bread machine.

4. Choose the "Cake" or "Quick bread" cycle from your bread machine's menu. This is a cycle that mixes and then bakes immediately.

5. Press "start" and allow the machine to mix for ½ to 1 minute. Begin timing AFTER the fast mixing starts if your machine mixes slowly at first.

6. Add the oil and allow the machine to mix for 1 minute.

7. Add the fruit juice and/or fruit. (A few bread machines have mix cycles that are longer than the ideal 3 to 4 minutes for non-yeast breads. If the mixing phase of this

cycle lasts more than four minutes on your machine, delay adding the liquids until about two minutes before the end of the mixing time. For instance, if your machine mixes for 6 minutes, instead of adding the liquids 1½ to 2 minutes after you start the machine, wait until it has been mixing for 4 minutes to add the liquids).

8. Use a rubber spatula to move flour from the corners of the pans to the center if it does not mix in by itself.

9. Add the optional raisins after the fruit and/or juice is completely mixed in.

10. If the dough is not evenly distributed in the pan at the end of the mixing time, reach in with a rubber spatula and gently spread the dough so it covers the bottom of the pan fairly evenly. Scrape down the sides of the pan if necessary.

11. Allow the machine to bake. When the cycle is complete, remove the bread pan from the machine. Turn it upside down and shake it to get the loaf of bread out.

12. Cool the bread completely on a cooling rack before slicing it. You can freeze the sliced bread and toast frozen slices when you want to eat them.

Makes one loaf of bread.

Muffins

These muffins are great for breakfast or snacks. For a special treat, stir blueberries into the batter before baking the muffins.

KAMUT (DAY 1)

2 cups kamut flour
¼ teaspoon salt
1 teaspoon baking soda
⅛ teaspoon unbuffered vitamin C
  powder
1½ cups pineapple juice concentrate,
  thawed, or water
¼ cup oil

BARLEY (DAY 1)

2 cups barley flour
¼ teaspoon salt
1 teaspoon baking soda
¼ teaspoon unbuffered vitamin C
  powder
1¼ cups water
¼ cup oil

AMARANTH (DAY 1,
borrow cloves from DAY 2)

1¾ cups amaranth flour
½ cup arrowroot
2 teaspoons baking soda
½ teaspoon unbuffered vitamin C
  powder
¼ teaspoon white stevia powde (optional,
  but don't use with fruit juice)
¼ teaspoon ground cloves (optional)
1 cup water OR pineapple juice
  concentrate, thawed
¼ cup oil

MILO-SWEET POTATO (DAY 1)

⅔ cup sweet potato or white sweet
  potato cut into ¼ to ½ inch cubes,
  or about 3 ounces of potato
¾ cup water plus additional water
2 cups milo flour
¼ teaspoon salt
1 teaspoon baking soda
¼ teaspoon unbuffered vitamin C
  powder
⅓ cup oil

MILO (DAY 1)

2½ cups milo flour
¼ teaspoon salt
1 teaspoon baking soda
¼ teaspoon unbuffered vitamin C
    powder
1¼ cups water OR 1 cup water PLUS
    1 extra large egg
⅓ cup oil

TEFF (DAY 2)

2 cups teff flour
¼ teaspoon salt
2 teaspoon baking soda
½ teaspoon unbuffered vitamin C
    powder
1½ cups water
¼ cup oil

SPELT (DAY 3)

2½ cups whole spelt flour or 2¾ cups
    white spelt flour
¼ teaspoon salt
1½ teaspoons baking soda
Unbuffered vitamin C powder – ⅜
    teaspoon if water is used OR ¼
    teaspoon if apple juice is used
1 cup water OR apple juice
    concentrate, thawed
⅓ cup oil

QUINOA (DAY 3)

1½ cups quinoa flour
½ cup tapioca flour
2 teaspoons baking soda
½ teaspoon unbuffered vitamin C
    powder
¼ teaspoon white stevia powder
    (optional, but it improves the
    flavor)
1½ teaspoons cinnamon (optional)
1 cup water
¼ cup oil

RYE (DAY 2)

2 cups rye flour or white rye flour
¼ teaspoon salt
¾ teaspoon baking soda
Unbuffered vitamin C powder – ¼
    teaspoon if water is used OR ⅛
    teaspoon if grape juice is used
1 cup water OR white grape juice
⅓ cup oil

BUCKWHEAT (DAY 2)

2 cups buckwheat flour (brown)
¼ teaspoon salt
2 teaspoon baking soda
½ teaspoon unbuffered vitamin C
    powder
1½ cups water
¼ cup oil

MILLET (DAY 3)

1½ cups millet flour
¾ cup tapioca flour
¼ teaspoon salt
¾ teaspoon baking soda
⅛ teaspoon unbuffered vitamin C
    powder
1 teaspoon cinnamon
¾ cup water OR apple juice
    concentrate - OR – ½ cup water
    OR apple juice concentrate PLUS
    1 extra large egg
¼ cup oil

RICE (DAY 4)

3 cups brown or white rice flour
½ teaspoon salt
2 teaspoons baking soda
½ teaspoon unbuffered vitamin C
    powder
1½ cups water OR 1¼ cups water
    PLUS 1 extra large egg
¼ cup oil

OAT (DAY 4)

2 cups oat flour
¼ teaspoon salt
1 teaspoon baking soda
¼ teaspoon unbuffered vitamin C
  powder
1 cup water
¼ cup oil

CHESTNUT (DAY 4)

1½ cups chestnut flour
1¼ cups water chestnut flour
1 teaspoon baking soda
¼ teaspoon unbuffered vitamin C
  powder
1 cup water
¼ cup oil

1. Choose one set of ingredients, from the previous page or above.

2. If you are making the milo-sweet potato muffins, peel the sweet potato and cut it into cubes. Put it in a saucepan with ¾ cup water. Bring it to a boil, reduce the heat, and simmer for 15 minutes. Puree the sweet potato and water with a blender, food processor, or hand blender. Measure the puree and add enough water to bring the volume up to 1¼ cups.

3. Turn on your oven to the temperature listed below for the type of muffins you are making:

   Kamut – 350°F
   Barley – 400°F
   Milo – 400°F
   Milo-sweet potato – 400°F
   Amaranth – 375°F
   Rye – 400°F
   Teff – 400°F
   Buckwheat – 400°F
   Spelt – 350°F
   Millet – 400°F
   Quinoa – 375°F
   Oat – 400°F
   Rice – 400°F
   Chestnut – 400°F

4. Rub oil all around the inside of 12 to 15 cups of a muffin pan. Put a little flour of the same kind you are using in the recipe in each cup of the pan and shake it around until the bottoms and sides of each cup are coated with flour – or, if you prefer, you can line the cups with paper liners. (The liners are especially nice for the more crumbly non-gluten grain and non-grain muffins).

5. OPTIONAL BLUEBERRY MUFFIN VARIATION: If you wish to make blueberry muffins, measure 1 cup of fresh or unthawed frozen blueberries. Rinse them in a strainer and set them aside to drain.

6. Stir together the flour(s), salt, baking soda, vitamin C powder, spices (if used), and stevia (if used) in a large bowl.

7. Thoroughly mix the oil, water, sweet potato puree, fruit juice, and eggs (if used) in another bowl or measuring cup.

8. Before the liquid ingredients have time to separate, pour them into the bowl with the dry ingredients.

9. Stir together the liquid and dry ingredients until they are just mixed. DO NOT OVERMIX.

10. OPTIONAL BLUEBERRY MUFFIN VARIATION: If you are making blueberry muffins, quickly fold the blueberries into the batter.

11. Quickly fill the prepared cups ⅔ to ¾ full with the batter.

12. Put the muffins into the oven and bake them for the shortest time listed below for the type of muffins you are making:

> Kamut – 20 to 25 minutes
> Barley – 30 to 35 minutes
> Milo – 15 to 20 minutes
> Milo-sweet potato – 15 to 20 minutes
> Amaranth – 20 to 25 minutes
> Rye – 18 to 22 minutes
> Teff – 20 to 25 minutes
> Buckwheat – 20 to 25 minutes
> Spelt – 20 to 25 minutes
> Millet – 15 to 20 minutes
> Quinoa – 20 to 25 minutes
> Oat – 30 to 35 minutes
> Rice – 20 to 25 minutes
> Chestnut – 20 to 25 minutes

13. Look at the muffins when the time is up. If they are lightly browned, stick a toothpick in the largest muffin. If it comes out dry, remove them from the oven.

14. If the muffins are not brown yet or if the toothpick comes out with batter (not dry crumbs) on it, bake them for a few more minutes. Then test them again.

15. When they muffins are done, turn them out on to a wire cooling rack and cool them completely.

16. Keep in mind that some of these muffins, especially those made with non-gluten grains, will be heavy or crumbly. However, if flours made from non-gluten grains are the best-tasting muffin flours you can eat, I am sure you will agree that muffins with a less-than-perfect texture are much better than no muffins at all.

Makes 10 to 15 muffins.

Fruited Muffins

Some flours are more challenging to make into muffins than others. Milo and chestnut muffins are especially crumbly. If you cannot tolerate using eggs as a binder in them as in the above recipe, you can use fruit to help them stay together instead. Quinoa can be "challenging" as far as taste goes, so fruit is a welcome addition to quinoa muffins too.

MILO-PINEAPPLE (Day 1)

2 cups milo flour
¼ teaspoon salt
1 teaspoon baking soda
¼ teaspoon unbuffered vitamin C powder
½ cup pineapple canned in its own juice or ½ cup fresh pineapple with juice to cover
½ cup pineapple juice concentrate, thawed
⅓ cup oil

QUINOA-APPLE (Day 3)

1¾ cups quinoa flour
¼ cup tapioca flour
2 teaspoons baking soda
½ teaspoon unbuffered vitamin C powder
1½ teaspoons cinnamon
1 cup unsweetened applesauce
¼ cup apple juice concentrate, thawed
¼ cup oil

CHESTNUT-PEACH (Day 4)

2¼ cups chestnut flour
¼ teaspoon salt
1 teaspoon baking soda
½ teaspoon unbuffered vitamin C powder
¼ teaspoon ground nutmeg (optional)
1¾ cups pureed peaches
¼ cup oil

1. Choose one set of ingredients from above.

2. Turn on your oven to 400°F for the milo muffins or to 375°F for the quinoa or chestnut muffins.

3. Rub oil all around the inside of 12 to 15 cups of a muffin pan. Put a little flour of the same kind you are using in the recipe in each cup of the pan and shake it around until the bottoms and sides of each cup are coated with flour – or, if you prefer, you can line the cups with paper liners. The liners are especially good for holding the milo and chestnut muffins together if you are going to store them in the freezer.

4. Puree the pineapple with its juice or the peaches with a blender, hand blender, or food processor. A hand blender is especially convenient because you can puree the fruit right in the measuring cup.

5. Stir together the flour(s), salt, baking soda, vitamin C powder, and spice (if used) in a large bowl.

6. Thoroughly mix the pureed fruit, fruit juice (if used), and oil in another bowl or measuring cup.

7. Before the liquid ingredients have time to separate, pour them into the bowl with the dry ingredients.

8. Stir together the liquid and dry ingredients until they are just mixed. DO NOT OVERMIX.

9. Quickly fill the prepared cups about ¾ full of batter.

10. Put the muffins into the oven and bake them for the shortest time listed below for the type of muffins you are making:

> Milo-pineapple – 15 to 20 minutes
> Quinoa-apple – 20 to 25 minutes
> Chestnut-peach – 18 to 23 minutes

11. Look at the muffins when the time is up. If they are lightly browned, stick a toothpick in the largest muffin. If it comes out dry, remove them from the oven.

12. If the muffins are not brown yet or if the toothpick comes out with batter (not dry crumbs) on it, bake them for a few more minutes. Then test them again.

13. When they muffins are done, put them on a wire cooling rack and cool them completely.

Makes 10 to 15 muffins.

Biscuits

KAMUT (DAY 1)

> 2 cups kamut flour
> 1 teaspoon baking soda
> ¼ teaspoon unbuffered vitamin C powder
> ½ teaspoon salt
> ¼ cup oil
> ½ cup water

BARLEY (Day l)

> 2 cups barley flour
> 1 teaspoon baking soda
> ¼ teaspoon unbuffered vitamin C powder
> ½ teaspoon salt
> ⅜ cup (¼ cup plus 2 tablespoons) oil
> ½ cup water

RYE (Day 2)

  2 cups rye flour
  1 teaspoon baking soda
  ¼ teaspoon unbuffered vitamin C
      powder
  ½ teaspoon salt
  ¼ cup oil
  ½ cup water

SPELT (Day 3)

  2 cups whole spelt flour or white
      spelt flour
  1 teaspoon baking soda
  ¼ teaspoon unbuffered vitamin C
      powder
  ½ teaspoon salt
  ¼ cup oil
  ½ cup water

OAT (Day 4)

  2 cups oat flour
  1 teaspoon baking soda
  ¼ teaspoon unbuffered vitamin C powder
  ½ teaspoon salt
  ¼ cup oil
  ½ cup water

1. Choose one set of ingredients from above or from the previous page.

2. Turn your oven on to 400°F.

3. Stir together the flour, baking soda, vitamin C powder, and salt in a large bowl.

4. Add the oil to the flour and stir it in. Use a pastry cutter to blend the oil into the flour until the mixture forms coarse crumbs.

5. Stir the water into the flour-oil mixture.

6. Use your hands to form the mixture into a dough.

7. Sprinkle a bread board with one to two tablespoons of the same kind of flour you used in the biscuits.

8. Transfer the dough to the bread board and knead it about 10 to 15 times.

9. Pat or roll the dough to about ½ inch thickness on the board.

10. Dip a glass or round cookie cutter into the flour. Then use it to cut the dough into biscuits.

11. Use a spatula to transfer the biscuits to an ungreased baking sheet.

12. Collect any dough scraps and pat or roll them into a piece of dough ½ inch thick; cut more biscuits as above and transfer them to the baking sheet.

13. Bake the biscuits for 20 to 25 minutes or until they are lightly browned.

Makes 7 to 10 biscuits.

Crackers

KAMUT (Day 1)

1½ cups kamut flour
½ teaspoon baking soda
¼ teaspoon unbuffered vitamin C
    powder
¼ teaspoon salt
¼ cup oil
½ cup water

MILO (Day 1)

1¼ cups milo flour
¾ cup arrowroot
1 teaspoon baking soda
¼ teaspoon unbuffered vitamin C
    powder
½ teaspoon salt
¼ cup oil
½ cup water

RYE (Day 2)

3 cups rye flour
1½ teaspoons baking soda
⅜ teaspoon unbuffered vitamin C
    powder
¾ teaspoon salt
1 teaspoon caraway seeds (optional)
2 teaspoons onion powder (optional)
¾ cup water
⅜ cup oil (¼ cup plus 2 tablespoons)

BUCKWHEAT (Day 2)

2 cups buckwheat flour
1 teaspoon baking soda
¼ teaspoon unbuffered vitamin C
    powder
½ teaspoon salt
¾ cup water
¼ cup oil

BARLEY (Day 1)

3 cups barley flour
1½ teaspoons baking soda
⅜ teaspoon unbuffered vitamin C
    powder
¾ teaspoon salt
⅔ cup water
⅜ cup oil (¼ cup plus 2 tablespoons)

AMARANTH (Day 1)

2 cups amaranth flour
⅔ cup arrowroot
1¼ teaspoons baking soda
⅜ teaspoon unbuffered vitamin C
    powder
¾ teaspoon salt
½ cup water
⅓ cup oil

TEFF (Day 2)

2 cups teff flour
1 teaspoon baking soda
¼ teaspoon unbuffered vitamin C
    powder
½ teaspoon salt
½ cup water
¼ cup oil

SPELT (Day 3)

2 cups whole-grain spelt flour
    OR white spelt flour
½ teaspoon salt
½ teaspoon baking soda
¼ teaspoon unbuffered vitamin C
    powder
¼ cup oil
½ cup water

QUINOA-SESAME (DAY 3)

2 cups quinoa flour
⅔ cup tapioca flour
3 tablespoons sesame seeds
1¼ teaspoons baking soda
⅜ teaspoon unbuffered vitamin C
    powder
¾ teaspoon salt
¾ cup plus 1 tablespoon water
⅓ cup oil

CHESTNUT (DAY 4)

2½ cups chestnut flour
1 cup water chestnut flour
½ teaspoon baking soda
¼ teaspoon unbuffered vitamin C
    powder
¼ teaspoon salt
¾ cup water
¼ cup oil

CASSAVA MEAL (DAY 3)

– Note special instructions below for forming the crackers

2 cups cassava meal
½ teaspoon baking soda
¼ teaspoon unbuffered vitamin C
    powder
¼ teaspoon salt
¾ cup water
¼ cup oil

QUINOA-APPLE (DAY 3)

2 cups quinoa flour
⅔ cup tapioca flour
1¼ teaspoons baking soda
¼ teaspoon unbuffered vitamin C
    powder
¾ cup plus 1 tablespoon apple juice
    concentrate, thawed
⅓ cup oil

RICE (DAY 4,
borrow arrowroot from DAY 1)

1 cup brown rice flour OR white rice
    flour
1 cup arrowroot or water chestnut
    starch
1 teaspoon baking soda
¼ teaspoon unbuffered vitamin C
    powder
½ teaspoon salt
½ cup water with arrowroot
    OR ⅝ cup with water chestnut
¼ cup oil

OAT (DAY 4)

– Note special mixing instructions below

4 cups quick oats, uncooked
½ teaspoon salt
⅓ cup oil
⅔ cup water

1. Choose one set of ingredients from the previous page or above.

2. Turn your oven on to 375°F if you are making the amaranth, barley, rye, cassava meal, or chestnut crackers. Turn it onto 350°F for all of the other kinds of crackers.

3. Lightly oil two baking sheets by putting a little oil on a paper towel and rubbing the baking sheets with it. (For the cassava meal crackers, oil a 12-inch by 15-inch pan instead of baking sheets).

4. For oat crackers, instead of following steps 5 through 7, stir the oats and salt together. Add the oil and mix it into the dry ingredients thoroughly. Stir in the water, then mix and knead the dough with your hands until it sticks together. Proceed as in step 9.

5. In a large bowl, mix together the flour(s), onion powder, caraway seeds, or sesame seeds (if called for), baking soda, vitamin C powder, and salt.

6. Stir the oil into the water or juice in a separate bowl or cup.

7. Pour the liquid ingredients into the flour mixture and stir; then mix the dough with your hands. If necessary, add 1 to 2 tablespoons additional water to help the dough stick together. (Do not add additional water to the cassava meal crackers; this dough is really a crumb collection rather than dough).

8. If you are making cassava meal crackers, do not follow steps 9 through 11. Instead, after mixing the ingredients, press the crumbly mixture firmly into a 12-inch by 15-inch pan. The crumb layer will be between ⅛ and ¼ inch thick. "Cut" the crumbs into 1½ inch squares using a knife.

9. For all the other crackers, divide the dough in half; put each half on one of the prepared baking sheets.

10. Lightly rub your rolling pin with oil. Roll the cracker dough out to about ⅛ inch thickness. The more fragile crackers, such as milo, chestnut, and rice, should be rolled thicker; spelt crackers can be rolled as thin as 1/16 inch if you wish.

11. Cut the dough into 1½ inch squares. If you wish, you may prick the spelt crackers with a fork. Sprinkle the crackers lightly with salt.

12. Bake the crackers for:
    Kamut: 13 to 17 minutes
    Barley: 15 to 20 minutes
    Milo: 20 to 25 minutes
    Amaranth: 15 to 20 minutes
    Rye: 15 to 20 minutes
    Teff: 15 to 20 minutes
    Buckwheat: 15 to 20 minutes
    Spelt: 10 to 15 minutes
    Quinoa-sesame: 15 to 25 minutes
    Quinoa-apple: 10 to 15 minutes
    Cassava meal: 35 to 40 minutes
    Oat: 20 to 25 minutes
    Rice: 18 to 22 minutes
    Chestnut: 8 to 12 minutes

13. Watch the crackers closely as the baking time nears completion. If the crackers on the edges of the sheets brown before the baking time is up, remove them from the baking sheet and continue to bake the rest of the crackers.

14. Use a spatula to remove the crackers from the baking sheets when they begin to brown.

15. Put the crackers on a paper towel to cool.

Makes 3 to 5 dozen crackers.

Non-Yeast
Sandwich Rolls

VARIATION #1

1. Choose one set of ingredients from the "Handmade Non-Yeast Bread" recipe, page 151.

2. Turn your oven on to 350°F.

3. Oil and flour, as in step 3 of the bread recipe, six to ten cups of a "Texas size" muffin tin or six to ten large glass custard cups.

4. Mix the batter as directed in steps 4 to 7 of the bread recipe.

5. Quickly fill the prepared cups ½ to ⅔ full with the batter.

6. Put the rolls into the oven and bake them for 30 to 40 minutes. When they are lightly browned, stick a toothpick in the largest roll. If it comes out dry, remove them from the oven. If there is still batter (not dry crumbs) clinging to the toothpick, bake the rolls for five more minutes and check them again.

7. When the rolls are done, put them on a wire cooling rack and cool them completely.

8. Slice them horizontally with a serrated knife. Toast them until crisp and use them to make sandwiches.

Makes six to ten rolls.

VARIATION #2

1. Chose one set of ingredients from the "Biscuits" recipe, page 164.

2. Turn your oven on to 400°F.

3. Mix and roll or pat the biscuit dough as in steps 3 to 9 of the biscuit recipe.

4. Cut the biscuits with a mug or large round cookie cutter as in step 10 of the biscuit recipe.

5. Use a spatula to transfer them to an ungreased baking sheet.

6. Bake them for 20 to 25 minutes, or until lightly browned.

7. Turn them out on to a wire cooling rack and cool them completely.

8. Slice them horizontally with a serrated knife. Toast them until crisp and use them to make sandwiches.

Makes four to five rolls.

Tortillas

If you will be making many tortillas and can tolerate teflon coatings, an electric tortilla maker will save you a lot of effort. Also, some of the very fragile tortillas, such as the rice, milo-arrowroot, and "Special Foods" tuber flour tortillas below, can be made using an electric tortilla maker but are quite difficult to roll out and cook in a pan. Large cooking stores often sell electric tortilla makers, or to order one see "Sources," page 300.

KAMUT (Day 1)

4 cups kamut flour
1 teaspoon salt
1⅝ cups (1½ cups
    plus 2 tablespoons) water

BARLEY (Day 1)

4 cups barley flour
1 teaspoon salt
1⅛ cups (1 cup plus 2 tablespoons)
    water

MILO-ARROWROOT (Day 1)

1¼ cups milo flour
1 cup arrowroot
½ teaspoon salt
¾ cup water

AMARANTH (Day 1)

4½ cups amaranth flour
1 teaspoon salt
1½ cups water

WHITE SWEET POTATO (Day 1)

2 cups white sweet potato flour (see
    "Sources," page 298)
½ teaspoon salt
1 cup water

RYE (Day 2)

4 cups rye flour
1 teaspoon salt
1½ cups water

TEFF (Day 2)

4 cups teff flour
1 teaspoon salt
1½ cups water

BUCKWHEAT (Day 2)

4 cups buckwheat flour
1 teaspoon salt
1¾ cups water

YAM-WATER CHESTNUT (Day 2, borrow water chestnut from Day 4)

1 cup true yam flour (see "Sources",
    page 298)
1 cup water chestnut flour
½ teaspoon salt
1½ cups very hot water

WHOLE-GRAIN SPELT (Day 3)

4 cups spelt flour
1 teaspoon salt
1¼ cups water

WHITE SPELT (Day 3)

3⅓ cups white spelt flour
¾ teaspoon salt
⅓ cup oil
½ cup water

QUINOA (Day 3)

4 cups quinoa flour
1 teaspoon salt
1½ cups water

CASSAVA (DAY 3)

2½ cups cassava flour (see "Sources," page 298)
¾ teaspoon salt
1 cup water

RICE (DAY 4)

4 cups brown rice or white rice flour
1 teaspoon salt
2 tablespoons oil
2 cups water

MALANGA-ARROWROOT (DAY 4, borrow arrowroot from DAY 1)

2 cups malanga flour (see "Sources," page 298)
2 cups arrowroot
¾ teaspoon salt
1⅓ cups very hot water

OAT (DAY 4)

3 cups oat flour
1 cup quick-cooking oats
1 teaspoon salt
1¼ cups water

CHESTNUT (DAY 4)

1 cup chestnut flour
1 cup water chestnut flour
¼ teaspoon salt
¾ cup very hot water

GARBANZO (EXTRA FOODS)

4 cups garbanzo flour
1 teaspoon salt
1 cup water

1. Choose one set of ingredients on the previous page or above.

2. If you are using an electric tortilla maker, begin heating it.

3. Combine the flour(s), oats (if used) and salt in a bowl. Stir in the water and oil (if called for). Mix the dough with a spoon and then knead it with your hands, adding an extra 1 to 2 tablespoons of water if needed, to form a dough that has the consistency of Play-doh.™ Tortillas made with "Special Foods" flours are especially unpredictable; you will probably have to add a different amount of water with each different batch of flour.

4. If you do not have an electric tortilla maker, begin heating a heavy frying pan over medium heat.

5. Divide the dough into balls about the size of a small plum, or larger if you want large tortillas.

6. To make tortillas by hand, roll each ball out on a well floured baking sheet to about ⅛ inch thickness.

7. Use a spatula to transfer the tortillas to the pan one at a time.

8. Cook until the tortilla begins to brown on the bottom (about 3 minutes); then turn it and cook the other side for another 3 minutes or until it is also beginning to brown.

9. To make tortillas with an electric tortilla maker, put each ball of dough into the press. Close it quickly and firmly IN ONE MOTION; then immediately release the pressure (but leave the iron closed) and allow the tortilla to cook for 1 to 2 minutes, or until it begins to brown. Turn the tortilla, lightly close the press, and cook the other side briefly for uniform browning.

NOTE ON USING AN ELECTRIC TORTILLA MAKER: If you press a tortilla and then decide you want it thinner and try to press it some more, it will break up into small pieces. However, once you have made one or two tortillas, you will know just how much pressure to use to produce a tortilla the size you want.

10. Cool the tortillas on paper towels or dish cloths.

11. Serve the more flexible tortillas rolled with any filling you desire. Serve the more fragile tortillas flat.

12. Keep in mind that some of these tortillas, especially those made with the more unusual flours, may be fragile. However, they taste good and are better than no tortillas at all.

Makes 10 to 15 tortillas

Pancakes

Pancakes are great as flatbreads and for making sandwiches. They are much less labor-intensive to make than tortillas.

KAMUT (DAY 1)

2 cups kamut flour
1 teaspoon baking soda
½ teaspoon unbuffered vitamin C powder
½ teaspoon salt
2 tablespoons oil
2¼ cups water

BARLEY (DAY 1)

2 cups barley flour
1 teaspoon baking soda
½ teaspoon unbuffered vitamin C powder
½ teaspoon salt
3 tablespoons oil
2¾ cups water initially plus an additional ¼ cup during cooking

MILO (DAY 1)

2 cups milo flour
1 cup arrowroot
1 teaspoon baking soda
½ teaspoon unbuffered vitamin C powder
½ teaspoon salt
¼ cup oil
1¾ cups water

AMARANTH (DAY 1, borrow cloves from DAY 2)

1½ cups amaranth flour
½ cup arrowroot
1 teaspoon baking soda
¼ teaspoon unbuffered vitamin C powder
1 teaspoon ground cloves (optional)
1½ cups water OR 1¼ cups water plus ¼ cup pineapple juice concentrate, thawed
2 tablespoons oil

RYE (Day 2)

2 cups rye flour
1 teaspoon baking soda
½ teaspoon unbuffered vitamin C
    powder
3 tablespoons oil
2¼ cups water or unsweetened white
    grape juice

BUCKWHEAT (Day 2)

2 cups buckwheat flour
1 teaspoon baking soda
½ teaspoon unbuffered vitamin C
    powder
½ teaspoon salt
2 tablespoons oil
2½ cups water

MILLET (Day 3)

2 cups millet flour
1½ cups tapioca flour
1 teaspoon baking soda
½ teaspoon unbuffered vitamin C
    powder
¼ teaspoon salt
¼ cup oil
1¾ cups water

TEFF (Day 2)

2 cups teff flour
1 teaspoon baking soda
½ teaspoon unbuffered vitamin C
    powder
½ teaspoon salt
2 tablespoons oil
2 cups water

SPELT (Day 3)

2 cups whole-grain spelt flour OR
    2⅛ cups (2 cups plus
    2 tablespoons) white spelt flour
1½ teaspoons baking soda
½ teaspoon unbuffered vitamin C
    powder
½ teaspoon salt
3 tablespoons oil
2 cups water OR 1¾ cups water plus
    ¼ cup thawed apple juice
    concentrate

QUINOA (Day 3)

1½ cups quinoa flour
½ cup tapioca flour
1 teaspoon baking soda
½ teaspoon unbuffered vitamin C
    powder
1½ teaspoons cinnamon
3 tablespoons oil
2 cups water OR 1½ cups water plus
    ½ cup apple juice concentrate,
    thawed

10. Close the iron and cook the waffles for about 15 minutes. Do not peek into the iron until the waffles should be done and the iron is no longer steaming, or you may split your waffles down the middle.

11. Remove the waffles from the iron when they are lightly browned.

12. Reheat your waffle iron until the light goes off before cooking more waffles.

13. Process the batter again for a few seconds before putting it into the iron.

14. If you do not eat your waffles immediately, cool them on a wire rack. These waffles freeze well and are good reheated in the toaster.

Makes 8 4-inch square waffles

Waffles

Waffles are not just for breakfast. Top them with nut butters or meat for a main dish sandwich. All of these waffles are made with "sturdy" flours for ease in removing them from the iron. For gluten-free waffles, see "Nut or Seed Waffles," above.

KAMUT (DAY 1)

2¼ cups kamut flour
1 teaspoon baking soda
¼ teaspoon unbuffered vitamin C powder with water as the only liquid OR ⅛ teaspoon if fruit juice is also used
½ teaspoon salt
¼ cup oil
2¼ cups water OR 2 cups water plus ¼ cup pineapple juice concentrate, thawed

RYE (DAY 2)

2¼ cups rye flour
1 teaspoon baking soda
¼ teaspoon unbuffered vitamin C powder with water as the only liquid OR ⅛ teaspoon if fruit juice is also used
½ teaspoon salt
¼ cup oil
2 cups water OR 1 cup water plus 1 cup unsweetened white grape juice

BARLEY (DAY 1)

2 cups barley flour
2 teaspoons baking soda
¾ teaspoon unbuffered vitamin C powder
½ teaspoon salt
2 tablespoons oil
2½ cups water

TEFF (DAY 2)

2½ cups teff flour
1 teaspoon baking soda
¼ teaspoon unbuffered vitamin C powder
½ teaspoon salt
¼ cup oil
1¾ cups water

BUCKWHEAT (DAY 2, borrow tapioca from DAY 3)

2 cups buckwheat flour
½ cup tapioca flour
1 teaspoon baking soda
¼ teaspoon unbuffered vitamin C powder
½ teaspoon salt
¼ cup oil
1¾ cups water

SPELT (DAY 3)

2½ cups whole grain spelt flour OR 2¾ cups white spelt flour
1 teaspoon baking soda
¼ teaspoon unbuffered vitamin C powder with water as the only liquid OR ⅛
    teaspoon if fruit juice is also used
½ teaspoon salt
¼ cup oil
2 cups water OR 1¾ cups water plus ¼ cup apple juice concentrate, thawed

1. Choose one set of ingredients from the previous page or above.

2. Brush your iron with the oil you will be using in your waffles. If you are having trouble with the waffles sticking to the iron, melted coconut oil, goat butter, or ghee are good choices to use to brush the iron and also to use in the recipe.

3. Heat the iron on "medium-high" or the waffle setting for 15 minutes before you begin cooking waffles. If the iron is not hot enough, you may have difficulty removing the waffles from the iron.

4. In a large bowl, mix the flour(s), baking soda, vitamin C powder, and salt.

5. In a separate bowl or cup, combine the oil, water, and fruit juice (if you are using it).

6. Stir the liquid ingredients into the flour mixture until thoroughly mixed.

7. Allow the batter to stand for about 10 minutes while the iron is heating before you begin cooking the waffles.

8. Put enough batter into the iron for it to reach to about 1 inch from the edge of the iron (about 1 cup for a large iron that makes four square waffles). Overfilling the iron may make the waffles difficult to remove.

9. Close the iron and cook the waffles for about 15 minutes. Do not peek into the iron until the waffles should be done and the iron is no longer steaming, or you may split your waffles down the middle.

10. Remove the waffles from the iron when they are browned.

11. Reheat your waffle iron until the light goes off before cooking more waffles.

12. If you do not eat your waffles immediately, cool them on a wire rack. These waffles freeze well and are good reheated in the toaster.

Makes 10 to 15 4-inch square waffles.

Granola

Make this ahead – it's great to have on hand when you need breakfast in a hurry.

KAMUT (DAY 1)

3 cups rolled kamut flakes
½ cup kamut flour
1 cup chopped walnuts or pecans
¼ teaspoon ground ginger (optional)
⅓ cup oil
¾ cup pineapple juice concentrate, thawed
⅔ cup chopped dried bananas, pineapple, or other dried fruit

BARLEY (DAY 1)

3 cups rolled barley flakes
½ cup barley flour
1 cup chopped walnuts or pecans
¼ teaspoon ground ginger (optional)
⅓ cup oil
¾ cup pineapple juice concentrate, thawed
⅔ cup chopped dried bananas, pineapple, or other dried fruit

AMARANTH (DAY 1)

1½ cups amaranth flour
½ cup tapioca flour
1½ cups chopped walnuts or pecans
¼ teaspoon ginger
⅓ cup oil
¾ cup mashed bananas
¼ cup pineapple juice concentrate, thawed
⅔ cup chopped dried bananas, pineapple, or other dried fruit

RYE (DAY 2)

2½ cups rolled rye flakes
½ cup rye flour
1 cup chopped cashews
¼ teaspoon ground cloves (optional)
⅓ cup oil
½ cup white or purple grape juice concentrate, thawed
¾ cup raisins or other chopped dried fruit

SPELT (DAY 3)

2½ cups rolled spelt flakes
½ cup spelt flour
1 cup chopped filberts
1 teaspoon cinnamon (optional)
⅓ cup oil
½ cup unsweetened applesauce
¼ cup apple juice concentrate, thawed
⅔ cup chopped dried pears or other dried fruit

QUINOA (DAY 3)

1½ cups quinoa flour
½ cup tapioca flour
1½ cups chopped filberts
½ cup sesame seeds
1½ teaspoons cinnamon
⅓ cup oil
¾ cup unsweetened applesauce
¼ cup apple juice concentrate, thawed
⅔ cup chopped dried pears or other dried fruit

Oat (DAY 4)

> 3 cups rolled oats
> ½ cup oat flour
> ½ cup chopped almonds
> ½ cup sunflower or pumpkin seeds
> ½ cup unsweetened coconut
> ¼ teaspoon ground nutmeg (optional)
> ¼ cup date sugar
> ⅓ cup oil
> ¾ cup pureed peaches or nectarines
> ⅔ cup chopped dates, apricots, or other dried
>   fruit

1. Choose one set of ingredients from the previous page or above.

2. Heat your oven to 300°F.

3. Lightly oil a 15 inch by 11 inch jelly roll pan, two 13 inch by 9 inch pans, or three cake pans.

4. In a large bowl, stir together the rolled grain (if called for), flour(s), nuts or seeds, spice, and date sugar (if called for).

5. In a separate bowl or cup, combine the pureed fruit (if called for), fruit juice (if called for), and oil.

6. Stir the liquid ingredients into the dry ingredients until they are thoroughly mixed.

7. Spread the granola mixture in the prepared pans and bake for the times below:

   > Kamut: 30 to 40 minutes
   > Barley: 30 to 40 minutes
   > Amaranth: 45 to 60 minutes
   > Rye: 30 to 40 minutes
   > Spelt: 35 to 45 minutes
   > Quinoa: 1 hour to 1 hour and 15 minutes
   > Oat: 35 to 45 minutes

8. Stir the granola and break it into chunks with your spoon if necessary every 10 to 15 minutes while it is baking.

9. When the granola is golden brown, remove it from the oven and allow it to cool completely in the pan(s).

10. Stir in the dry fruit.

11. Store the granola in airtight containers in a cool place, or freeze it to maintain freshness for longer periods of time.

Makes 6 to 7 cups of granola.

Yeast Breads

Yeast breads are something that many of us on allergy diets cannot have. However, if you are allergic to wheat but not to yeast, or as your health improves to the point that you can tolerate yeast occasionally, you will enjoy the recipes in this chapter. Instructions are given for making yeast breads by hand, with a little help from your mixer, or with a bread machine.

The ingredients used in yeast bread are some type of flour, water, yeast, usually a small amount of sweetener to feed the yeast, and salt to moderate the growth of the yeast. The proper application of heat, and the development of a good structure (usually gluten) in the dough transform these ingredients into bread.

Yeast is a single-celled microorganism, and is what makes yeast breads rise and become the light, fluffy, flavorful delights we expect them to be. The yeast does this by producing carbon dioxide gas, which is trapped in the structure of the bread, and causes it to expand.

Several factors influence this process. The most important is the temperature at which the yeast grows and multiplies. When yeast breads are made by hand, the dough should be kept at about 85 to 90°F during the rising process, both initially after the dough is made, and after the dough is shaped and put in the pan to rise before baking.

The proper temperature of the water used to dissolve the yeast varies depending on the method you are using to make the dough. When making bread by hand or using a mixer, the temperature of the water should be about 115°F to 120°F because the bread will cool as it kneads. When using a bread machine, the water should be at or slightly above room temperature, about 80°F, because the bread machine will heat up the dough as it kneads. The other ingredients that are put into the bread should all be at about room temperature.

If you are making bread by the hand/mixer method, you will need a warm place for it to rise. This can be a draft-free, warm corner of your kitchen. If you do not have such a spot, there are three almost-foolproof ways to create a cozy place for your yeast bread to rise (or "proof"). One is to heat your electric oven to 350°F for 5 minutes, turn it off, and leave the door open until it cools to about 90°F. (A yeast thermometer is a handy tool for checking both the temperature of your rising place and the water used to dissolve the yeast). Then close the door, and you will have a warm, draft-free rising place for your bread. Second, if you have a gas stove, the pilot light keeps the inside of the oven at just the right temperature for bread dough to rise. The third way is to use the proofing box you may have made to incubate yogurt or sourdough bread as a rising place. See page 58 for more about proofing boxes.

In addition to the proper temperature, other factors influence the growth of yeast. One is the availability of food. Most bread recipes contain some type of sugar (fruit sugar in this book) to nourish the yeast, although sourdough and some Italian and French breads do not. (In these breads, the yeast is nourished more slowly as the enzymes in the flour break down some of the starch into sugar). Acidity influences the growth of the yeast. Yeast prefers slightly acid conditions, but too much acid, such as you have when you try to make the dough very sweet using fruit sweeteners, can inhibit the growth of the yeast. Salt also moderates the growth of yeast. Bread made without salt will rise much faster and higher and may fall during baking if it overproofs.

The gas made by the yeast must be trapped by the bread dough to cause the dough to rise. In breads made with spelt, and to a lesser degree kamut and rye, the gluten naturally present in the flour is developed into a network of fibers that traps the gas during the kneading process. Kneading causes small molecules of the gluten proteins to form long chains and sheets. This makes the dough feel smooth and elastic, and when you poke your finger into it, it will spring back. The gas made by the yeast is trapped in this gluten structure, and the result is light, fluffy bread.

There are several methods of kneading bread dough to properly develop the gluten structure. The most basic is old fashioned hand kneading. The yeast bread recipes in this book can be made this way if desired; hand kneading is a therapeutic activity if you have the energy for it. If you are interested in making your bread with less effort, you can knead it using a heavy-duty mixer. Of course, a bread machine does all of the kneading automatically, as well as controlling the rising time and temperature and baking the bread.

If you wish to make gluten-free breads, such as rice, buckwheat, quinoa, or amaranth bread, or breads that contain only a small amount of gluten, such as barley or oat bread, you will have to add something to trap the gas and strengthen the structure of the bread. The most common ingredients to add are guar gum or xanthum gum. Both are soluble fibers that form into chains during kneading. They are not as strong as gluten, so if the dough rises too much, your bread will fall during baking. Other ingredients, such as tapioca flour and eggs, also help to strengthen the structure of gluten-free or low-gluten breads. The structure of these breads is best developed by a mixer or bread machine. Because gluten-free bread dough is much softer, ranging in consistency from being a heavy batter to a soft dough, all of the "kneading" can be done by your mixer even if it is not a heavy duty mixer.

To make yeast bread by the mixer/hand method, put ½ to ⅔ of the flour, the yeast, the salt, and any other dry ingredients in your mixer bowl. Mix on low speed for about 30 seconds. Warm the liquid ingredients to 115 to 120°F. With the mixer running on low speed, add the liquid ingredients to the bowl in a slow stream. Continue mixing until they are thoroughly mixed. At this point, if you do not have a heavy-duty mixer, beat gluten-containing doughs for five to ten minutes. (Beat low-gluten or non-gluten doughs for three minutes, allow them to rise in the bowl, beat them for three minutes again, and then transfer them to the loaf pan for the final rise).

If you are making gluten-containing bread and have a heavy duty mixer with dough hooks, you can mix in the rest of the flour and knead the bread as directed in your mixer's direction book. If you do not have a heavy-duty mixer, by hand stir in as much of the remaining flour as you can, and then turn the dough out onto a floured board to knead it. Knead it by pushing on it with the heels of your hands, folding it over, turning it 90°, and then repeating the process over and over for about ten minutes, gradually adding more flour, until the dough is smooth and elastic. The "feel" of the bread will tell you when enough flour has been added; it will no longer be sticky and will be very resilient. Hand-kneaded bread will absorb a little more flour than called for in most bread machine recipes. Other ingredients, such as nuts and raisins, may be added during the hand kneading time.

Put the dough into an oiled bowl and turn it over to oil the other side of the dough. Cover it with plastic wrap or a towel and allow it to rise in a warm place, as described above, until it has doubled in volume. This will take 45 to 60 minutes for most kinds of breads. If quick-rise yeast is used instead of active dry yeast, the rising time will be about one third shorter.

Punch the dough down and form it into a loaf, rolls, or whatever shape you desire. Place it into an oiled pan and allow it to rise in a warm place until doubled again. The second rise will take less time than the first rise. To tell when gluten-containing dough is ready to bake, poke it gently with your finger. If it does not spring back, it is ready. Gluten-free or non-gluten doughs should be judged by looking at their size. They are ready to bake when they have barely doubled in volume. It is better to bake them when they are only 1¾ times their original volume than to let them overproof, or they may collapse during baking.

If you are allowing the bread to rise in your oven, take it out when it has risen enough. Preheat the oven to 350°F or 375°F for most loaf breads or 375°F for most rolls. Bake from 15 to 20 minutes for rolls. Light, fluffy, gluten-containing breads will take 45 minutes to an hour to bake. Dense whole grain, low-gluten, or non-gluten breads can take over an hour to bake. The bread is done when it is brown and pulls away from the sides of the pan. To keep the crust from getting soggy, remove the bread from the pan immediately after baking. For light, fluffy, gluten-containing breads, if you tap the bottom of the loaf and it sounds hollow, it is done. The more dense breads may not sound hollow but should be well browned. If sweet breads brown too rapidly during baking, cover them with a piece of foil part way through the baking time.

If you will be making bread often, a bread machine is a great time and labor saving device to have. Almost any machine on the market will make good spelt or kamut bread. If you wish to make other kinds of bread, you will need to have a machine on which you can control the length of time the bread rises for the last time before it bakes. At the time of this writing, Zojirushi makes a programmable bread machine that is excellent for allergy breads. The Breadman Ultimate machine is also programmable but kneads so vigorously that it overdevelops the gluten in spelt bread and also produces inferior non-grain and non-gluten-grain breads. Several companies make machines with "bake only" cycles that can be used with the dough cycle to achieve control of the second rising time. However, you have to be present at the right time to switch the machine from the dough cycle to the bake cycle. For more about bread machine baking, refer to *Easy Breadmaking For Special Diets.* (See the last page of this book for more information).

When you use a bread machine to make yeast breads, accurate measuring of all of the ingredients is VITALLY important. Refer to page 150 for instructions on how to measure accurately. Also, it is important to learn to judge the consistency of the dough by looking at it and touching it. For high-gluten doughs, such as kamut and spelt, after several minutes of kneading, the dough should form a smooth, silky ball. It should feel slightly tacky, but not sticky, when you reach into the machine and touch it. Do not judge a bread dough and begin adding flour or water in the first few minutes of kneading; allow the gluten time to develop. (The exception to this is if the machine sounds as if it is really laboring to knead. In this case, add water one tablespoon at a time immediately). After several minutes of kneading, if the dough is too wet or too dry, add either flour one tablespoon at a time or water one teaspoon at a time until the right consistency is reached, allowing the machine to knead for a minute or two after each addition. Using this method, you can compensate for the inevitable variations in flour quality or moisture content due to weather changes.

Record any changes you make in the bread machine recipes and how they turn out. If you live in an exceptionally dry or wet climate, you may find that you routinely have to use more water or flour than the recipe calls for.

The consistency of lower-gluten doughs varies from recipe to recipe; it is difficult to generalize about their consistencies. Rye doughs are very sticky. Some gluten-free doughs may look and feel more like heavy batters than doughs. The first time you make each low-gluten or non-gluten bread, follow the recipe exactly and observe the consistency of the dough carefully. Measuring accurately and using high quality ingredients should produce a good loaf. However, when making lower gluten breads in a bread machine, sometimes the loaf will over-rise and collapse during baking. The next time you make the bread, increase the flour or decrease the liquid to make a stiffer dough, or preferably, if your machine allows, decrease the time of the second rise. After making a few loaves of each kind of bread, you will gain enough experience to be able to easily compensate for any variations in your flour.

Using high quality commercial flours for yeast breads is essential to success. For spelt breads, always use Purity Foods flour. I have found more variability in spelt flour from different sources than for any other kind of flour. Purity Foods flour is the only one that consistently produces excellent bread. It is milled from a European strain of spelt which is higher in protein and gluten than most spelt, and thus makes better bread. Arrowhead Mills is a good brand to buy for the other types of flour.

Most experts recommend letting your bread cool before you cut it and eat it. However, around our house, it smells so good than some people cannot wait that long. I have found that if I use a good bread knife and a gentle sawing motion to cut it, I can cut it immediately without smashing the loaf, although the cut edge may not be as nice as if it had completely cooled off. You may be able to purchase a good bread knife, such as a Henckels, in a discount store, as I did, for a fraction of the price that they sell for in cooking catalogues or stores.

Homemade bread keeps best when stored at room temperature or in the freezer. It gets stale more quickly in the refrigerator. Always let your bread cool completely before storing it. A good, economical way to store bread is in a plastic bag on the kitchen counter. The crust will soften in a plastic bag. Some people use paper or waxed paper bags to store bread if they want the crust to stay crisp.

If you have been buying frozen rice yeast bread from your health food store, the recipes in this chapter will give you more variety, as well as saving you a considerable amount of money.

Mixer/Hand Made
Yeast Breads

KAMUT (Day 1)

2 cups kamut flour
1 package (2¼ teaspoons) active dry
    or quick-rise yeast
¾ teaspoon salt
1¼ cups water
¼ cup pineapple juice concentrate,
    thawed
1½ tablespoons oil
1¼ to 1½ cups additional kamut
    flour

AMARANTH (Day 1 – borrow pear and peach in Fruit Sweet™ or Pear Sweet™ from Days 3 and 4)

2¼ cups amaranth flour
1 cup arrowroot
1 package (2¼ teaspoons) quick-rise
    yeast
1 teaspoon salt
4 teaspoons guar gum
1⅛ cups water
3 tablespoons Fruit Sweet™ or
    Pear Sweet™
3 tablespoons oil

BUCKWHEAT (Day 2 – borrow arrowroot from Day 1 or tapioca starch from Day 3)

2 cups buckwheat flour
1¼ cups arrowroot or tapioca starch
1 package (2¼ teaspoons) quick-rise
    yeast
1 tablespoon guar gum
1 teaspoon salt
1¼ cups water
¼ cup grape juice concentrate,
    thawed (white or purple)
3 tablespoons oil
Additional buckwheat flour to coat
    the pan

RYE (Day 2)

2½ cups rye flour
1 package (2¼ teaspoons) quick-rise
    yeast
1 teaspoon salt
⅓ cup water
1 cup white grape juice
3 tablespoons oil
1½ to 2 cups additional rye flour

BARLEY (Day 1)

3 cups barley flour
1½ packages (3¼ teaspoons) quick-
    rise yeast
1½ teaspoons salt
3¼ teaspoons guar gum
1¾ cups water
⅜ cup (¼ cup plus 2 tablespoons)
    pineapple juice concentrate,
    thawed
¼ cup oil
3 cups additional barley flour

WHOLE SPELT (Day 3)

2 cups whole spelt flour
1 package (2¼ teaspoons) active dry
    or quick-rise yeast
¾ teaspoon salt
3 tablespoons apple juice concentrate,
    thawed
⅔ cup plus 3 tablespoons water
1 tablespoon oil
1 teaspoon liquid lecithin or
    additional oil
1⅛ to 1½ cups additional whole spelt
    flour

WHITE SPELT (DAY 3)

2 cups white spelt flour
1¾ teaspoons active dry or quick-rise
    yeast
¾ teaspoon salt
3 tablespoons apple juice concentrate,
    thawed
⅝ cup (½ cup plus 2 tablespoons)
    water
2½ teaspoons oil
1 teaspoon liquid lecithin or
    additional oil
⅞ to 1 cup additional white spelt
    flour

OAT (DAY 4)

2¾ cups oat flour
½ cup date sugar
1 package (2¼ teaspoons) quick-rise
    yeast
2¼ teaspoons guar gum
½ teaspoon salt
1½ cups water
3 tablespoons oil
Additional oat flour or oatmeal to
    coat the pan

QUINOA (DAY 3)

2 cups quinoa flour
1 package (2¼ teaspoons) quick-rise
    yeast
2¼ teaspoons guar gum
1 teaspoon cinnamon (optional)
¼ teaspoon salt
1 cup water
½ cup apple juice concentrate,
    thawed
3 tablespoons oil
½ cup raisins (optional)
Additional quinoa flour or sesame
    seeds to coat the pan

EGG-FREE BROWN RICE (DAY 4, borrow tapioca from day 3, arrowroot from DAY 1, and the pineapple and pear in Fruit Sweet™ or Pear Sweet™ from days 1 and 3)

2¾ cups brown rice flour
¾ cup tapioca flour or arrowroot
1 package (2¼ teaspoons) active dry
    or quick-rise yeast
1 tablespoon guar gum
1 teaspoon salt
1½ cups water
3 tablespoons honey, Fruit Sweet™
    or Pear Sweet™
3 tablespoons oil
Additional rice flour to coat the pan

RICE (DAY 4, borrow apple and tapioca from DAY 3 or pineapple and arrowroot from DAY 1)

2 cups brown or white rice flour
⅓ cup potato flour
⅓ cup tapioca flour or arrowroot
1 package (2¼ teaspoons) active dry or quick-rise yeast
4 teaspoons guar gum
⅛ teaspoon unbuffered vitamin C powder
1 teaspoon salt
2 tablespoons oil
3 extra-large eggs (¾ cup) at room temperature
¼ cup apple or pineapple juice, thawed
½ cup water at about 115°F
Additional rice flour to coat the pan

Choose one set of ingredients from the previous two pages.

DIRECTIONS FOR KAMUT, RYE, AND SPELT BREADS:

1. Put the first amount of flour listed, the yeast, and the salt in a large mixer bowl.

2. Mix on low speed for about 30 seconds.

3. In a small saucepan, warm the liquid ingredients, such as the water, juice, oil, and lecithin, to 115-120°F. (Measure the temperature with a yeast thermometer).

4. With the mixer running on low speed, add the liquids to the dry ingredients in a slow stream.

5. Continue mixing until the dry and liquid ingredients are thoroughly mixed.

6. If your mixer is not a heavy-duty mixer, at this point beat the dough on medium speed for 5 to 10 minutes. With some types of bread you will be able to tell that the gluten is developing because the dough will begin to climb up the beaters. Then knead the rest of the flour in by hand, kneading for about 10 minutes, or until the dough is very smooth and elastic. If you wish to add raisins to the dough, do it during this hand kneading period.

7. If your mixer is a heavy-duty mixer, after the liquids are thoroughly mixed in, with the mixer still running, begin adding the rest of the flour around the edges of the bowl ½ cup at a time, mixing well after each addition before adding more flour, until the dough forms a ball and cleans the sides of the bowl. Knead the dough on the speed directed in your mixer manual for 5 to 10 minutes, or until the dough is very elastic and smooth. Turn the dough out onto a floured board and knead it by hand briefly to check the consistency of the dough, kneading in a little more flour if necessary. Raisins should be added to the dough by hand after the mixer is finished kneading it.

8. For kamut bread, form the dough into a loaf and put it into an oiled loaf pan. Let it rise only once (in the pan) as in step 13. Proceed with step 14.

9. For rye and spelt bread, put the dough into an oiled bowl and turn it once so that the top of the ball is also oiled. Cover it with a towel and let it rise in a warm (85°F to 90°F) place until it has doubled in volume, about 45 minutes to l hour. (Rye bread will take much longer to rise if made with regular rather than quick-rise yeast).

10. Punch the dough down and shape it into a loaf.

11. For rye bread, oil a loaf pan. For spelt bread, oil a loaf pan, line the bottom and long sides of it with waxed or parchment paper, and oil the paper.

12. Put the loaf into the prepared pan.

13. Allow the bread to rise in a warm place until double again. This will take about 35 minutes to an hour.

14. If your warm rising spot is in your oven, remove the loaf from the oven.

15. Preheat your oven to 375°F.

16. Bake the bread for the following times, or until the loaf is nicely browned.

> Kamut: 40 to 45 minutes
> Rye: 45 to 60 minutes
> Whole spelt: 40 to 45 minutes
> White spelt: 40 to 45 minutes

17. Remove the bread from the pan immediately after you take it out of the oven. It should sound hollow when tapped on the bottom with your knuckles.

18. Cool the bread on a cooling rack before slicing it.

DIRECTIONS FOR BARLEY, AMARANTH, BUCKWHEAT, QUINOA, OAT AND RICE BREADS:

1. If you are using eggs, remove them from the refrigerator and allow them to warm to room temperature. If you forget to take them out of the refrigerator ahead, float them in a bowl of warm water for about 5 minutes while you are gathering the other ingredients.

2. Put the amount of flour(s) listed at the top of the ingredient list, the yeast, the salt, the guar gum, and the other dry ingredients in a large mixer bowl.

3. Mix on low speed for about 30 seconds.

4. In a small saucepan, warm the liquid ingredients, such as the water, juice or sweetner, oil, and lecithin, to 115-120°F. (Measure the temperature with a yeast thermometer). Do not warm the eggs.

5. With the mixer running on low speed, add the liquids to the dry ingredients in a slow stream. If you are using eggs, beat them slightly and add them to the bowl.

6. Continue mixing until the dry and liquid ingredients are thoroughly mixed.

7. Beat the dough on medium speed for 3 minutes.

8. For barley bread, add the rest of the flour to the bowl a little at a time. Use the mixer to beat in the first few additions of flour; knead the rest in with your hands. Knead the dough on a floured board for 5 to 10 minutes. Form the dough into a loaf and put it into an oiled loaf pan. Let it rise only once (in the pan) as in step 13 below. Proceed with step 14.

9. For the other kinds of bread, scrape the dough from the beaters and the sides of the bowl into the bottom of the bowl.

10. Cover the bowl, put it in a warm (85°F to 90°F) place and let the dough rise for 1 to 1½ hours.

11. Beat the dough again for three minutes at medium speed.

12. Oil a loaf pan and coat the inside of it generously with the flour you used to make the bread, oatmeal (for oat bread), or sesame seeds (for quinoa bread).

13. Put the dough in the pan and allow it to rise in a warm place until it just barely doubles again, about 30 to 40 minutes if you used active dry yeast or 20 to 30 minutes if you used quick-rise yeast. DO NOT allow the bread to over-rise at this point, or it may collapse during baking.

14. If your warm rising spot is in your oven, remove the loaf from the oven.

15. Preheat your oven to 350°F for oat bread or to 375°F for all the other kinds of bread.

16. Bake the bread for the following times or until it is slightly browned.

> Barley: 65 to 85 minutes
> Amaranth: 55 to 65 minutes
> Buckwheat: 55 to 65 minutes
> Quinoa: 60 to 70 minutes
> Oat: 65 to 75 minutes
> Rice: 35 to 45 minutes
> Egg-free brown rice: 35 to 45 minutes

17. For the oat and quinoa breads, loosely cover the loaf with foil after the first 20 minutes of baking to prevent excessive browning.

18. Remove the bread from the pan immediately after you take it out of the oven.

19. Cool the bread on a cooling rack before slicing it.

RAISIN BREAD VARIATION: Add ½ cup raisins and 1 teaspoon cinnamon to any of the recipes above. Add the cinnamon to the flour as you begin to make the dough and knead or stir in the raisins by hand right before allowing the dough to rise.

Makes 1 loaf of bread

Bread Machine Yeast Breads

Add the ingredients listed below to your bread machine pan in the order your machine's book specifies, either from the top of the list down, or from the bottom of the list up. Then choose the cycle, start your machine, and soon you will have bread!

KAMUT (DAY 1)

Ingredients:	1½ pound loaf	1 pound loaf
Water	1⅔ cups	1¼ cups
Pineapple juice concentrate, thawed	⅓ cup	¼ cup
Oil	2 tablespoons	1½ tablespoons
Liquid lecithin (or may use additional oil)	1 tablespoon	½ tablespoon
Salt	1 teaspoon	¾ teaspoon
Kamut flour	4⅓ cups	3¼ cups
Active dry yeast	3 teaspoons	2¼ teaspoons

Cycle: Basic yeast bread

BARLEY (DAY 1, borrow the pear and peach in the Fruit Sweet™ or Pear Sweet™ from DAYS 3 & 4)

Ingredients:	1½ pound programmable machine
Water	2 cups
Fruit Sweet™, Pear Sweet™ or honey	2 tablespoons
Oil	1½ tablespoons
Liquid lecithin (or may use additional oil)	½ tablespoon
Salt	1 teaspoon
Guar gum	3 teaspoons
Barley flour*	3⅓ cups
Active dry yeast	2¼ teaspoons

Cycle: Programmable machines: Use the times on the standard cycle except set Rise 1 to the lowest time possible, Rise 2 = 30 minutes, and Bake = 60 minutes.

Machines with "bake only" cycle: Run the dough cycle. After 30 minutes of rising time, check the bread. If (or when) it is almost double in volume, start the bake cycle.

*When using the Zojirushi, reserve 1 cup of the barley flour to add ¼ cup at a time during Knead 1 and assist the kneading with a spatula.

AMARANTH (DAY 1, borrow the pear and peach in the Fruit Sweet™, or Pear Sweet™ from DAYS 3 & 4)

Ingredients:	1½ pound programmable machine
Water	1⅛ cups
Fruit Sweet™, Pear Sweet™ or honey	3 tablespoons
Oil	2 tablespoons
Liquid lecithin (or may use additional oil)	1 tablespoon
Salt	1 teaspoon
Guar gum	4 teaspoons
Amaranth flour*	2½ cups
Arrowroot	¾ cup
Active dry yeast	2¼ teaspoons

Cycle: Programmable machines: Use the times on the standard cycle except set
Rise 1 = 5 minutes, Rise 2 = 30 minutes, and Bake = 60 minutes.
Machines with "bake only" cycle: Run the dough cycle. After 30 minutes of rising time, check the bread. If (or when) it is almost double in volume, start the bake cycle.

With any machine, spread the dough evenly in the pan after the last kneading period. This is a very dense bread. *When using the Zojirushi, reserve 1 cup of the amaranth flour to add ¼ cup at a time during Knead 1 and assist the kneading with a spatula.

BUCKWHEAT (DAY 2, borrow arrowroot from DAY 1 or tapioca from DAY 3)

Ingredients:	1½ pound programmable machine
Water	1¼ cups
White grape juice concentrate, thawed	¼ cup
Oil	3 tablespoons
Salt	1 teaspoon
Guar gum	1 tablespoon
Buckwheat flour*	2 cups
Arrowroot or tapioca flour	1¼ cups
Active dry yeast	2¼ teaspoons

Cycle: Programmable machines: Use the times on the standard cycle except set
Rise 1 = 5 minutes, Rise 2 = 30 minutes, and Bake = 60 minutes.
Machines with "bake only" cycle: Run the dough cycle. After 30 minutes of rising time, check the bread. If (or when) it is almost double in volume, start the bake cycle.

*When using the Zojirushi, reserve 1 cup of the buckwheat flour to add ¼ cup at a time during Knead 1 and assist the kneading with a spatula.

RYE (DAY 2, borrow tapioca from DAY 3)

Ingredients:	1½ pound loaf	1 pound loaf
Water	⅓ cup	¼ cup
White grape juice	1 cup	⅔ cup
Oil	1½ tablespoon	1 tablespoon
Liquid lecithin (or may use additional oil)	½ tablespoon	½ tablespoon
Salt	1½ teaspoon	1 teaspoon
Unbuffered vitamin C powder	⅛ teaspoon	Scant ⅛ teaspoon
Rye flour	2½ cups	1⅔ cups
Tapioca flour	¾ cup	½ cup
Guar gum	4 teaspoons	3 teaspoons
Active dry yeast	2¼ teaspoons	1½ teaspoons

Cycle: Basic yeast bread. With some machines, you will have to assist the mixing and kneading of this dough with a spatula. For all machines, spread the dough evenly in the pan as soon as the last kneading time is finished. This is a very dense bread.

WHOLE SPELT (DAY 3)

Ingredients:	1½ pound loaf	1 pound loaf
Water	1 cup	¾ cup
Apple juice concentrate, thawed	¼ cup	3 tablespoons
Oil	1 tablespoon	2 teaspoons
Liquid lecithin (or may use additional oil)	½ tablespoon	1 teaspoon
Salt	¾ teaspoon	½ teaspoon
Whole spelt flour	3⅓ cups	2½ cups
Active dry yeast	2¼ teaspoons	1½ teaspoons

Cycle: Basic yeast bread

WHITE SPELT (DAY 3)

Ingredients:	1½ pound loaf	1 pound loaf
Water	¾ cup	⅔ cup
Apple juice concentrate, thawed	3 tablespoons	2 tablespoons
Oil	2½ teaspoons	2 teaspoons
Liquid lecithin (or may use additional oil)	1 teaspoon	1 teaspoon
Salt	¾ teaspoon	½ teaspoon
White spelt flour	2⅞ cups	2⅜ cup
Active dry yeast	1¾ teaspoons	1¼ teaspoons

Cycle: Basic yeast bread

WHITE SPELT RAISIN (DAY 3, borrow raisins from DAY 2 and date sugar from DAY 4)

Ingredients:	1½ pound loaf	1 pound loaf
Water	1¼ cups	¾ cup + 1 tablespoon
Oil	1½ tablespoons	1 tablespoon
Liquid lecithin (or may use additional oil)	½ tablespoon	1 teaspoon
Date sugar	⅓ cup	¼ cup
Salt	1 teaspoon	¾ teaspoon
Cinnamon	1½ teaspoons	1 teaspoon
White spelt flour	3¾ cups	2⅝ cups
Active dry yeast	2¼ teaspoons	1¼ teaspoons
Raisins (add later, see note below)	½ cup	⅓ cup

Cycle: Raisin bread or basic yeast bread. Put all of the ingredients except the raisins into your machine. When the "beep" of the raisin bread cycle sounds, or 5 to 8 minutes before the end of the last kneading time, add the raisins to the machine.

QUINOA (DAY 3, borrow raisins from DAY 2)

Ingredients:	1½ pound programmable machine
Water	1 cup
Apple juice concentrate, thawed	⅓ cup
Oil	2 tablespoons
Liquid lecithin (or may use additional oil)	1 tablespoon
Salt	¾ teaspoon
Cinnamon	1 teaspoon
Guar gum	4 teaspoons
Quinoa flour*	2½ cups
Tapioca flour	¾ cup
Active dry yeast	2¼ teaspoons
Raisins (optional – see note)	½ cup

Cycle: Programmable machines: Use the times on the standard cycle except set
     Rise 1 = 5 minutes, Rise 2 = 30 minutes, and Bake = 60 minutes.
   Machines with "bake only" cycle: Run the dough cycle. After 30 minutes of rising
     time, check the bread. If (or when) it is almost doubled in volume, start the bake
     cycle.

Add the raisins 5 to 10 minutes before the end of Knead 2 or the last kneading time. This is a very dense bread. *When using the Zojirushi, reserve 1 cup of the quinoa flour to add ¼ cup at a time during Knead 1 and assist the kneading with a spatula.

OAT (DAY 4, borrow arrowroot from DAY 1)

Ingredients:	1½ pound programmable machine
Water	1½ cups
Oil	2 tablespoons
Liquid lecithin (or may use additional oil)	1 tablespoon
Salt	½ teaspoon
Guar gum	1 tablespoon
Date sugar	½ cup
Oat flour*	2½ cups
Arrowroot	½ cup
Active dry yeast	2¼ teaspoons

Cycle: Programmable machines: Use the times on the standard cycle except set
Rise 1 = 5 minutes, Rise 2 = 30 minutes, and Bake = 60 minutes
Machines with "bake only" cycle: Run the dough cycle. After 30 minutes of rising
time, check the bread. If (or when) it is almost double in volume, start the bake
cycle.

*When using the Zojirushi, reserve 1 cup of the oat flour to add ¼ cup at a time during Knead 1 and assist the kneading with a spatula.

RICE (DAY 4, borrow apple and tapioca from DAY 3)

Ingredients:	1½ pound loaf	1 pound loaf
Water	½ cup + 1 tablespoon	½ cup
Apple juice concentrate, thawed	¼ cup	3 tablespoons
Oil	2 tablespoons	1½ tablespoons
Extra large eggs	3 eggs OR ¾ cup	2 eggs OR ½ cup
Salt	1 teaspoon	¾ teaspoon
Vitamin C powder	⅛ teaspoon	Scant ⅛ teaspoon
Guar gum	4 teaspoons	3 teaspoons
Brown or white rice flour	2 cup	1½ cups
Potato flour	⅓ cup	¼ cup
Tapioca flour	⅓ cup	¼ cup
Active dry yeast	2¼ teaspoons	1½ teaspoons

Cycle: Basic yeast bread. This is a dense bread.

EGG-FREE RICE (DAY 4 – borrow the pineapple and pear in the Fruit Sweet™ or Pear Sweet™ from Days 1 & 3)

Ingredients:	1½ pound programmable machine
Water	1½ cups
Fruit Sweet™, Pear Sweet™ or honey	3 tablespoons
Oil	2 tablespoons
Liquid lecithin (or use additional oil)	1 tablespoon
Salt	1 teaspoon
Guar gum	1 tablespoon
Brown rice flour*	2¾ cups
Tapioca flour	¾ cup
Active dry yeast	2¼ teaspoons

Cycle: Programmable machines: Use the times on the standard cycle except set Rise 1 = 5 minutes, Rise 2 = 30 minutes, and Bake = 60 minutes.

Machines with "bake only" cycle: Run the dough cycle. After 20 minutes of rising time, check the bread. If it is almost doubled in volume, start the bake cycle. Otherwise, check it again in five minutes. After 30 minutes of rising time, start the bake cycle even if it has not quite doubled in volume.

*When using the Zojirushi, reserve 1 cup of the rice flour to add ¼ cup at a time during Knead 1 and assist the kneading with a spatula. **Rise 2 should last just until the dough has barely doubled and should end before the top of the dough begins to collapse. This is a dense bread.

DIRECTIONS:

1. Choose one set of ingredients from above. Choose the loaf size appropriate for your machine. If you have a 2-pound machine, you may double the amounts of the ingredients in the 1-pound column for any of the breads except kamut. For kamut bread, use the 1½-pound ingredient list in a 2-pound machine.

2. Add the ingredients (except raisins) to your bread machine pan in the order directed by your machine's instruction booklet. This will either be from the top of the list down or from the bottom of the list up.

3. Start the cycle specified with the ingredient list. Follow any special directions for each type of bread given with the ingredient list.

4. When your bread is finished baking, remove it from the pan.

5. Cool it on a wire rack before slicing it.

Makes one loaf of bread.

> NOTE: For low-gluten and gluten-free breads made in a programmable machine, if the loaf over-rises and collapses during baking, the final rising time may need to be "tweaked." See page 183 for more about this.

Any day Buns or Rolls

Any Day

Ingredients from the "Mixer/Hand Made Yeast Breads" recipe, page 184, or the
"Bread Machine Yeast Breads" recipe, page 189

1. Make any bread dough from the "Mixer/Hand Made Yeast Breads" recipe or use the dough cycle on your bread machine to make dough from the "Bread Machine Yeast Breads" recipe.

2. For kamut and barley breads, skip the first rise and go directly to step 3 or 4. For all other kinds of breads, allow mixer or handmade dough to rise once or allow the dough cycle of your bread machine to complete. Punch down the dough.

3. For kamut, handmade barley, rye, or spelt doughs, divide the dough into balls. If you wish to use these buns for sandwiches, make about 8 balls; for dinner rolls, make 12 to 20 balls depending on the size you prefer. Put the balls on an oiled baking sheet.

4. For amaranth, machine-made barley, buckwheat, quinoa, oat, or rice doughs, put the dough into an oiled muffin tin, filling each well about ¾ full. If you wish to have sandwich buns, use a "Texas size" muffin tin and fill each well ⅓ to ½ full.

5. Allow the buns or rolls to rise in a warm place until they are about double in volume. This will take from 25 minutes to an hour, depending on which bread dough you make and whether you use regular active dry or quick-rise yeast. Do not allow the low-gluten doughs to over-rise or they may collapse during baking.

6. If they are rising in your oven, remove them from the oven.

7. Preheat your oven to 375°F.

8. Bake the buns or rolls until they are nicely browned. The time will vary widely depending on the size and dough from which they are made. Most light rolls or buns, such as kamut and spelt, take 15 to 25 minutes. Rye buns and most of the rolls will take 20 to 35 minutes. Very dense buns, such as handmade barley buns, take 45 to 50 minutes.

9. Remove the buns or rolls from the baking sheet or muffin tin immediately after they come from the oven.

10. Cool them on a wire cooling rack.

11. For sandwich buns, use a serrated knife to slice them in half horizontally.

Makes 8 to 20 buns or rolls.

Hand Shaped Breads

The easiest way to make these breads is using a bread machine. However, you can decrease the amount of water you use (as directed below) and make the dough by the mixer/hand method at the beginning of this chapter. Then shape and bake the bread as directed below.

ITALIAN OR FRENCH BREAD (Day 3)

1¼ cup water
1½ tablespoons apple juice concentrate, thawed
1½ teaspoons salt
3¾ cups white spelt flour
1 package (2¼ teaspoons) active dry yeast

CHALLAH (Day 3 – borrow the pineapple and peach in the Fruit Sweet™ from days 1 and 4)

1 cup water
¼ cup Fruit Sweet™, Pear Sweet™ or honey
1 tablespoon oil
½ tablespoon liquid lecithin (or you may use additional oil)
1 teaspoon salt
A small pinch of saffron (optional – for color)
3¾ cups white spelt flour
1 package (2¼ teaspoons) active dry yeast
2 teaspoons sesame seeds
    (for the top of the bread – do not add them to the dough)

"Egg white" wash for French bread or Challah:

¼ cup water
1 teaspoon tapioca flour

1. Choose one set of bread ingredients from above.

2. If you are making this bread using a bread machine, add the ingredients to your machine in the order your machine's directions specify, either from the top of the list down or from the bottom of the list up. Start the dough cycle.

3. If you are making this bread by the mixer/hand method, decrease the amount of water by ⅛ cup (2 tablespoons). Make the dough according to the instructions given for spelt breads on page 186. Put the dough in a bowl, put it in a warm place, and allow it to rise once.

4. If you are making French bread or challah, prepare the "egg white" wash while the dough is rising. Stir together the water and tapioca flour in a small saucepan. Cook over medium heat until the mixture comes to a boil, clears, and thickens.

5. At the end of the dough cycle, or when the handmade dough has finished rising once, remove dough from the machine or bowl.

6. Knead it briefly on an oiled or very lightly floured board.

7. Generously oil a baking sheet.

8. For French or Italian bread, shape the dough into a long or round loaf and put it on the prepared baking sheet.

9. For challah or braided Italian bread, divide the dough into three pieces, roll them into 15" ropes, and braid the dough. Place the loaf on the prepared baking sheet.

10. Brush the French bread or challah with the "egg white" wash. Sprinkle the challah with the sesame seeds. Slash the top of the French bread diagonally with a knife in several places.

11. Let the loaf rise in a warm place until double, 30 to 45 minutes.

12. If your bread is rising in your oven, remove it from the oven.

13. Preheat your oven to 400°F for French or Italian bread or to 375°F for challah.

14. If you are making French or Italian bread, you can put a few potatoes in the oven to bake along with the bread for added moisture to help the crust become crisp.

15. If you are making Italian bread, spray the bread with water right before baking, and at 5 and 10 minutes into the baking time.

16. If you are making French bread, carefully brush it with the "egg white" wash again right before baking it.

17. Bake the bread for the following times or until it is nicely browned.

   Italian or French bread: 20 to 40 minutes, depending on the shape of the loaf
   Challah: 25 to 30 minutes

18. Use a spatula to loosen and remove the loaf from the baking sheet.

19. Cool the bread on a cooling rack immediately after taking it from the oven.

Makes 1 loaf

Sweet Rolls

You can make the dough for these rolls using a bread machine or by the mixer/hand method at the beginning of this chapter. Then shape and bake them as directed below.

KAMUT DOUGH (DAY 1 – borrow the pear and peach in the Fruit Sweet™ or Pear Sweet™ from **DAYS 3&4)**

> 1⅛ cups (1 cup plus 2 tablespoons) water
> ⅜ cup (¼ cup plus 2 tablespoons) Fruit Sweet™, Pear Sweet™ or honey
> 1 tablespoon oil
> 1 tablespoon liquid lecithin (or you may use additional oil)
> ½ teaspoon salt
> 3¼ cups kamut flour
> 1 package (2¼ teaspoons) active dry yeast

WHOLE SPELT DOUGH (DAY 3 – borrow the pineapple and peach in the Fruit Sweet™ from **DAYS 1&4)**

> 1 cup water
> ⅓ cup Fruit Sweet™, Pear Sweet™ or honey
> 1 tablespoon oil
> 1 tablespoon liquid lecithin (or you may use additional oil)
> ½ teaspoon salt
> 3¾ cups whole spelt flour
> 1 package (2¼ teaspoons) active dry yeast

WHITE SPELT DOUGH (DAY 3 – borrow the pineapple and peach in the Fruit Sweet™ from days 1 and 4)

> ⅔ cup water
> ⅓ cup Fruit Sweet™, Pear Sweet™ or honey
> 1 tablespoon oil
> 1 tablespoon liquid lecithin (or you may use additional oil)
> ¾ teaspoon salt
> 3¼ cups white spelt flour
> 1¾ teaspoons active dry yeast

Additional ingredients for hot cross buns:

> ½ cup currants (borrow from **DAY 2**) or dried blueberries
> "Egg white" wash, page 196

Additional ingredients for CINNAMON ROLLS (borrow raisins from **DAY 2**, date from **DAY 4:** for **KAMUT ROLLS** borrow the cinnamon from **DAY 3**):

> 2 teaspoons oil
> ½ cup date sugar
> 2 teaspoons cinnamon
> ½ cup raisins

Additional ingredients for MONKEY BREAD (borrow date from **DAY 4:** for **KAMUT BREAD** borrow the cinnamon from **DAY 3**):

> Oil
> ½ cup date sugar
> 2 teaspoons cinnamon

1. Choose one set of dough ingredients from the previous page.

2. If you are making these rolls using a bread machine, add the ingredients to your machine in the order your machine's directions specify, either from the top of the list down or from the bottom of the list up. Start the dough cycle. For the hot cross buns, add the currants or blueberries to the machine 5 to 10 minutes before the end of the kneading time or when the "add raisins" beep sounds.

3. If you are making these rolls by the mixer/hand method, decrease the amount of water by ⅛ cup (2 tablespoons). Make the dough according to the instructions given for kamut or spelt breads on page 186. For the hot cross buns, add the currants or blueberries to the dough during the hand kneading time. Put the dough in a bowl, put it in a warm place, and allow it to rise once.

4. Remove the dough from the machine when the dough cycle is finished or from the bowl after the first rising time is done.

HOT CROSS BUNS SHAPING AND BAKING DIRECTIONS:

1. Knead the dough a few times on a lightly oiled board.

2. Roll it to ½ inch thickness with a lightly oiled rolling pin.

3. Cut rounds of dough with a 2½ inch biscuit cutter or glass.

4. Place the rounds on a lightly oiled baking sheet.

5. Allow them to rise in a warm place until double, about 40 minutes.

6. Make the "egg white" wash as directed on page 196 while they are rising.

7. Snip a shallow cross in the top of each bun with a very sharp scissors or knife.

8. Brush the tops of the rolls with the "egg white" wash.

9. Preheat your oven to 375°F.

10. Bake the rolls for 15 minutes, or until lightly browned.

Makes about 12 buns.

CINNAMON ROLLS SHAPING AND BAKING DIRECTIONS:

1. Remove the dough from the machine and use a lightly oiled rolling pin to roll it out to a 12 inch by 15 inch rectangle on a lightly oiled board.

2. Brush the rectangle with oil.

3. Sprinkle it with the sweetener, cinnamon, and raisins.

4. Starting at the long side, roll the dough up jelly roll fashion.

5. Cut the roll into 12 to 15 slices and put them cut side down in an oiled 13 inch by 9 inch pan.

6. For individual cinnamon rolls, cut the dough into 15 slices and put each slice cut side down into an oiled muffin cup.

7. Allow the rolls to rise in a warm place until double, about 35 to 50 minutes.

8. Preheat your oven to 375°F.

9. Bake the rolls for 20 to 30 minutes or until lightly browned.

Makes 12 to 15 cinnamon rolls

MONKEY BREAD SHAPING AND BAKING DIRECTIONS:

1. Oil a 10 inch tube pan or a 2 to 3-quart round casserole dish.

2. Knead the dough briefly on a lightly floured board.

3. Divide the dough into 45 to 50 1-inch balls.

4. Stir together the sweetener and cinnamon in a small bowl. Put a few tablespoons of oil in another small bowl.

5. Dip each ball in the oil and roll it in the mixture of the sweetener and cinnamon.

6. Place the balls in the prepared pan.

7. Sprinkle any remaining cinnamon-sweetener mixture over the top of the balls.

8. Let the bread rise in a warm place until double, about 35 to 50 minutes.

9. Preheat your oven to 375°F.

10. Bake the money bread for 35 to 45 minutes or until brown.

11. Remove it from the pan immediately and cool it on a wire cooling rack.

Makes one circular monkey bread

Simple Fruit Desserts

The desserts in this chapter contain fruit only. They are also very easy to make and delicious.

Any day Fruit Sorbet

Because most of these desserts do not contain any sweeteners in addition to the fruit, use the ripest fruit you can find.

BANANA (DAY 1)

6 to 8 ripe bananas

QUICK BLUEBERRY (DAY 1)

2 ripe bananas
4 cups frozen unsweetened
    blueberries (about 1 pound)

APPLE (DAY 3)

1¾ cups unsweetened applesauce
1 cup apple juice concentrate
¾ teaspoon cinnamon

PEAR (DAY 3)

4 to 5 ripe pears (about 1¾ to 2
    pounds)

CANTALOUPE (DAY 4)

2 small cantaloupes

ANY DAY CRANBERRY (DAY 1 with pineapple, DAY 3 with apple, EXTRA FOODS with stevia)

½ pound fresh cranberries
    (2½ to 3 cups)
1 cup apple or pineapple juice
    concentrate, thawed,
    OR 1 cup water plus ⅛ to a scant
    ¼ teaspoon white stevia extract
    powder

PINEAPPLE (DAY 1)

1 20-ounce can of juice-packed
    pineapple OR 3 to 4 cups fresh
    pineapple with juice

MANGO (DAY 2)

3 ripe mangoes

QUICK STRAWBERRY OR RASPBERRY (DAY 3)

¾ cup unsweetened applesauce
4 to 5 cups frozen unsweetened
    strawberries or raspberries (1 to
    1½ pounds)

PEACH, APRICOT, or NECTARINE (DAY 4)

1 16- to 20-ounce can of water or
    juice-packed peaches or apricots
    OR about 2 pounds of fresh
    peaches, apricots, or nectarines

ANY DAY KIWI (DAY 1 with pineapple, DAY 3 with apple, EXTRA FOODS with stevia)

9 to 10 kiwi fruits
1 cup apple or pineapple juice
    concentrate, thawed
    OR 1 cup water plus ⅛ teaspoon
    white stevia powder

FANCY RASPBERRY (DAY 3)

10 to 12 ounces fresh raspberries or frozen raspberries, thawed

1 cup thawed apple juice concentrate plus ½ cup water OR ½ cup Pear Sweet™ plus 1 cup water

FANCY PEACH (DAY 4)

2 to 2 ¼ pounds fresh or frozen peaches or 1 16- to 20-ounce can juiced-packed peaches to make 2 cups peach puree

½ cup Fruit Sweet™, Pear Sweet™, or honey

ANY DAY ORANGE SORBET (EXTRA FOODS)

1½ teaspoons agar flakes or gelatin

1¾ cups water, divided

¾ cup orange juice concentrate, thawed

Choose one set of ingredients from the previous page or above.

DIRECTIONS FOR THE QUICK BLUEBERRY, STRAWBERRY, OR RASPBERRY SORBETS:

1. If you are using bananas, peel them and break them into chunks.

2. Put the bananas or applesauce into a blender or a food processor with the metal puree-ing blade.

3. If you are using them, puree the bananas until they are smooth.

4. Turn the machine on. Add the frozen berries a few at a time, processing after each addition.

5. Serve the sorbet immediately or freeze any that is left over.

DIRECTIONS FOR BANANA, PEAR, OR FRESH PEACH, APRICOT, OR NECTARINE SORBET:

1. If you are using the bananas, peel them and break them into chunks.

2. If you are using the other fruits, peel them, core the pears or remove the pits from the other fruits, and cut them into chunks.

3. Put the chunks on a baking sheet and put them into the freezer.

4. When they are frozen solid, proceed as in step 6 below, under "Directions For All Other Kinds of Sorbet," or transfer the chunks to a plastic bag and store them in the freezer until you wish to make sorbet. This is a good way to keep from wasting bananas if you find you have too many ripe ones to use at one time.

DIRECTIONS FOR PINEAPPLE SORBET AND PEACH OR APRICOT SORBET MADE WITH CANNED FRUIT:

1. The night before you wish to make sorbet, put the whole can of fruit in the freezer. (You may want to keep a can of fruit in your freezer all the time so you are always ready to make sorbet). If you are using fresh pineapple with juice, put it in a container and put it in the freezer.

2. The next morning run warm water on the can or container, remove both ends of the can with a can opener, and slide the fruit out. Break the frozen fruit and juice into chunks and proceed as in step 7 below under "Directions For All Other Kinds of Sorbet."

DIRECTIONS FOR FANCY PEACH OR RASPBERRY SORBET:

1. Puree the fruit with a food processor, blender, or hand blender.

2. If you are using the raspberries, press the puree through a wire mesh strainer with the back of a spoon to remove the seeds. Measure out ¾ cup seedless puree.

3. Combine the 2 cups peach puree or ¾ cup raspberry puree with the sweetener or juice and water.

4. Put the mixture into ice cube trays and freeze for several hours or overnight until the fruit mixture is completely frozen.

5. About 10 minutes before you want to serve the sorbet, remove the frozen fruit cubes from the freezer and allow them to stand for 5 minutes at room temperature.

6. Proceed as in step 7 below under "Directions for All Other Kinds of Sorbet."

DIRECTIONS FOR ORANGE SORBET:

1. In a saucepan, sprinkle the agar flakes or gelatin over ¾ cup of the water.

2. Heat over medium heat until the mixture boils and the agar or gelatin dissolves. Cool to room temperature.

3. Combine the agar or gelatin mixture, orange juice concentrate, and remaining 1 cup of water.

4. Put the mixture into ice cube trays and freeze for several hours or overnight until the fruit mixture is completely frozen.

5. About 20 minutes before you want to serve the sorbet, remove the frozen fruit cubes from the freezer and allow them to stand for 10 to 15 minutes at room temperature.

6. Proceed as in step 7 below under "Directions for All Other Kinds of Sorbet."

DIRECTIONS FOR CRANBERRY SORBET:

1. Combine the cranberries and fruit juice or water in a saucepan.

2. Bring the mixture to a boil, reduce the heat, and simmer it, stirring it occasionally, for about 20 minutes, or until the cranberries have popped and lost their shape.

3. If you are using the stevia, stir in ⅛ teaspoon of stevia thoroughly. Taste the mixture to determine if you have added enough stevia. If it is still too tart for you, add up to ⅛ teaspoon more.

4. Put the cranberries into ice cube trays and freeze for several hours or overnight until the fruit mixture is completely frozen.

5. Proceed as in step 6 immediately below to process the cranberries.

DIRECTIONS FOR ALL OTHER KINDS OF SORBET:

1. Peel the fruit and remove any seeds if you are using fresh fruit.

2. Cut the fruit into chunks.

3. Put the fruit and any additional ingredients into a blender or food processor with the metal pureeing blade and process until smooth.

4. If you are making apple sorbet, stir together the applesauce, juice, and cinnamon.

5. Put the puree into ice cube trays and freeze for several hours or overnight until the fruit mixture is completely frozen.

6. About 20 minutes before you want to serve the sorbet, remove the frozen fruit cubes or chunks from the freezer and allow them to stand for 10 to 15 minutes at room temperature.

7. Put a few cubes or frozen fruit chunks into your blender or food processor with the metal pureeing blade and puree until smooth.

8. Add more cubes or chunks one or two at a time, processing until smooth after each addition.

9. Serve the sorbet immediately or freeze any that is left over.

Makes 6 servings

Quick Fruit Sorbet

Day 1 – PINEAPPLE
Day 2 – GRAPE
Day 3 – APPLE
Extra foods – ORANGE

> ¾ cup, or 1 6-ounce can of frozen pineapple, grape, white grape, apple, or orange juice concentrate
> 1 tray of ice cubes (made with about 2 cups of water)

1. Put the fruit juice concentrate into a food processor with the metal pureeing blade.

2. Process briefly until smooth.

3. Add the ice cubes one or two at a time, processing until the sorbet is smooth after each addition.

4. Serve the sorbet immediately or freeze any that is left over. This sorbet tends to become very hard if frozen for a long time.

Makes about 6 servings

Frozen Fruit Treats

This recipe was my son John's idea. His grandma originally made it for him with grapes.

ANY DAY, depending on the fruit used

> BANANA CHUNKS (DAY 1), GRAPES (DAY 2), APPLE CHUNKS (DAY 3),
>   STRAWBERRIES (DAY 3), pitted BLACK CHERRIES (DAY 4),
>   PEACH CHUNKS (DAY 4), MELON BALLS (DAY 4),
>   BLUEBERRIES (EXTRA FOODS), ORANGE SEGMENTS (EXTRA FOODS), or
>   other small pieces of fruit
> Toothpicks

1. Peel large fruits and cut them into bite-sized chunks.

2. Skewer pieces of fruit on the toothpicks, putting three or four pieces of fruit on each toothpick.

3. Lay the toothpicks with fruit on a dish.

4. Put the dish in the freezer and freeze for several hours or until the fruit is hard.

Makes as many servings as you would like

Baked Apples or Pears

DAY 3

> 4 large baking apples or pears
> ½ cup thawed apple juice concentrate, apple juice, or water with the apples
>   OR pear juice or water with the pears
> ½ teaspoon cinnamon (optional)

1. Core the apples or pears.

2. Put them in a 2½-quart glass casserole dish with a lid.

3. Pour the juice or water into the casserole.

4. Sprinkle the cinnamon down the holes in the center of the fruit.

5. Turn your oven on to 350°F. There is no need to preheat the oven for this recipe.

6. Bake for 40 to 50 minutes for the apples or 1 to 1½ hours for the pears or until the fruit is tender when pierced with a fork.

7. Serve hot or refrigerate the fruit.

Makes 4 servings.

Other Desserts

The desserts in this chapter are more complex than those in the last chapter and therefore may be more difficult to digest. Allergy patients with severe yeast problems should ask their doctors whether they should wait until they have made some progress on the road to recovery before eating these desserts. However, since these desserts are made without sugar, they are much better for you than anything you can buy in your grocery store. Also, because they are made with whole grains, vegetables, and fruits, they can add valuable nutrients to your diet.

These desserts will be occasional treats rather than staples of your diet. For that reason, and also because some ingredients are especially useful in dessert recipes (for example, date sugar is "made" for cake), there is more "borrowing" of foods from other rotation days than in other chapters of this book.

Fruited Cake

KAMUT-PINEAPPLE (DAY 1)

1 cup pineapple canned in its own juice or fresh pineapple with enough juice to cover it
1 cup pineapple juice concentrate, thawed
¼ cup oil
2¾ cups kamut flour
1½ teaspoons baking soda
½ teaspoon unbuffered vitamin C powder
6 slices of juice-packed canned or fresh pineapple (optional)
6 small pieces of dried banana (optional)

BARLEY-PINEAPPLE (DAY 1)

1 cup juice-packed canned pineapple or fresh pineapple with enough juice to cover it
1 cup pineapple juice concentrate, thawed
¼ cup oil
3 cups barley flour
1½ teaspoons baking soda
½ teaspoon unbuffered vitamin C powder
6 slices of juice-packed canned or fresh pineapple (optional)
6 small pieces of dried banana (optional)

BARLEY-DATE (DAY 1 – borrow date from DAY 4)

4 cups barley flour
1 cup date sugar
2 teaspoons baking soda
½ teaspoon unbuffered vitamin C powder
1½ cups chopped dates
1½ cups chopped walnuts
2 cups pineapple concentrate, thawed (or borrow apple juice concentrate from DAY 3 for a more "neutral" tasting cake)
¾ cup oil

WHITE SPELT-DATE (DAY 3 – borrow date from DAY 4)

5 cups white spelt flour
1¼ cups date sugar
2½ teaspoons baking soda
½ teaspoon unbuffered vitamin C powder
1½ cups chopped dates
½ cup chopped nuts
1⅔ cups apple juice concentrate, thawed
½ cup oil

SPELT-APPLE (Day 3 – borrow raisins and cloves from Day 2 and nutmeg from Day 4)

- 1 cup apple juice concentrate
- 2¼ cups whole spelt flour
- 1½ teaspoons baking soda
- ¾ teaspoon cinnamon
- ⅛ teaspoon nutmeg (optional)
- ⅛ teaspoon cloves (optional)
- ⅛ teaspoon salt
- ¾ cup grated peeled apple (about 1 small apple)
- ½ cup unsweetened applesauce
- ⅜ cup (¼ cup plus 2 tablespoons) oil
- ¾ cup raisins (optional)

OAT-DATE (Day 4 – borrow cloves from Day 2 and cinnamon from Day 3)

- 1½ cups quick rolled oats (uncooked)
- 1½ cups boiling water
- ¾ cup oil
- ¾ cup cool water
- 1½ cups oat flour
- 1 cup date sugar
- 1¼ teaspoons baking soda
- ½ teaspoon unbuffered vitamin C powder
- 1 teaspoon salt
- 2 teaspoon cinnamon
- ½ teaspoon ground cloves
- 1 cup chopped pitted dates
- ½ cup finely chopped nuts

1. Choose one set of ingredients from the previous page or above.

2. If you are making the kamut-pineapple or barley-pineapple cake, put the canned or fresh pineapple with its juice (but not the optional six slices) in a blender or food processor and puree it until smooth. Add the pineapple juice concentrate and oil and blend again briefly.

3. If you are making the spelt-apple cake, put the apple juice concentrate in a small saucepan. Bring it to a boil and cook it over medium heat until its volume is reduced to ½ cup. (Pour it into a measuring cup to check its volume occasionally as it is cooking). Allow it to cool.

4. If you are making the oat-date cake, stir together the oats and boiling water in a large bowl. Allow them to cool for 5 to 10 minutes. Add the oil and cool water and stir the mixture vigorously until it is fairly smooth and the lumps are gone.

5. Preheat your oven to 325°F for the spelt-apple cake or to 375°F for any of the other kinds of cake.

6. For the barley-date cake or white spelt-date cake, prepare two 8 inch by 4 inch loaf pans. For the other cakes, prepare an 8 inch round or square cake pan. If you are making the kamut-pineapple or barley-pineapple cake, oil the pan; put the pineapple slices into the bottom of the pan in a single layer with the banana pieces in the center of the slices. If you are making any of the other cakes, oil the pan and shake flour in it so that the bottom and sides are coated with flour.

7. In a large bowl, stir together the dry ingredients such as the flour, date sugar, baking soda, vitamin C powder, salt, spices, dates, raisins, and nuts.

8. In a separate small bowl, combine the remaining ingredients such as the juice, oil, applesauce, and grated apple. (You will have already combined the liquid ingredients for the kamut-pineapple, barley-pineapple, and oat-date cakes).

9. Add the liquid ingredients to the dry ingredients and stir until they are just mixed in.

10. Pour the batter into the prepared pan(s).

11. Bake the cakes until they are lightly browned and a toothpick inserted into the center of the cake comes out dry or for the following times:

> Kamut-pineapple: 35 to 45 minutes
> Barley-date: 30 to 40 minutes
> Barley-pineapple: 30 to 40 minutes
> Spelt-apple: 40 to 50 minutes
> White spelt-date: 30 to 40 minutes
> Oat-date: 55 to 60 minutes

12. Cool the kamut-pineapple or barley-pineapple cake in the pan for 10 minutes; then run a knife around the edges of the pan and invert the cake onto a serving dish.

13. The other cakes are best served from the pan. Frost them with the optional frosting below, if you wish.

Makes an 8 inch one layer cake or two 8 by 4 inch loaf cakes

OPTIONAL FROSTING FOR FRUITED CAKES:

(**DAY 4** when made with oat flour; to use on **DAYS 1&3**, borrow dates from **DAY 4**)

> ⅔ cup water
> 1½ tablespoons barley (**DAY 1**), kamut (**DAY 1**), spelt (**DAY 3**),
>   or oat (**DAY 4**) flour
> 1 cup date sugar

1. Combine the flour and water in a small saucepan.

2. Bring them to a boil, reduce the heat, and simmer, stirring often, until they form a thick sauce.

3. Remove the pan from the heat.

4. If the date sugar is lumpy, press it through a sieve to remove any lumps.

5. Add the date sugar to the sauce and stir it in thoroughly until the frosting is smooth.

6. Frost the cake immediately before the frosting cools.

Makes enough frosting for one 8 inch or 9 inch cake or two loaf cakes.

Vegetable Cake

KAMUT-CARROT (DAY 1 – borrow cinnamon from DAY 3 and cloves and raisins from DAY 2)

2½ cups kamut flour
2 teaspoons baking soda
1½ teaspoons cinnamon
¼ teaspoon cloves
1 cup raisins (optional)
1½ cups grated carrots
1 cup pineapple juice concentrate, thawed
1 cup water
¼ cup oil

RYE-CARROT (DAY 2 – borrow optional pineapple from DAY 1 and cinnamon from DAY 3)

2½ cups rye flour
2 teaspoons baking soda
½ teaspoon vitamin C powder (Omit it if you use the pineapple juice).
1½ teaspoons cinnamon
¼ teaspoon cloves
1 cup raisins (optional)
1½ cups grated carrots
2 cups white grape juice OR 1 cup thawed white grape or pineapple juice concentrate plus 1 cup water
¼ cup oil

WHITE SPELT-CARROT (DAY 3 – borrow cloves and raisins from DAY 2 and date sugar from DAY 4)

2¼ cups white spelt flour
¾ cup date sugar
1½ teaspoons baking soda
⅜ teaspoon unbuffered vitamin C powder
1¼ teaspoons cinnamon
¼ teaspoon cloves
¼ teaspoon salt
¾ cup raisins (optional)
1 cup grated carrots
⅜ cup (¼ cup plus 2 tablespoons) oil
⅞ cup (¾ cup plus 2 tablespoons) water

WHOLE SPELT-ZUCCHINI (DAY 3 – borrow pineapple from DAY 1, cloves from DAY 2, zucchini and coconut from DAY 4)

2 cups whole spelt flour
1¼ teaspoons baking soda
¼ teaspoon salt
¾ teaspoon cinnamon
¼ teaspoon ground cloves
⅓ cup grated unsweetened coconut
1⅓ cups grated zucchini
⅔ cup very small pieces of fresh pineapple or pineapple tidbits canned in their own juice, drained
¾ cup plus 1 tablespoon pineapple juice concentrate, thawed
⅓ cup oil

MILLET-ZUCCHINI (Day 3 – borrow cloves and raisins from **Day 2** and date, both squashes, and nutmeg from **Day 4**; this cake is quite fragile).

    1½ cups millet flour
    1 cup tapioca starch
    ½ cup date sugar
    2 teaspoons baking soda
    ½ teaspoon unbuffered vitamin C powder
    1½ teaspoons cinnamon
    ¼ teaspoon cloves
    ¼ teaspoon nutmeg
    ¼ teaspoon salt
    1½ cups pureed cooked butternut squash
    ¼ cup water
    ¼ cup oil
    1 cup grated zucchini

OAT-CARROT (Day 4 – borrow cinnamon from **Day 3** and cloves and optional raisins from **Day 2**)

    2½ cups oat flour
    1 cup date sugar
    1¾ teaspoons baking soda
    ½ teaspoon unbuffered vitamin C
        powder
    1½ teaspoons cinnamon
    ¼ teaspoon cloves
    ¼ teaspoon salt
    ¾ cup commercially chopped pitted
        dates (coated with oat flour),
        hand-chopped dates, or raisins
    1 cup water
    ½ cup oil
    1 cup grated carrots

QUINOA-CARROT (Day 3 – borrow cloves and raisins from **Day 2**)

    2½ cups quinoa flour
    ½ cup tapioca flour
    1½ teaspoons baking soda
    1 teaspoon cinnamon
    ¼ teaspoon cloves
    1 cup raisins (optional)
    1 cup grated carrots
    1½ cups apple juice concentrate
    ⅜ cup (¼ cup plus 2 tablespoons) oil

1. Choose one set of ingredients from the previous page or above.

2. Peel the carrots if you are using them. Grate the carrots or zucchini using the largest hole on a cheese grater or a food processor. Drain the zucchini on paper towels to absorb excess moisture.

3. Prepare two 8 inch by 4 inch loaf pans if you are making the quinoa cake or one 8 inch or 9 inch square cake pan for any of the other kinds of cake. Rub the inside of the pan(s) with oil. Shake flour in the pan(s) so that the sides and bottom are coated with flour.

4. Preheat your oven to 325°F for the spelt-zucchini cake or to 350°F for any other type of cake.

5. In a large bowl stir together the dry ingredients such as the flour(s), date sugar, baking soda, vitamin C powder, spices, coconut, and raisins or dates.

6. In a small bowl stir together the liquid or "wet" ingredients such as the juice, water, oil, and pineapple. Stir in the grated vegetables.

7. Add the liquid ingredient-vegetable mixture to the dry ingredients and stir until they are just mixed.

8. Pour the batter into the prepared cake pan(s).

9. Bake the cake until it is lightly browned and a toothpick inserted into its center comes out dry or for the following times:

> Kamut-carrot: 45 to 55 minutes
> Rye-carrot: 45 to 55 minutes
> White spelt-carrot: 30 to 35 minutes
> Spelt-zucchini: 50 to 55 minutes
> Millet-zucchini: 40 to 50 minutes
> Quinoa-carrot: 40 to 50 minutes
> Oat-carrot: 40 to 45 minutes

10. Cool the cake(s) completely on a cooling rack.

11. If you wish to, frost the cake(s) with the optional "cream cheese" frosting below.

Makes one 8 or 9 inch square one layer cake or two loaf cakes

OPTIONAL "CREAM CHEESE" FROSTING FOR VEGETABLE CAKES:

(**DAY 1** if you use goat yo-cheese and yogurt, **DAY 3** if you use sheep yo-cheese and yogurt, or **EXTRA FOODS** if you use cow cream cheese and milk; borrow date from **DAY 4**)

> ½ cup goat or sheep yo-cheese (recipe, page 63) or 4 ounces of cream cheese at room temperature
> 2 tablespoons of goat or sheep yogurt or 1½ tablespoons of cow's milk
> ¾ cup very fine date sugar

1. If your date sugar is coarse, put it in a food processor with the metal pureeing blade and process it for two to three minutes or until it is fine. Measure the date sugar after processing.

2. Using an electric mixer, beat together the yo-cheese or cream cheese with the yogurt or milk.

3. While the mixer is running, beat in the date sugar about ¼ cup at a time.

4. Spread the frosting on the cooled cake.

5. Store any cake frosted with this frosting in the refrigerator.

Makes enough frosting for one 8 or 9 inch one-layer cake or two loaf cakes

High Mineral Gingerbread

Blackstrap molasses contains all the minerals of sugar cane that are refined out to make white sugar. By combining blackstrap molasses with fruit juice, you get the milder flavor of "regular" molasses plus extra minerals.

AMARANTH (Day 1, borrow cinnamon from Day 3)

1½ cups amaranth flour
½ cup arrowroot
1 teaspoon baking soda
¼ teaspoon unbuffered vitamin C powder
¾ teaspoon ginger
1 teaspoon cinnamon
¾ cup pineapple juice concentrate, thawed
¼ cup blackstrap molasses
¼ cup oil

SPELT (Day 3, borrow ginger from Day 1)

2 cups whole spelt flour
1 teaspoon baking soda
¼ teaspoon unbuffered vitamin C powder
¾ teaspoon ginger
1 teaspoon cinnamon
¾ cup apple juice concentrate, thawed
¼ cup blackstrap molasses
¼ cup oil

QUINOA (Day 3, borrow ginger from Day 1)

1¼ cups quinoa flour
½ cup tapioca starch
1 teaspoon baking soda
¼ teaspoon unbuffered vitamin C powder
¾ teaspoon ginger
1 teaspoon cinnamon
¾ cup apple juice concentrate, thawed
¼ cup blackstrap molasses
¼ cup oil

1. Choose one set of ingredients from above.
2. Preheat your oven to 350°F.
3. Rub the inside of an 8 inch or 9 inch round or square cake pan with oil. Shake flour in it so the bottom and sides of the pan are coated.
4. In a large bowl, stir together the flour(s), baking soda, vitamin C powder, and spices.
5. In another bowl or cup, stir together the molasses, juice, and oil.
6. Add the liquid ingredients to the dry ingredients and stir them together until they are just mixed.
7. Put the batter into the prepared pan.
8. Bake the cake for 30 to 35 minutes or until a toothpick inserted in its center comes out dry.

Makes one 8 inch or 9 inch square or round one layer cake

Any day Spice Cake

BARLEY-DATE (DAY 1, borrow cloves and allspice from **DAY 2**, cinnamon from **DAY 3**, and date from **DAY 4**)

- 2 cups barley flour
- ½ cup date sugar
- 1 teaspoon baking soda
- ¼ teaspoon unbuffered vitamin C powder
- 1 teaspoon cinnamon
- ¼ teaspoon cloves
- ¼ teaspoon allspice
- 2 cups pureed or thoroughly mashed bananas
- ⅜ cup (¼ cup plus 2 tablespoons) oil

BARLEY-FOS (DAY 1, borrow cloves and allspice from **DAY 2**, cinnamon from **DAY 3**)

- 2¼ cups barley flour
- 1 cup FOS
- 1 teaspoon baking soda
- ¼ teaspoon unbuffered vitamin C powder
- 1 teaspoon cinnamon
- ¼ teaspoon cloves
- ¼ teaspoon allspice
- 2 cups pureed or thoroughly mashed bananas
- ⅜ cup (¼ cup plus 2 tablespoons) oil

MILO-DATE (DAY 1, borrow cloves and allspice from **DAY 2**, cinnamon from **DAY 3**, and date from **DAY 4**)

- 2 cups milo flour
- ½ cup date sugar
- 1 teaspoon baking soda
- ¼ teaspoon unbuffered vitamin C powder
- 1 teaspoon cinnamon
- ¼ teaspoon cloves
- ¼ teaspoon allspice
- 1½ cups pureed or thoroughly mashed bananas
- ⅜ cup (¼ cup plus 2 tablespoons) oil

MILLET (DAY 3 – borrow cloves and allspice from day 2)

- 1¼ cups millet flour
- 1¼ cups tapioca flour
- 1¼ teaspoons baking soda
- ¼ teaspoon unbuffered vitamin C powder
- 1 teaspoon cinnamon
- ¼ teaspoon cloves
- ⅛ teaspoon allspice
- ⅞ cup apple juice concentrate, thawed, OR ¼ to ⅜ teaspoon white stevia extract powder (to taste) plus ⅞ cup water
- ¼ cup oil

AMARANTH (DAY 1 – borrow cinnamon from **DAY 3**, grape, cloves and allspice from **DAY 2**, and the pear and peach in Fruit Sweet™ or Pear Sweet™ from **DAYS 3 & 4**)

- 2¼ cups amaranth flour
- ¾ cup arrowroot
- 2 teaspoons baking soda
- ½ teaspoon unbuffered vitamin C powder
- 1 teaspoon cinnamon
- ¼ teaspoon cloves
- ⅛ teaspoon allspice
- ½ cup Grape Sweet™, Pear Sweet™ or Fruit Sweet™ OR ¼ to ½ teaspoon white stevia extract powder (to taste)
- Water – ½ cup with the Grape Sweet™, Pear Sweet™ or Fruit Sweet™ OR 1 cup with the stevia
- ¼ cup oil

OAT-DATE (DAY 4 – borrow bananas from **DAY 1**, cloves and allspice from **DAY 2** and cinnamon from **DAY 3)**

> 2 cups oat flour
> ½ cup date sugar
> 1 teaspoon baking soda
> ¼ teaspoon unbuffered vitamin C powder
> 1 teaspoon cinnamon
> ¼ teaspoon cloves
> ¼ teaspoon allspice
> 1½ cups pureed or thoroughly mashed bananas
> ⅜ cup (¼ cup plus 2 tablespoons) oil

1. Choose one set of ingredients from the previous page or above.
2. If you will be using bananas, thorougly mash them or puree them. A hand blender is helpful for this task because you can puree them right in the measuring cup.
3. If you will be using date sugar and it is quite lumpy, press it through a sieve with the back of the spoon to get rid of the lumps.
4. Preheat the oven to 350°F for the amaranth or millet cakes or to 375°F for the barley, milo, or oat cakes.
5. Prepare an 8 inch by 4 inch loaf pan for the amaranth or millet cakes or an 8 or 9 inch round cake pan for the barley, milo, or oat cakes. Rub the inside of the pan with oil and shake flour in it so the bottom and sides are coated with flour.
6. Stir together the dry ingredients such as the flour(s), date sugar, FOS or stevia, baking soda, vitamin C powder and spices in a large bowl.
7. In a separate bowl or cup, stir together the liquid ingredients such as pureed bananas, water, apple juice concentrate, Grape Sweet™, Pear Sweet™ or Fruit Sweet™ and oil.
8. Stir the liquid ingredients into the dry ingredients until they are just mixed in. (The amaranth batter will be stiff).
9. Put the batter into the baking pan.
10. Bake the cakes until a toothpick inserted into the center of the cake comes out dry or for the following times:

    Barley: 25 to 30 minutes
    Milo: 25 to 30 minutes
    Amaranth: 30 to 40 minutes
    Millet: 30 to 40 minutes
    Oat: 25 to 30 minutes

    The stevia sweetened cakes will not brown very much. The other cakes will be lightly browned when they are done.
11. Cool the cake thoroughly before frosting it. If you wish to frost this cake, use the frosting recipes for the fruited or vegetable cakes on pages 208 or 211.
12. Serve the cake from the pan.

Makes one 8 inch or 9 inch round one-layer cake or one loaf cake.

Any day Carob
or Chocolate Cake

BARLEY (DAY 1, borrow apple from DAY 3)

2½ cups barley flour
⅓ cup carob powder or cocoa
1½ teaspoons baking soda
½ teaspoon unbuffered vitamin C powder
¼ teaspoon salt
1¼ cups apple juice concentrate, thawed
¼ cup oil

RYE (DAY 2)

2¼ cups rye flour
⅓ cup carob powder
1½ teaspoons baking soda
¼ teaspoon salt
1 cup white or purple grape juice concentrate, thawed
½ cup oil

WHITE SPELT (DAY 3)

2⅓ cups white spelt flour
¼ cup cocoa or carob powder
1¼ teaspoons baking soda
¼ teaspoon salt
¼ teaspoon unbuffered vitamin C powder
1 cup plus 3 tablespoons apple juice concentrate, thawed
3 tablespoons oil

QUINOA (DAY 3)

1½ cups quinoa flour
¾ cup tapioca flour
⅓ cup carob powder
1½ teaspoons baking soda
¼ teaspoon salt
1 cup apple juice concentrate, thawed
½ cup oil

QUINOA-STEVIA (DAY 3)

1½ cups quinoa flour
½ cup tapioca flour
½ cup carob powder
2 teaspoons baking soda
½ teaspoon unbuffered vitamin C powder
¼ teaspoon salt
¼ to ½ teaspoon white stevia powder, or to taste
1¼ cups water
¼ cup oil

RICE (DAY 4)

1½ cups rice flour
½ cup date sugar
¼ cup carob powder
1 teaspoon baking soda
¼ teaspoon unbuffered vitamin C powder
¼ teaspoon salt
1 cup water OR ¾ cup water plus 1 extra large egg
¼ cup oil

1. Choose one set of ingredients from above.

2. Prepare an 8 inch by 4 inch loaf pan for the quinoa-stevia cake or rice cake or an 8 or 9 inch square or round cake pan for any of the other cakes. Rub the inside of the pan with oil and shake flour in it so the bottom and sides are coated with flour.

3. If your carob or cocoa is lumpy, press it through a sieve with the back of a spoon to remove the lumps.

4. Preheat the oven to 350°F.

5. Stir together the dry ingredients such as the flour(s), carob or cocoa, stevia, date sugar, baking soda, vitamin C powder, and salt in a large bowl.

7. In a separate bowl or cup stir together the water or fruit juice concentrate and oil.

8. Stir the liquid ingredients into the dry ingredients until they are just mixed in.

9. Put the batter into the prepared baking pan.

10. Bake the cake for 25 to 40 minutes or until a toothpick inserted into the center of the cake comes out dry. (Overbaking of chocolate or carob cakes makes them seem very dry).

11. Cool the cake completely before frosting it with one of the frostings below if you wish to frost the cake.

Makes one 8 inch or 9 inch round or square one-layer cake or one loaf cake.

NUT FROSTING FOR CAROB OR CHOCOLATE CAKES:

DAY 1 (borrow coconut from DAY 4 and the pear and peach in the
        Fruit Sweet™ from DAYS 3 & 4)
DAY 2 (borrow coconut from DAY 4)
DAY 3 (borrow coconut from DAY 4 and the pineapple and peach in the
        Fruit Sweet™ from DAYS 1 & 4)
DAY 4 (borrow the pineapple and pear in the Fruit Sweet™ from DAYS 1 & 3)

    ⅜ cup Fruit Sweet™ (DAYS 1, 3, OR 4), Grape Sweet™ (DAY 2),
       Pear Sweet™ (DAY 3), or honey (EXTRA FOODS)
  1 cup finely shredded unsweetened coconut
  1 cup finely chopped nuts appropriate for the rotation day

1. Put the sweetener into a small saucepan and bring it to a boil.

2. Thoroughly stir in the coconut and nuts.

3. Spread the frosting on the cake immediately before the frosting cools.

Makes enough frosting for one 8 inch or 9 inch square or round one-layer cake

COCONUT FROSTING FOR CHOCOLATE OR CAROB CAKES:

DAY 1 (borrow coconut from **DAY 4**
    and the pear and peach in the Fruit Sweet™ from **DAYS 3 & 4**)
DAY 2 (borrow arrowroot from **DAY 1**
    or tapioca from **DAY 3** and coconut from **DAY 4**)
DAY 3 (borrow coconut from **DAY 4**
    and the pineapple and peach in the Fruit Sweet™ from **DAYS 1 & 4**)
DAY 4 (borrow the pineapple and pear in the Fruit Sweet™
    or Pear Sweet™ from **DAYS 1 & 3**)

    ½ cup water
    ½ cup Fruit Sweet™ (**DAYS 1, 3, OR 4**), Grape Sweet™ (**DAY 2**),
        Pear Sweet™ (**DAY 3**), or honey (**EXTRA FOODS**)
    3 tablespoons arrowroot (**DAY 1**)
        OR 2½ tablespoons tapioca flour (**DAY 3**) or water chestnut flour (**DAY 4**)
    2 cups very finely shredded unsweetened coconut
        OR 3 cups regular unsweetened shredded coconut

1. Stir together the water, sweetener, and starch in a saucepan.

2. Cook the mixture over medium heat, stirring it every few minutes, until it thickens and begins to boil.

3. Stir in the coconut before the sweetener mixture can cool off.

4. Immediately spread the frosting on the top of the cake.

    NOTE: This frosting is best made with very finely shredded coconut; but if you cannot get it, you can use regular shredded coconut. To buy very finely shredded coconut by mail order, see "Sources of Special Foods," page 299.

Makes enough frosting for one 8 inch or 9 inch square or round one-layer cake

Any day Pie

CRUSTS:

KAMUT (DAY 1)

2¾ cups kamut flour
½ teaspoon salt
⅔ cup oil
4 to 5 tablespoons water

BARLEY (DAY 1)

3 cups barley flour
½ teaspoon salt
½ cup oil
6 to 7 tablespoons water

AMARANTH (DAY 1)

1½ cups amaranth flour
¾ cup arrowroot
½ teaspoon salt
½ cup oil
4 to 5 tablespoons water

RYE (DAY 2)

2½ cups rye flour
½ teaspoon salt
⅔ cup oil
4 to 5 tablespoons water

TEFF (DAY 2)

3 cups teff flour
½ teaspoon salt
½ cup oil
5 to 6 tablespoons water

BUCKWHEAT (DAY 2)

3 cups buckwheat flour
½ teaspoon salt
¾ cup oil
6 to 8 tablespoons water

SPELT (DAY 3)

3 cups spelt flour
½ teaspoon salt
½ cup oil
5 to 6 tablespoons water

WHITE SPELT (DAY 3)

2½ cups white spelt flour
½ teaspoon salt
⅜ cup (¼ cup plus 2 tablespoons) oil
4 to 6 tablespoons water

QUINOA (DAY 3)

2 cups quinoa flour
1 teaspoon baking soda
¼ teaspoon unbuffered vitamin C
    powder
½ teaspoon salt (optional)
½ teaspoon cinnamon (optional)
½ cup oil
4 to 6 tablespoons water

OAT (DAY 4)

3 cups oat flour
½ teaspoon salt
½ cup oil
4 to 5 tablespoons water

RICE (DAY 4)

3 cups brown or white rice flour
½ teaspoon salt
½ cup oil
6 to 8 tablespoons water

COCONUT (DAY 4)

2 cups unsweetened shredded or very
    finely shredded coconut (See
    "Sources," page 299 for finely
    shredded coconut).
Coconut oil – ¼ cup with shredded
    coconut OR ⅜ cup (¼ cup plus 2
    tablespoons) with finely shredded
    coconut

Choose one set of ingredients from the previous page.

DIRECTIONS FOR COCONUT PIE CRUST:

1. Preheat your oven to 300°F.

2. Melt approximately the amount of coconut oil you will need in a small saucepan over low heat.

3. Measure the coconut oil.

4. Measure the coconut into a glass pie dish.

5. Pour the coconut oil onto the coconut. Mix the oil and coconut thoroughly using a spoon and your hands.

6. Press the mixture evenly onto the bottom and sides of the dish.

7. Bake the crust for 12 to 15 minutes or until it begins to brown.

8. Cool the crust completely on a wire cooling rack.

9. Fill the crust with any completely cooked filling below, such as pumpkin, carob, or coconut filling. You may also use any fruit filling if you cook it until it is thickened and the fruit is tender; then allow it to cool slightly before putting it in the coconut crust.

Makes one coconut pie crust

DIRECTIONS FOR MAKING ANY OTHER PIE CRUST FOR ONE CRUST PIES:

1. Choose one set of ingredients from above.

2. If you are making a pie for which you bake the crust before filling it, preheat your oven to 350°F for the quinoa crust or to 400°F for any of the other kinds of pie crust. If you will be baking the crust with the filling in it, preheat your oven to the temperature given for the filling below.

3. Stir together the dry ingredients such as the flour(s), salt, baking soda, vitamin C powder and cinnamon in a large bowl.

4. Add the oil and blend it in thoroughly with a pastry cutter.

5. Add the smallest amount of water listed above and mix the dough until it begins to stick together, adding more water if necessary.

6. Divide the dough in half.

7. Press each half of the dough into a glass pie dish.

8. If you are making a type of pie that directs that the crust be baked before adding the filling to it, gently prick the crusts with a fork. Bake the crusts until they begin to brown on the bottom or for the following times:

> Kamut: 13 to 18 minutes
> Barley: 15 to 18 minutes
> Amaranth: 15 to 18 minutes
> Rye: 15 to 20 minutes
> Teff: 15 to 18 minutes
> Buckwheat: 15 to 18 minutes
> Spelt: 18 to 22 minutes
> White spelt: 13 to 17 minutes
> Quinoa: 20 to 25 minutes
> Oat: 15 to 20 minutes
> Rice: 15 to 18 minutes

9. Completely cool the crusts on a wire cooling rack before filling them.

10. If you are making only one pie, freeze the second crust.

Makes two single pie crusts

DIRECTIONS FOR MAKING CRUST FOR TWO CRUST PIES:

1. Follow the directions for mixing pie dough in steps 1 through 6 under "Directions For Making Any Other Pie Crust For One Crust Pies" above.

2. Press one half of the crust into the bottom of a glass pie dish.

3. Add the prepared filling (recipes below) to the crust.

4. Crumble the other half of the crust over the filling.

5. Bake as directed for the filling, below.

Makes enough crust for one two-crust pie

> NOTE ON WHITE SPELT CRUST: White spelt pie crust is sturdy enough to be rolled out on a pastry cloth if you wish. Flour the pastry cloth and cloth-covered rolling pin well. Roll half of the dough to about ⅛ inch thick. Use the pastry cloth to fold the crust in half. Then transfer it to the pie dish and unfold it. For a two-crust pie, roll out the second half of the dough. Put the top crust over the filling and cut the edge so it overlaps the bottom crust by about ½ inch. Fold the edge of the top crust under the bottom crust and press the three-layer edge together with a fork. Pierce the top crust with the fork to allow steam to escape. Bake as directed in the filling recipe.

PIE FILLINGS:

BLUEBERRY (DAY 1)

¾ cup pineapple juice concentrate,
   thawed
2 tablespoons arrowroot
1 pound fresh or frozen unsweetened
   blueberries

APPLE (DAY 3)

⅞ cup (¾ cup plus 2 tablespoons)
   apple juice concentrate
6 to 7 apples, peeled, cored, and sliced
   (about 5 cups of slices)
1 teaspoon cinnamon
2 tablespoons tapioca flour OR 3
   tablespoons quick-cooking tapioca

GRAPE (DAY 2; borrow tapioca from DAY 3)

½ cup unsweetened purple grape juice
   concentrate, thawed
3 tablespoons quick-cooking tapioca
4 cups seedless grapes

CHERRY (DAY 4; borrow tapioca from DAY 3 and apple from DAY 3 or the pineapple and pear in the Fruit Sweet™ or Pear Sweet™ from DAYS 1&3)

1½ cups apple juice concentrate OR ¾
   cup Fruit Sweet™ or Pear Sweet™
¼ cup quick-cooking tapioca OR 3
   tablespoons water chestnut starch
2 16-ounce cans unsweetened tart red
   pie cherries, drained

PEACH (DAY 4; borrow apple, tapioca, and cinnamon from DAY 3)

⅞ cup (¾ cup plus 2 tablespoons) apple juice concentrate
5 cups of peeled, pitted, and sliced fresh peaches OR 5 cups of drained, canned,
   water-packed peaches OR 1½ pounds of unsweetened frozen peaches
¼ teaspoon cinnamon (optional)
3 tablespoons water chestnut or tapioca starch

PUMPKIN (ANY DAY, depending on the sweetener used; borrow pumpkin and nutmeg from DAY 4, ginger from DAY 1, cloves and allspice from DAY 2, and cinnamon from DAY 3)

1 envelope unflavored gelatin OR 1 tablespoon agar flakes
Sweetener and liquid – choose from the following list by rotation day:
   DAY 1: 1 cup pineapple juice concentrate, thawed
   DAY 2: 1 cup white grape juice concentrate, thawed OR ½ cup Grape Sweet™
      plus ½ cup water
   DAY 3: 1 cup apple juice concentrate, thawed, OR ½ cup Pear Sweet™
      plus ½ cup water
   DAY 4: 1 cup water plus 1 cup date sugar
   EXTRA FOODS: 1 cup water plus ¼ teaspoon white stevia extract powder

1 16-ounce can pumpkin
1 teaspoon cinnamon
1 teaspoon nutmeg
¼ teaspoon cloves
¼ teaspoon allspice
¼ teaspoon ginger

CAROB (**Day 1** if made with goat's milk and arrowroot, **Day 3** if made with Pear Sweet™, sheep's milk and tapioca, or **Day 4** if made with coconut milk and water chestnut starch; **Days 1, 3** or **4** with the Fruit Sweet™, borrow pineapple, pear, or peach from their days)

Goat's, sheep's, or coconut milk – 2 cups with the honey, Pear Sweet™ or Fruit Sweet™ OR 2¼ cups with the stevia

⅓ cup honey, Pear Sweet™ or Fruit Sweet™ OR ⅛ teaspoon white stevia extract

5 tablespoons arrowroot, tapioca starch, or water chestnut starch

¼ cup carob powder

2 teaspoons corn-free natural vanilla (optional)

COCONUT (**Day 4**; borrow the pineapple and pear in the Fruit Sweet™ or Pear Sweet™ from **Days 1 & 3**, the arrowroot from **Day 1**, or the tapioca from **Day 3**)

1 15-ounce can unsweetened coconut milk (See "Sources," page 299)

¼ cup honey, Pear Sweet™ or Fruit Sweet™ OR ⅛ teaspoon white stevia extract

5 tablespoons water chestnut starch, tapioca flour, or arrowroot

Unsweetened grated coconut (optional)

Choose one set of filling ingredients from the previous page or above.

DIRECTIONS FOR BLUEBERRY, GRAPE, CHERRY, OR PEACH PIE:

1. For a one-crust pie, make, bake, and cool a pie crust according to the directions above. For a two-crust pie, make the pastry dough for a double crust pie and press the bottom crust into a pie dish.

2. If you are making a cherry pie with apple juice, boil the apple juice down to ¾ cup in volume and allow it to cool.

3. Preheat your oven to 400°F if you are making a two-crust pie.

4. In a saucepan, stir together the fruit juice or sweetener and the starch or quick-cooking tapioca. If you are using the tapioca, let it soak in the juice for 5 minutes before proceeding.

5. Add the fruit to the pan and cook the mixture over medium heat, stirring often, until it thickens and comes to a boil.

6. Reduce the heat to very low and simmer the pie filling for 5 minutes, stirring often.

7. For a one crust pie, cool the filling for 10 minutes, put it into the cooled, baked pie crust, and refrigerate the pie.

8. For a two crust pie, put the filling into the unbaked bottom crust you have ready. Crumble the rest of the pie crust dough over the filling. Bake the pie for 10 minutes at 400°F, then turn down the oven temperature to 350°F and bake it for 30 to 50 minutes more or until the bottom crust of the pie begins to brown.

DIRECTIONS FOR APPLE PIE:

1. For a one-crust pie, make, bake, and cool a pie crust according to the directions above. For a two-crust pie, make the pastry dough for a double crust pie and press the bottom crust into a pie dish.

2. Combine the apples, cinnamon, and ⅝ cup of the apple juice in a saucepan. Bring them to a boil, reduce the heat, and simmer until the apples are tender – about 20 minutes.

3. While the apples are simmering, combine the remaining ¼ cup apple juice with the tapioca starch or quick-cooking tapioca. Allow the quick-cooking tapioca to soak in the apple juice for at least five minutes.

4. Preheat your oven to 400°F.

5. Stir the tapioca mixture into the apples when they are tender. Cook over medium heat, stirring often, until the filling thickens and returns to a boil.

6. For a one crust pie, cool the filling for 10 minutes, put it into the cooled, baked pie crust, and refrigerate the pie.

7. For a two crust pie, put the filling into the unbaked bottom crust you have ready. Crumble the rest of the pie crust dough over the filling. Bake the pie for 10 minutes at 400°F, then turn down the oven temperature to 350°F and bake it for 40 to 50 minutes more, or until the bottom crust of the pie begins to brown.

DIRECTIONS FOR PUMPKIN PIE:

1. Make, bake, and cool a pie crust for a one crust pie.

2. Measure the water or fruit juice concentrate into a saucepan. Sprinkle the gelatin or agar over the surface of the liquid.

3. Bring the liquid to a boil, reduce the heat to medium, and boil it until the gelatin or agar is dissolved.

4. If you are using the stevia, add it to the agar or gelatin mixture. Stir it until it is completely dissolved.

5. Add the pumpkin, date sugar (if you are using it), Grape Sweet™ or Pear Sweet™ (if you are using it), and spices to the pan and stir thoroughly.

5. When the filling is well mixed, put it into the cooled baked pie crust.

6. Refrigerate the pie.

DIRECTIONS FOR CAROB OR COCONUT PIE:

1. Make, bake, and cool a pie crust for a one crust pie.

2. If you are making the carob pie, press the carob powder through a sieve with the back of the spoon to remove any lumps.

3. Stir together the carob (if you are using it), starch, and stevia (if you are using it) in a saucepan.

4. Add about ½ cup of the milk to the saucepan and stir until the mixture is smooth.

5. Stir in the rest of the milk and the honey, Pear Sweet™ or Fruit Sweet™.

6. Cook the pie filling over medium heat, stirring, until it thickens and boils. Stir in the optional vanilla.

7. Cool the filling for about 5 minutes.

8. Pour the filling into the prepared pie shell.

9. Sprinkle the coconut pie with coconut if you wish.

10. Refrigerate the pie until it is very cold.

PUDDING VARIATION: Pour the cooked filling into a serving bowl rather than a pie crust and serve warm or cold.

Makes one pie

Any day Fruit Cobbler

FRUIT FILLINGS:

BLUEBERRY (DAY 1)

    4 cups fresh blueberries OR a 1 pound bag of unsweetened frozen blueberries

    ½ cup pineapple juice concentrate, thawed

    5 teaspoons arrowroot

RHUBARB (DAY 2 – borrow arrowroot from **DAY 1** or tapioca from **DAY 3)**

    4 cups sliced rhubarb (just under 1 pound)

    1 cup white grape juice concentrate OR ½ cup Grape Sweet™

    5 teaspoons arrowroot or tapioca flour

EASY APPLE (DAY 3, borrow date from **DAY 4)**

    4 cups peeled and sliced apples (about 5 apples)

    ½ cup date sugar

    ¼ cup tapioca starch

    ½ teaspoon cinnamon

    4 tablespoons water

EASY BLUEBERRY (DAY 1 – borrow date from **DAY 4)**

    4 cups fresh blueberries or 1 pound frozen unsweetened blueberries

    ½ cup date sugar

    ¼ cup arrowroot

    4 tablespoons water ONLY if you are using fresh fruit

APPLE (DAY 3)

    4 to 5 apples, peeled, cored, and sliced to make 3½ to 4 cups of slices

    ½ cup apple juice concentrate, thawed

    5 teaspoons tapioca starch OR 2 tablespoons quick-cooking tapioca

    ½ teaspoon cinnamon

STRAWBERRY (DAY 3)

    1 pound of fresh strawberries or a 1-pound bag of unsweetened frozen strawberries

    ½ cup apple juice concentrate, thawed

    3 tablespoons tapioca flour

TART CHERRY (DAY 4 – borrow the apple and tapioca from **DAY 3** or the pineapple and pear in the Fruit Sweet™ or Pear Sweet™ from **DAYS 1&3)**

> 2 1-pound cans water-packed tart pie cherries, drained, OR 4 cups fresh pitted pie cherries
>
> 1½ cups apple juice concentrate or ¾ cup Fruit Sweet™ or Pear Sweet™
>
> 5 teaspoons water chestnut starch or tapioca starch OR 3 tablespoons quick-cooking tapioca

EASY PEACH (DAY 4 – borrow arrowroot from **DAY 1** or tapioca starch from **DAY 3)**

> 4 cups fresh peeled and sliced peaches OR 1 pound frozen unsweetened peaches
>
> ½ cup date sugar
>
> ¼ cup water chestnut starch, arrowroot, or tapioca starch
>
> 2 tablespoons water ONLY if you are using fresh fruit

BLACK CHERRY (DAY 4 – borrow the pineapple and arrowroot from **DAY 1** or the apple and tapioca from **DAY 3)**

> 4 cups pitted fresh dark (bing) cherries OR one 1-pound bag frozen unsweetened dark cherries
>
> ½ cup apple or pineapple juice concentrate, thawed
>
> 5 teaspoons water chestnut starch, arrowroot, or tapioca starch

PEACH (DAY 4 – borrow the pineapple and arrowroot from **DAY 1** or the apple and tapioca from **DAY 3)**

> 4 cups sliced fresh peaches OR 1 1-pound bag unsweetened frozen peaches
>
> ½ cup apple or pineapple juice concentrate, thawed
>
> 5 teaspoons water chestnut starch, arrowroot or tapioca starch OR 3 tablespoons quick-cooking tapioca

TOPPINGS:

EASY ROLLED GRAIN TOPPING (ANY DAY depending on the grain used – borrow date from **DAY 4** and cinnamon from **DAY 3):**

> 1 cup rolled kamut (**DAY 1**), barley (**DAY 1**), rye (**DAY 2**), spelt (**DAY 3**), millet (**DAY 3**), or oats (**DAY 4**)
>
> ½ cup date sugar
>
> 1 teaspoon cinnamon (optional)
>
> ¼ cup oil
>
> 2 tablespoons water

KAMUT SHORTCAKE TOPPING (Day 1)

¾ cup kamut flour
¾ teaspoon baking soda
⅛ teaspoon unbuffered vitamin C powder
⅜ cup (¼ cup plus 2 tablespoons) pineapple juice concentrate, thawed
⅛ cup (2 tablespoons) oil

RYE SHORTCAKE TOPPING (Day 2)

¾ cup rye flour
¾ teaspoon baking soda
⅛ teaspoon unbuffered vitamin C powder
⅜ cup (¼ cup plus 2 tablespoons) white grape juice concentrate, thawed
⅛ cup (2 tablespoons) oil

TEFF SHORTCAKE TOPPING (Day 2)

¾ cup teff flour
¾ teaspoon baking soda
⅛ teaspoon unbuffered vitamin C powder
⅜ cup (¼ cup plus 2 tablespoons) white grape juice concentrate, thawed
⅛ cup (2 tablespoons) oil

SPELT SHORTCAKE TOPPING (Day 3)

⅞ cup (¾ cup plus 2 tablespoons) whole spelt flour OR 1 cup white spelt flour
¾ teaspoon baking soda
⅛ teaspoon unbuffered vitamin C powder
⅜ cup (¼ cup plus 2 tablespoons) apple juice concentrate, thawed
⅛ cup (2 tablespoons) oil

BARLEY SHORTCAKE TOPPING (Day 1)

⅞ cup (¾ cup plus 2 tablespoons) barley flour
¾ teaspoon baking soda
⅛ teaspoon unbuffered vitamin C powder
⅜ cup (¼ cup plus 2 tablespoons) pineapple juice concentrate, thawed
⅛ cup (2 tablespoons) oil

AMARANTH SHORTCAKE TOPPING (Day 1)

¾ cup amaranth flour
¼ cup arrowroot
¾ teaspoon baking soda
⅛ teaspoon unbuffered vitamin C powder
⅜ cup (¼ cup plus 2 tablespoons) pineapple juice concentrate, thawed
⅛ cup (2 tablespoons) oil

BUCKWHEAT SHORTCAKE TOPPING (Day 2)

¾ cup buckwheat flour
¾ teaspoon baking soda
⅛ teaspoon unbuffered vitamin C powder
⅜ cup (¼ cup plus 2 tablespoons) white grape juice concentrate, thawed
⅛ cup (2 tablespoons) oil

QUINOA SHORTCAKE TOPPING (Day 3)

⅝ cup (½ cup plus 2 tablespoons) quinoa flour
⅛ cup (2 tablespoons) tapioca flour
¾ teaspoon baking soda
⅛ teaspoon unbuffered vitamin C powder
⅜ cup (¼ cup plus 2 tablespoons) apple juice concentrate, thawed
⅛ cup (2 tablespoons) oil

RICE SHORTCAKE TOPPING (DAY 4 – borrow pineapple from DAY 1 or apple from DAY 3)

⅞ cup (¾ cup plus 2 tablespoons) rice flour
¾ teaspoon baking soda
⅛ teaspoon unbuffered vitamin C powder
⅜ cup (¼ cup plus 2 tablespoons) apple or pineapple juice concentrate, thawed
⅛ cup (2 tablespoons) oil

Choose one set of filling ingredients and one set of topping ingredients from the previous pages or above.

DIRECTIONS FOR EASY BLUEBERRY, EASY APPLE, AND EASY PEACH FILLINGS:

1. Stir together the date sugar, starch and cinnamon in a 2½- to 3-quart casserole dish.

2. Add the fruit to the dish and stir to coat the fruit with the starch mixture.

3. If you are using fresh fruit, sprinkle 4 tablespoons water over the blueberries or apples or 2 tablespoons water over the peaches. Omit the water if you are using frozen fruit.

4. For the easiest possible dessert, top this fruit mixture with an easy rolled grain topping and bake as directed for the topping, below.

DIRECTIONS FOR THE OTHER FRUIT FILLINGS:

1. If you are making the rhubarb, raspberry, or tart cherry filling using fruit juice concentrate, put the fruit juice into a saucepan. Bring it to a boil, reduce the heat to medium, and boil it down to one half its original volume (½ cup for the rhubarb or raspberry or ¾ cup for the cherry filling). Allow the juice to cool to lukewarm and proceed with step 3 below.

2. If you are using the Fruit Sweet™, Pear Sweet™ or Grape Sweet™ to make rhubarb, raspberry, or tart cherry filling or if you are making any of the other fillings, put the juice or sweetener into a saucepan.

3. Stir the starch or tapioca into the juice or sweetener.

4. If you are using the quick-cooking tapioca, allow it to soak for at least 5 minutes.

5. Add the fruit to the pan and stir.

6. Heat the mixture over medium heat until it thickens and comes to a boil. Boil and stir it for one minute.

7. Put the fruit into a 2½- to 3-quart casserole dish.

8. Preheat your oven to 325°F for the easy rolled grain topping or to 350°F for any of the other toppings.

8. Prepare the topping of your choice and put it on top of the fruit as directed below.

9. Bake for 25 to 35 minutes or until the topping begins to brown.

DIRECTIONS FOR THE EASY ROLLED GRAIN TOPPINGS:

1. Turn on the oven to 325°F.
2. Stir together the rolled grain, date sugar, and cinnamon in a bowl.
3. Add the oil and stir it in until it is mixed in well.
4. Stir in 2 tablespoons of water.
5. Sprinkle the grain mixture on top of the prepared fruit filling in the casserole dish.
6. Bake for 30 to 40 minutes or until the topping browns.

DIRECTIONS FOR ANY OF THE SHORTCAKE TOPPINGS:

1. Turn on the oven to 350°F.
2. In a medium bowl, stir together the flour(s), baking soda, and vitamin C powder.
3. Stir together the juice and oil in another bowl or cup.
4. Add the liquid ingredients to the dry ingredients and stir until they are just mixed in.
5. Drop the topping onto the prepared fruit filling in the casserole dish.
6. Bake for 25 to 35 minutes or until the topping is slightly browned.

Makes 4 to 6 servings

SHORTCAKE VARIATION:

1. Choose one set of shortcake topping ingredients from above.
2. Preheat your oven to 350°F.
3. Rub oil in an 8 by 4 inch loaf pan. (If you want a larger shortcake, double the ingredient amounts and use a 8 by 8 inch square or 8 to 9 inch round cake pan). Shake flour in the pan so that the bottom and sides of the pan are coated with flour.
4. Mix the shortcake topping as directed immediately above.
5. Spread the batter in the prepared pan.
6. Bake for 25 to 30 minutes or until it is lightly browned.
7. Serve the shortcake from the pan. Cut it into squares and serve it topped with fresh fruit.

Makes 3 to 4 servings

Cookies

There is nothing like a cookie to make being on a restricted diet more fun. All of the recipes in this chapter are made without sugar (most are sweetened with fruit), so they may be acceptable on your diet and are certainly much better for you than giving in to a "normal" treat. However, as with all desserts, people with yeast problems should check with their doctors about whether they should wait until they have improved to enjoy these treats. The cookie recipes in this chapter are fairly simple: if you want to make cookies like Fig Newtons™, Oreos™, or pizzelles, refer to *Allergy Cooking With Ease.*

Since cookies are an occasional treat rather than a dietary staple that you will want to eat every fourth day, there is more "borrowing" of foods from other rotation days in this chapter than in other chapters of this book. Spices are often borrowed from other days, but they tend to be foods that we do not use often anyway. Fruit Sweet™ is a good sweetener for cookies because it is more concentrated than frozen fruit juice concentrates. It is made from peach, pear, and pineapple juice concentrates, so it does not taste like any one fruit. However, to use it you must borrow two fruits from other rotation days. For instance, if you are going to use it on **DAY 1**, pineapple is one of your fruits for that day, and you can borrow pear from **DAY 3** ("split" the family and you can still eat apples on day three) and peach from **DAY 4** (eat cantaloupe on **DAY 4**).

Drop Cookies

Drop cookies are easy to make and you can use almost any kind of flour. Many of the versions below call for milk-free unsweetened carob chips, but you can omit them for a basic cookie, or substitute nuts or dried fruit instead.

KAMUT-PINEAPPLE (DAY 1)

1 cup juice-packed canned pineapple with its juice or fresh pineapple with juice to cover
¾ cup pineapple juice concentrate, thawed
½ cup oil
2 cups kamut flour
½ teaspoon baking soda
1 cup shredded unsweetened coconut

BASIC KAMUT (DAY 1 – borrow the pear and peach in the Fruit Sweet™ from DAYS 3 & 4)

1¾ cups kamut flour
½ teaspoon baking soda
⅛ teaspoon salt
¾ cup Fruit Sweet™
½ cup oil
¾ cup milk-free unsweetened carob chips or chopped nuts (optional)

KAMUT-ORANGE (DAY 1)

2 cups kamut flour
½ teaspoon baking soda
1 cup orange juice concentrate,
    thawed
⅓ cup oil
1 teaspoon corn-free natural orange
    flavor (optional – see "Sources,"
    page 299)

BASIC BARLEY (DAY 1 – borrow the pear and peach in the Fruit Sweet™ or Pear Sweet™ from DAYS 3 & 4)

3½ cups barley flour
1 teaspoon baking soda
¼ teaspoon unbuffered vitamin C
    powder
½ teaspoon salt
1 cup oil
1 cup Fruit Sweet™ or Pear Sweet™
1 cup milk-free unsweetened carob
    chips or chopped nuts (optional)

BASIC AMARANTH (DAY 1 – borrow the pear and peach in the Fruit Sweet™ or Pear Sweet™ from DAYS 3 & 4)

2¼ cups amaranth flour
¾ cup arrowroot
1 teaspoon baking soda
¼ teaspoon unbuffered vitamin C
    powder
¼ teaspoon salt
1¼ cup pineapple juice concentrate,
    thawed, OR ¾ cup Fruit Sweet™
    or Pear Sweet™ plus ½ cup water
¼ cup oil
¾ cup milk-free unsweetened carob
    chips or chopped nuts (optional)

KAMUT-CAROB (DAY 1 – borrow the pear and peach in the Fruit Sweet™ or Pear Sweet™ from DAYS 3 & 4)

2⅔ cups kamut flour
⅓ cup carob powder
1 teaspoon baking soda
¼ teaspoon unbuffered vitamin C
    powder
1 cup oil
1 cup Fruit Sweet™, Pear Sweet™ or
    honey
1 cup milk-free unsweetened carob
    chips or chopped nuts (optional)

BARLEY-MOLASSES (DAY 1 – borrow the pear and peach in the Fruit Sweet™ or Pear Sweet™ from DAYS 3 & 4)

3 cups barley flour
1 teaspoon baking soda
¼ teaspoon unbuffered vitamin C
    powder
¼ teaspoon salt
½ teaspoon ginger
1 cup light molasses OR ¾ cup Fruit
    Sweet™ or Pear Sweet™
    plus ¼ cup blackstrap molasses
½ cup oil

BASIC MILO (DAY 1, borrow cinnamon from DAY 3)

3 cups milo flour
1 teaspoon baking soda
¼ teaspoon unbuffered vitamin C
    powder
¼ teaspoon salt
¼ teaspoon ginger or 1 teaspoon
    cinnamon (optional)
1½ cups thoroughly mashed or pureed
    bananas (about 4 bananas)
½ cup oil
1 cup milk-free unsweetened carob
    chips or chopped nuts (optional)

TEFF-APPLESAUCE (DAY 2, borrow apple from DAY 3)

2 cups teff flour
½ teaspoon baking soda
⅛ teaspoon salt
½ cup unsweetened applesauce
¾ cup apple juice concentrate, thawed
½ cup oil
¾ cup chopped nuts (optional)

BASIC TEFF (DAY 2)

3 cups teff flour
1 teaspoon baking soda
¼ teaspoon unbuffered vitamin C powder
¼ teaspoon salt
¾ cup Grape Sweet™
⅜ cup (¼ cup plus 2 tablespoons) water
⅜ cup (¼ cup plus 2 tablespoons) oil
¾ cup milk-free unsweetened carob chips or chopped nuts (optional)

BASIC WHITE SPELT (DAY 3 – borrow the pineapple and peach in the Fruit Sweet™ from DAYS 1 & 4)

3½ cups white spelt flour
1 teaspoon baking soda
¼ teaspoon unbuffered vitamin C powder
½ teaspoon salt
1 cup Fruit Sweet™ or Pear Sweet™
1 cup oil (or for a lower fat version, ⅔ cup oil plus ⅓ cup water)
1 teaspoon corn-free natural vanilla flavoring (optional)
1 cup milk-free unsweetened carob chips or chopped nuts (optional)

BASIC RYE (DAY 2)

4 cups rye flour
1½ teaspoons baking soda
½ teaspoon unbuffered vitamin C powder
¼ teaspoon salt
1 cup Grape Sweet™
½ cup water
½ cup oil
1 cup milk-free unsweetened carob chips or chopped nuts (optional)

BASIC BUCKWHEAT (DAY 2)

3 cups buckwheat flour
1 teaspoon baking soda
¼ teaspoon unbuffered vitamin C powder
¼ teaspoon salt
¾ cup Grape Sweet™
¾ cup (¼ cup plus 2 tablespoons) water
⅜ cup (¼ cup plus 2 tablespoons) oil
¾ cup milk-free unsweetened carob chips or chopped nuts (optional)

BASIC QUINOA (DAY 3)

2 cups quinoa flour
⅔ cup tapioca starch
1 teaspoons baking soda
Unbuffered vitamin C powder – ¼ teaspoon with the apple juice OR ⅜ teaspoon with the stevia
1⅓ cups apple juice concentrate OR ⅞ cups water plus ½ to ¾ teaspoon white stevia powder, to taste
⅓ cup oil
1 cup milk-free unsweetened carob chips or chopped nuts (optional)

BASIC MILLET (Day 3)

2¼ cups millet flour
½ teaspoon baking soda
½ cup unsweetened applesauce
¾ cup apple juice concentrate, thawed
½ cup oil
¾ cup milk-free unsweetened carob chips or chopped nuts (optional)

CARROT (Day 3, borrow rasins from Day 2)

2 cups quinoa or spelt flour
⅔ cup tapioca starch
1 teaspoon baking soda
Unbuffered vitamin C powder – ¼ teaspoon with the apple juice OR ⅜ teaspoon with the stevia
1 teaspoon cinnamon
⅞ cups (¾ cups plus 2 tablespoons) apple juice concentrate, thawed OR ⅞ cup (¾ cups plus 2 tablespoons) water plus ½ to ¾ teaspoon white stevia extract powder, to taste
⅓ cup oil
1½ cups grated carrots
½ cup chopped dried pears or raisins (optional)

CAROB-TAPIOCA (Day 3)

1½ cups carob powder
1½ cups tapioca starch
1 teaspoon baking soda
¼ teaspoon unbuffered vitamin C powder
1 cup apple juice concentrate, thawed OR ¾ teaspoon white stevia powder plus 1 cup water
½ cup oil

BASIC WHOLE SPELT (Day 3)

2⅓ cups whole spelt flour
½ teaspoon baking soda
¼ teaspoon salt
1¼ cup apple juice concentrate
½ cup oil
¾ cup milk-free unsweetened carob chips or chopped nuts (optional)

BASIC RICE (Day 4 – borrow arrowroot from Day 1 or tapioca from Day 3 and the pineapple and pear in the Fruit Sweet™ or Pear Sweet™ from Days 1 & 3)

1½ cups brown or white rice flour
1¼ cups water chestnut starch, 1½ cups arrowroot, or 1½ cups tapioca starch
1½ teaspoons baking soda
⅜ teaspoon unbuffered vitamin C powder
¾ teaspoon salt
¾ cup Fruit Sweet™, Pear Sweet™ or rice syrup
3 tablespoons water
⅜ cup oil
¾ cup milk-free unsweetened carob chips or chopped nuts (optional)

BASIC OAT (Day 4 – borrow the pineapple and pear in the Fruit Sweet™ or Pear Sweet™ from Days 1 & 3)

3½ cups oat flour
1 teaspoon baking soda
¼ teaspoon unbuffered vitamin C powder
½ teaspoon salt
1 cup oil
1 cup Fruit Sweet™ or Pear Sweet™
1 cup milk-free unsweetened carob chips or chopped nuts (optional)

BASIC CHESTNUT (DAY 4 – borrow the pineapple and pear in the Fruit Sweet™ or Pear Sweet™ from **DAYS 1 & 3**; these cookies are very fragile)

    1½ cups chestnut flour
    1½ cups water chestnut flour
    ¾ teaspoon baking soda
    ¼ teaspoon unbuffered vitamin C powder
    ¾ cup Fruit Sweet™ or Pear Sweet™
    ¾ cup oil
    1 cup milk-free unsweetened carob chips or chopped nuts (optional)

1. Choose one set of ingredients from the previous pages or above.

2. If you are making the kamut-pineapple cookies, puree the pineapple in a food processor, blender, or hand blender. Add the pineapple juice concentrate and oil and puree again for a few seconds.

3. If you are making the basic milo cookies, thoroughly mash the bananas or puree them using a blender, food processor, or hand blender. Measure the bananas, add the oil to them, and stir thoroughly or puree for a few more seconds.

4. If you are making the whole spelt cookies or the quinoa cookies using the apple juice, put the apple juice concentrate into a saucepan. Bring it to a boil and boil it down in volume to ¾ cup for the spelt cookies or to ⅞ cup (¾ cup plus 2 tablespoons) for the quinoa cookies. Allow it to cool before proceeding with the recipe.

5. Preheat your oven to 375°F for the basic barley, amaranth, rye, teff, buckwheat, white spelt, oat, or rice cookies or to 350°F for any of the other cookies.

6. For the kamut-pineapple, basic kamut, milo, rye, whole spelt, and rice cookies, lightly rub your baking sheets with oil.

7. In a large bowl stir together the dry ingredients, such as the flour(s), carob powder, baking soda, vitamin C powder, stevia, cinnamon, and salt.

8. In a separate bowl or cup, combine the liquid ingredients such as the sweetener, water, oil, and flavoring. If you are making carrot cookies, add the carrots to the liquid ingredients. (You will have already combined the liquid ingredients for the kamut-pineapple and milo cookies).

9. Add the liquid ingredients to the dry ingredients and stir until they are just mixed in.

10. Fold in the carob chips, nuts, dry fruit, or coconut.

11. Drop the dough by teaspoonfuls onto baking sheets, allowing room for the softer doughs to spread out as they bake.

12. For the stiffer doughs, such as the kamut-pineapple, kamut-orange, barley-molasses, milo, rye, teff, buckwheat, quinoa, carob-tapioca, rice, or chestnut cookies, flatten the balls of dough out to ¼ inch thickness by pressing them with your fingers held together or with the oiled bottom of a glass.

13. Bake the cookies until they begin to brown or for the following times:

> Kamut-pineapple: 15 to 20 minutes
> Basic kamut: 9 to 13 minutes
> Kamut-orange: 12 to 16 minutes
> Kamut-carob: 10 to 12 minutes
> Basic barley: 8 to 10 minutes
> Barley-molasses: 10 to 15 minutes
> Basic milo: 12 to 17 minutes
> Basic amaranth: 10 to 13 minutes
> Basic rye: 10 to 15 minutes
> Teff-apple: 15 to 20 minutes
> Basic teff: 10 to 13 minutes
> Basic buckwheat: 9 to 12 minutes
> Basic whole spelt: 10 to 14 minutes
> Basic white spelt: 6 to 9 minutes
> Basic lower fat white spelt: 8 to 12 minutes
> Basic millet: 15 to 20 minutes
> Basic quinoa: 10 to 15 minutes
> Carrot: 12 to 15 minutes
> Carob-tapioca: 10 to 12 minutes
> Basic oat: 8 to 10 minutes
> Basic rice: 8 to 11 minutes
> Basic chestnut: 8 to 10 minutes

The carob-tapioca cookies and stevia sweetened cookies will not brown much and should be baked until they are set and dry to the touch instead of brown.

14. Cool the barley, white spelt, and oat cookies on the baking sheets for about 5 minutes before removing them.

15. Use a spatula to transfer the cookies to sheets of paper towel and allow them to cool completely.

Makes about 3 dozen cookies

Easy Shortbread

KAMUT (DAY 1)

2½ cups kamut flour
½ teaspoon baking soda
½ cup oil
⅝ cup (½ cup plus 2 tablespoons)
    pineapple juice concentrate,
    thawed

AMARANTH (DAY 1)

1¼ cups amaranth flour
1 cup arrowroot
½ teaspoon baking soda
⅜ cup (¼ cup plus 2 tablespoons) oil
½ cup pineapple juice concentrate,
    thawed

TEFF (DAY 2)

2 cups teff flour
½ teaspoon baking soda
⅛ teaspoon unbuffered vitamin C
    powder
½ cup oil
½ cup thawed white grape juice
    concentrate OR ¼ cup Grape
    Sweet™ plus ¼ cup water

WHOLE SPELT (DAY 3)

1½ cups whole spelt flour
1 cup tapioca starch
½ teaspoon baking soda
⅜ cup (¼ cup plus 2 tablespoons) oil
½ cup apple juice concentrate,
    thawed

OAT-DATE (DAY 4)

2¼ cups oat flour
½ cup date sugar
½ teaspoon baking soda
⅛ teaspoon unbuffered vitamin C
    powder
⅜ cup (¼ cup plus 2 tablespoons) oil
½ cup water

BARLEY (DAY 1)

2⅛ cups (2 cups plus 2 tablespoons)
    barley flour
½ teaspoon baking soda
½ oil
½ cup pineapple juice concentrate,
    thawed

RYE (DAY 2)

2 cups rye flour
½ teaspoon baking soda
⅛ teaspoon unbuffered vitamin C
    powder
½ cup oil
½ cup thawed white grape juice
    concentrate OR ¼ cup Grape
    Sweet™ plus ¼ cup water

BUCKWHEAT (DAY 2)

2 cups buckwheat flour
½ teaspoon baking soda
⅛ teaspoon unbuffered vitamin C
    powder
½ cup oil
¾ cup thawed white grape juice
    concentrate OR ⅜ cup Grape
    Sweet™ plus ⅜ cup water

QUINOA (DAY 3)

1¼ cups quinoa flour
1 cup tapioca starch
½ teaspoon baking soda
⅜ cup (¼ cup plus 2 tablespoons) oil
½ cup apple juice concentrate,
    thawed

OAT-PINEAPPLE (DAY 4, borrow
pineapple from DAY 1)

2½ cups oat flour
½ teaspoon baking soda
⅜ cup (¼ cup plus 2 tablespoons) oil
½ cup pineapple juice concentrate,
    thawed

RICE (DAY 4)

2¼ cups rice flour
½ cup date sugar
½ teaspoon baking soda
⅛ teaspoon unbuffered vitamin C
  powder
½ cup oil
½ cup water

CHESTNUT (DAY 4)

1 cup chestnut flour
1 cup water chestnut flour
½ teaspoon baking soda
⅛ teaspoon unbuffered vitamin C
  powder
⅜ cup (¼ cup plus 2 tablespoons) oil
⅜ cup (¼ cup plus 2 tablespoons)
  water

1. Choose one set of ingredients from the previous page or above.

2. Preheat your oven to 350°F.

3. If you are using date sugar and it is lumpy, press it through a sieve with the back of a spoon to remove the lumps.

4. In a large bowl, stir together the dry ingredients such as the flour(s), date sugar, baking soda, and vitamin C powder.

5. In a separate bowl or cup, stir together the oil and juice or water.

6. Add the liquid ingredients to the dry ingredients, mixing with a spoon and your hands until the dough sticks together. If the dough is too dry to stick together, add 1 to 2 tablespoons of water.

7. Turn the dough out onto a baking sheet.

8. Using a rolling pin, roll the dough out to ¼ inch thickness.

9. Cut the dough into 2 to 2½ inch diamonds or squares with a sharp knife.

10. Put the baking sheet into the oven and bake the cookies until they are lightly browned or for the following times:

     Kamut: 20 to 25 minutes
     Barley: 18 to 23 minutes
     Amaranth: 15 to 20 minutes
     Rye: 15 to 20 minutes
     Teff: 15 to 20 minutes
     Buckwheat: 15 to 20 minutes
     Spelt: 15 to 20 minutes
     Quinoa: 15 to 20 minutes
     Oat-pineapple: 15 to 20 minutes
     Oat-date: 15 to 20 minutes
     Rice: 20 to 25 minutes
     Chestnut: 15 to 20 minutes

11. Cut the cookies again on the same lines, if necessary, after you remove them from the oven.

12. Remove the cookies from the baking sheet with a spatula. Put them on paper towels to cool completely.

Makes 2 to 3 dozen cookies

Cookie Cutter Cookies

KAMUT-MOLASSES (DAY 1 – borrow the pear and peach in the Fruit Sweet™ or Pear Sweet™ from DAYS 3 & 4 and nutmeg from DAY 4)

2¼ cups kamut flour
¾ teaspoon baking soda
¼ teaspoon unbuffered vitamin C powder
½ teaspoon ginger
¼ teaspoon nutmeg
¾ cup light molasses OR ¼ cup blackstrap molasses plus ½ cup Fruit Sweet™ or Pear Sweet™
¼ cup oil

AMARANTH-MOLASSES (DAY 1 – borrow the pear and peach in the Fruit Sweet™ or Pear Sweet™ from DAYS 3 & 4 and nutmeg from DAY 4)

2½ cups amaranth flour
½ cup arrowroot
¾ teaspoon baking soda
¼ teaspoon unbuffered vitamin C powder
½ teaspoon ginger
¼ teaspoon nutmeg
¾ cup light molasses OR ¼ cup blackstrap molasses plus ½ cup Fruit Sweet™ or Pear Sweet™
½ cup oil

BARLEY-STEVIA OR FOS (DAY 1)

3 cups barley flour
⅜ to ½ teaspoon white stevia powder, to taste, OR 1 cup FOS*
½ teaspoon baking soda
⅛ teaspoon unbuffered vitamin C powder
½ cup oil
½ cup water

SPELT-STEVIA OR FOS (DAY 3)

3⅛ cups (3 cups plus 2 tablespoons) whole spelt flour
⅜ to ½ teaspoon white stevia powder OR 1 cup FOS*
½ teaspoon baking soda
⅛ teaspoon unbuffered vitamin C powder
½ cup oil
½ cup water

SPELT-MOLASSES (DAY 3 – borrow the pineapple and peach in the Fruit Sweet™ from DAYS 1 & 4, ginger from DAY 1 and nutmeg from DAY 4)

3 cups whole spelt flour
¾ teaspoon baking soda
¼ teaspoon unbuffered vitamin C powder
½ teaspoon ginger
¼ teaspoon nutmeg
¾ cup light molasses OR ¼ cup blackstrap molasses plus ½ cup Fruit Sweet™ or Pear Sweet™
½ cup oil

1. Choose one set of ingredients from the previous page.

2. *If you are using the FOS, please read pages 20 and 250 of this book and be aware that FOS can support the growth of a few types of "unfriendly" bacteria that may contribute to dysbiosis. If you do not have these bacteria, FOS may be better for you than sugar but should be used with caution.

3. Preheat your oven to 350°F.

4. In a large bowl stir together the dry ingredients such as the flour(s), baking soda, vitamin C powder, spices, FOS and stevia.

5. In a separate bowl or cup, stir together the liquid ingredients such as the Fruit Sweet™ or Pear Sweet™, molasses, water, and oil.

6. Add the liquid ingredients to the dry ingredients and mix them in using a spoon and then your hands to make a stiff dough. You may add an additional teaspoon or two of water if necessary to get the dough to stick together.

7. If you are making the amaranth cookies, or to save work on the other cookies, omit steps 8 through 10 and instead roll the dough directly on a baking sheet and cut it into squares with a knife.

8. For cookie cutter cookies, roll the dough out to between ⅛ inch and ¼ inch thickness on a floured board using a floured rolling pin.

9. Cut the dough into cookies with cookie cutters.

10. Transfer the cookies to an ungreased baking sheet with a spatula.

11. Decorate the cookies with raisins or small pieces of dried fruit, if desired.

12. Bake the cookies until they begin to brown or for the following times:

    Kamut: 11 to 15 minutes
    Barley: 15 to 20 minutes
    Amaranth: 12 to 16 minutes
    Spelt: 10 to 15 minutes

    The stevia sweetened cookies will not brown much; they should be baked until they are set and feel dry to the touch.

13. Remove the cookies from the baking sheet with a spatula and put them on paper towels to cool completely.

Makes 2 to 3 dozen cookies

Nut Butter Cookies

BARLEY (DAY 1 – borrow the pear and peach in the Fruit Sweet™ or Pear Sweet™ from **DAYS 3 & 4)**

  1½ cups barley flour
  1 cup rolled barley flakes
  1 teaspoon baking soda
  ½ cup natural peanut butter
  ¼ cup oil
  1 cup Fruit Sweet™ or Pear Sweet™

RYE (DAY 2)

  2 cups rye flour
  ½ teaspoon baking soda
  ⅛ teaspoon unbuffered vitamin C powder
  ⅔ cup cashew butter
  ¼ cup oil
  ¾ cup Grape Sweet™

1. Choose one set of ingredients from above.

2. Preheat your oven to 375°F for the barley cookies or 400°F for the rye cookies.

3. In a large bowl, stir together the dry ingredients such as the flour, barley flakes, baking soda, and vitamin C powder.

4. In a separate bowl or cup, thoroughly stir together the nut butter, oil and sweetener.

5. Add the nut butter mixture to the dry ingredients and stir until it is just mixed in.

6. Drop the dough by teaspoonfuls about 2 inches apart on an ungreased baking sheet.

7. The barley cookies will spread by themselves. Flatten the rye cookies by smashing them with your fingers or the tines of a fork.

8. Bake the cookies until they begin to brown or for the following times:

  Barley: 7 to 10 minutes
  Rye: 8 to 10 minutes

9. Allow the barley cookies to cool on the baking sheet for about 5 minutes.

10. Remove the cookies from the baking sheet using a spatula and put them on paper towels to cool completely.

Makes 3 dozen cookies

Two Way Oatmeal Cookies

STEVIA SWEETENED OATMEAL COOKIES (DAY 4, borrow cinnamon from DAY 3)

> 3 cups oatmeal
> 1 cup oat flour
> ½ teaspoon salt
> 4 teaspoons cinnamon
> ½ teaspoon white stevia extract powder
> ¾ cup water
> ⅜ cup (¼ cup plus 2 tablespoons) oil

OATMEAL TREASURES (DAY 4 – borrow the pineapple and pear in the Fruit Sweet™ or Pear Sweet™ from DAYS 1 & 3, the cinnamon from DAY 3, and the raisins from DAY 2)

> 3½ cups oat flour
> 1 cup oatmeal
> 1 teaspoon cinnamon
> 1 teaspoon baking soda
> ½ cup oil
> 1 cup honey plus ½ cup water OR 1½ cups Fruit Sweet™ or Pear Sweet™
> ¾ cup raisins, chopped dates or commercially chopped dates coated with oat flour
> ¾ cup milk-free unsweetened carob chips (optional)

1. Choose one set of ingredients from above.
2. Preheat your oven to 350°F.
3. Lightly rub a baking sheet with oil.
4. In a large bowl stir together the dry ingredients such as the flour, oatmeal, cinnamon, baking soda, salt, and stevia.
5. In a separate bowl or cup, stir together the liquid ingredients such as oil, water, honey, Fruit Sweet™ or Pear Sweet™
6. Add the liquid ingredients to the dry ingredients and stir until they are mixed.
7. Fold in the dry fruit and carob chips if you are using them.
8. For the stevia sweetened cookies, roll the dough into walnut sized balls and put them on the prepared baking sheet. Flatten the balls to about ¼ inch thickness with your fingers held together or with an oiled glass bottom.
9. For the oatmeal treasures, drop heaping teaspoonfuls of dough about 2 inches apart on the prepared baking sheet.
10. Bake the cookies for the following times:
    > Stevia sweetened oatmeal cookies: 15 to 20 minutes;
    >   these cookies will not brown much
    > Oatmeal treasures: 12 to 16 minutes, or until lightly browned
11. Allow the oatmeal treasures to cool on the baking sheet for about five minutes.
12. Remove the cookies from the baking sheet with a metal spatula and put them on paper towels to cool completely.

Makes 3 to 4 dozen cookies

Any Day Brownies

AMARANTH (DAY 1)

1 cup amaranth flour
¼ cup arrowroot
⅓ cup carob powder
1 teaspoon baking soda
¼ teaspoon unbuffered vitamin C
   powder
⅛ teaspoon white stevia extract
   powder
¼ cup oil
¾ cup water
¼ cup chopped nuts (optional)

RYE (DAY 2)

1⅔ cups rye flour
¼ cup carob powder
1 teaspoon baking soda
⅔ cup grape juice concentrate,
   thawed
⅓ cup oil
½ cup chopped nuts (optional)

QUINOA (DAY 3)

1 cup quinoa flour
¼ cup tapioca starch
⅓ cup carob powder
1 teaspoon baking soda
¼ teaspoon unbuffered vitamin C
   powder
¼ cup oil
¾ cup apple juice concentrate,
   thawed, OR ¾ cup water plus ⅛
   teaspoon white stevia extract
   powder
¼ cup chopped nuts (optional)

OAT (DAY 4)

1 cup oatmeal
¾ cup oat flour
¼ cup carob powder or cocoa
1 cup date sugar
1 teaspoon baking soda
¼ teaspoon unbuffered vitamin C
   powder
½ cup oil
½ cup water
½ cup chopped nuts (optional)

1. Choose one set of ingredients from above.

2. Preheat your oven to 350°F.

3. Prepare a baking pan by rubbing the inside of it with oil and shaking flour in it so the bottom and sides are coated with flour. For the amaranth and quinoa brownies, use an 8 inch by 4 inch or 9 inch by 5 inch loaf pan. For the rye and oat brownies, use an 8 inch or 9 inch square baking pan.

4. If your carob powder contains lumps, press it through a strainer with the back of a spoon to remove the lumps before measuring it.

5. Stir together the dry ingredients such as the flour(s), carob powder, baking soda, vitamin C powder, date sugar, stevia, and optional nuts in a large bowl.

6. In a separate bowl or cup stir together the fruit juice or water and the oil.

7. Stir the liquid ingredients into the dry ingredients until they are just mixed.

8. Spread the batter in the prepared pan.

9. Bake the brownies until they are set and a toothpick inserted into the center of the pan comes out dry, or for the following times:

> Amaranth: 18 to 20 minutes
> Rye: 18 to 20 minutes
> Quinoa: 18 to 20 minutes
> Oat: 25 to 35 minutes

Do not overbake these brownies – they should still be moist inside.

10. Cool the brownies in the pan before cutting them into squares. The oat brownies are fragile. It is easiest to serve all of these brownies from the pan.

Makes 10 amaranth or quinoa brownies or 16 rye or oat brownies

FOS Scotch Shortbread
Day 4

> 1½ cups quick-cooking oats, uncooked
> ½ cup FOS*
> ½ cup oat flour
> ¼ teaspoon salt
> 3 tablespoons oil
> 2 tablespoons water

1. *Before using this recipe, please read pages 20 and 250 of this book and be aware that FOS can support the growth of a few "unfriendly" bacteria that may contribute to dysbiosis. If you do not have these bacteria, FOS may be better for you than sugar, but should be used with caution.

2. Preheat your oven to 350°F.

3. Prepare an 8 inch or 9 inch square baking pan by rubbing the inside of it with oil.

4. Stir together the oats, FOS, flour, and salt in a bowl.

5. Stir the oil into the dry ingredients until it is thoroughly mixed in.

6. Stir the water into the oat mixture.

7. Press the mixture into the bottom of the prepared baking pan.

8. Bake for 25 to 30 minutes or until lightly browned.

9. Remove the pan from the oven, run a knife around the edges of the pan, and cut the cookies into 2 inch squares.

10. Allow the cookies to cool in the pan for five to ten minutes; then remove them with a spatula or serve them from the pan.

Makes 16 cookies

Coconut Cookies

DAY 4 – borrow the pineapple and pear in the Fruit Sweet™ or Pear Sweet™ from **DAYS 1 & 3** and the tapioca from **DAY 3**

2 cups finely shredded unsweetened coconut (see "Sources, page 299)
¼ cup tapioca starch or water chestnut flour
¼ teaspoon corn-free natural vanilla flavoring (optional)
½ cup Fruit Sweet™ or Pear Sweet™ OR ⅜ cup coconut milk plus ½ cup FOS*
Coconut oil

1. *If you are using the FOS, please read pages 20 and 250 of this book and be aware that FOS can support the growth of a few types of "unfriendly" bacteria that may contribute to dysbiosis. If you do not have these bacteria, FOS may be better for you than sugar, but should be used with caution.

2. Preheat your oven to 325°F.

3. Melt a teaspoon or two of coconut oil and rub a baking sheet with it. If necessary, you can substitute another kind of oil. However, these cookies are fragile and are more easily removed from the baking sheet if it is greased with coconut oil.

4. In a bowl, stir together the coconut, starch, and FOS if you are using it.

5. In a separate bowl or cup, combine the coconut milk, Pear Sweet™ or Fruit Sweet™ with the vanilla.

6. Stir the liquid ingredients into the coconut mixture.

7. Press the mixture into walnut-sized balls with your hands.

8. Put the balls on the prepared baking sheet and flatten them to about ½ inch thickness with your fingers held together.

9. Bake the cookies until they begin to brown – for 12 to 15 minutes if they are made with Fruit Sweet™ or Pear Sweet™ or for 15 to 20 minutes if they are made with FOS.

10. Allow them to cool on the baking sheet for a few minutes.

11. Carefully remove them from the baking sheet with a metal spatula. Put them on a dish or wire cooling rack to cool; they will stick to paper towels.

Makes about 1½ dozen cookies

Snacks and Beverages

People on restricted diets, especially children, often miss "fun" things to eat for snacks. This chapter will give you some ideas for nutritious between-meal foods.

Oven Sweet Potato or White Potato Chips

DAY 1 if made with sweet potatoes
EXTRA FOODS if made with white potatoes

> 1 pound white potatoes, sweet potatoes, or white sweet potatoes
> ¼ teaspoon salt, or to taste

1. Preheat your oven to 350°F.
2. Peel and very thinly slice the potatoes.
3. Place them on a wire rack with a baking sheet underneath it.
4. Sprinkle the potatoes with salt.
5. Put them into the oven and bake them for 30 minutes.
6. Remove them from the oven.
7. Turn your broiler on to 400°F.
8. Put the potatoes about 5 inches from the heating element of your broiler and broil them for 2 to 3 minutes, or until they just begin to brown. Watch them carefully.
9. Remove them from the oven and turn them over on the rack.
10. Broil them on the other side for another 2 to 3 minutes or until they begin to brown, again watching them carefully.

Makes about one half pound of chips

Lentil Spread

Extra foods; walnuts are **Day 1**

    1 pound dry lentils
    Water
    1 to 2 onions, peeled and chopped (optional, but the onion gives the spread most of
        its flavor)
    1 tablespoon oil (only needed if using onion)
    ½ cup walnuts or other nuts
    2 to 2½ teaspoons salt
    1 teaspoon pepper, or more to taste

1. The day before you plan to make this spread, wash and sort over the lentils, discarding any shriveled ones.

2. Put the lentils in a saucepan and cover them with twice their volume of water.

3. Soak the lentils overnight.

4. The next morning rinse the lentils three times and drain them.

5. Add four cups of water to the drained lentils in the saucepan.

6. Bring the lentils to a boil and simmer them for one to two hours or until they are soft.

7. While they are cooking, if you wish to use the onion, saute it slowly in the oil until it is golden brown, about 20 to 30 minutes.

8. Pour the lentils into a colander and allow them to drain and cool slightly.

9. Put the nuts in a blender or food processor with the metal pureeing blade and grind them using a pulsing action.

10. Add the lentils, onions, and seasonings to the nuts in the food processor and puree all of the ingredients together. (You will have to do this in small batches if you are using a blender).

11. Refrigerate the spread or freeze it in serving-sized portions.

12. Serve this spread with raw vegetables as a dip, on crackers, or in sandwiches. It tastes somewhat like liverwurst or pate.

Makes about 5 cups of spread

Garbanzo Dip

Extra foods; mustard is **Day 2**

1¾ cups cooked garbanzo beans (See the recipe on page 104 for how to cook them or use 1 drained 16-ounce can).
⅓ cup water
¼ to ½ teaspoon salt, or to taste
2 teaspoons tart-tasting unbuffered vitamin C powder
⅛ teaspoon dry mustard (optional)
⅛ teaspoon pepper (optional)

1. Put the beans in a blender or food processor with the metal pureeing blade. Process them using a pulsing action until they are finely ground.

2. Add all of the other ingredients and puree until smooth. (You may have to do this in small batches if you are using a blender).

3. Refrigerate the dip.

4. Serve this dip spread on crackers or rice cakes or use it as a dip for raw vegetables or cooked artichokes.

Makes about 2 cups of dip

Mineral Munchies

This is a tasty way to eat dulse, the mildest tasting of the seaweeds. You will get a lot of iron and other minerals from it as well as from the spicy arugula.

Day 2

Fresh arugula
Dry dulse

1. Wash the arugula leaves and pat them dry.

2. Put a small piece of dulse in each leaf and roll it up.

3. Consume it immediately, or to serve others, skewer the leaf with a toothpick to keep it rolled up.

Fruit Snacks

BANANA (Day 1)

6 large bananas

MANGO (Day 2)

3 mangoes

GRAPE (Day 2, borrow pears from Day 3 or Day 3, borrow grapes from Day 2)

2 pounds pears OR 2 1-pound cans water-packed canned pears, drained
⅔ cups grape juice concentrate, thawed

APPLE (Day 3)

3 cups unsweetened applesauce
1 teaspoon cinnamon

STRAWBERRY OR RASPBERRY (Day 3)

½ pound fresh strawberries or raspberries OR ½ of a 1-pound bag of frozen unsweetened strawberries or raspberries
2 cups unsweetened applesauce

PEACH (Day 4)

2 pounds fresh peaches OR 1½ 1-pound bags of frozen unsweetened peaches OR 3 1-pound cans of water-packed canned peaches, drained

KIWI (Extra foods)

12 kiwis

1. Choose one set of ingredients from above.

2. If you are using frozen fruit, allow it to thaw at least partially.

3. If you are using fresh fruit, peel and seed it and cut it into chunks.

4. If you are using canned fruit, drain it.

5. Put the fruit in a blender or a food processor with the metal pureeing blade. (You may need to process it in small batches if you are using a blender).

6. Puree the fruit.

7. Add any other ingredients, such as cinnamon or grape juice concentrate, and process again briefly. You will have about 3 cups of puree.

8. Cover food dehydrator trays or cookie sheets, platters, and trays with heavy plastic wrap.

9. Put ⅓ cup to ⅜ cup portions of the pureed fruit onto the plastic wrap and spread the puree out into 7 inch circles so that it is about ¼ inch thick.

10. If you have a dehydrator, put the trays into it and dry the fruit for about 10 to 12 hours at 135°F.

11. If you do not have a dehydrator, put the cookie sheets, platters, or trays out in the sun, covered with netting, on a hot day and dry for 10 to 12 hours.

12. After 10 hours, check the fruit. If it does not have any sticky spots, it is finished. If it

still has sticky spots, allow it to keep drying. Check it every hour or so. It should not become so dry that it is brittle.

13. When the fruit is dry, cut the plastic wrap so that the individual circles are separated. Roll the circles up while they are still warm or stack them and store them in a plastic bag.

Makes about 8 fruit snacks

Four Way Rhubarb

Use this recipe to make rhubarb concentrate (for leavening and salad), rhubarb tea, rhubarb jam, or rhubarb pudding.

DAY 2
RHUBARB CONCENTRATE AND TEA

1 pound rhubarb (about 4 cups of ½-inch slices)
2 cups water
Additional water for tea

RHUBARB JAM

1 pound rhubarb (about 4 cups of ½-inch slices)
2 cups water
⅛ teaspoon white stevia extract powder

RHUBARB PUDDING (borrow tapioca from DAY 3)

1 pound rhubarb (about 4 cups of ½-inch slices)
1¼ cups water, divided
3 tablespoons minute tapioca
⅛ teaspoon white stevia powder

1. Clean the rhubarb and cut it into ½ inch slices.

2. Place the rhubarb slices in a saucepan with 2 cups of water for rhubarb concentrate, tea, or jam or with ¾ cup of water for rhubarb pudding.

3. Bring the rhubarb to a boil, reduce the heat, and simmer it covered. For rhubarb pudding, cook it for 10 to 15 minutes or until the rhubarb is tender. For rhubarb concentrate, tea, or jam, cook it for one hour.

DIRECTIONS FOR RHUBARB PUDDING:

1. If you are making rhubarb pudding, while the rhubarb is simmering, combine the tapioca with the remaining ½ cup water and allow them to stand for at least 5 minutes.

2. When the rhubarb is tender, add the tapioca mixture to the rhubarb, return it to a boil, and simmer for 5 minutes.

3. Thoroughly stir in the stevia.

4. Cool the pudding for at least 20 minutes before serving. It will thicken as it cools.

5. Refrigerate the pudding.

Makes 4 to 6 servings of pudding

DIRECTIONS FOR RHUBARB CONCENTRATE OR TEA:

1. For rhubarb concentrate or tea, pour the rhubarb that has simmered for one hour into a strainer or colander with a bowl underneath it and let it stand for about ½ hour to thoroughly strain the liquid from the rhubarb pulp.

2. The drained liquid is rhubarb concentrate. It can be used for leavening or in salads as directed in the recipes in this book. (Use the pulp to make the jam below).

3. To use rhubarb concentrate to make rhubarb tea, put 4 to 6 tablespoons (to taste) of the concentrate into a 10-ounce mug and fill with boiling water. Rhubarb tea is a tangy tea somewhat like rosehip or hibiscus tea.

4. Refrigerate rhubarb concentrate to use within a day or two or freeze any leftover rhubarb concentrate for future use.

Makes about 2 cups of rhubarb concentrate or 6 to 8 cups of rhubarb tea

DIRECTIONS FOR RHUBARB JAM:

1. After the rhubarb has simmered for one hour, put it into a strainer or colander with a bowl underneath it and let it stand for about ½ hour to thoroughly strain the liquid from the rhubarb pulp.

2. Use the rhubarb pulp that remains in the strainer to make jam. (Use the liquid as rhubarb concentrate to make tea or in baking or salads as directed above).

3. Puree the reserved rhubarb pulp in a food processor or blender until smooth.

4. Sprinkle ⅛ teaspoon white stevia powder into the processor or blender and puree again for a minute or so.

5. Refrigerate the jam.

Makes about 1 cup jam

Special Occasion Foods

This chapter contains recipes for desserts and candies which are so close to "normal" that your guests will not be able to tell that they do not contain sugar or wheat. White spelt flour will make cakes and cookies that are better than those from the bakery, and FOS (fructooligosaccharides) makes candy that even an allergic child's friends will like.

*WARNING: If you are going to use FOS, you should be aware that it will support the growth of a few of the unfriendly bacteria which can cause dysbiosis. Be sure that FOS-containing treats will not be eaten by anyone who has problems with these organisms. If you do not have these "unfriendly" bacteria, FOS may be better for you than sugar, but should be used with caution. (See page 20 for more about FOS and dysbiosis). Even healthy people will get diarrhea from FOS if they eat it in very large amounts because it is not absorbed. Indulge in the candies in this chapter in small amounts only. If you cannot buy FOS or FOS syrup at your health food store, see "Sources," page 300, for mail order sources.

FOS-ettes

EXTRA FOODS

> ½ to ¾ cup FOS*
> ½ teaspoon corn-free natural flavoring (strawberry, lemon, vanilla, maple, mint, etc.)
> 1½ teaspoons hot water

1. Before using this recipe, read the warning about FOS in the paragraph above.

2. Put ½ cup FOS in a small bowl.

3. Make a well in the center of the FOS and measure the flavoring into the well.

4. Add the water to the well and begin stirring in the middle of the bowl, mixing the flavoring and water and then gradually mixing in the FOS.

5. When you have stirred in as much FOS as you can with the spoon, use your hand to knead in enough of the remaining FOS to form a stiff fondant. Add more FOS to the bowl as needed.

6. Roll the fondant into about 24 ½-inch balls. (This will result in about 1 teaspoon of FOS per ball. You may make larger balls if you wish).

6. Roll each ball in additional FOS to coat it.

7. Place the balls on a dish and allow them to stand uncovered overnight or longer.

MINT PATTIES OR MAPLE CREAMS VARIATION:

1. Make FOS-ettes fondant as above using mint or maple flavoring.

2. For maple creams, shape the fondant as above. If you are making mints, divide the fondant into 15 pieces and form each piece into a 1 inch disc.

3. Allow the candy to stand overnight.

4. Melt ½ cup milk-free unsweetened carob chips over boiling water in the top of a double boiler.

5. Dip the mint patties or maple creams in the melted carob.

6. Place the candies on an oiled baking sheet or dish until the carob hardens.

Makes 24 FOS-ettes or maple creams or 15 mint patties

Suckers

EXTRA FOODS

> 1 cup FOS*
> ½ cup plus 1 tablespoon FOS* syrup
> ¼ to ½ teaspoon corn-free natural flavoring
> Coconut oil, ghee, or goat's butter
> About 12 sucker sticks

1. *Before using this recipe, please read pages 20 and 250 of this book and be aware that FOS can support the growth of a few "unfriendly" bacteria that may contribute to dysbiosis. If you do not have these bacteria, FOS may be better for you than sugar, but should be used with caution.

2. Combine the FOS and FOS syrup in a saucepan and bring them to a boil.

3. Cover the pan with a lid and cook for three minutes over medium high heat to wash down crystals that may be on the sides of the pan into the bottom of the pan.

4. Uncover the pan. Attach a candy thermometer to the side of the pan so the tip is submerged in the syrup but it does not touch the bottom of the pan. Cook the candy on medium heat without stirring it to the hard crack stage (305-310°F).

5. While the candy is cooking, grease a cookie sheet with coconut oil, ghee, or goat's butter. Lay sticks on it at about 4 inch intervals.

6. When the candy reaches the hard crack stage, stir in the flavoring.

7. Drop large spoonfuls of the candy over the sticks on the prepared sheet.

8. Allow the suckers to cool completely. Wrap them with plastic wrap or cellophane.

Makes about a dozen 3 to 4 inch suckers

Salt Water Taffy

Extra foods

    1 cup FOS*
    1 cup FOS* syrup
    1 tsp salt
    ¼ to ½ teaspoon corn-free natural flavoring
    Coconut oil, ghee, or goat's butter

1. *Before using this recipe, please read pages 20 and 250 of this book and be aware that FOS can support the growth of a few "unfriendly" bacteria that may contribute to dysbiosis. If you do not have these bacteria, FOS may be better for you than sugar, but should be used with caution.

2. Stir together the FOS, FOS syrup, and salt in a saucepan. Attach a candy thermometer to the side of the pan so the tip is submerged in the syrup but it does not touch the bottom of the pan.

3. Bring the candy mixture to a boil and cook it over medium heat without stirring it until the candy thermometer reaches the hard ball stage (265-270°F).

4. While the candy is cooking, generously grease a marble slab or large platter with coconut oil, ghee, or goat butter. Also grease a cookie sheet with the same fat.

5. When the candy has reached the hard ball stage, pour it onto the prepared marble slab or platter.

6. Sprinkle the flavoring on top of the candy.

7. As the candy cools, lift the edges to the middle of the mass with a metal spatula.

8. When it is cool enough to handle, grease your hands with the same type of fat you used to grease the platter. Pick up the candy, and pull and fold it repeatedly it until it becomes opaque and shiny and is almost completely cooled. This will take about 20 minutes.

9. Pull it into a rope and put it on the prepared cookie sheet.

10. Cut it into pieces with a greased pair of kitchen shears.

11. Allow it to stand uncovered for several hours; then it may be stored in a tin.

Makes about 1 pound of taffy

Caramels

DAY 1 if goat's butter and milk are used
EXTRA FOODS if cow's butter and cream are used

> 1 cup FOS*
> 1 cup FOS* syrup
> ½ cup goat's or cow's butter
> 1 cup goat's milk or cream OR heavy whipping cream (cow's), divided

1. *Before using this recipe, please read pages 20 and 250 of this book and be aware that FOS can support the growth of a few "unfriendly" bacteria that may contribute to dysbiosis. If you do not have these bacteria, FOS may be better for you than sugar, but should be used with caution.

2. Stir together the FOS, FOS syrup, butter, and ½ cup of the milk or cream in a saucepan. Attach a candy thermometer to the side of the pan so the tip is submerged in the liquid but it does not touch the bottom of the pan.

3. Generously grease an 8 inch square baking pan with cow's or goat's butter.

4. Bring the candy mixture to a boil and cook it over medium heat, stirring it constantly, until the candy thermometer reaches the firm ball stage (242°F).

5. Remove the pan from the heat and gradually stir in the rest of the cream.

6. Return the pan to the heat and cook it until the candy thermometer reaches 247-250°F.

7. Pour the candy into the prepared pan.

8. Allow it to cool at room temperature for 2 to 3 hours or until it is firm.

9. When it is firm, turn the candy out onto a cutting board and cut into squares with a knife.

10. Store it on buttered wax paper or parchment paper in a tin.

Makes about 1½ pounds of caramels

FOS Candy Canes

EXTRA FOODS

> 1½ cups FOS*
> ½ cup FOS* syrup
> ⅛ teaspoon cream of tartar
> Coconut oil, ghee, or goat's butter
> ¼ teaspoon peppermint flavoring

1. *Before using this recipe, please read pages 20 and 250 of this book and be aware that FOS can support the growth of a few "unfriendly" bacteria that may contribute to dysbiosis. If you do not have these bacteria, FOS may be better for you than sugar, but should be used with caution.

2. Combine the FOS, FOS syrup, and cream of tartar in a saucepan.

3. Cook the mixture over medium heat until the FOS crystals dissolve, stirring occasionally.

4. Cover the pan with a lid and cook for three minutes over medium high heat to wash down crystals that may be on the sides of the pan into the bottom of the pan.

5. Uncover the pan. Attach a candy thermometer to the side of the pan so the tip is submerged in the syrup but it does not touch the bottom of the pan.

6. Cook the candy on medium heat without stirring it to the hard crack stage (305-310°F).

7. While the solution is boiling, thoroughly grease a marble slab or a large platter with coconut oil, ghee, or goat's butter.

8. When the candy thermometer reaches the right temperature, immediately pour the candy onto the marble slab or platter.

9. As the edges of the candy cool, lift them toward the center with a metal spatula.

10. When the candy is partially cooled, sprinkle the peppermint on the surface of the candy and continue to lift the candy from the edges to the center with the spatula.

11. Grease your hands with coconut oil, goat's butter, or ghee.

12. When the candy is just cool enough to handle, form it into a ball and pull it until it takes on a sheen, about 20 pulls.

13. Pull the candy into a rope, cut it into 8 to 10 pieces, and form them into cane shapes.

14. Put the candy canes on the marble slab or platter to harden.

Makes 8 to 10 10-inch candy canes

Nut Butter Cups

Day 2 if made with cashew butter and Grape Sweet™
Extra foods if made with peanut butter

¼ cup natural peanut butter, cashew butter, or other nut butter
¼ cup Fruit Sweet™, Grape Sweet™, Pear Sweet™, honey, or FOS* syrup
1¾ cups (about 10 ounces) carob chips

1. If you are going to make these candies with FOS,* before beginning please read pages 20 and 250 of this book and be aware that FOS can support the growth of a few "unfriendly" bacteria that may contribute to dysbiosis. If you do not have these bacteria, FOS may be better for you than sugar, but should be used with caution.

2. Thoroughly stir together the nut butter and sweetener in a bowl.

3. Put water into the bottom of a double boiler to a depth of about one inch and bring it to a boil.

4. Remove the double boiler from the heat and put 1 cup of the carob chips in the top of the double boiler.

5. Stir the carob chips until they are melted.

6. Grease the wells of a mini-muffin tin with coconut oil, goat's butter or ghee.

7. Fill each well about ⅓ full of melted carob and swirl the tin so the sides of the cups are also coated with carob.

8. Refrigerate the tin for a few minutes until the carob is firm.

9. Fill each cup with the nut butter mixture to about half full.

10. Melt the remaining carob chips as in steps 3, 4, and 5 above.

11. Add 1 to 2 teaspoons melted carob to the tops of the cups, sealing it to the carob on the sides of the cups.

Makes about 12 candies

Easy Fudge

DAY 1 – borrow the pear and peach in the FruitSweet™ or Pear Sweet™ from days 3 and 4

    1 cup Fruit Sweet™, Pear Sweet™ or honey
    3 tablespoons oil
    ¾ cup carob powder
    1¼ cups powdered goat's milk
    3 tablespoons finely chopped nuts (optional)

1. Lightly rub an 8 or 9 inch square baking dish with oil.

2. In a bowl, stir together the Fruit Sweet™, Pear Sweet™ or honey and the oil.

3. Add the carob powder and powdered milk to the bowl and beat the fudge with a spoon until it is smooth.

4. Mix in the nuts, if you wish to use them.

5. Spread the fudge in the prepared dish.

6. Refrigerate the fudge.

7. Just before serving time, cut the fudge into ¾ inch squares with a sharp knife.

8. Leave the fudge in the dish and store it in the refrigerator because its consistency is soft.

Makes about 1 pound of fudge

Spelt "Graham" Crackers

Day 3 – borrow goat butter from **Day 1** and the pineapple and peach in the
Fruit Sweet™ from **Days 1&4**

> 2½ cups whole spelt flour
> ½ teaspoon salt
> ¾ teaspoon baking soda
> ¼ teaspoon unbuffered vitamin C powder
> ½ cup goat butter or ghee
> ½ cup Fruit Sweet™ or Pear Sweet™

1. An hour or so before you plan to make these crackers, take the goat butter or ghee out of the refrigerator to soften.

2. Rub two baking sheets with oil and lightly flour them.

3. Preheat your oven to 350°F.

4. Stir together the spelt flour, salt, baking soda, and vitamin C in a bowl.

5. Cut the butter or ghee into the flour mixture with a pastry cutter until the mixture resembles coarse crumbs.

6. Stir the sweetener into the flour mixture until it is thoroughly mixed in.

7. Divide the dough in half and put each half on one of the prepared baking sheets.

8. Flour the dough and a rolling pin and roll the dough to about ⅛ inch thickness on the baking sheets.

9. Cut the dough into 1½ inch by 3 inch rectangles and prick them with a fork.

10. Bake the crackers for 8 to 10 minutes, or until they begin to brown.

11. Remove them from the baking sheets and put them on paper towels to cool.

Makes 3 to 4 dozen crackers

Spritz

Day 3 – borrow goat butter from **Day 1** and the
pineapple and peach in the Fruit Sweet™ from **Days 1&4**

> 1 cup goat butter or ghee
> ⅔ cup Fruit Sweet™ or Pear Sweet™
> 1 teaspoon corn-free natural vanilla or almond flavoring
> 3⅔ cups white spelt flour
> ¼ teaspoon salt
> ⅜ teaspoon baking soda
> ⅛ teaspoon unbuffered vitamin C powder

1. An hour or so before you plan to make these cookies, take the goat butter or ghee out of the refrigerator to soften.

2. Preheat your oven to 375°F.

3. Cream the butter or ghee on medium speed with an electric mixer.

4. Add the Fruit Sweet™ or Pear Sweet™ and flavoring and beat thoroughly.

5. Stir the baking soda, vitamin C and salt into the flour in another bowl.

6. Add the flour mixture to the mixer bowl about ½ cup at a time, beating after each addition, until it has all been added.

7. Put the dough into a cookie press. Follow the directions that came with the press.

8. Press out cookies or long spritz strips onto an ungreased baking sheet.

9. Bake the cookies for 6 to 11 minutes, depending on the size and thickness of the cookies.

Makes about 4 dozen small cookies

Biscotti

DAY 3 – borrow the pineapple and peach in the Fruit Sweet™ from DAYS 1 & 4 and almonds from DAY 4

    3 cups white spelt flour
    ¼ teaspoon salt
    ¾ teaspoon baking soda
    ¼ teaspoon unbuffered vitamin C crystals
    ½ cup sliced almonds
    ¾ cup Fruit Sweet™ or Pear Sweet™
    ⅓ cup oil
    1 teaspoon corn-free natural almond flavoring
    1 teaspoon corn-free natural vanilla flavoring

1. Preheat your oven to 350°F.

2. Lightly rub a baking sheet with oil.

3. In a large bowl, stir together the flour, salt, baking soda, vitamin C, and almonds.

4. In a separate bowl or cup, stir together the sweetener, oil, and flavorings.

5. Add the liquids to the dry ingredients and stir until they are just mixed.

6. Transfer the dough to a floured board and knead it about 20 times.

7. Form the dough into a loaf about 12 inches long, 3½ inches wide, and 1 inch high on the prepared baking sheet.

8. Bake the loaf for 20 to 25 minutes, or until it just barely starts to brown.

9. Remove the baking sheet from the oven.

10. Using a serrated knife, slice the loaf down the middle and then into about 1 inch slices crosswise.

11. Lay the slices on their sides on the baking sheet.

12. Return the sheet to the oven.

13. Bake the cookies for 5 to 10 minutes; when they begin to brown, turn them over so the other side of each slice is down. Bake them for another 5 to 10 minutes.

14. Remove them from the baking sheet to paper towels to cool.

Makes about 2 dozen cookies

Almost Normal German Chocolate Cake

DAY 3 – for the frosting, borrow the peach and pineapple in the Fruit Sweet™ from DAYS 1&4, the coconut from DAY 4, and the pecans and goat milk and butter from DAY 1

CAKE:

7 cups white spelt flour
¾ cup cocoa
3½ teaspoons baking soda
1⅛ teaspoons unbuffered vitamin C powder
3½ cups apple juice concentrate, thawed
½ cup plus 1 tablespoon oil

FROSTING:

⅝ cup Fruit Sweet™ or Pear Sweet™
2 egg yolks
3 tablespoons goat's or cow's butter
⅝ cup goat milk
3 tablespoons tapioca flour
1 teaspoon corn-free natural vanilla flavoring
¾ cup chopped pecans
About ¾ cup unsweetened finely shredded coconut, or up to 1¼ cups if it is coarsely shredded

1. Preheat your oven to 350°F.

2. Rub oil on the inside of three 8 inch round cake pans. Shake flour inside them so the bottom and sides are coated. Cut waxed or parchment paper to fit the bottoms of the pans and put a circle of paper into the bottom of each pan.

3. Stir together the flour, cocoa, baking soda, and vitamin C in a very large bowl.

4. In a separate bowl or cup, combine the apple juice concentrate and oil.

5. Stir the liquids into the flour mixture until they are just mixed in.

6. Divide the batter between the three prepared pans.

7. Bake the cake for 25 minutes, or until a toothpick inserted into the centers of the pans comes out dry. Overbaking causes chocolate cakes to be dry.

8. Remove the cake from the oven and cool the layers in the pans for 15 minutes.

9. Invert the layers onto cooling racks, then invert them again so they are right-side-up on the racks.

10. Allow the cake layers to cool completely before frosting the cake. Remove the waxed or parchment paper from the bottoms of the layers when they are completely cool.

11. To make the frosting, combine the sweetener, egg yolks, and goat butter in a saucepan.

12. Cook over medium heat, stirring often, to bring it to a simmer. Then simmer, stirring often, for 5 minutes or until it begins to thicken.

13. Stir together the goat milk and tapioca flour thoroughly. Add them to the sweetener mixture and cook, stirring, until the mixture is very thick.

14. Stir in the vanilla, pecans, and enough of the coconut to make a very thick frosting.

15. Spread the top of one cake layer with about ⅓ of the frosting. Put another cake layer on top of the first and spread it with ⅓ of the frosting. Repeat with the third cake layer.

16. Store this cake in the refrigerator.

Makes one three-layer cake

Orange Cake

DAY 3 – borrow date from **DAY 4**

CAKE:

> 5½ cups white spelt flour
> 2¼ teaspoons baking soda
> ½ teaspoon unbuffered vitamin C powder
> 2¼ cups apple juice concentrate, thawed
> ¾ cup oil
> 1½ tablespoons grated orange peel

FROSTING:

> 2 cups of sheep's yo-cheese (see recipe on page 63) or cow's
>   low-fat or regular cream cheese
> ¼ cup orange juice concentrate, thawed
> 2 cups date sugar

1. Grate the outermost layer of the peel from an orange using the finest holes on a cheese grater. (This is called the orange zest).

2. Preheat your oven to 350°F.

3. Rub oil on the inside of two 8 inch round cake pans. Shake flour inside them so the bottom and sides are coated. Cut waxed or parchment paper to fit the bottoms of the pans and put a circle of paper into the bottom of each pan.

4. Stir together the flour, baking soda, and vitamin C in a large bowl.

5. In a separate bowl or cup, combine the apple juice concentrate, oil, and orange peel.

6. Stir the liquids into the flour mixture until they are just mixed in.

7. Divide the batter between the prepared pans.

8. Bake the cake for 25 to 30 minutes or until a toothpick inserted into the centers of the pans comes out dry.

9. Remove the cake from the oven and cool the layers in the pans for 15 minutes.

10. Invert the layers onto cooling racks, then invert them again so they are right-side-up on the racks.

11. Allow the cake layers to cool completely before frosting the cake. Remove the waxed or parchment paper from the bottoms of the layers when they are completely cool.

12. To make the frosting, if your date sugar is not very fine, process it in a food processor or blender until it is finely ground.

13. Put the yo-cheese or cream cheese in your mixer bowl.

14. Beat the cheese with the orange juice until it is smooth.

15. Gradually beat in the date sugar.

16. Put one cake layer on a serving dish and spread the top of it with frosting.

17. Put the second layer on top of the first layer.

18. Frost the top and sides of the cake.

19. Store this cake in the refrigerator.

Makes one two-layer cake

A Personal Postscript:
Three Generations of Food Allergies

A surprising number of people who have my books ask me about my experiences with different allergy treatments and diets. Since every book is a reflection of the life of its author, the experiences my family has had with food allergies contribute to my opinions (some of them unconventional) about foods, diets, and other treatments discussed in this book. Therefore, I am including a personal postscript about my family's history of food allergies.

GRANDPA'S STORY

My father had an ulcer when he was a young man. At that time, the treatment for ulcers included a diet rich in dairy products. He recovered from the ulcer, but in his early thirties began having dizzy spells. These were finally diagnosed as milk allergy. He eliminated all dairy products from his diet and enjoyed good health for many years. Thirty years later, when he developed prostate cancer and wanted to give his immune system all the support he could, he underwent provocative testing for food allergies. He had not developed any new allergies even though he had not rotated his foods.

When my father became allergic to milk, my mother read food labels when she went grocery shopping and became an expert on cooking without milk. Thus, I grew up knowing that some ingredients that most people consider essential to a recipe really are not necessary. When I got married, my husband watched me make mashed potatoes and asked, "Where is the milk?" I actually had to learn to use milk in cooking.

My father's milk allergy also taught me that one can accept dietary restrictions cheerfully and appreciate improved health rather that dwelling on limitations and restrictions.

JOEL'S STORY

My son Joel was born in January, 1983. His early infancy was difficult because of "tummy trouble" which his doctor said bordered on being colic. He was exclusively breast-fed for the first several months of his life. I was on an elimination, but not a rotation diet at that time and noticed that whenever I ate citrus fruits he became more fussy. So I eliminated citrus from my diet until he was weaned. When I was retested for food allergies when Joel was about two years old, I found that I was allergic to citrus. At that time I learned that when a nursing mother passes traces of a food to which she is allergic to her child in her milk, along with antibodies to that food, the baby can experience allergic symptoms even if he is not allergic to that food.

After Joel was a few months old, his "tummy trouble" passed. He had sensitive skin and was prone to rashes. If he spit up in his sleep, he would awaken with mild eczema on the cheek that he had slept on.

When we introduced wheat into Joel's diet when he was almost a year old, he developed diarrhea. His dad thought that perhaps I was imagining the problem because of my wheat allergy, so we tried wheat again a few weeks later. That time Dad changed his diapers and agreed with my assessment of the situation. So Joel never ate wheat.

At the age of eighteen months, Joel developed eczema on his legs whenever he played outside in the grass. His doctor recommended long pants and ointments, and the problem was controlled.

When Joel was twenty-two months old, he sampled some eggnog in the grocery store. By the time we reached the checkout he was clawing at his arms, which were covered with eczema. Since he had eaten all the ingredients in the eggnog except eggs without problems, we assumed that the eggs were the culprit. Until this time we had never fed him eggs, nor had I eaten them when pregnant or nursing him. But after this experience we assumed that he was allergic to eggs. So Joel never ate eggs again.

Shortly after Joel's second birthday, I learned about rotation diets and began rotating my foods. However, since two year olds have definite ideas about what they will eat and when, we did not try to put Joel on rotation also; rather he just continued to avoid wheat and eggs. We also did not let him eat chocolate because whenever he ate it he would "climb the walls."

At age four Joel began having eczema in the winter when he had no exposure to grass. I knew that his extreme fondness for milk and peanut butter could indicate food allergy, so we eliminated them from his diet. However, his eczema did not clear up, so in May, 1987 we took him to my allergist. Blood tests showed several possible problem foods. Using elimination and challenge testing at home, we confirmed that he was allergic to wheat, milk, eggs, rice, corn, potatoes, peanuts, and chocolate.

We put Joel on a rotation diet that eliminated his problem foods for about six months. Then we began reintroducing them, and he was able to tolerate most of them at five day intervals on a carefully rotated basis. He could eat corn once or twice a month, but he developed eczema if he ate it as often as weekly. But in general, as long as he followed his diet, he did quite well.

At age eleven, Joel's eczema became a persistent problem in spite of dietary manipulation, and he sneezed and had watery eyes whenever he left the purified air of our home. At that time I had been on low dose immunotherapy (described on page 11) for almost a year, so Joel had seen what it was like to be "on restrictions" for a shot. We knew that we had to do something about his allergies but did not want to subject him to the rigors of the low dose immunotherapy protocol without his full consent and cooperation. So we sat down and read the patient instruction booklet ("the pink book") together and let him make the choice between low dose immunotherapy and conventional allergy treatment. He chose low dose immunotherapy, fully aware of "the rules." He obeyed these rules at shot time more consistently and with more maturity than some adults do.

When Joel was tested before beginning low dose immunotherapy, the tests showed that, along with many inhalant allergies, Joel had developed an allergy to yeast. Joel received his first low dose immunotherapy injection in June, 1994. At about a week after his shot, I noticed that his morning cough was lessening. At ten days after his shot, his eczema totally cleared up for the first time in months. Because I thought it would return as soon as we liberalized his diet when we went "off restrictions," I took pictures of his arms on the eleventh day after his shot. When we got "off restrictions," he began eating everything (literally!) and his eczema did not return until his shot began to wear off about five weeks later.

After his first year of low dose immunotherapy, Joel was able to go progressively longer between shots before they began to wear off. By the time he was in high school, he was taking them only once a year in the summer. He was totally unrestricted except around the time of his shots. He ate a sugar-free healthy diet at home, but when having fun with his friends was able to enjoy whatever they were eating, including things he thought he'd never eat again like pizza, popcorn, and ice cream.

Joel is now an adult, a totally independent, self-sufficient graduate student with an electrical engineering fellowship, and is living half-way across the country from us. His allergies are no longer a problem and have not kept him from doing anything he wanted in life. He still takes a shot once a year. We fully expect him to have a healthy, normal, unrestricted life. This is indeed one of the greatest blessings any parent of an allergic son or daughter can experience.

MY STORY

I was an allergic child. I began taking conventional allergy shots for inhalants at age ten. When I was in my early twenties, I developed joint problems which I was initially told were rheumatoid arthritis, although the rheumatologist I later consulted called the problem arthralgia. I was treated with ibuprofen, and later with naproxen, two nonsteroidal anti-inflammatory drugs.

In the fall of 1978, I had an acute and severe intestinal "bug." For about two months afterwards, I got diarrhea whenever I ate raw vegetables or fruits. But the problem eventually went away and I forgot about the "bug" until many years later when I began to wonder if this "bug" was either the beginning of a parasitic infestation or a first episode of Crohn's disease.

In the spring of 1979, I began having trouble with dizziness and headaches. Because of my father's similar experience with milk allergy, I tried eliminating milk from my diet, but it did not help. I consulted several doctors, had CAT scans and other tests, and tried many medications to no avail. The cause was finally determined in October, 1980, when provocative testing showed that I was allergic to wheat, eggs, beef, tomatoes, lettuce, and chocolate. When I eliminated these foods from my diet, I became aware of several other foods that I had not been tested for that were also problems. The elimination diet cleared up my dizziness, headaches, and even the joint problems. I was instructed to try to reintroduce allergenic foods into my diet after six months of avoidance. When I did so, I was not able to tolerate any of the foods. After moving back to the purer environment of Colorado in late 1981, I felt quite healthy and we started our family.

In late 1984, I began experiencing food allergy symptoms again. I consulted a new allergist, who I had heard successfully treated food allergies with neutralization. (See pages 10 to 11 for more about neutralization). Of the 21 foods he tested me for, I was allergic to 18. My new problem foods included all grains, cow's milk, citrus fruits, beans, chicken, pork, lamb, turkey, and several other foods. I began a rotation diet which included none of my problem foods and felt much better. After a few weeks of taking food neutralizing drops, I was told to try reintroducing foods into my diet. I was unable to tolerate any of them. However, I was happy to feel better on my new rotated diet of unusual foods. Although food neutralization did not work for me, I was not a complete neutralization failure; the drops I was given for inhalants and chemicals were helpful.

I was healthy until 1991 when I developed severe diarrhea, fever, anemia, and weight loss. Stool tests showed the presence of *Candida albicans* but no *Salmonella, Shigella,* or parasites. My doctor gave me Nystatin and, on the assumption that I might have contracted "enteropathogenic *E. coli*," (the strain of *E. coli* often involved in food poisoning) also treated me with the antibiotic Cipro™. I felt better, but within a day of stopping the Cipro™ was back where I started. After many tests, the problem was diagnosed as Crohn's disease, an inflammatory bowel disease.

The gastroenterologist who diagnosed the Crohn's disease told me that the Crohn's had caused my food allergies. At the time I did not believe it, because I knew I had food allergies for eleven years before the Crohn's was diagnosed. But later, I remembered the intestinal "bug" I had thirteen years previously, and wondered if it had been an episode of Crohn's disease. The doctor also told me that diet had no influence on the disease. However, since I was on a rotation diet, and thus able to isolate and identify reactions to foods, my body told me that what I ate did indeed have a profound effect on the severity of my symptoms.

The milder drugs used to treat Crohn's disease did not help me much, so I was put on cortisone. It was effective but had unpleasant side effects. When my dosage was tapered and I eventually stopped taking it, the diarrhea gradually increased. However, I did not tell anyone because I did not want to take any more cortisone.

About that time, in the spring of 1992, I visited my allergist for the routine yearly testing necessary to keep my allergy shots current. The tests showed a major increase in my reaction to *Candida albicans* which I assumed was a result of the antibiotics and cortisone I had taken. However, when I discussed the test results with the doctor, he thought the *Candida* problem might have preceded and contributed to the Crohn's rather that having been caused by its treatment. He put me on a low-yeast diet and Diflucan,™ and my diarrhea improved as much as it had on cortisone, without any of the unpleasant side effects.

For several months, I did fairly well, as Crohn's patients go, on a low-fiber rotated diet of buffalo, duck, several kinds of fish, and vegetables cooked to mush. However, any deviation, such as ¼ cup of unsweetened applesauce, would cause a flare-up of the Crohn's disease. Then, in November, 1992, I began getting headaches from buffalo. Problems with duck followed, and then I lost my tolerance for the kinds of fish I had been eating and some vegetables. By January, 1993, I would go to the fish counter of our health food store, buy types of fish I had never eaten before, and react to them the first time I ate them. Since I no longer had any no-fiber flesh foods to eat, I reintroduced amaranth, quinoa, exotic tuber starches (malanga, cassava, white sweet potato, and true yam), and three nut butters into my diet. Home-ground nut butters gave me diarrhea because I could not grind them to complete smoothness, so I was limited to the three very finely ground commercial nut butters I could tolerate. Thus, on one of my rotation days I was eating only quinoa and carrots and felt like I was about to starve. As far as diarrhea went, I was not doing as well with the higher fiber diet.

One takes desperate measures in desperate times, so in spite of the fact that at that time the nearest doctor using low dose immunotherapy (see page 11 for more information) was 420 miles away, necessitating an 840 mile round trip on shot day because we could not find a chemically safe place to stay near his office, I began low dose immunotherapy in March, 1993. With my first shot, I noticed a dramatic improvement in my inhalant allergies, was able to add a few foods to my diet and had less diarrhea than in months. I continued to make small gains with low dose immunotherapy for about a year. Then, with my March, 1994 shot, my pollen allergies worsened and I "lost" some foods. For the next year I continued to do poorly and lose progressively more foods. Since severe food allergies can take up to two years to respond to low dose immunotherapy, we tinkered with my shots and considered that I might just be a slow responder. In 1995, we began exploring possible interferences with low dose immunotherapy, such as hormonal factors, and finally considered the possibility of intestinal dysbiosis. (See pages 17 to 20 for an explanation of dysbiosis).

In September, 1995, I had my first CDSA with parasitology. (CDSA stands for comprehensive digestive stool analysis. (See page 19 for more information about this test).

It showed severe dysbiosis with bacterial pathogens, but no parasites were detected even though the test included a purged stool specimen. No *Lactobacillus* nor *Bifidobacterium* was present. I began treatment with botanical antibacterial therapies, probiotics, and nutritional factors to help the intestine heal. I had another CDSA in November, which showed severe dysbiosis again. My score was two points worse and I had *Salmonella*. I then took several additional botanical therapies plus a course of Cipro.™ My third CDSA in February, 1996 was four points better and the *Salmonella* was gone, but the results were still not good. My doctor was researching more effective treatments for dysbiosis. While I waited for him to come up with an answer, I consulted a nutritionist who helped me begin to correct some nutritional imbalances and improve my digestion. I also began to learn everything I could to help myself.

At the same time, after seeing the results of my third CDSA, another doctor's nurse-practitioner called Great Smokies Diagnostic Laboratory, where the test was done, for advice. She asked them how I could still have large amounts of the unfriendly bacteria *Klebsiella* in every CDSA after having taken five months of botanical medicines that their testing showed it was sensitive to and a course of Cipro,™ to which it was also sensitive on testing. They asked her if I were taking FOS. (Fructooligosaccharides, described on pages 20 and 250). When she replied, "Yes," they told her to have me stop taking it because it supports the growth of *Klebsiella*. I stopped it two weeks before my March, 1996 low dose immunotherapy injection, while still taking the botanical antibacterial remedies. My March shot worked better than any shot had in the previous two years. I suspect that stopping the FOS allowed the botanical medicines to finally knock down the *Klebsiella*.

As my food tolerance improved, I was able to tolerate homemade goat's acidophilus milk. (For the recipe, see page 61). When I stopped taking the antibacterial botanical remedies to do my fourth CDSA in June, 1996, my symptoms did not worsen as they had every time I had stopped the botanical remedies previously. My score was down into the "mild dysbiosis" range with no bacterial pathogens present. I had good amounts of *Bifidobacterium* but still had no *Lactobacillus*.

My doctor recommended taking yet another brand of probiotic supplement containing a DDS-1 strain of *Lactobacillus*. I had taken dozens of bottles of several different brands of DDS-1 containing supplements in the previous nine months, but began taking the new brand. Also at this time, I was first able to purchase sheep's milk yogurt. (See "Sources," page 294). Because I now had milk products from two animals to rotate I was able to eat more of the fermented milks than I previously could.

My fifth CDSA in November, 1996 still showed no *Lactobacillus*, the *Klebsiella* was back, and my score was again in the "severe dysbiosis" range. My doctor said, "There is something here that I'm not seeing," and ordered a stool test performed by a different lab that also included a saliva test for antibodies to organisms that might be difficult to detect in a stool culture or parasite test. This test showed antibodies to the parasite *Entamoeba his-*

tolytica. I underwent several courses of treatment with anti-parasitic drugs taken two or three at a time plus long-term botanical remedies to eradicate the parasite. I repeated the saliva antibody test several times to determine if the drugs were effective and had negative results followed by positive results several times. My CDSAs continued to show *Klebsiella* most of the time and never had any *Lactobacillus* present.

When someone living in the "clean" United States has a parasite, the question is "How did you get it?" I believe that I was infected with *Entamoeba histolytica* over twenty years before it was diagnosed while we were living in California and I was working in a hospital with Asian immigrants. My problems which were later diagnosed as food allergies began a few months after having a three-month episode of diarrhea which was probably the initial parasitic infection. When I asked the doctor who originally diagnosed my food allergies why I had suddenly begun having problems with foods, he should have looked for the real answer to that question and treated me for the parasite. It probably would have been easier to eradicate then than it was after a long-term infection. Don't rule out parasites just because you haven't traveled to a Third World country! The world and its parasites can come to you wherever you live. Eating in a restaurant may expose you to food cooked by an immigrant who may not even realize he or she has parasites and who is in too much of a hurry for thorough hand-washing after a bathroom visit. Parasitic infection can be a trigger for a host of problems including food and chemical sensitivities.

The treatment of the parasite was definitely a major turning point for me, and as my health improved, I became less involved with health issues and much more involved with life. Therefore, I don't have as much of a paper trail of lab test results and dates of what I did when with what results. However, I remember that I did continue to explore new therapies that led to further improvement. In the late 1990's, a new probiotic, Culturelle™, became available. (For more information about this supplement and *Lactobacillus GG*, see page 27). After taking this supplement, my CDSAs finally showed the presence of *Lactobacillus.* However, they still also show *Klebsiella* and moderate dysbiosis. I tried the specific carbohydrate diet (SCD) as described by Elaine Gottschall in *Breaking the Vicious Cycle* and followed it strictly for a few years in addition to avoiding my food allergens and following a rotation diet. The SCD greatly improved my intestinal function. I still follow it most of the time but can eat starch occasionally and in moderation without problems now.

I have continued to take low dose immunotherapy at about 6-month intervals. What looked like a terrible problem in 2001, the withdrawal of EPD from the United States, turned out to be a good thing for me. EPD was replaced with LDA, which contains an Americanized antigen mix and gives more complete coverage to Americans than a mix based on British allergenic exposures. I have done much better on LDA than I did on EPD. The addition of perfumes to LDA has really eliminated my chemical sensitivities, and the list of foods I can eat continues to expand. (For more about EPD and LDA, see page 11).

I am still not completely "cured" and no longer waste time wanting to be. I am no longer starving and I have not had a Crohn's flare-up in over ten years; that is good enough for me. I'm in my 50's now. My most important job in life, that of raising my children, is almost finished as my younger son John is about to go to college. I'm ready to make the quantum leap from "a lot healthier than I was" to "better than I've ever been" when I go to heaven. Like the Apostle Paul, "I have fought the good fight, I have finished the race, I have kept the faith. Now there is in store for me a crown of righteousness, which the Lord, the righteous Judge, will award to me on that day."[1] The older I get, the more eager I am to escape all the unrighteousness and injustices of this world. The poor are getting poorer and the rich are getting richer and oppressing the poor (and even the middle class, like my family) more and more at every turn. There are "wars and rumors of wars" around the world and it seems that those in power encourage war. I'm not sure I want to see what's coming next in the world and I know where I'm going when I leave this world. I have also seen enough tragedy and disability among older members of our extended families to really mean it when I say that I never want to be a burden on my family.

Many people with food allergies are desperate for more than just food and help with their medical problems. My final recommendation is for a "supplement" that can give you the hope for the future that I have. I know it's politically incorrect to espouse one religion, and I am very much against cramming Christianity bundled with "democracy" and "capitalism" (i.e. greed and oppression) down the throats of the whole world, but I'd like to encourage you to just consider the claims of Jesus Christ with an open mind, much like taking a new probiotic and seeing how it works for you. Get a Bible (possibly an easily understood version like the Living Bible) and read the Gospel of John, one chapter per day. This experiment will take about 10 minutes a day for three weeks and could lead you to a greater "cure" than all of the treatments, supplements, and diets discussed in this book put together.

Finally, as you are traveling along your road back to health you may feel like this: "We were under great pressure, far beyond our ability to endure, so that we despaired even of life. Indeed, in our hearts we felt the sentence of death. But this happened that we might not rely on ourselves, but on God."[2] My hope for you is not only that you will get to the root of your health problems and solve them, but that you will also come to realize that in everything, both good experiences and bad, both temporal and eternal things, you must rely not on yourselves but on God. It is wonderful to eat and be satisfied; those of us who have had times with very little food because of our allergies appreciate eating and being satisfied like few people outside the Third World do. But the goal of life is beyond eating and being satisfied. It is to serve and "praise the Lord your God" – for blessings such as food we can eat or, in any circumstances, whether we can eat or not, for His gifts of life and His love.

FOOTNOTES/
1. II Timothy 4:7-8.
2. II Corinthians 1:8-9

Classification of Food Plants
with Rotation Group Numbers[1]

DIVISION MYCOPHYTA (MOLDS AND YEASTS)

Subdivision Eumycotina

Class Ascomycetes

Subclass Hemiascomycetes

Order Saccharomycetaceae

FAMILY SACCHAROMYCETACEAE / 1

BAKER'S YEAST, BREWER'S YEAST
(*Saccharomyces cerevisiae*)

Saccharomyces boulardii (probiotic supplement)

Saccharomyces kefir (used to make kefir)

Order Eurotiales

FAMILY EUROTIACEAE / 2

CITRIC ACID PRODUCING MOLDS
(*Aspergillus species*)

Aspergillus orazeae
(plant-based digestive enzymes)

FOS PRODUCING MOLD
(*Aspergillus species*)

CHEESE MOLDS

Penicillium roqueforti

Penicillium camemberti

Penicillium species (other cheeses)

Subclass Protoascomycetes

Order Pezizales

FAMILY ELVELLACEAE / 3

MOREL (SPONGE MUSHROOM)

Order Tuberales

TRUFFLE FAMILY / 4

TRUFFLE

Class Basidiomycetes

Subclass Holobasidiomycetes

Order Agaricales

FAMILY AGARICACEAE / 5

COMMON (CULTIVATED) MUSHROOM

FIELD MUSHROOM, MEADOW MUSHROOM

HORSE MUSHROOM

OYSTER MUSHROOM

PAROSOL (UMBRELLA) MUSHROOM

SHITAKE MUSHROOM

FAMILY BOLETACEAE / 6

PORCINO (CEP) MUSHROOM

FAMILY RUSSULACEAE / 7

GREEN RUSSULA

FAMILY CANTHARELLACEAE / 8

CHANTERELLE

Order Lycoperdales

FAMILY LYCOPERDACEAE / 9

PUFFBALL

Subclass Hemibasidiomycetes

Order Auriculariales

FAMILY AURICULARIACEAE / 10

WOOD EAR

DIVISION RHODOPHYTA

Class Rhodophyceae

Subclass Florideophycidae

Order Nemalionales

FAMILY GELIDIACEAE / 11

AGAR (*Gelidium species*)

Order Gigartinales

FAMILY GRACILARIACEAE / 12

AGAR (*Gracillaria species*)

EDIBLE SEAWEEDS of *Gracillaria species*

FAMILY GIGARTINACEAE / 13
    CARAGEEN *(Chondrus species)*
    IRISH MOSS (an edible seaweed)
    ARAME
Order Palmariales
FAMILY PALMARIACEAE / 14
    DULSE (an edible seaweed)

Subclass Bangiophycidae
Order Bangiales
FAMILY BANGIACEAE / 15
    NORI (an edible seaweed)

DIVISION PHAEOPHYTA
Class Phyophyceae
Order Laminariales
FAMILY LAMINARIACEAE / 16
    KOMBU
    EDIBLE SEAWEEDS of *Laminaria species*
FAMILY ALARIACEAE / 17
    WAKAME
MANY FAMILIES OF BROWN ALGAE / 18
    KELPS (edible seaweed - many species)
    ALGIN OR ALGINIC ACID (food additive)

DIVISION CHLOROPHYTA
Class Cholorphyceae
Order Chlorococcales
FAMILY OOCYSTACEAE / 19
    CHLORELLA SPECIES (a nutritional
      supplement)

DIVISION CYANOPHYTA
Class Cyanophyceae
Order Oscilliatoriales
FAMILY NOSTOCINACEAE / 20
    SPIRULINA SPECIES
      (a nutritional supplement)

DIVISION PTEROPSIDA
Class Gymnospermae
Order Cycadales
CYCAD FAMILY / 21
    FLORIDA ARROWROOT

Order Coniferales
PINE FAMILY / 22
    JUNIPER (used to make gin)
    PINE NUTS
Order Ginkoales
GINKO FAMILY / 23
    GINKO BILBOA (herbal supplement)

SUBDIVISION ANGIOSPERMAE
Class Dicotyledones
Subclass Apetale
Order Piperales
PEPPER FAMILY / 24
    BLACK PEPPER, WHITE PEPPER
Order Proteales
PROTEA FAMILY / 25
    MACADAMIA NUT
Order Urticales
MULBERRY FAMILY / 26
    HEMP
    MULBERRY
    FIG
    BREADFRUIT
HOPS FAMILY / 27
    HOPS (used in making beer)
Order Polygonales
BUCKWHEAT FAMILY / 28
    BUCKWHEAT
    RHUBARB
    SORREL
Order Juglandales
WALNUT FAMILY / 29
    BLACK WALNUT
    WHITE WALNUT (BUTTERNUT)
    ENGLISH WALNUT
    PECAN
    HICKORY NUT
Order Fagales
BEECH FAMILY / 30
    CHESTNUT
BIRCH FAMILY / 31
    FILBERT
    NATURAL WINTERGREEN FLAVOR
    XYLITOL (from birch trees)

Order Chenopodiales
GOOSEFOOT FAMILY / 32
    BEET, SUGAR BEET (and beet sugar), CHARD
    SPINACH
    QUINOA
AMARANTH FAMILY / 33
    AMARANTH

Order Ranales
WATER LILY FAMILY / 34
    LOTUS (and flour)
CUSTARD APPLE FAMILY / 35
    ATEMOYA
    CUSTARD APPLE
    CHERIMOYA
    PAPAW
NUTMEG FAMILY / 36
    NUTMEG
    MACE
BARBERRY FAMILY / 37
    BARBERRY
    MANDRAKE (also called MAYAPPLE)
    GOLDENSEAL (herbal supplement)
LAUREL FAMILY / 38
    AVOCADO
    BAY LEAF
    CINNAMON
    SASSAFRAS

Order Papaverales
POPPY FAMILY / 39
    POPPYSEED
    CAPER[2]
MUSTARD FAMILY / 40
    ARUGULA
    Brassica oleracea variants:
        BROCCOLI
        BRUSSEL SPROUTS
        CABBAGE (all varieties except Chinese)
        CAULIFLOWER
        COLLARDS, KALE
        KOHLRABI
    BOK CHOI
    CANOLA (OIL AND SEEDS)
    CHINESE CABBAGE

    CRESS (CURLY, GARDEN, UPLAND, AND WATER)
    HORSERADISH
    MUSTARD GREENS
    MUSTARD SEED
    RADISH, BLACK RADISH, DAIKON
    RAPINI, ITALIAN KALE
    RUTABAGA
    TURNIP

Subclass Polypetale
Order Rosales
GOOSEBERRY FAMILY / 41
    GOOSEBERRY
    TRUE CURRANT
ROSE FAMILY / 42
    BLACKBERRY
    BOYSENBERRY
    DEWBERRY
    LOGANBERRY
    LONGBERRY
    RASPBERRY
    STRAWBERRY
    YOUNGBERRY
APPLE FAMILY[3] / 43
    APPLE, APPLE CIDER, CIDER VINEGAR
    LOQUAT
    PEAR
    QUINCE
    ROSEHIP
PLUM FAMILY / 44
    ALMOND
    APRICOT
    CHERRY
    CHOKECHERRY
    NECTARINE, PEACH
    PLUM
PEA FAMILY / 45
    Subfamily Mimosaceae
        GUAR GUM
        GUM ACACIA
        GUM ARABIC
        GUM TRAGACANTH
    Subfamily Caesalpinoideae
        TAMARIND (a seasoning)

Subfamily Papilionoideae / 45, continued
ADZUKI BEAN
ALFALFA
ANASAZI BEAN
ASPARAGUS (YARD-LONG) BEAN
BLACK-EYED PEA (COWPEA)
BLACK BEAN
CHICKPEA (GARBANZO BEAN)
FAVA BEAN
GREEN PEA, SNOW PEA
KUDZU
LENTIL
LIMA BEAN
LICORICE
LOCUST (CAROB) BEAN
LUPINE BEAN (and flour)
MUNG BEAN
PEANUT
Phaseolus vulgaris variants:
GREEN (SNAP) BEAN
KIDNEY BEAN
NAVY BEAN
PINTO BEAN
WAX BEAN
WHITE BEAN
SOYBEAN

Order Gerinales
FLAX FAMILY / 46
FLAXSEED (and oil)
OXALIS FAMILY / 47
CARAMBOLA
SPURGE FAMILY / 48
CASTOR OIL
SWEET CASSAVA, MANIOC, MANDIOCA
TAPIOCA (made from bitter cassava)
RUE (CITRUS) FAMILY / 49
CITRON
CLEMENTINE
GRAPEFRUIT
KUMQUAT
LEMON
LIME
MANDARIN, TANGERINE
ORANGE
PUMELLO

TANGELO (tangerine-grapefruit hybrid)
UGLI FRUIT (grapefruit-clementine hybrid)
Order Salpindales
CASHEW FAMILIY / 50
CASHEW
MANGO
PISTACHIO
HOLLY FAMILY / 51
YERBA MATE (beverage)
MAPLE FAMILY / 52
MAPLE SUGAR and SYRUP

Order Rhamnales
GRAPE FAMILY / 53
GRAPE and grape products such as CREAM
OF TARTAR, COMMERCIAL DRIED
"CURRANTS," RAISINS, WINE, and
WINE VINEGAR

Order Malvales
MALLOW FAMILY / 54
AMERICAN HEMP
COTTONSEED (oil)
HIBISCUS
OKRA
STERICULA FAMILY / 55
CHOCOLATE, COCOA
COLA NUT

Order Guttiferales
DILLENIA FAMILY / 56
KIWI FRUIT

Order Parietales
TEA FAMILY / 57
BLACK TEA, GREEN TEA
PASSIONFLOWER FAMILY / 58
PASSION FRUIT
PAPAYA FAMILY / 59
PAPAYA

Order Myrtales
MYRTLE FAMILY / 60
ALLSPICE
CLOVES
EUCALYPTUS
FEIJOA
GUAVA
EVENING PRIMROSE FAMILY / 61
EVENING PRIMROSE OIL

POMEGRANATE FAMILY / 62
POMEGRANATE, GRENADINE (derived from pomegranate)
SAPUCAYA FAMILY / 63
BRAZIL NUT
PARADISE NUT

Order Umbellales
GINSENG FAMILY / 64
GINSENG, ALL VARIETIES
PARSLEY FAMILY / 65
ANISE
CARAWAY
CARROT
CELERY, CELERY SEED AND LEAF, CELERIAC
CHERVIL
CORIANDER, CILANTRO
CUMIN
DILL
FENNEL
PARSLEY, PARSLEY ROOT
PARSNIP

Subclass Sympetale
Order Ericales
BLUEBERRY FAMILY / 66
BLUEBERRY
CRANBERRY
HUCKLEBERRY

Order Ebenales
EBONY FAMILY / 67
PERSIMMON
SAPODILLA FAMILY / 68
CHICLE (CHEWING GUM BASE)
GUTTA PERCHA (DENTAL MATERIAL)
SAPOTE
Order Gentianales
OLIVE FAMILY / 69
BLACK OLIVE, GREEN OLIVE, OLIVE OIL
GENTIAN FAMILY / 70
Gentiana lutea (herbal supplement)

Order Polemoniales
MORNING GLORY FAMILY / 71
JICAMA[4]
SWEET POTATO, COMMERCIAL "YAM", WHITE SWEET POTATO (BONIATO, CAMOTE)
MINT FAMILY / 72
BASIL
MARJORAM
MENTHOL
MINT
OREGANO
PEPPERMINT
ROSEMARY
SAGE
SAVORY
SPEARMINT
THYME
POTATO FAMILY / 73
EGGPLANT
PAPRIKA
PEPINO (MELON PEAR)
PEPPER - ANAHEIM, BANANA, BELL, CAYENNE, CHERRY, CHILI, JALAPENO
TAMARILLO
TOBACCO
TOMATO
TOMATILLO
WHITE POTATO

Order Rubiales
MADDER FAMILY / 74
COFFEE

Order Curcurbitales
GOURD FAMILY / 75
CHAYOTE
CUCUMBER
MELONS (except watermelon) - CANTALOUPE, CASABA, CRENSHAW, HONEYDEW, MUSKMELON, PERSIAN MELON
PUMPKIN (and PUMPKIN SEEDS), SPAGHETTI SQUASH
SUMMER SQUASH (CROOKNECK, STRAIGHTNECK, YELLOW, ZUCCHINI), CALABAZA
WATERMELON

WINTER SQUASH (ACORN, BUTTERCUP, BUTTERNUT, DELICATA, HUBBARD, PATTYPAN)

Order Campanulales

COMPOSITE FAMILY / 76 to 79[5]

  Group Tubuliflorae

    Tribe Heliantheae / 76

      DAHLIA (DACOPA BEVERAGE)

      JERUSALEM ARTICHOKE

      SUNFLOWER (SEEDS AND OIL)

    Tribe Anthemideae / 77

      CHAMOMILE

      STEVIA (SWEETENER)

      TARRAGON

      Artemesia annua (herbal supplement)

    Tribe Cynareae / 78

      BURDOCK

      CARDOON

      GLOBE ARTICHOKE

      SAFFLOWER (OIL)

      Echinacea (herbal supplement)

  Group Liguliflorae

    Tribe Cichorieae / 79

      CHICORY, RADICCHIO

      DANDELION

      ENDIVE, BELGIAN ENDIVE, ESCAROLE

      LETTUCE, ROMAINE

      SALSIFY

Order Tubiflorae

Suborder Solanineae

PEDALIUM FAMILY / 80

  SESAME (SEEDS, OIL, AND MEAL)

Order Plantasinales

PLANTAGINACEAE FAMILY / 81

  PSYLLIUM SEED (fiber supplement)

Subclass Caryophyllidae

Order Caryophyllales

CACTUS FAMILY / 81.5

  CACTUS (NOPALES)

  PRICKLY PEAR

Class Monocotyledones

Order Graminales

SEDGE FAMILY / 82

  GROUNDNUT

  WATER CHESTNUT

GRAIN FAMILY / 83 to 99[6]

  Subfamily Poateae

    Tribe Bambuseae

      BAMBOO SHOOTS / 83

    Tribe Hordeae

      BARLEY / 84

      KAMUT / 85[7]

      RYE / 86

      SPELT / 87[7]

      TRITICALE (a hybrid of wheat and rye) / 88

      WHEAT / 89[7]

    Tribe Aveneae

      OATS / 90

    Tribe Festuceae

      LEMON GRASS / 91

      TEFF / 91

    Tribe Orizeae

      RICE / 92

      WILD RICE / 93

  Subfamily Panicateae

    Tribe Paniceae

      MILLET / 94

    Tribe Andropogoneae

      MILO (JOWAR), SORGHUM / 95

      MOLASSES / 96

      SUGAR CANE AND CANE SUGAR / 97

    Tribe Tripsaceae

      CORN / 98

      JOB'S TEARS / 99

Order Palmales

PALM FAMILY / 100

  CABBAGE-PALM

  COCONUT (MEAL AND OIL)

  DATE AND DATE SUGAR

  SAGO (STARCH AND SOURCE OF VITAMIN C)

Order Arales
ARUM FAMILY / 101
  CERIMAN (TROPICAL FRUIT)
  DASHEEN ARROWROOT
  MALANGA
  POI
  TARO

Order Xyridales
PINEAPPLE FAMILY / 102
  PINEAPPLE

Order Liliales
LILY FAMILY / 103
  ALOE VERA
  ASPARAGUS
  CHIVES
  GARLIC
  LEEKS
  ONION
  SARSAPARILLA
  SHALLOT
YAM FAMILY / 104
  NAME (TRUE YAM)
AGAVE FAMILY / 105
  AGAVE (source of tequila)
  AGUAMIEL (sweetener derived from the maguey plant)
  YUCCA
IRIS FAMILY / 106
  SAFFRON
TACCA FAMILY / 107
  FIJI ARROWROOT

Order Scitaminales
CANNA FAMILY / 108
  QUEENSLAND ARROWROOT
BANANA FAMILY / 109
  BANANA
  MUSA ARROWROOT
  PLANTAIN
GINGER FAMILY / 110
  CARDAMON
  EAST INDIAN ARROWROOT
  GINGER
  TURMERIC

ARROWROOT FAMILY / 111
  WEST INDIAN ARROWROOT

Order Orchidales
ORCHID FAMILY / 112
  VANILLA
  LYCHEE

FOOTNOTES

1. The classification of plants was derived from the sources listed below and represents a consensus of the opinions of the authors listed:

> Alexopoulos, Constantine John, *Introductory Mycology,* Second Edition, John Wiley and Sons, Inc., New York, 1962.

> Alexopoulos, C. J. and H. C. Bold, *Algae and Fungi,* The Macmillan Company, New York, 1967.

> Clements, Frederic E. and Cornelius L. Shear, *The Genera of Fungi,* Hafner Publishing Company, New York, 1931.

> Lobban, Christopher S. and Michael J. Wynne, *The Biology of Seaweeds,* Blackwell Scientific Publications, Oxford, England, 1981.

> Phaff, H. J., M. W. Miller, and E. M. Mrak, *The Life of Yeasts,* Harvard University Press, 1966.

> Rendle, Alfred Barton, *The Classification of Flowering Plants,* Volumes 1 and 2, Second Edition, Cambridge University Press, London, 1967.

> Round, F. E., *The Biology of Algae,* Second Edition, Edward Arnold Publishers Limited, Bath, England, 1973.

> Schneider, Elizabeth, *Uncommon Fruits and Vegetables,* Harper & Row Publishers, New York, 1986.

> Taylor, Norman, *Taylor's Encyclopedia of Gardening,* Fourth Edition, Houghton Mifflin Company, Boston, 1961.

2. Capers are sometimes classified in the Cappari-daceae family, another family in the order Papaverales. According to this classification, they would be rotated separately from poppy-seeds.

3. The fruits the apple family are sometimes considered a tribe of the family rose family, which contains most berries. Because these foods are so closely related, if you are very sensitive to them, you may wish to rotate them on the same day.

4. Some botanists classify jicama in the legume family rather than the morning glory family. Because of cross-reactivity with sweet potatoes, allergy doctors place it in the morning glory family, as it is in this classification scheme. If you are very sensitive to the foods in these families, you may want to rotate them together.

5. Some allergy doctors feel that the tribes in the composite family are different enough antigenically to be treated as separate families for the purpose of a rotation diet. Therefore, they are assigned different rotation group numbers.

6. The grains are given different rotation group numbers even though they are all in the same family because some doctors allow their patients to eat a different grain each day on rotation. See pages 9 and 35 for more information about how to rotate grains.

7. Wheat, kamut, and spelt are different species within the same genus *(Triticum)* and thus are very closely related.

Classification of Food Animals

with Rotation Group Numbers[1]

PHYLUM MOLLUSCA
Class Gastropoda

Order Prosobranchia
ABALONE FAMILY / 201
   ABALONE

Order Pulmonata
SNAIL FAMILY / 202
   EDIBLE SNAILS

Class Pelecypoda

Order Filibranchia
MUSSEL FAMILY / 203
   MUSSEL
SCALLOP FAMILY / 204
   SCALLOP
OYSTER FAMILY / 205
   OYSTER

Order Eulamellibranchia
THICK-SHELLED CLAM FAMILY / 206
   THICK-SHELLED CLAM
SOFT-SHELLED CLAM FAMILY / 207
   SOFT-SHELLED CLAM
COCKLE FAMILY / 208
   COCKLE

Class Cephalopoda
Order Dibranchia
SQUID FAMILY / 209
   SQUID
   CUTTLEFISH
Order Octopoda
OCTOPUS FAMILY / 210
   OCTOPUS

PHYLUM ARTHROPODA
Subphylum Mandibulata
Class Crustacea
Subclass Malocostraca

Order Decapoda
PRAWN FAMILY / 211
   PRAWN
   SHRIMP
LOBSTER FAMILY / 212
   CRAYFISH
   LOBSTER
CRAB FAMILY / 213
   CRAB (ALL VARIETIES)

PHYLUM CHORDATA
Subphylum Vertebrata
Class Ostichethyes
Superorder Chondrostei

Order Acipenseroidei
STURGEON FAMILY / 214
   STURGEON (CAVIAR)

Superorder Teleostei
Order Isopondyli
HERRING FAMILY / 215
   HERRING
   MENHADEN
   SARDINE
   SHAD
ANCHOVY FAMILY / 216
   ANCHOVY
Suborder Salmonoidea
SALMON FAMILY / 217
   SALMON (ALL VARIETIES)
   TROUT (ALL FRESHWATER VARIETIES)
SMELT FAMILY / 218
   SMELT
WHITEFISH FAMILY / 219
   WHITEFISH

Order Haplomi
PIKE FAMILY / 220
   BLACKFISH
   MUSKELLUNGE

Suborder Mugiloidea
MULLET FAMILY / 245
   MULLET
SILVERSIDE FAMILY / 246
   SILVERSIDE
Suborder Scorpaenoidea
SCORPIONFISH FAMILY / 247
   SCORPIONFISH

Order Heterosomata
Suborder Pleuronectoidea[3]
TURBOT FAMILY / 248
   TURBOT
   CALIFORNIA HALIBUT (LEFT-EYED)
HALIBUT FAMILY / 248
   HALIBUT (RIGHT-EYED)
FLOUNDER FAMILY / 248
   DAB
   FLOUNDER
   PLAICE
SOLE FAMILY / 248
   SOLE

Order Lophiformes
Suborder Lophoidei
ANGLERFISH FAMILY / 249
   MONKFISH

Class Amphibia
Order Salientia
FROG FAMILY / 250
   FROG

Class Reptilia
Order Chelonia
TURTLE FAMILY / 251
   TERRAPIN, TURTLE
Order Crocodylia
ALLIGATOR FAMILY / 252
   ALLIGATOR
CROCIDILE FAMILY / 253
   CROCODILE
Order Squamata
Superorder Serpentes
MANY SNAKE FAMILIES / 254
   SNAKES

Class Aves
Order Struthioniformes
OSTRICH FAMILY / 255
   OSTRICH
Order Casuariiformes
EMU FAMILY / 256
   EMU
Order Anseriformes
DUCK FAMILY / 257
   DUCK (AND DUCK EGGS)
   GOOSE (AND GOOSE EGGS)
Order Galliformes
GROUSE FAMILY / 258
   GROUSE (ALSO CALLED PARTRIDGE)
PHEASANT FAMILY / 259
   CHICKEN (AND CHICKEN EGGS)
   CORNISH HEN
   PHEASANT
   QUAIL
TURKEY FAMILY / 260
   TURKEY (AND TURKEY EGGS)
GUINEA FOWL FAMILY / 261
   GUINEA HEN (AND GUINEA HEN EGGS)
Order Columbiformes
DOVE FAMILY / 262
   DOVE
   PIGEON (ALSO CALLED SQUAB)

Class Mammmalia
Order Marsupialia
OPOSSUM FAMILY / 263
   OPOSSUM
KANGAROO FAMILY / 264
   KANGAROO
Order Lagomorpha
HARE FAMILY / 265
   RABBIT
Order Rodentia
Suborder Sciuromorpha
SQUIRREL FAMILY / 266
   SQUIRREL

Footnotes

1. The classification of animals was derived from the sources listed below and represents a consensus of the opinions of the authors listed:

    The Larousse Encyclopedia of Animal Life, McGraw-Hill Book Company, New York, 1967.

    The New Larousse Encyclopedia of Animal Life, Bonanza Books, New York, 1981.

    Rothschild, Nathaniel, Baron, *A Classification of Living Animals,* John Wiley and Sons, Inc., New York, New York, 1961.

2. The fish name "ono" can be used for either wahoo (most common) or yellow-fin tuna (ahi).

3. The fish in the suborder Pleuronectoidea are sometimes classified together as one food family and therefore are given the same rotation group number. If you are sensitive to these fish, rotate all of them on the same day.

4. Some doctors allow their patients to "rotate" meats of the cattle family as though they were not all in the same family; therefore they are given separate rotation group numbers.

An Alphabetical Index to
The Food Classifications
with Rotation Group Numbers

A

Abalone - 201, page 277

Acidophilus milk - the same rotation group as the animal the milk came from

Agar, *Gelidium species* - 11, page 269

Agar, *Gracillaria species* - 12, page 269

Agave (used to make tequila) - 105, page 275

Aguamiel (sweetener from the maguey plant) - 105, page 275

Ahi - 242, page 278

Albacore - 242, page 278

Alfalfa - 45, page 272

Algin or alginic acid - 18, page 270

Alligator - 252, page 279

Allspice - 60, page 272

Almond - 44, page 271

Aloe vera - 103, page 275

Amaranth - 33, page 271

American hemp - 54, page 272

Anchovy - 216, page 277

Anise - 65, page 273

Antelope - 276, page 280

Apple - 43, page 271

Apricot - 44, page 271

Arame - 13, page 270

Arrowroot, Dasheen - 101, page 275

Arrowroot, East Indian - 110, page 275

Arrowroot, Fiji - 107, page 275

Arrowroot, Florida - 21, page 270

Arrowroot, Musa - 109, page 275

Arrowroot, Queensland - 108, page 275

Arrowroot, West Indian - 111, page 275

Artemesia annua (herbal supplement) - 77, page 274

Artichoke, globe - 78, page 274

Artichoke, Jerusalem - 76, page 274

Arugula - 40, page 271

Asparagus - 103, page 275

Atemoya - 35, page 271

Avocado - 38, page 271

B

Bamboo shoots - 83, page 274

Banana - 109, page 275

Barberry - 37, page 271

Barley - 84, page 274

Basil - 72, page 273

Bass, black - 235, page 278

Bass, freshwater - 235, page 278

Bass, sea - 231, page 278

Baker's yeast - 1, page 269

Bay leaf - 38, page 271

Bean, adzuki, asparagus, black, fava, garbanzo, green, kidney, lima, lupine, mung, navy, pinto, soy, wax, white, etc. - 45, page 272

Bear - 269, page 280

Beef - 277, page 280

Beet - 32, page 271

Beet sugar - 32, page 271

Belgian endive - 79, page 274

Berries - see listings under individual berry names

Bison (American buffalo) - 278, page 280

Blackberry - 42, page 271

Blackfish - 220, page 277

Blueberry - 66, page 273

Bluefish - 238, page 278

Boar, wild - 272, page 280

Bok choi - 40, page 271

Boniato (white sweet potato) - 71, page 273

Bonito - 241, page 278

Boysenberry - 42, page 271

Brazil nut - 63, page 273

Breadfruit - 26, page 270

Brewer's yeast - 1, page 269

Broccoli - 40, page 271

Brussels sprouts - 40, page 271

Buckwheat - 28, page 270

Buffalo, American (bison) - 278, page 280

Buffalo, cape, water, etc. - 279, page 280

Burdock - 78, page 274

Butter, cow's milk - 277, page 280

Butterfish - 230, page 278

Butternut (white walnut) - 29, page 270

C

Cabbage, all varieties - 40, page 271

Cabbage-palm - 100, page 274

Cactus - 81.5, page 274

Calabaza - 75, page 273

Camel - 273, page 280

Camote - 71, page 273

Cane sugar - 97, page 274

Canola (oil and seeds) - 40, page 271

Cantaloupe - 75, page 273

Cape Catensis – 226, page 278

Caper - 39, page 271

Cardoon - 78, page 274

Carageen - 13, page 270

Carambola - 47, page 272

Caraway - 65, page 273

Cardamon - 110, page 275

Cardoon - 78, page 274

Caribou - 274, page 280

Carob bean, carob bean gum - 45, page 272

Carob flour or powder (from carob bean pod) - 45, page 272

Carp - 222, page 278

Carrot - 65, page 273

Casaba melon - 75, page 273

Cashew - 50, page 272

Cassava - 48, page 272

Castor oil - 48, page 272

Catfish, freshwater - 223, page 278

Catfish, sea - 224, page 278

Cauliflower - 40, page 271

Celeriac - 65, page 273

Celery - 65, page 273

Celery leaf or seed - 65, page 273

Ceriman - 101, page 275

Chamomile - 77, page 274

Chanterelle - 8, page 269

Chard - 32, page 271

Chayote - 75, page 273

Cheese - 2, page 269, and the rotation group of the animal the milk came from

Cheese molds - 2, page 269

Cherimoya - 35, page 271

Cherry - 44, page 271

Chervil - 65, page 273

Chestnut - 30, page 270

Chestnut, water - 82, page 274

Chicken - 259, page 279

Chicken eggs - 259, page 279

Chickpea (garbanzo bean) - 45, page 272

Chicle (chewing gum base) - 68, page 273

Chicory - 79, page 274

Chives - 103, page 275

Chlorella species (nutritional supplement) - 19, page 270

Chocolate - 55, page 272

Chokecherry - 44, page 271

Chub - 222, page 278

Cider, apple - 43, page 271

Cider vinegar - 43, page 271, also yeast - 1, page 269

Cilantro - 65, page 273

Cinnamon - 38, page 271

Citric acid (molds that produce it) - 1, page 269

Citron - 49, page 272

Clam, soft-shelled - 207, page 277

Clam, thick-shelled - 206, page 277

Clementine - 49, page 272

Cloves - 60, page 272

Cockle - 208, page 277

Cocoa - 55, page 272

Coconut, coconut meal, coconut oil - 100, page 274

Cod - 226, page 278

Coffee - 74, page 273

Cola nut - 55, page 272

Collards - 40, page 271

Coriander - 65, page 273

Corn - 98, page 274

Cornish hen - 259, page 279

Cottonseed (and oil) - 54, page 272

Crab, all varieties - 213, page 277

Cranberry - 66, page 273

Crappie - 235, page 278

Crayfish - 212, page 277

Cream of tartar - 53, page 272

Crenshaw melon - 75, page 273

H

Haddock - 226, page 278

Hake - 226, page 278

Halibut, California (left-eyed) - 248, page 279

Halibut (right-eyed) - 248, page 279

Harvestfish - 230, page 278

Hemp – 26, page 270

Hemp, American – 54, page 272

Herring - 215, page 277

Hibiscus - 54, page 272

Hickory nut - 29, page 270

Hoki - 226, page 278

Honeydew melon - 75, page 273

Hops - 27, page 270

Horse - 271, page 280

Horseradish - 40, page 271

Huckleberry - 66, page 273

I

Irish moss - 13, page 270

J

Jack - 237, page 278

Jicama - 71, page 273

Job's tears - 99, page 274

Juniper (gin) - 22, page 270

K

Kale - 40, page 271

Kamut - 85, page 274

Kangaroo - 264, page 279

Kefir - 1, page 269, and the same rotation group as the animal the milk came from

Kelp - 18, page 270

Kiwi fruit - 56, page 272

Kohlrabi - 40, page 271

Kombu - 16, page 270

Kudzu - 45, page 272

Kumquat - 49, page 272

L

Lamb (sheep) - 283, page 280

Leek - 103, page 275

Lemon - 49, page 272

Lemon grass - 91, page 274

Lentil - 45, page 272

Lettuce, all types - 79, page 274

Licorice - 45, page 272

Lime - 49, page 272

Lion - 270, page 280

Llama - 273, page 280

Lobster - 212, page 277

Locust (carob) bean and locust (carob) bean gum - 45, page 272

Loganberry - 42, page 271

Longberry - 42, page 271

Loquat - 43, page 271

Lotus (flour) - 34, page 271

Lupine, bean and flour - 45, page 272

Lychee - 112, page 275

M

Macadamia nut - 25, page 270

Mace - 36, page 271

Mackerel - 240, page 278

Mahi mahi (dolphinfish) - 232, page 278

Malanga - 101, page 275

Mandarin - 49, page 272

Mandioca - 48, page 272

Mandrake - 37, page 271

Mango - 50, page 272

Manioc - 48, page 272

Maple sugar - 52, page 272

Maple syrup - 52, page 272

Marjoram - 72, page 273

Marlin - 244, page 278

Mayapple - 37, page 271

Melon, casaba, crenshaw, honeydew, Persian - 75, page 273

Menhaden - 215, page 277

Menthol - 72, page 273

Milk, cow's - 277, page 280

Milk, goat's - 282, page 280

Milk, sheep's - 283, page 280

Milk, other - in the same families as the animals that produce them

Millet - 94, page 274

Milo - 95, page 274

Minnow - 222, page 278

Mint - 72, page 273

Molasses - 96, page 274

Molds, cheese - 2, page 269

Molds, citric acid producing - 2, page 269

Using Commercially Prepared Foods

Commercially prepared foods can be great savers of time spent in the kitchen for those of us on allergy diets. However, commercial foods may contain hidden allergens which you should avoid. You MUST READ LABELS very carefully to find foods you can use. The use of commercial foods can be challenging, but it is not impossible.

This reference section contains a list of some commercial products that might be foods you can use on your diet. Please READ THE LABELS on these items before you purchase them; manufacturers change the ingredients they use in their foods often and may have changed them since the time of this writing. Large health food stores carry many of the items listed. Addresses are given when available to help your health food store find you foods they do not already carry. Some of the companies listed welcome individual orders. Visit the company websites listed below for more information.

This section also contains a list of derivatives of common allergenic foods which can be ingredients you need to avoid in commercially prepared foods. This list may not be exhaustive; other ingredients might be derived from your problem foods which are not listed below.

HIDDEN ALLERGENS AND FOOD DERIVATIVES TO AVOID IN COMMERCIALLY PREPARED FOODS

MILK:
Casein, sodium caseinate, or caseinate
Curds
Lactalbumin
Lactoglobulin
Lactose
Milk products such as butter, cheese, cream, etc.
Powdered, evaporated, or condensed milk
Whey

EGGS:
Albumin
Egg pasta
Globulin
Meringue
Ovomucoid
Ovomucin
Ovovitellin or vitellin
Powdered or dried egg, egg yolk, or egg white
Sauces such as mayonnaise, hollandaise, or tartar sauce

Also, some wines may be clarified with egg white.

WHEAT:
Alcoholic beverages such as beer, whiskey, and gin
Bulgur
Couscous
Flour, graham flour, gluten flour, wheat flour, semolina flour
Gluten
Grain-based coffee substitutes, such as Postum™
Hydrolyzed vegetable protein (HVP)
Modified food starch
Monosodium glutamate (MSG)
Pasta, including those such as Jerusalem artichoke pasta made with semolina flour
Wheat germ, bran, or berries, cracked wheat
White (grain) vinegar

CORN:
Adhesive stamps and envelopes (Do not lick them; apply water with a sponge instead.)
Alcoholic beverages, especially sweet wines
Baking powder (most contain cornstarch)
Corn flour, cornmeal, corn syrup, corn oil
Corn starch (a filler in many supplements and medications)
Dextrose
Dextrin
Flavorings such as vanilla may contain corn syrup
Fructose
Glucose

Grits
Hominy
Maltodextrin
Modified food starch, food starch
Powdered sugar (contains cornstarch)
Vitamin C (Some brands labeled as
"synthetic" are actually manufactured from
corn.)

Also, some plastic wraps and plastic or
paper cups and plates may be coated with
corn oil.

SOY:

Lecithin
Margarine
Miso
Shortening
Soy flour, soy oil, soy meal, soy milk
Tamari, soy sauce, worcestershire sauce
Tempeh
Textured vegetable protein
Tofu

YEAST:

All alcoholic beverages
Black (fermented) teas
Cheese
Malted products
Soft drinks which may contain fermented
products such as root beer and ginger ale
Soy sauce and condiments which contain
soy sauce
Vinegar (all kinds) and condiments which
contain vinegar, such as mustard, pickles, etc.
Vitamins and vitamin enriched processed
foods
Yeast breads (Sourdough is NOT yeast-free,
but contains "wild" yeasts which some yeast-
sensitive people can tolerate.)

If your doctor puts you on a yeast-free
diet, he or she may also advise you to avoid
leftovers, fruit juices, mushrooms, dried fruits
and spices, sugar, and many other foods.

COMMERCIALLY PREPARED FOODS YOU MIGHT BE ABLE TO USE

Most of these companies make products in addition
to those listed below. Visit their websites for up-to-
date information about all of their products.

BREADS:

Most of the breads below are sourdough breads.
They contain wild yeast from the air even though it
may not be listed as an ingredient.

Food For Life White Rice Bread: White rice flour,
water, honey, soy oil, guar gum, xanthum gum,
cellulose, yeast, sea salt

Food for Life Baking Company, Inc.
P.O. Box 1434
Corona, CA 92878
(951) 279-5090
(800) 797-5090
www.foodforlife.com

French Meadow Spelt Bread: Spelt, water,
and sea salt

French Meadow Bakery
(also makes kamut and rye breads)
2610 Lyndale Avenue South
Minneapolis, MN 55408
(612) 870-4740
1-877-NOYEAST
www.frenchmeadow.com

Nokomis Bakery Spelt and Kamut Sourdough Breads

Nokomis Bakery
2463 County Road ES
East Troy, WI 53120
(800) 367-0358
www.nokomisbakery.com

Pacific Bakery Kamut Bread: Organic kamut,
water, sea salt
Pacific Bakery Spelt Bread: Spelt, water, sea salt

Pacific Bakery
P.O. Box 950
(760) 757-6020
www.pacificbakery.com

Rudi's Spelt Bread: Organic spelt flour, water, honey, yeast, canola oil, salt, lecithin

> Rudi's Organic Bakery
> 3300 Walnut, Unit C
> Boulder, CO 80301
> (303) 447-0495
> (877) 293-0876
> www.rudisbakery.com

Rudolph's 100% Rye Bread: Organic rye flour, water, sourdough culture, salt

> Rudolph's Specialty Bakeries Ltd.
> 390 Alliance Avenue
> Toronto, Ontario, Canada M6N 2H8
> (416) 763-4315
> www.rudolphsbreads.com

CRACKERS AND FLATBREADS:

Amaranth Flatbread: amaranth flour, water, garbanzo flour, safflower oil, sea salt

> Nu-World Amaranth, Inc.
> P.O. Box 2202
> Naperville, IL 60567
> (630) 369-6819
> www.nuworldfoods.com

Rice cakes, many brands:
Watch out for other grains, popcorn, cheese, and sweeteners that may be included in the ingredients.

RICE CRACKERS:

Edward & Sons Brown Rice Snaps (a variety of flavors available)

> Edward & Sons Trading Company
> P.O. Box 1326
> Carpenteria, CA 93014
> (805) 684-8500
> www.edwardandsons.com

Hol-Grain Brown Rice Crackers:
Brown rice is the only ingredient

> Conrad Rice Mill, Inc.
> P.O. Box 10640
> New Iberia, LA 70560
> (337) 364-7242
> (800) 551-3245
> www.conradricemill.com

Westbrae Natural Unsalted Brown Rice Wafers: Brown rice, sesame seeds

> Westbrae Natural Foods
> The Hain Celestial Group, Inc.
> 4600 Sleepytime Drive
> Boulder, CO 80301
> (800) 434-4246
> www.westbrae.com

RYE CRACKERS:

RyVita Tasty Dark Rye or Tasty Light Rye Crackers: Whole grain rye, salt

> InterNatural Foods, LLC.
> 15 Prospect Street
> Paramus, NJ 07652
> (201) 909-0808
> www.internaturalfoods.com/Ryvita/Ryvita.html
(These are widely available in health food stores.)

Wasa Original Crispbread: Light Rye variety contains whole grain rye flour, water, salt

> GermanDeli.com
> 2890 Market Loop
> Southlake, TX 76092
> (877) GERMANY
> www.germandeli.com/wasacrispbread.html
(These are widely available in health food stores.)

CEREALS, HOT:

Rolled grains from health food store bulk bins are a good choice. Watch out for mixed grains in packaged hot cereals. A few packaged hot cereals are listed which are made from a single grain.

Lundberg Hot & Creamy Rice Cereal: 100% Rice

> Lundberg Family Farms
> 5370 Church Street
> Richvale, CA 95974
> (530) 882-4551
> www.lundberg.com

Pocono Cream of Buckwheat: 100% Buckwheat

> Birkett Mills
> 163 Main Street
> Penn Yan, NY 14527
> (315) 536-3311
> www.thebirkettmills.com

CEREALS, COLD:

Except for puffed grains, most cold cereals are made from mixed grains. A few types of cold cereals that contain more simple ingredients are listed here.

Puffed Amaranth: Amaranth only

Nu-World Amaranth, Inc.
P.O. Box 2202
Naperville, IL 60567
(630) 369-6819
www.nuworldfoods.com

Arrowhead Mills Puffed Rice: Brown rice only

Arrowhead Mills Puffed Millet: Millet only

Arrowhead Mills Organic Spelt Flakes: Spelt, apple, pear and peach juice concentrates, sea salt, vitamin C, vitamin E

Arrowhead Mills
The Hain Celestial Group, Inc.
4600 Sleepytime Drive
Boulder, CO 80301
(800) 434-4246
www.hain-celestial.com

Barbara's Brown Rice Crisps: Brown rice, pineapple juice concentrate, pear juice concentrate, peach juice concentrate, sea salt

Barbara's Breakfast O's: Whole oat flour, brown rice flour, pineapple juice concentrate, pear juice concentrate, oat bran, peach juice concentrate, sea salt (This cereal contains two grains, but they are both on day 4 of the rotation diet in this book).

Barbara's Bakery, Inc.
3900 Cypress Drive
Petaluma, CA 94954
(707) 765-2273
www.barbarasbakery.com

Erewhon Kamut Flakes: Kamut, pear juice concentrate, sea salt (By splitting the apple and pear family and assigning pear to day 1, this cereal fits day 1 of the rotation diet in this book).

Erewhon Crispy Brown Rice Cereal: Brown rice, barley malt, sea salt (also comes salt-free)

Erewhon Cereals
U.S. Mills, Inc.
200 Reservoir Street
Needham, MA 02494-3146
(781) 444-0440
www.usmillsinc.com

PASTA:

Read pasta labels carefully to be sure that they only contain the grains you can eat. Most buckwheat (soba) pasta contains wheat, jerusalem artichoke pasta contains semolina, which is a kind of wheat, and wheat-free quinoa pasta contains corn.

BARLEY:
Orgran Stoneground Barley and Spinach Pasta: Barley flour, spinach, water
Made by Roma Food Products, Australia
Imported into North America by:

Cemac Foods Corporation
1821 East Sedgley Avenue
Philadelphia, PA 19124
(215) 288-7440
www.cemacfoods.com

Orgran
47-53 Aster Avenue
Carrum Downs
Victoria 3201
AUSTRALIA
International phone : +61 3 9776 9044
www.orgran.com

BUCKWHEAT:
Eden 100% Soba Japanese Buckwheat Pasta: Buckwheat only

BEAN:
Eden Mung Bean Pasta: Bean starch only

Eden Foods, Inc.
701 Tecumseh Road
Clinton, MI 49236
(517) 456-7424
(888) 424-EDEN (3336)
www.edenfoods.com

CORN:
Westbrae Natural Corn Pasta: Corn flour only

Westbrae Natural Foods
The Hain Celestial Group, Inc.
4600 Sleepytime Drive
Boulder, CO 80301
(800) 434-4246
www.westbrae.com

QUINOA
Quinoa Pasta: Quinoa flour, corn flour

> The Quinoa Corporation
> Post Office Box 279
> Gardena, CA. 90248
> (310) 217-8125
> www.quinoa.net

RICE:
Ener-G Rice Macaroni, Lasagne, Spaghetti, or Shells: Rice flour, water

> Ener-G Foods, Inc.
> P. O. Box 84487
> Seattle, WA 98124
> (206) 767-6660
> (800) 331-5222
> www.ener-g.com

SPELT:
Vita-Spelt Spaghetti, Shells, Medium Shells, Elbow Macaroni, Rotini, Lasagne, Angel Hair: spelt flour, water (Egg Noodles contain egg)

> Purity Foods, Inc.
> 2871 W. Jolly Road
> Okemos, MI 48864
> (517) 351-9231
> www.purityfoods.com

Uncommon pastas (amaranth, barley, lentil, millet, milo, oat, quinoa, rye, white sweet potato, cassava, malanga, true yam): each type contains only the specified flour and water

> Special Foods
> 9207 Shotgun Court
> Springfield, VA 22153
> (703) 644-0991
> www.specialfoods.com

FRUIT AND VEGETABLE PRODUCTS:

CANNED BEANS:
Westbrae Natural Organic Cooked Beans (black beans, kidney beans, great northern beans, red beans, pinto beans, garbanzo beans, soybeans, lentils, split peas)

> Westbrae Natural Foods
> The Hain Celestial Group, Inc.
> 4600 Sleepytime Drive
> Boulder, CO 80301
> (800) 434-4246
> www.westbrae.com

CANNED FRUITS AND VEGETABLES
(Read the labels carefully - some brands of organic "health food" vegetables contain cane sugar.):

S & W water-packed fruits and vegetables: contain the specified fruit or vegetable and water

> S & W Fine Foods, Inc.
> P.O. Box 193575
> San Francisco, CA 94119-3575
> (800) 252-7033
> www.swfinefoods.com

Santa Cruz Organic Applesauce: organic apples only

> Santa Cruz Naturals, Inc.
> P.O. Box 369
> Chico, CA 95927
> (530) 899-5010
> www.scojuice.com

LIVE CULTURE SAUERKRAUT AND CULTURED VEGETABLES:
Rejuvenative Foods Sauerkraut: cabbage, macrobiotic high-mineral sea salt

Rejuvenative Foods Dill-flavored Sauerkraut: cabbage, lemon juice, dill

> Rejuvenative Foods
> P.O. Box 8464
> Santa Cruz, CA 95061
> (408) 462-6715
> (800) 805-7957
> www.rejuvenative.com

FROZEN FRUITS AND VEGETABLES:
Cascadian Farms Organic Frozen Fruits and Vegetables - many types

> Cascadian Farms
> 719 Metcalf
> Sedro Wolley, WA 98284
> (360) 855-0100
> www.cfarm.com

ALL-FRUIT JAMS, SPREADS, AND SAUCES:

Knudsen's all natural or organic fancy fruit spreads: most contain the specified fruit, white grape juice concentrate, fruit pectin; the apple butter contains apples and apple juice concentrate.

Knudsen and Sons, Inc.
Speedway Avenue
Chico, CA 95926
(530) 899-5000
www.knudsenjuices.com

Wax Orchards Fruit Syrups, Spreads, Butters, and Sweeteners

Wax Orchards, Inc.
22744 Wax Orchards Road S.W.
Vashon Island, WA 98070
(800) 634-6132
www.waxorchards.com

SOUPS:

Read soup labels carefully. Many soups contain wheat or wheat starch, modified food starch, sugar, yeast, MSG, etc. A few of the better soups are listed here.

Shelton's All-Natural Chicken Broth, salt-free: chicken broth, onion, celery, spices (salted version also contains chicken fat and sea salt)

Shelton's Premium Poultry
204 N. Loranne Avenue
Pomona, CA 91767
(909) 623-4361
(800) 541-1833
www.sheltons.com

Hain Pure Foods "Healthy Naturals" Soups:
Chicken Broth: chicken broth, chicken fat, carrots, sea salt, onion powder, spices
Vegetarian Split Pea Soup: water, split peas, carrots, green peas, celery, onion powder, spices
Vegetarian Lentil Soup: water, lentils, celery, tomato paste, potato flour, onions, olive oil, garlic, spices
Black Bean Soup: water, black beans, tomato paste, celery, onions, sea salt, garlic, spices

The Hain Celestial Group, Inc.
4600 Sleepytime Drive
Boulder, CO 80301
(800) 434-4246
www.hain-celestial.com

ALTERNATIVE MILK PRODUCTS:

BUTTER:

Mt. Sterling Cheese Corp. Pure Goat Milk Butter: goat cream only

Mt. Sterling Cheese Corporation
P.O. Box 103
Mt. Sterling, WI 54645
(608) 734-3151
http://grantcounty.org/visitor/farm.html

CHEESES (Soy, rice, almond, and hemp cheeses usually contain casein from cow's milk):

Goat cheese: Mt. Sterling Cheese's Cheddar, Jack, etc. contain pasteurized goat milk, salt, culture, and microbial enzymes (address above)

MILK:

Read the labels carefully because rice milks often contain legumes and soy milks often contain grains.

Meyenberg Goat Milk - available canned, powdered, ultrapasteurized and aseptic packed

Meyenberg Goat Milk
Jackson-Mitchell
P.O. Box 934
Turlock, CA 95381
(800) 891-GOAT
www.meyenberg.com

Nut Milks such as almond and hazelnut:

Pacific Natural Foods, Inc.
19480 SW 97th Avenue
Tualatin, OR 97062
(503) 692-9666
www.pacificfoods.com

Pacific Foods Organic Oat Non-Dairy Drink
Plain flavor: filtered water, organic oat groats, oat bran, tricalcium phosphate, sea salt, guar gum, xanthan gum, carrageenan, carob bean gum, riboflavin (b2), vitamin a palitate, vitamin d2.

Pacific Natural Foods, Inc.
19480 SW 97th Avenue
Tualatin, OR 97062
(503) 692-9666
www.pacificfoods.com

Rice Dream Rice Milk: filtered water, brown rice, safflower oil, vanilla, sea salt

> Imagine Foods, Inc.
> 350 Cambridge Avenue, Suite 350
> Palo Alto, CA 94306
> (415) 327-1444
> www.imaginefoods.com

Pacific Rice Non-Dairy Drink: water, brown rice, tricalcium phosphate, *L. acidophilus, L. bifidus,* guar gum, xanthum gum, carageen, sea salt, vitamins A and D

> Pacific Natural Foods, Inc.
> 19480 S.W. 97th Avenue
> Tualatin, OR 97062
> (503) 692-9666
> www.pacificfoods.com

Edensoy Soy Milk: Purified water, organic soybeans, malted cereal extract, Job's tears, barley, kombu, sea salt

> Eden Foods, Inc.
> 701 Tecumseh Road
> Clinton, MI 49236
> (517) 456-7424
> (888) 424-EDEN (3336)
> www.edenfoods.com

Westsoy Soy Milk: filtered water, organic soybeans, brown rice syrup, vanilla, carageen, sea salt

> Westbrae Natural Foods
> The Hain Celestial Group, Inc.
> 4600 Sleepytime Drive
> Boulder, CO 80301
> (800) 434-4246
> www.westbrae.com

YOGURT:

Hollow Road Farms Sheep's Milk Yogurt: pasteurized sheep's milk, *L. bulgaricus, S. thermophilus, L. acidophilus, L. bifidus*

> Hollow Road Farms
> Old Chatham Sheepherding Company
> 155 Shaker Museum Road
> Old Chatham, NY 12136
> (518) 794-7333
> (888) SHEEP60
> www.blacksheepcheese.com

Redwood Hill Farm Goat Milk Yogurt: pasteurized whole goat milk, tapioca, and living cultures (*L. bulgaricus, S. thermophilus, L. acidophilus, L. bifidus*)

> Redwood Hill Farm
> 2064 Highway 116 North, Building 1
> Sebastopol, CA 95472
> (707) 823-8250
> www.redwoodhill.com

White Wave Soy Yogurt: Filtered water, whole organic soybeans, organic evaporated cane juice, fruit – strawberries, cherries, blueberries, peaches, etc., rice starch, dextrose, natural flavors, tricalcium phosphate, pectin, citric acid, locust bean gum, annatto and turmeric (for color), yogurt cultures (*L. bulgaricus, S. thermophilus, L. acidophilus, B. bifidum, L. casei, L. rhamnosus*).

> White Wave Soy Foods, Inc.
> 1990 N. 57th Court
> Boulder, CO 80301
> (303) 443-3470
> www.whitewave.com

Table of Measurements

When your recipe says to use ⅜ cup or ⅛ teaspoon, what do you do? Or what if you want to divide a recipe in half? The easiest and most accurate thing to do is to have a liquid measuring cup with ⅛ cup markings, a set of dry measuring cups that contains a ⅛ cup measure, and a set of measuring spoons that has a ⅛ teaspoon. There are even sets that have ½ tablespoon! You can order such kitchen equipment from the King Arthur Flour Baker's Catalogue. (See "Sources," page 300). But in the meantime, use this table to make your recipes work.

⅛ teaspoon	= ½ of your ¼ teaspoon measure			
⅜ teaspoon	= ¼ teaspoon + ⅛ teaspoon			
⅝ teaspoon	= ½ teaspoon + ⅛ teaspoon			
¾ teaspoon	= ½ teaspoon + ¼ teaspoon			
⅞ teaspoon	= ½ teaspoon + ¼ teaspoon + ⅛ teaspoon			
1 teaspoon	= ⅓ tablespoon	. . . .	=	⅙ fluid ounce
1½ teaspoons	= ½ tablespoon	. . . .	=	¼ fluid ounce
3 teaspoons	= 1 tablespoon	. . . .	=	½ fluid ounce
½ tablespoon	= 1½ teaspoons	. . . .	=	¼ fluid ounce
1 tablespoon	= 3 teaspoons	. . . .	=	½ fluid ounce
2 tablespoons*	= ⅛ cup	. . . .	=	1 fluid ounce
4 tablespoons	= ¼ cup	. . . .	=	2 fluid ounces
5⅓ tablespoons	= ⅓ cup	. . . .	=	2⅔ fluid ounces
8 tablespoons	= ½ cup	. . . .	=	4 fluid ounces
16 tablespoons	= 1 cup	. . . .	=	8 fluid ounces
⅛ cup	= 2 tablespoons*	. . . .	=	1 fluid ounce
¼ cup	= 4 tablespoons	. . . .	=	2 fluid ounces
⅜ cup	= ¼ cup + 2 tablespoons*	. . . .	=	3 fluid ounces
⅝ cup	= ½ cup + 2 tablespoons*	. . . .	=	5 fluid ounces
¾ cup	= ½ cup + ¼ cup	. . . .	=	6 fluid ounces
⅞ cup	= ¾ cup + 2 tablespoons*	. . . .	=	7 fluid ounces
	OR ½ cup + ¼ cup + 2 tablespoons*			
1 cup	= ½ pint	. . . .	=	8 fluid ounces
1 pint	= 2 cups	. . . .	=	16 fluid ounces
1 quart	= 4 cups OR 2 pints	. . . .	=	32 fluid ounces
1 gallon	= 4 quarts	. . . .	=	128 fluid ounces

*In my experience, measuring tablespoons are all a little scanty of 1/16 cup (The ones from King Arthur come the closest to the correct volume), so 2 tablespoons is a little short of ⅛ cup. Therefore, if you need to measure, for example, ⅜ cup of liquid, it will probably be more accurate to "eyeball" an amount halfway between ¼ cup and ½ cup than to use ¼ cup plus two tablespoons. The best way to measure ⅜ cup is to fill your measuring cup to the third ⅛-cup line if it is marked in ⅛-cup intervals or to the 3 ounce line if it is marked in ounces.

Recommended Reading

Bland, Jeffrey, Ph.D. *Digestive Enzymes,* Keats Publishing, Inc., New Caanan, CT 06840, 1993.

Braly, James, M.D. *Dr. Braly's Food Allergy & Nutrition Revolution,* Keats Publishing, Inc., New Caanan, CT 06840, 1992.

Chaitow, Leon and Natasha Trenev, *Probiotics,* Hohm Press, P.O. Box 2501, Prescott, AZ 86302, 1990.

Crook, William G. M.D., *Detecting Your Hidden Allergies,* Professional Books, Inc., Box 3246, Jackson, TN 38303, 1988.

Crook, William G. M.D., *The Yeast Connection and the Woman,* Professional Books, Inc., Box 3246, Jackson, TN 38303, 1995.

Crook, William G. M.D. and Marjorie H. Jones, R.N., *The Yeast Connection Cookbook,* Professional Books, Inc., Box 3246, Jackson, TN 38303, 1989.

Dumke, Nicolette M. *Allergy Cooking with Ease,* Revised Edition. Adapt Books, Allergy Adapt, Inc., 1877 Polk Avenue, Louisville, CO 80027, 2007.

Dumke, Nicolette M. *Easy Breadmaking for Special Diets.* Adapt Books, Allergy Adapt, Inc., 1877 Polk Avenue, Louisville, CO 80027, 1995; Revised edition, 2007.

Dumke, Nicolette M. *Easy Cooking for Special Diets: How to Cook for Weight Loss/Blood Sugar Control, Food Allergy, Heart Healthy, Diabetic and "Just Healthy" Diets – Even if You've Never Cooked Before.* Adapt Books, Allergy Adapt, Inc., 1877 Polk Avenue, Louisville, CO 80027, 2007.

Dumke, Nicolette M. *The Low Dose Immunotherapy Handbook: Recipes and Lifestyle Advice for Patients on LDA and EPD Treatment.* Adapt Books, Allergy Adapt, Inc., 1877 Polk Avenue, Louisville, CO 80027, 2003.

Gates, Donna, *The Body Ecology Diet,* B.E.D. Publications, Inc., P.O. Box 550556, Atlanta, GA 30355, 1995.

Gates, Donna, *The Magic of Kefir,* B.E.D. Publications, Inc., P.O. Box 550556, Atlanta, GA 30355, 1996.

Gittleman, Ann Louise, *Guess What Came to Dinner: Parasites and Your Health,* Avery Publishing Group, Inc., Garden City Park, NY, 1993.

Grant, Doris and Jean Joice, *Food Combining for Health,* Healing Arts Press, 1 Park Street, Rochester, VT 05767, 1989.

Golos, Natalie, and Frances Golos Golbitz, *If This Is Tuesday, It Must Be Chicken,* Keats Publishing, Inc., New Caanan, CT 06840, 1983.

Jones, Marjorie H., R.N., *The Allergy Self-Help Cookbook,* Rodale Press, Emmaus, PA 1984.

Lewis, Sondra K. with Lonette Dietrich Blakely. *Allergy and Candida Cooking: Understanding and Implementing Plans for Healing.* Canary Connect Publications, 605 Holiday Road, Coralville, IA 52241-1016, 2006.

Licata, Vincent, *Yogurt and Acidophilus for Health and Vitality,* Continental Health Research, 300 N. Broadway, Santa Ana, CA 92701, 1972.

Lipski, Elizabeth, M.S., C.C.N., *Digestive Wellness,* Keats Publishing, Inc., New Caanan, CT 06840, 1996.

Philpott, William H. M.D., *Victory Over Diabetes,* Keats Publishing, Inc., New Caanan, CT 06840, 1983.

Randolph, Theron G. M.D., *An Alternative Approach to Allergies,* Harper & Row/Bantam Books, New York, NY, 1980.

Rosenbuam, Michael, M.D. and Murray Susser, M.D., *Solving the Puzzle of Chronic Fatigue Syndrome,* Life Sciences Press, P.O. Box 1174, Tacoma, WA 98401, 1992.

Sources of Special Foods, Products, and Services

Those of us with food allergies need many products and services that may not always be easy to find. This section lists sources of special foods, products, and services. Also see pages 289 to 294 for sources of commercially prepared foods. Most of these companies sell products and services in addition to those listed below. Visit their websites for up-to-date information about all of their products and services.

CULTURES

Acidophilus milk culture/probiotic supplement:

Culturelle™:

CAG Functional Foods
P.O. Box 2820
Omaha, NE 68103
(888) 828-4242
www.culturelle.com

Consumers may order Culturelle™ from:
N.E.E.D.S
6666 Manlius Center Road
East Syracuse, NY 13057
1-800-634-1380
www.needs.com

Ultradophilus™:

Metagenics San Clemente
100 Ave La Pata
San Clemente, CA 92673
(800) 692-9400
www.metagenics.com

Kefir cultures and the GoodLife™ kefir bug:

The Body Ecology Diet
1266 West Paces Ferry Road, Suite 505
Atlanta, GA 30327
(800) 896-7838

Sourdough cultures:

Sourdoughs International, Inc.
P.O. Box 670
(208) 382-4828
www.sourdo.com

Yogurt and acidophillus milk cultures, including Hansen's:

New England Cheesemaking Supply Company
Box 85
Ashfield, MA 01330-0085
(413) 628-3808

DISINFECTANTS

Nutribiotic™ for disinfecting raw produce:
N.E.E.D.S
6666 Manlius Center Road
East Syracuse, NY 13057
1-800-634-1380
www.needs.com

DAIRY PRODUCTS, ALTERNATIVE -
See pages 293 to 294

FLOURS, GRAINS, GRAIN ALTERNATIVES
(For breads, crackers, flatbreads, and cereals, see pages 289 to 291).

Amaranth:

Nu-World Amaranth, Inc.
P. O. Box 2202
Naperville, IL 60540
(630) 369-6819
www.nuworldfoods.com

Buckwheat:

Arrowhead Mills
The Hain Celestial Group, Inc.
4600 Sleepytime Drive
Boulder, CO 80301
(800) 434-4246
www.hain-celestial.com

Cassava meal (also called manioc flour):

Sundial Herbal Products
3609 Boston Post Road
Bronx, NY 10466
(718) 798-3962
www.sundialherbs.com/html
/other_products.html

Chestnut flour:

Gold Mine Natural Food Company
7805 Arjons Drive
San Diego, CA 92126
(800) 475-FOOD
www.goldminenaturalfood.com

Kamut flour:

Arrowhead Mills
The Hain Celestial Group, Inc.
4600 Sleepytime Drive
Boulder, CO 80301
(800) 434-4246
www.hain-celestial.com

Millet or Milo flour, organic:

Purcell Mountain Farms
HCR 62 BOX 284
Moyie Springs, ID 83845
866-440-2326
www.purcellmountainfarms.com

Potato flour:

Bob's Red Mill
Natural Foods Inc.
5209 S.E. International Way
Milwaukie, OR 97222
(503) 654-3215
(800) 349-2173
www.bobsredmill.com

Quinoa:

The Quinoa Corporation
P.O. Box 279
Gardena, CA. 90248
(310) 217-8125
www.quinoa.net

Rice or Rye flour:

Arrowhead Mills
The Hain Celestial Group, Inc.
4600 Sleepytime Drive
Boulder, CO 80301
(800) 434-4246
www.hain-celestial.com

Spelt:

Purity Foods, Inc.
2871 W. Jolly Road
Okemos, MI 48864
(517) 351-9231
www.purityfoods.com

Tapioca flour:

Ener-G Foods, Inc.
P. O. Box 84487
Seattle, WA 98124
(206) 767-6660
(800) 325-9788
www.ener-g.com

NOW Natural Foods *(order from them through your health food store)*
395 S. Glen Ellyn Road
Bloomingdale, IL 60108
(800) 283-3500
www.nowfoods.com

Teff flour:

Bob's Red Mill
Natural Foods Inc.
5209 S.E. International Way
Milwaukie, OR 97222
(503) 654-3215
(800) 349-2173
www.bobsredmill.com

Tuber flours (white sweet potato, cassava, malanga, true yam, lotus, water chestnut, etc.):

Special Foods
9207 Shotgun Court
Springfield, VA 22153
(703) 644-0991
www.specialfoods.com
(Water chestnut flour may also be purchased at Oriental grocery stores).

FOODS, MISCELLANEOUS

Baking powder, corn-free:

Featherweight Baking Powder
The Hain Celestial Group, Inc.
4600 Sleepytime Drive
Boulder, CO 80301
(800) 434-4246
www.hain-celestial.com

Carob chips, milk-free unsweetened:

NOW Natural Foods *(order from them through your health food store)*
395 S. Glen Ellyn Road
Bloomingdale, IL 60108
(800) 283-3500
www.nowfoods.com

Coconut, finely shredded unsweetened:

Jerry's Nut House, Inc.
2101 Humboldt Street
Denver, CO 80205
(303) 861-2262

Coconut milk, unsweetened:

Asian Food Grocer
131 West Harris Avenue
San Francisco, CA 94080
(888) 482-2742 or (650) 873-7600
www.asianfoodgrocer.com

Flavorings, natural, corn- and alcohol-free:

The Spicery Shoppe
1525 Brook Drive
Downers Grove, IL 60515
(630) 932-8100 or (800) 323-1301

Guar gum:

Bob's Red Mill
Natural Foods Inc.
5209 S.E. International Way
Milwaukie, OR 97222
(503) 654-3215 or (800) 349-2173
www.bobsredmill.com

Oils, cold pressed:

Omega Nutrition
6515 Aldrich Road
Bellingham, WA 98226
(800) 661-3529 (FLAX) or (360) 384-1238
www.omeganutrition.com

Unbuffered vitamin C powder, corn-free, for baking and salads:

N.E.E.D.S
6666 Manlius Center Road
East Syracuse, NY 13057
1-800-634-1380
www.needs.com

Xanthum gum:

NOW Natural Foods *(order from them through your health food store)*
395 S. Glen Ellyn Road
Bloomingdale, IL 60108
(800) 283-3500
www.nowfoods.com

Yeast, regular and quick-rise, corn- and preservative-free:

Red Star Yeast
Universal Foods Corporation
Consumer Service Center
433 E. Michigan Street
Milwaukee, WI 53202
(414) 271-6755
www.redstaryeast.com

GAME MEAT

Game Sales International, Inc.
P.O. Box 5314
2456 E. 13th Street
Loveland, CO 80537
(303) 667-4090 or (800) 729-2090

Coastal Procurement (Alligator)
3100 Ridgelake Drive
Metairie, LA 70002
(504) 734-9444

HEALTH PROFESSIONALS

Physicians who specialize in the diagnosis and treatment of food allergies:

American Academy of Environmental Medicine
7701 East Kellogg, Suite 625
Wichita, KS 67207
(316) 684-5500
www.aaem.com

American College for Advancement in Medicine
23121 Verdugo Drive, Suite 204
Laguna Hills, CA 92653
(888) 439-6891, (800) 532-3688 or
(949) 583-7666
www.acam.org

Nutritionists:

International & American Associations of Clinical Nutritionists
15280 Addison Road, Ste. 130
Addison, TX 75001
(972) 407-9089
www.iaacn.org

KITCHENWARE, including measuring spoons and cups with ⅛ teaspoon and ⅛ cup measures, electric tortilla maker, yogurt maker, bread machines, etc.

King Arthur Flour Baker's Catalogue
P.O. Box 876
Norwich, VT 05055-0876
(800) 827-6836
www.bakerscatalogue.com

LABORATORIES:

Blood tests for food allergies:

Immuno Laboratories, Inc.
6801 Powerline Road
Fort Lauderdale, FL 33309
(800) 231.9197 or (954) 691.2500
www.betterhealthusa.com

Optimal Health Resource Laboratories, Inc.
(self-testing offered also)
2700 North 29th Avenue. Suite #205
Hollywood, FL 33020
(888) 751-3388 or (954) 920-3728
www.yorkallergyusa.com

Comprehensive Digestive Stool Analysis:

Great Smokies Diagnostic Laboratories
63 Zillicoa Street
Asheville, NC 28801
(800) 522-4762 or (828) 253-0621
www.gsdl.com
(Also gives physician referrals, does tests of intestinal permeability, parasitology, and many other tests.)

Parasitology testing:

Parasitology Center, Inc. (PCI)
903 S. Rural Rd. #101-318
Tempe, AZ 85281
(480) 767-2522

Saliva tests for antibodies to parasites, *Clostridium difficile, Helicobacter pylori,* and other organisms that may be difficult to detect by stool testing:

DiagnosTechs, Inc.
6620 S. 192nd Place, Bldg. J.
Kent, WA 98032
800-878-3787 or (425) 251-0596
www.diagnostechs.com

PASTA - See pages 291 to 292

SUPPLEMENTS, HYPOALLERGENIC:

N.E.E.D.S
6666 Manlius Center Road
East Syracuse, NY 13057
1-800-634-1380
www.needs.com

NEEDS carries a wide variety of hypoallergenic supplements and products referred to in this book including probiotics, digestive enzymes, Nutribiotic™ for disinfecting raw produce, etc.

ROTATION DIETS, CUSTOMIZED:

Allergy Adapt, Inc.
1877 Polk Avenue
Louisville, CO 80027
303-666-8253
www.food-allergy.org

SWEETENERS

FOS:

Flora Inc.
P.O. Box 73
805 E. Badger Road
Lynden, WA 98264
www.florahealth.com
(Visit this website to find a health food store where you may purchase FOS).

Fruit Sweet™, Pear Sweet™ and Grape Sweet™ :

Wax Orchards Inc.
22744 Wax Orchards Road., S.W.
Vashon Island, WA 98070
(800) 634-6132
www.waxorchards.com

Stevia:

NOW Natural Foods (order from them through your health food store)
395 S. Glen Ellyn Road
Bloomingdale, IL 60108
(800) 283-3500
www.nowfoods.com

Index to Recipes According to Grain Use

* GLUTEN FREE

General Index

Recipes appear in italics; informational sections appear in standard type

Books to Help You With Your Special Diet

The Ultimate Food Allergy Cookbook and Survival Guide: How to Cook with Ease for Food Allergies and Recover Good Health gives you everything you need to survive and recover from food allergies. It contains medical information about the diagnosis of food allergies, health problems that can be caused by food allergies, and your options for treatment. The book includes a rotation diet that is free from common food allergens such as wheat, milk, eggs, corn, soy, yeast, beef, legumes, citrus fruits, potatoes, tomatoes, and more. Instructions are given on how to personalize the standard rotation diet to meet your individual needs and fit your food preferences. Contains 500 recipes that can be used with (or without) the diet. Extensive reference sections include a listing of commercially prepared foods for allergy diets and sources for special foods, services, and products.

ISBN 1-887624-08-2 or 978-1-887624-08-4 . . . .$24.95

Customized rotation diets will be available starting in 2007. Visit www.food-allergy.org any time after that to check on availability, price, and ordering information.

Allergy Cooking With Ease (Revised Edition). This classic all-purpose allergy cookbook was out of print and now is making a comeback in a revised edition. It includes all the old favorite recipes of the first edition plus many new recipes and new foods. Contains over 300 recipes for baked goods, main dishes, soups, salads, vegetables, ethnic dishes, desserts, and more. Informational sections of the book are also totally updated, including the extensive "Sources" section.

ISBN 1-887624-10-4 or 978-1-887624-10-7 . . . .$19.95

Easy Breadmaking for Special Diets contains over 200 recipes for allergy, heart healthy, low fat, low sodium, yeast-free, controlled carbohydrate, diabetic, celiac, and low calorie diets. It includes recipes for breads of all kinds, bread and tortilla based main dishes, and desserts. Use your bread machine, food processor, mixer, or electric tortilla maker to make the bread YOU need quickly and easily.

Revised Edition: ISBN 1-887624-11-2 or 978-1-887624-11-4 . . . .$19.95

Original Edition – ISBN 1-887624-02-3 . . . .$14.95

Easy Cooking for Special Diets: How to Cook for Weight Loss/Blood Sugar Control, Food Allergy, Heart Healthy, Diabetic and "Just Healthy" Diets – Even if You've Never Cooked Before. This book contains everything you need to know to stay on your diet plus 265 recipes complete with nutritional analyses and diabetic exchanges. It also includes basics such as how to grocery shop, equipping your kitchen, how to handle food safely, time management, information on nutrition, and sources of special foods.

ISBN 1-887624-09-0 or 978-1-887624-09-1 . . . . $24.95

The Low Dose Immunotherapy Handbook: Recipes and Lifestyle Tips for Patients on LDA and EPD Treatment gives 80 recipes for patients on low dose immunotherapy treatment for their food allergies. It also includes organizational information to help you get ready for your shots.

ISBN: 1-887624-07-4 or 978-1-887624-07-7 . . . . $9.95

How to Cope With Food Allergies When You're Short on Time is a booklet of time saving tips and recipes to help you stick to your allergy diet with the least amount of time and effort.

$4.95 or FREE with the order of two other books on these pages

You can order these books by mail using the order form on the next page or on-line by going to www.food-allergy.org.

Online credit card orders can be placed with Amazon.com at www.amazon.com.

Order Form

ITEM	QUANTITY	PRICE	TOTAL
The Ultimate Food Allergy Cookbook and Survival Guide*		$24.95	
Allergy Cooking with Ease*		$19.95	
Easy Breadmaking for Special Diets*		$14.95	
Easy Cooking for Special Diets*		$24.95	
The Low Dose Immunotherapy Handbook		$ 9.95	
How to Cope With Food Allergies When You're Short on Time		$ 4.95 or FREE	

Order any 2 of the first four books above and get *How to Cope with Food Allergies when You're Short on Time* **FREE!**

SUBTOTAL		
SHIPPING (see table below)		
Colorado residents add 4.1% sales tax		
TOTAL		

Ship to:

NAME: _____

STREET ADDRESS: _____

CITY, STATE, ZIP _____

PHONE NUMBER (in case of questions about order): _____

Please make check payable to:
Allergy Adapt, Inc. and send it and this order to:
Allergy Adapt, Inc., 1877 Polk Ave., Louisville, CO 80027

SHIPPING TABLE

IF YOU ARE ORDERING JUST ONE BOOK, FOR SHIPPING ADD:

The Ultimate Food Allergy Cookbook and Survival Guide* . . . . .add $4.00

Allergy Cooking With Ease* . . . . .add $4.00

Easy Breadmaking for Special Diets* . . . . .add $3.50

Easy Cooking for Special Diets* . . . . .add $4.00

The Low Dose Immunotherapy Handbook . . . . .add $2.00

How to Cope With Food Allergies When You're Short on Time . . . . .add $1.50

TO ORDER MORE THAN ONE BOOK, FOR SHIPPING ADD:

Up to 3 starred* books and 2 non-starred books . . . . .add $6.00

4 starred* books and up to 2 non-starred books . . . . .add $9.00

Call 303-666-8253 or e-mail foodalle@food-allergy.org if you have questions about shipping calculations or questions on large order discounts.

Printed in the United States
128127LV00003B/1-52/A